LEGAL RULE ALIGNMENT
IN THE GUANGDONG-HONG KONG-MACAO GREATER BAY AREA
A STUDY ON PRIVATE LENDING CASES

粤港澳大湾区
法律规则衔接研究

深圳前海合作区人民法院／编著
卞飞／主编

民间借贷篇

（中英文版）

法律出版社
LAW PRESS · CHINA
北京

图书在版编目(CIP)数据

粤港澳大湾区法律规则衔接研究. 民间借贷篇 / 深圳前海合作区人民法院编著. -- 北京 : 法律出版社, 2024

ISBN 978-7-5197-8921-3

Ⅰ. ①粤… Ⅱ. ①深… Ⅲ. ①区域经济合作－法律－研究－广东、香港、澳门②民间借贷－法律－研究－广东、香港、澳门 Ⅳ. ①D922.290.4

中国国家版本馆 CIP 数据核字(2024)第 051082 号

粤港澳大湾区法律规则衔接研究
——民间借贷篇
YUEGANG'AO DAWANQU FALÜ GUIZE XIANJIE YANJIU
—MINJIAN JIEDAIPIAN

深圳前海合作区人民法院 编著

责任编辑 陈昱希 赵雪慧
装帧设计 鲍龙卉

出版发行 法律出版社
编辑统筹 法规出版分社
责任校对 张红蕊
责任印制 耿润瑜
经　　销 新华书店

开本 710 毫米×1000 毫米 1/16
印张 27.5 **字数** 600 千
版本 2024 年 9 月第 1 版
印次 2024 年 9 月第 1 次印刷
印刷 天津嘉恒印务有限公司

地址:北京市丰台区莲花池西里 7 号(100073)
网址:www.lawpress.com.cn
投稿邮箱:info@lawpress.com.cn
举报盗版邮箱:jbwq@lawpress.com.cn

销售电话:010-83938349
客服电话:010-83938350
咨询电话:010-63939796

书号:ISBN 978-7-5197-8921-3
定价:98.00 元

凡购买本社图书,如有印装错误,我社负责退换。电话:010-83938349

粤港澳大湾区法律规则衔接研究
民间借贷篇

编 委 会

主　　编: 卞　飞

撰 稿 人: 卞　飞　刘　哲　罗　晓　张晓程
张怡扬　张　楠　孙　旭　涂莹洁

专家顾问: 王鸣峰　叶伟锋　姬厚实

Legal Rule Alignment in the Guangdong-Hong Kong-Macao Greater Bay Area

A Study on Private Lending Cases

Editorial Committee

Chief Editor: Bian Fei

Authors: Bian Fei, Liu Zhe, Luo Xiao, Zhang Xiaocheng, Zhang Yiyang, Zhang Nan, Sun Xu, Tu Yingjie

Expert Consultants: William M.F. Wong, Ray W.F. Yip, Michael Ji

前　言

粤港澳大湾区发展中，法治建设是关键要素，也是重要保障。内地、香港特区和澳门特区分属三种法律体系，独一无二的“一国两制三法域”的特点在一定程度上制约了经济要素的自由流动和经济合作纵深发展，也使在推动区域法治一体化建设时没有先例可循，需要自我探索、自我创新。《粤港澳大湾区发展规划纲要》提出，要不断深化粤港澳互利合作。《全面深化前海深港现代服务业合作区改革开放方案》进一步提出，要在前海合作区内探索不同法系、跨境法律规则衔接。通过推动跨境法律规则衔接，打破制度壁垒、透明优化规则、降低发展成本，已成为提升湾区整体竞争力的必然路径。

深圳前海法院成立于国家推进粤港澳大湾区建设的关键时期，是内地对港开展司法交流的桥头堡。自成立以来，前海法院坚持以打造透明公平高效的法治化营商环境为愿景，全方位、系统化、分阶段推进粤港澳大湾区商事诉讼规则和实体规则衔接，初步形成推动跨境商事法律规则衔接的“前海范式”。为进一步推动规则衔接向纵深发展，我们编写推出“粤港澳大湾区法律规则衔接研究”系列丛书。丛书涵盖诉讼规则和实体规则两个层面，既具有理论前沿性，又具有实践价值，期待为商事主体开展跨境投资提供指引，为大湾区打造一体化、法治化营商环境提供动能。

我们充分关注商事主体愿景，让法律规则公开透明，增强投资信心。我们瞄准商事主体最关心关切的、影响市场要素自由流动的核心领域，以及影响涉港澳审判的关键因素，由点带面、渐进有序地探索推进法律规则衔接的有效路径。以商事纠纷较为集中的合同类、公司类纠纷类型为“小切口”，清单式呈现内地与香港特区在成文法、司法裁判等方面的异同点，让商事主体开展跨境商事活动“有规可循”，消解他们因不熟悉规则而存在的顾虑；探索制定融合两地商事法律规则且具有实践指导意义的范本，为跨境商事活动提供合同样本，推动法律规则衔接在市场活动中的灵活运用。回应跨境商事主体对诉讼权利保障的期待，聚焦诉讼程序中的管辖、送达、举证、审判等重要流程节点，在总结提炼前海法院已有探索实践经验的基础上提出有益建议，以期打造更为高效便捷的跨境诉讼环境。

我们致力寻找最大公约数，求大同存小异，凝聚融合发展信心。在全球经济高度融合发展的背景下，虽然内地和香港特区的具体法律规则存在不同，但在立法旨趣、基本原则上日益具有趋同性。在商事诉讼规则方面，主要体现在便利当事人诉讼、促进替代性纠纷解决、倡导诚实理性诉讼等方面；在商事实体规则方面，体现在尊重商事主体意思自治、遵循公司自治、促进资源要素有效分配等方面。规则衔接并非要消除差异，而是要尊重差异、互鉴互融。寻找到两地商事法律规则的共通之处，为推进规则衔接搭建桥梁，更有助于提升商事主体开展跨境投资以及大湾区一体化融合发展的信心。

我们立足司法实践，回应审判所需，打造涉港商事审判优选地。在涉港审判中，香港法的查明与适用一直是重要的课题。前海法院已适用香港法审理案件137件，是全国适用香港法审理案件最多的法院。由于两地法律渊源差异较大，香港法的查明需耗费当事人较高的经济成本，而法官在适用香港法时也时常面临不熟悉香港法和普通法思维，或缺乏自主查明渠道等难题。我们围绕受理案件类型较多的公司类以及借贷合同、国际货物运输合同等类型，系统深入研究香港成文法和判例，形成体系化成果，直接服务涉港审判中香港法的查明适用，不仅为涉港案件当事人节约了大量经济成本，更有助于提升涉港审判的竞争力，打造涉港审判的优选地。

我们积极拓宽“朋友圈”，开放包容互鉴，凝聚法治共识。前海法院成立“粤港澳商事法律规则衔接研究中心”，与香港中文大学、香港城市大学、香港大学、澳门大学等港澳高校开展合作，聘请港澳学者担任专家研究员，接收内地与港澳高校学生作为司法研修生，让熟知港澳法律的专业人士参与到司法研究中。通过共同研究推动跨境法律规则衔接，促进思路互动、规则互通、方法互鉴、举措互学，提升港澳专业人士和港澳青年对内地法治建设的认同感，为大湾区建设凝聚更强大的合力。

潮起两岸，风劲扬帆。新时代的画卷里，粤港澳大湾区融合发展的美好愿望正在变成生动现实。前海法院将不负厚望、续写篇章、久久为功，为推动粤港澳经济互补和协同发展、促进区域一体化建设贡献智慧和力量。

卞　飞

2024 年 7 月

Preface

In developing the Guangdong – Hong Kong – Macao Greater Bay Area (hereinafter referred to as the Greater Bay Area), the rule of law is a crucial element and an important safeguard. The legal systems in the Chinese Mainland, Hong Kong Special Administrative Region (HKSAR), and Macao Special Administrative Region (Macao SAR) are different from each other. Such unique feature of "one country, two systems, and three jurisdictions" restricts the free flow of the economy and the in – depth development of economic cooperation to a certain extent. As a result, the Greater Bay Area lacks a precedent to be followed in promoting the construction of regional integration of the rule of law, which requires self – exploration and self – innovation. *The Outline Development Plan for the Guangdong – Hong Kong – Macao Greater Bay Area* proposes to constantly deepen mutual beneficial cooperation among the Chinese Mainland, HKSAR and Macao SAR. Furthermore, the *Plan for Comprehensively Deepening the Reform and Opening Up of the Qianhai Shenzhen – Hong Kong Modern Service Industry Cooperation Zone* explores the cross – border articulation of legal rules among different legal systems in the Qianhai Cooperation Zone. Promoting the alignment of cross – border legal rules breaks down institutional barriers, optimizes the transparency of rules, reduces development costs, and becomes an inevitable path to enhance overall competitiveness.

Shenzhen Qianhai Cooperation Zone People's Court (hereinafter referred to as the Qianhai Court), a gateway for judicial exchanges between the Chinese Mainland and HKSAR, was established during the crucial period when China promoted the Greater Bay Area construction. Since its establishment, the Qianhai Court has always kept creating a transparent, fair and efficient business environment under the rule of law as its vision. In a comprehensive, systematic, and multi – phased manner, the Qianhai Court also boosts the alignment of commercial litigation rules and substantive rules of the Greater Bay Area, initially forming the "Qianhai Paradigm" for promoting the alignment of cross – border commercial legal rules. In promoting and deepening the alignment of the legal rules of Guangdong, HKSAR, and Macao SAR, we wrote, edited, and launched a series of books entitled *Legal Rule Alignment in the Guangdong – Hong Kong – Macao Greater Bay Area*. The book series, covering both litigation and substantive rules, is theoretically cutting – edge and practically valuable; the series is expected to provide guidance for commercial entities to carry out cross – border investment, providing impetus to create an integrated, rule – of – law business environment in the Greater Bay Area.

We fully notice the expectations of commercial entities and thus publicize and clarify legal rules to increase their confidence in investment. We aim at the core areas that commercial subjects are most concerned about and that affect the free flow of market factors, as well as the key factors affecting trials involving HKSAR and Macao SAR. The Qianhai Court, from an entry point to an overall picture, explores the practical path of promoting the alignment of legal rules in a gradual and orderly manner. The Qianhai Court takes contractual and corporate disputes, which are more common in commercial disputes, as a "small entry point" to single out a list of the similarities and differences between the Chinese Mainland and HKSAR in terms of statute law and judicial decisions, so that commercial entities can have rules to follow in carrying out cross – border commercial activities, and their concerns due to lack of familiarity with different rules can be alleviated. The Qianhai Court explores the formulation of a model that integrates the legal rules of the two regions and of practical guidance, and provides contract templates for cross – border commercial activities, so as to vitalize the flexible application of the legal rules alignment in market activities. The Court not only responds to the expectations of cross - border commercial subjects for the protection of their litigation rights, focusing on the important process points of litigation procedures, such as jurisdiction, service, proof, and trial, but also puts forward useful suggestions intending to create a more efficient and convenient environment for cross - border litigation by summarizing and refining the Qianhai Court experience.

We are committed to finding the greatest common part among different legal systems, seeking common ground while reserving minor differences, and building confidence in integration and development. Against the background of the highly integrated development of the global economy, there is an increasing similarity in converging the legislative intent and basic principles between the Chinese Mainland and HKSAR, despite some differences in the specific legal rules. In terms of commercial litigation rules, similarity is mainly reflected in facilitating litigation for the parties concerned, promoting alternative dispute resolution, and advocating honest and rational litigation; in terms of substantive commercial rules, similarity is reflected in respecting the autonomy of commercial entities, following corporate independence, and promoting the effective allocation of resource factors. The alignment of rules is not to eliminate differences but to respect differences, exchange mutual appreciation and integration. Finding commonalities in the commercial legal rules of the two regions builds a bridge to promote the alignment of rules to boost the confidence of commercial entities in carrying out cross - border investment as well as the integrated development of the Greater Bay Area.

Based on judicial practice, we respond to the needs of trials and build a preferred hub for Hong Kong - related commercial trials. The ascertainment and application of Hong Kong (SAR) Law have always been important issues in Hong Kong - related trials. Also, the Qianhai Court has applied Hong Kong (SAR) Law to 137 cases, the largest number of cases applied to Hong Kong (SAR) Law in the Chinese Mainland. However, there are significant differences in the sources of law between the two regions, so the ascertainment of Hong Kong (SAR) Law may cost more expenditure from the commercial entities. In applying Hong Kong (SAR) Law, judges always encounter difficulties such as being unfamiliar with Hong Kong (SAR) Law and having a common law mindset or a lack of independent ascertainment channels. We systematically conduct in - depth research on Hong Kong statutory laws and case laws in relation to the companies, loan contracts, and international transportation of goods contracts, which are the major types of cases received by the Court. The Court has thus formed a systematized result to provide direct services for ascertaining and applying Hong Kong (SAR) Law in Hong Kong - related trials. Such a result not only saves a large amount of monetary costs for the parties involved in Hong Kong - related cases but also enhances competitiveness and builds a preferred hub for Hong Kong - related trials.

We actively broaden our "circle of friends", open to inclusive and mutual understanding, and forge a consensus on the rule of law. The Qianhai Court sets up the "Guangdong, Hong Kong and Macao Commercial Law Rules Alignment Research Center", cooperating with Hong Kong and Macao universities such as the Chinese University of Hong Kong, City University of Hong Kong, University of Hong Kong, and University of Macao. The Court also recruits Hong Kong and Macao scholars as expert researchers, and accepts students from the Chinese Mainland, Hong Kong, and Macao universities as judicial trainees, enabling professionals who are familiar with Hong Kong and Macao laws to participate in the judicial research. Through joint research and promotion of the alignment of cross - border legal rules, we continue to promote the interaction of ideas, the sharing of rules, the mutual understanding of methods and the learning of initiatives. We are also dedicated to enhancing the sense of identity of Hong Kong and Macao professionals and young people with the rule of law construction in the Chinese Mainland so as to build a stronger synergy for the Greater Bay Area construction.

As tides rise, the wind is strong enough to set forth for a journey. In the scroll of the new era, the glorious hope for the integration and development of the Greater Bay Area is turning into a splendid reality. The Qianhai Court will live up to its high expectations, continue to write new chapters, and make long-term efforts to contribute wisdom and strength in order to promote the financial collaboration and cooperative development of the Greater Bay Area, and to boost the integration construction of the regions.

Bian Fei

July 2024

阅 读 指 南

为了方便不同语言背景的读者，本书提供了中英文对照版本。此外，为了满足读者不同阅读需求，我们为您提供以下几种阅读方式：

如果您喜欢要点式阅读，推荐您翻到第 23 页（中文目录前），我们向您提供“列举清单式”的法律要点比较一览；

如果您喜欢沉浸式阅读，推荐您翻到第 3 页（中文目录后），我们向您提供“全面详尽式”的民间借贷规则衔接研究。

Reading Guide

For the convenience of readers with different language backgrounds, this book provides Chinese and English versions. In addition, to meet the diverse reading preferences of our readers, we provide you with the following reading options:

If you like to read in a point-by-point manner, we recommend you to turn to page 23 (before the Chinese Contents), where we provide you with an enumerative table of comparisons on key legal points.

If you like to read in an immersive manner, we recommend you to turn to page 3 (after the Chinese Contents), where we provide you with a comprehensive and detailed study on rule alignment with regard to private lending cases.

序　　言

民间借贷是自然人、法人和非法人组织之间进行资金融通的行为。在粤港澳大湾区建设背景下，深圳与香港特区的交流互动日益频繁，资金融通更为便利。民间借贷作为多层次信贷市场的重要组成部分，凭借其形式灵活、手续简便、融资快捷等特点为两地人民群众的生产生活带来了诸多便利。与此同时，两地因民间借贷而产生的争端频发，前海法院受理的涉港民间借贷纠纷案件的数量居高不下。内地通过《民法典》《民间借贷司法解释》等法律法规构建起民间借贷法律规则体系；与之不同的是，香港特区民间借贷法律规则不仅有《放债人条例》等成文法，还包括蕴含着丰富的民间借贷理念、适用规则的判例法。庞杂的民间借贷判例需要不断抽丝剥茧，才能梳理出核心的法律规则。这种多元、零散的法律形式，陌生、复杂的普通法思维给跨境投资者在理解和应用法律时带来一定的挑战，同时也会影响内地法院在涉港商事审判中对香港特区民间借贷法律的查明、理解与适用。为此，前海法院以内地和香港特区民间借贷法律规则为视域，针对相同的“小切口”进行有参照性的类比分析，这既能为投资者提供清晰明了的商事活动指南，又能为审判者带来可理解性强、适用性高的法律“查明意见”。

本书主要以民间借贷的法律要素为基本脉络，通过对内地和香港特区民间借贷相关法律的全方位比较与衔接进行研究。本书一共分为八个章节，分别是：第一章民间借贷的相关概念比较、第二章职业放贷人的法律规则比较、第三章本金与利息的法律规则比较、第四章利率司法保护上限的法律规则比较、第五章合同条款约定不明的法律规则比较、第六章与担保合同关系的法律规则比较、第七章夫妻债务制度的法律规则比较、第八章诉讼时效的法律规则比较。第一章主要介绍了两地不同的立法体例以及不完全对应的法律概念，进一步厘定本书的比较范围，以此奠定全文衔接研究的基础。第二章至第五章分别从职业放贷人、本金与利息、利率保护限额、合同条款约定不明等方面来比较内地和香港特区法律规则的异同。从比较情况来看，两地均认可民间借贷的法律效力、均不认可职业放贷人（或无牌放债人）放贷的法律效力；但两地在利率保护限额、违反法律强制性规定后的法律效果等方面存在较大差异，其他部分差异较小。第六章至第八章分别从与民间借贷有密切联系的担保合同、夫妻债务制度、诉讼时效等方面来比较内地和香港特区的法律规则的异同。从比较情况来看，两地均认可主合同无效则担保合同亦无效、民间借贷并非当然为夫妻共同债务；但两地在诉讼时效方面存在较大差异，其他部分差异较小。

从内地与香港特区民间借贷的法律规则和实践运用的全方位比较研究可知，两地的法律既具有较强的紧密性和互通性，也存在一定的差异。本书通过对成文法和相关案例的全面比较研究，形成对两地民间借贷法律规则异同比较的可视化、可理解的成果，以期能够为跨境投资者提供全面准确、清晰明了的民间借贷法律规则指南，为大湾区商事法律规则的多维度衔接和融合铺设基石，并在此过程中积累宝贵经验。同时，由于民间借贷的概念、观点、理论和体系根植于所处地域的社会、经济和历史等复杂背景，并据此不断修正和重构，故本书难以做到巨细无遗、面面俱到。因此，如本书有疏漏、舛误之处，敬请批评指正。

Prologue

Private lending refers to the conduct of capital financing between natural persons, legal persons, and unincorporated organisations. Against the background of the construction of the Guangdong-Hong Kong-Macao Greater Bay Area, the exchanges and interactions between Shenzhen and Hong Kong Special Administrative Region (Hong Kong) have been becoming increasingly frequent, making capital financing more convenient. In the Chinese Mainland and Hong Kong, as an important part of the multi-level credit market, private lending brings various conveniences to the production and people's life with its flexible forms, simple procedures, and quick financing. At the same time, disputes frequently arise from private lending between the Chinese Mainland and Hong Kong, and the number of Hong Kong-related private lending cases accepted by the Shenzhen Qianhai Cooperation Zone People's Court remains at a considerably high level. The Chinese Mainland has established a legal system for private lending through laws and regulations such as the *Civil Code of the People's Republic of China* and the *Provisions of the Supreme People's Court on Several Issues Concerning the Application of Laws in the Trial of Private Lending Cases*. However, the rules on private lending in Hong Kong include not only statutory laws such as the *Money Lenders Ordinance*, but also case laws containing various concepts and applicable rules. The complexity of case laws requires in-depth analysis to sort out the core principles. Cross-border investors have come across certain challenges in understanding and applying the laws in Hong Kong since the case laws are diverse and fragmented while the common law thinking is unfamiliar and complex to them. Meanwhile, it also affects the courts in the

Chinese Mainland in the ascertainment, understanding and application of Hong Kong laws in respect of private lending in commercial trials. Therefore, the Shenzhen Qianhai Cooperation Zone People's Court carries out comparative analysis based on the same "micro entry point" within the scope of private lending rules in the Chinese Mainland and Hong Kong, providing investors with clear and straightforward business activity guidelines as well as furnishing the judges with understandable and highly applicable "law ascertainment opinions".

This book follows the basic elements of private lending to conduct comprehensive research of comparison and rule alignment between the private lending laws in the Chinese Mainland and Hong Kong. There are eight chapters in this book: *Chapter Ⅰ Comparison of Relevant Concepts of Private Lending*, *Chapter Ⅱ Comparison of Legal Rules on Professional Money Lenders*, *Chapter Ⅲ Comparison of Legal Rules on Principal and Interest*, *Chapter Ⅳ Comparison of Legal Rules on the Statutory Interest Rate Cap*, *Chapter Ⅴ Comparison of Legal Rules on Unclear Contractual Terms*, *Chapter Ⅵ Comparison of Legal Rules on Security Contracts*, *Chapter Ⅶ Comparison of Legal Rules on Marital Debts*, *Chapter Ⅷ Comparison of Legal Rules on Limitations*. Chapter Ⅰ gives a detailed introduction to the different legislation and concepts of private lending in the Chinese Mainland and Hong Kong, clarifying the scope of comparison while laying down the foundation for the rule alignment of the whole book. Rules on professional money lenders, principal and interest, statutory interest rate cap, and unclear contractual terms are illustrated and compared from Chapter Ⅱ to Chapter Ⅴ respectively. It is found that both Chinese Mainland and Hong Kong recognise the legal effect of private lending but negate the validity of lending by professional (unlicensed) money lenders. Additionally, there are significant differences in the statutory interest rate cap and the legal effect of violation of mandatory provisions between the Chinese Mainland and Hong Kong, while few differences are found in other aspects. Chapter Ⅵ, Chapter Ⅶ and

Chapter Ⅷ focus on the comparison of legal rules closely relevant to private lending, namely the rules on security contracts, martial debts and limitations. It is found that, when a loan contract is determined as void (or unenforceable), the laws in the Chinese Mainland and Hong Kong both negate the validity and enforceability of security contracts. In terms of community debt, the positions are similar in the Chinese Mainland and Hong Kong that private lending debts are not ipso facto community debt. The rules on limitations are quite different between the Chinese Mainland and Hong Kong, while the rules on other aspects are not of much difference.

From the all-round comparative study of the legal rules and practical applications of private lending in the Chinese Mainland and Hong Kong, it is clear that the two jurisdictions share strong closeness and interoperability as well as certain differences. Through the comprehensive comparative study of statutory laws and relevant case laws, this book presents a visual and comprehensible analysis of comparing the similarities and differences in the private lending rules in the two jurisdictions. The book aims to provide cross-border investors with a comprehensive, accurate and clear guideline to the legal rules on private lending, thus accumulating valuable experience and laying a foundation for the multidimensional integration and the alignment of commercial legal rules within the Greater Bay Area. As an objective fact, the concepts, views, theories and systems of private lending are deeply rooted in the intricate complexities of the social, economic and historical grounds in which they are situated. Legal rules on private lending have been continuously undergoing revision and reconstruction in light of these factors; inevitably, this book may not cover every nuance and detail. Any criticisms and corrections, therefore, regarding oversights or inaccuracies in this book would be mostly appreciated.

凡　　例

一、内地

1. 内地法律文件名称中的“中华人民共和国”省略，其余一般不省略。例如，《中华人民共和国民法典》，简称《民法典》；

2. 《最高人民法院关于审理民间借贷案件适用法律若干问题的规定》，根据其修正的版本不同，分别简称为《民间借贷司法解释》《民间借贷司法解释（2020 修正）》《民间借贷司法解释（2020 第二次修正）》；

3. 《最高人民法院关于适用〈中华人民共和国民法典〉有关担保制度的解释》，简称《担保制度司法解释》；

4. 《最高人民法院关于审理涉及夫妻债务纠纷案件适用法律有关问题的解释》，简称《夫妻债务司法解释》；

5. 《最高人民法院关于审理民事案件适用诉讼时效制度若干问题的规定》，简称《诉讼时效规定》；

6. 《全国法院民商事审判工作会议纪要》，简称《九民纪要》。

二、香港特区

1. 第 4A 章《高等法院规则》（Cap. 4A Rules of the High Court），简称《高等法院规则》；

2. 第 20 章《卖据条例》（Cap. 20 Bills of Sale Ordinance），简称《卖据条例》；

3. 第 163 章《放债人条例》（Cap. 163 Money Lenders Ordinance），简称《放债人条例》；

4. 第 163A 章《放债人规例》（Cap. 163A Money Lenders Regula-

tions），简称《放债人规例》；

5. 第182章《已婚者地位条例》（Cap. 182 Married Persons Status Ordinance），简称《已婚者地位条例》；

6. 第219章《物业转易及财产条例》（Cap. 219 Conveyancing and Property Ordinance），简称《物业转易及财产条例》；

7. 第336H章《区域法院规则》（Cap. 336H Rules of the District Court），简称《区域法院规则》；

8. 第347章《时效条例》（Cap. 347 Limitation Ordinance），简称《时效条例》。

TABLE OF STATUTES

I. Chinese Mainland

1. "People's Republic of China" is omitted from the names of Chinese Mainland legislation, while the rest are generally not omitted. For instance, the *Civil Code of the People's Republic of China* is abbreviated as the *Civil Code*;

2. The *Provisions of the Supreme People's Court on Several Issues Concerning the Application of Laws in the Trial of Private Lending Cases* is abbreviated in various revised versions as the *Provisions on Private Lending*, the *Provisions on Private Lending (2020 First Amendment)* and the *Provisions on Private Lending (2020 Second Amendment)*, respectively;

3. The *Interpretation of the Supreme People's Court on the Application of the Relevant Guarantee System of the Civil Code of the People's Republic of China* is abbreviated as the *Interpretation of the Relevant Guarantee System*;

4. The *Interpretation of the Supreme People's Court on Issues concerning the Application of Law in the Trial of Cases Involving Marital Debt Disputes* is abbreviated as the *Interpretation on Marital Debt*;

5. The *Provisions of the Supreme People's Court on Several Issues concerning the Application of Statute of Limitations during the Trial of Civil Cases* is abbreviated as the *Provisions on Statute of Limitations*;

6. The *Minutes of the National Courts' Civil and Commercial Trial Work Conference* is abbreviated as the *Conference Minutes*.

II. Hong Kong Special Administrative Region (Hereinafter Abbreviated as Hong Kong)

1. Cap. 4A *Rules of the High Court* is abbreviated as *Rules of the High Court*;

2. Cap. 20 *Bills of Sale Ordinance* is abbreviated as the *Bills of Sale Ordinance*;

3. Cap. 163 *Money Lenders Ordinance* is abbreviated as the *Money Lenders Ordinance*;

4. Cap. 163A *Money Lenders Regulations* is abbreviated as the *Money Lenders Regulations*;

5. Cap. 182 *Married Persons Status Ordinance* is abbreviated as the *Married Persons Status Ordinance*;

6. Cap. 219 *Conveyancing and Property Ordinance* is abbreviated as the *Conveyancing and Property Ordinance*;

7. Cap. 336H *Rules of the District Court* is abbreviated as *Rules of the District Court*;

8. Cap. 347 *Limitation Ordinance* is abbreviated as the *Limitation Ordinance*.

法律要点比较一览

<table>
<tr><th colspan="4">职业放贷人的法律规则比较</th></tr>
<tr><th>法律要点</th><th>异同点</th><th>内地</th><th>香港特区</th></tr>
<tr><td rowspan="3">职业放贷人的认定标准</td><td>相同点</td><td colspan="2">1. 对于未持有相关金融资质（放债人牌照）的放贷行为均不认可，在法律上均予以否定性的评价。
2. 对于职业放贷人（无牌放债人）的认定均没有统一的衡量标准。内地对于职业放债人的认定仍处于探索阶段，各地法院根据本地的经济发展情况制定职业放贷人认定标准。香港特区对放债人的认定散落在判例法之中，暂无统一的成文法认定标准。
3. 都从出借人、借款人、出借行为三个维度对职业放贷人（无牌放债人）进行认定。在认定的方法上，两地均采取结合个案证据及具体案情作出综合性判断的方法进行认定。</td></tr>
<tr><td rowspan="2">不同点</td><td colspan="2">在认定职业放贷人（无牌放债人）时，对于出借行为的认定侧重点不同。</td></tr>
<tr><td>内地多以法院受理的民间借贷案件数量作为重要考量因素。</td><td>香港特区多以出借人实际放贷次数作为重要考量因素。</td></tr>
<tr><td rowspan="3">职业放贷人的法律后果</td><td>相同点</td><td colspan="2">对于职业放贷人（无牌放债人）的放贷行为均不认可，都持有否定的法律评价并规定相应不利法律后果。</td></tr>
<tr><td rowspan="2">不同点</td><td colspan="2">1. 对职业放贷人（无牌放债人）的放贷行为的否定评价结果不同。</td></tr>
<tr><td>内地法律明确规定属于职业放贷行为的民间借贷合同无效，借款人一般需要向出借人返还本金以及支付相应的资金占用费。资金占用费的金额一般参照一年期 LPR 认定。</td><td>香港特区的《放债人条例》规定无牌放债人订立的借款合同不可被强制执行。</td></tr>
</table>

续表

<table>
<tr><th>法律要点</th><th>异同点</th><th>内地</th><th>香港特区</th></tr>
<tr><td rowspan="2"></td><td rowspan="2"></td><td colspan="2">2. 对职业放贷人（无牌放债人）的放贷行为的处理路径不同。</td></tr>
<tr><td>由于内地法律明文规定职业放贷人的借款合同属于无效合同，因此内地法院对职业放贷人的借款合同的处理没有自由裁量权。</td><td>香港特区的法院可以基于公平原则行使自由裁量权，对无牌放债人的借款合同予以有限的保护。但是，香港特区法院对该自由裁量权的行使十分谨慎。</td></tr>
<tr><th colspan="4">本金与利息的法律规则比较</th></tr>
<tr><th>法律要点</th><th>异同点</th><th>内地</th><th>香港特区</th></tr>
<tr><td rowspan="7">本金与利息的内涵</td><td>相同点</td><td colspan="2">1. 对民间借贷借款本金的认定均采用保守性和限制性立法视角，限定只有实际出借的款项才可被视为借款本金。
2. 对于砍头息等预先扣除款在认定借款本金时会从本金数额中予以扣除。</td></tr>
<tr><td rowspan="6">不同点</td><td colspan="2">1. 利息的内涵不同。</td></tr>
<tr><td>内地法律下利息、违约金、其他费用等总计不能超过一年期LPR四倍的法定限额，但利息与违约金、其他费用等属于不同的法律概念。</td><td>香港特区法律规定放债行为中除了本金及税项以外，超出本金的款项（无论以何种名目）均认定为利息。</td></tr>
<tr><td colspan="2">2. 砍头息等预先扣除款在认定借款利息时的司法处理方式不同。</td></tr>
<tr><td>内地法律未规定将砍头息从本金数额中扣除后再将其纳入利息数额中。</td><td>香港特区法律规定将预先扣除款或预先约定扣除款从本金数额扣除后，还可能再次纳入利息数额中。</td></tr>
<tr><td colspan="2">3. 对借新还旧合同的司法限制不同。</td></tr>
<tr><td>内地法律要求最后一期合同期限届满之时的本金与利息总额之和不得超过以最初本金为基数计算的本金与利息总额之和，以防止出现超出司法限额征收利息的情况。</td><td>香港特区法律仅要求每一期借新还旧合同均须符合法律规定，除此之外在其他方面未有明确要求。</td></tr>
</table>

续表

法律要点	异同点	内地	香港特区
借期内利息的法律规则	不同点	当利息未作约定或约定不明时，确定利息的方式不同。	
		内地法律对借款主体是否为自然人加以区分，规定自然人之间的借款对利息未作约定或约定不明均视为没有利息，只有除自然人之间借款以外的借款对利息约定不明时才会按当地或当事人的交易方式、交易习惯、市场报价利率等因素确定利息。	香港特区法律对借款主体是否为自然人不作区分，对利息约定不明时均通过交易过程、贸易习惯等进行推断，只有对利息未作约定且无法推断时才视为无息，并且还存在衡平法规定的特殊情形。
逾期利息的法律规则	相同点	均尊重当事人意思自治，对借款合同中明确约定的逾期利息，在不超过法定限额的情况下，予以司法保护。	
	不同点	1. 对逾期利息的性质认定不同。	
		内地法律优先考虑当事人合同约定，逾期利息的性质根据合同约定可以是违约金，也可以是损害赔偿。	香港特区根据普通法原则认定逾期利息的性质为违约损害赔偿。
		2. 对逾期利率高于借期利率的司法保护不同。	
		内地法律对逾期利率高于借期利率的情况，在不超过司法保护限额（一年期 LPR 四倍）的前提下，予以保护。	香港特区法律对此没有明确规定，但过高的逾期利率在司法实践中有可能被认定为惩罚性赔偿而不能获得法律保护。
		3. 未约定逾期利息时的计算标准不同。	
		内地法律规定借款合同对逾期利息未作约定时，逾期利率可参照借期内利率确定；对借期内利率也未作约定时，则按照一年期 LPR 的标准计算逾期利息。	香港特区法律将未约定情况下逾期利息的计算标准划分为判决前逾期利息计算标准和判决后逾期利息计算标准，判决前逾期利息通常按港元最优惠利率（目前为 5.625%）+1 的标准进行计算，判决后逾期利息则按判定利率（目前为 8.875%）标准进行计算。

续表

利率司法保护上限的法律规则比较			
法律要点	**异同点**	**内地**	**香港特区**
利率司法保护限额	相同点	对借贷交易的利率限额均通过成文法的形式进行了明确的法律规定，且两地通过修订法律的形式下调了贷款利率保护的上限。	
	不同点	对借贷交易的贷款利率保护上限规定不同，香港特区的利率保护上限明显高于内地。	
		内地的民间借贷利率司法保护上限为一年期 LPR 四倍（截至 2024 年 7 月 22 日年利率为 13.4%），且 LPR 数值是浮动而非固定的。	香港特区利率司法保护规则为：除豁免情形外，超过年利率 48%，即属犯罪；超过年利率 36%，可以推定交易属于敲诈性。
超过利率司法保护上限的法律后果	相同点	均规定当借贷交易利率超过利率司法保护上限，出借人应承担相应的不利法律后果。	
	不同点	超过利率司法保护上限的借贷交易的法律后果不同。	
		内地法律规定不保护超出上限部分的利息（截至 2024 年 7 月 22 日年利率为 13.4%），但法院对于借款本金以及司法保护范围内的利息与费用予以支持。	香港特区法律规定，超过年利率 48% 的借贷交易即属犯罪，不得强制执行，即法院对本金、利息等均不予支持。对于超过年利率 36% 的借贷交易，如法院推定其属敲诈性，可不予强制执行或重新商议并确定应执行的利率；如法院行使酌情权信纳其不属敲诈性，则借款协议可正常执行。
合同条款约定不明的法律规则比较			
法律要点	**异同点**	**内地**	**香港特区**
清偿顺序无约定或约定不明	相同点	对借款人还款的本息清偿顺序的规定基本一致，均为有约定的从约定，无约定且双方均未指定还款分配比例的，推定先偿还利息后偿还本金。	
	不同点	当事人的指定抵充权有所不同。	
		内地法律规定，只要当事人双方无约定，还款按照实现债权的有关费用、利息、主债务的先后顺序予以清偿抵充。	香港特区法律规定，如果当事人双方无约定，则借款人有权先指定还款的本金与利息分配比例；如果借款人也

续表

法律要点	异同点	内地	香港特区
			未作指定，则出借人有权决定分配比例（但不得抵扣非法合同或不公平请求下的债务）；只有在当事人双方均未指定分配比例时，才按照“先息后本”顺序清偿。
借款期限无约定或约定不明	相同点	对于借款期限无约定或者约定不明情况的处理方式基本一致：首先可由出借人与借款人协商确定；无法协商一致的，可以根据对合同的解释、交易习惯等确定；仍无法确定借款期限的，出借人可以要求借款人在合理期限内立即返还借款。	
	不同点	对于出借人立即偿还借款的“合理期限”的定义有所不同。	
		内地法下的“合理期限”在司法实践中需要综合考量出借人的性质、借款人的偿付能力等因素进行判定，在考量时并不严格限制这一期限的用途，法官有较大的自由裁量权。	香港法下的“合理期限”主要是指支付款项所需要的合理时间。

与担保合同关系的法律规则比较

法律要点	异同点	内地	香港特区
借款合同无效时担保合同的效力	相同点	1. 在绝大多数情形下，内地和香港特区的法律都认为担保具有从属性。内地法律明确规定担保合同具有从属性，担保合同不能独立于借款合同的存在而存在。香港特区法律规定，保证、按揭、押记以及质押等担保的设立都从属于借款合同，担保责任的范围取决于借款合同所限定的责任范围。 2. 一般而言，当借款合同被认定无效（不可被强制执行）时，均否定担保合同的效力及其可执行性。内地法律明确规定，借款合同无效，担保合同亦随之无效。香港特区法律规定，借款合同因出借人无牌放债或约定过高利率而被认定无法强制执行，担保合同亦无法被强制执行。借款合同因《放债人条例》之外的原因而被认定为无效或无法被强制执行，担保人所提供的保证、按揭、押记或质押亦无法被强制执行。	

续表

法律要点	异同点	内地	香港特区
	不同点	1. 对借款合同无效、担保合同亦无效的例外规定不一致。	
		内地法律要求担保合同严格遵循从属性，未对借款合同无效、担保合同亦无效的法律规则作出例外规定。	香港特区法律对保证所遵循的责任共存原则存在法定例外规定。当以弥偿的方式提供担保，由于弥偿具有独立性，弥偿合同的效力不受借款合同无效的影响。
		2. 当担保合同因借款合同无效而被认定为无效（不可被强制执行）时，对担保人需要承担责任的例外情形规定不一致。	
		内地法律规定，当借款合同导致担保合同无效时，担保人只在有过错的情况下才承担赔偿责任，且其所承担的责任不应超过借款人不能清偿部分的1/3。	根据香港特区法律，当担保人以弥偿的方式提供担保，弥偿合同有效成立且合同约定的弥偿条件已成就时，出借人可以继续要求弥偿人向其承担弥偿责任。
让与担保的效力问题	相同点	1. 都存在让与担保（以交易行为提供担保）的实践，其表现形式基本一致。并且，两地的法律都承认让与担保（以交易行为提供担保）具有担保效力。在两地的借贷活动中，借款人采取将担保物的所有权转至出借人名下，或另行订立买卖合同的方式，为先前或后续签订的借款合同提供担保。两地的法律都认可此种财产转让交易行为或签订买卖合同的方式，能够发挥担保的功能和效力。 2. 在处理后让与担保纠纷上存在相似之处。在解决后让与担保纠纷时，两地的法律都认为应当对出借人与借款人订立买卖合同这一交易的实质进行认定，即判断出借人和借款人是否具有进行买卖行为的真实意思表示。如认定出借人与借款人订立买卖合同是双方的真实意思表示，则出借人要求借款人继续履行买卖合同的主张一般会得到法院支持。内地法律明确规定，如当事人所提交的证据可证明买卖合同存在，但不足以证明民间借贷事实存在的，法院一般认定双方订立的买卖合同是其真实的意思表示，按照买卖合同法律关系审理。香港特区的判例法明确指出，交易性质的认定应当关注交易的实质而非其形式，即应当根据案件事实认定出借人和借款人之间的买卖合同是否为成立在先的借款合同提供担保，而不应当被买卖合同的外在表现形式迷惑。	

续表

法律要点	异同点	内地	香港特区
	不同点	在司法实践中对让与担保的分类存在不同。	
		内地司法实践中，根据合同标的物所有权转让的先后顺序，让与担保的类型可具体细分为让与担保和后让与担保两种方式，其中让与担保还可被进一步细分为买卖式担保和所有权转让式担保。	香港特区法律对借贷活动中出现的以交易行为作为担保的行为不作具体的类型区分，而是注重根据案件的具体情形断定交易行为的真正性质，一般未将借款合同订立的时间点以及财产转让的时间点作为判断的决定性因素。

夫妻债务制度的法律规则比较

法律要点	异同点	内地	香港特区
夫妻债务制度	相同点	1. 夫妻双方通过共同签字等共同意思表示所负担的债务由夫妻双方共同承担。 2. 夫妻一方以个人名义超出家庭日常生活需要对外所借款项一般不认定为夫妻共同债务。	
	不同点	1. 在夫妻财产制度上存在区别。	
		内地以夫妻共同财产制为原则，以约定财产制为例外。	香港特区以分别财产制为原则，仅在特殊情况下可认定夫妻共同持有某一项财产。
		2. 在夫妻债务制度上存在区别。	
		内地对夫妻双方共同意思表示所负的债务及夫妻一方以个人名义因家庭日常生活需要所负的债务一般认定为夫妻共同债务；超出家庭日常生活需要所负的债务一般不认定为夫妻共同债务，除非债权人有证据证明该债务用于夫妻共同生活、共同生产经营或者基于夫妻双方共同意思表示而负担。	香港特区法律没有单独对夫妻共同债务作出专门的定义或规定，夫妻一方对外负担的债务一般认定为个人债务，且香港特区夫妻之间无日常家事代理权。

续表

<table>
<tr><th colspan="4">诉讼时效的法律规则比较</th></tr>
<tr><th>法律要点</th><th>异同点</th><th>内地</th><th>香港特区</th></tr>
<tr><td rowspan="9">诉讼时效</td><td>相同点</td><td colspan="2">1. 诉讼时效制度在时效届满的法律效果上大致相同，均阻却权利人通过诉讼程序获得救济的途径，但并不否定权利的存在。
2. 均通过成文法规定诉讼时效的抗辩需由当事人专门提出。</td></tr>
<tr><td rowspan="8">不同点</td><td colspan="2">1. 诉讼时效期间不同。</td></tr>
<tr><td>内地规定了普遍适用的 3 年普通诉讼时效期间；内地并未针对特定的担保而专门规定不同的诉讼时效期间。</td><td>香港特区对不同类别诉讼的时效期间进行了列举。对于借款纠纷而言，内地的诉讼时效为 3 年，香港特区则为 6 年。香港特区针对藉按揭和押记而获得保证的款项规定了专门的诉讼时效期间（本金 12 年、利息 6 年）。</td></tr>
<tr><td colspan="2">2. 在特定情况下，诉讼时效的起算时点因关于请求权产生的规定不一致而有所不同。</td></tr>
<tr><td>对于没有约定期限的借款合同，内地法律规定了还款的合理期限，诉讼时效自合理期限届满之日起算。</td><td>对于没有约定期限的借款合同，香港特区的诉讼时效自借款发放之日起算。</td></tr>
<tr><td colspan="2">3. 突破原有诉讼时效期间的规定不同。</td></tr>
<tr><td>内地关于诉讼时效中断、中止的规定具有普遍适用的效力，而诉讼时效的延长仅适用于最长诉讼时效，且未列举具体场景，仅赋予法院在极特殊情况下对最长诉讼时效进行延长。</td><td>香港特区没有专门的诉讼时效中断、中止的规定，但对诉讼时效的延长或延后规定了具体适用的场景。</td></tr>
<tr><td colspan="2">4. 最长诉讼时效期间不同。</td></tr>
<tr><td>内地法律对最长诉讼时效期间作出了普遍适用的规定。</td><td>香港特区未作此类普遍适用的规定。</td></tr>
</table>

TABLE OF COMPARISONS

<table>
<tr><th colspan="4">Comparison of Legal Rules on Professional Money Lenders</th></tr>
<tr><th>Key Points</th><th>Comparison</th><th>Chinese Mainland</th><th>Hong Kong</th></tr>
<tr><td rowspan="3">Criteria for Determination of Professional Money Lenders</td><td>Similarity</td><td colspan="2">1. The laws in the Chinese Mainland and Hong Kong do not endorse the conduct of lending without a financial qualification (or a money lender's licence) and both hold a negative attitude towards it.
2. There is no consolidated standard for determination of a professional (unlicensed) money lender in the Chinese Mainland and Hong Kong. The Chinese Mainland is still at an exploratory stage in determination of professional money lenders and the courts at all levels formulate contextualised criteria for determination of professional money lenders in light of the level of economic developments in local area. The criteria for determination in Hong Kong are scattered in case law and no consolidated criteria is summarised and fixed by the statutes.
3. The laws in the Chinese Mainland and Hong Kong both determine whether a person is a professional (unlicensed) money lender from the following three aspects: the lenders, the borrowers and the conduct of lending. Both jurisdictions adopt a comprehensive approach to determine this issue by taking into account the specific evidence and peculiar features of each case.</td></tr>
<tr><td rowspan="2">Difference</td><td colspan="2">Different in emphasis on the ascertainment of lending conduct.</td></tr>
<tr><td>The courts in the Chinese Mainland consider the number of private lending cases as a significant factor.</td><td>The courts in Hong Kong stress on the factor of the actual number of loans made by the lenders.</td></tr>
</table>

Continue

Key Points	Comparison	Chinese Mainland	Hong Kong
Legal Consequences of the Conduct of Professional Money Lenders	Similarity	The Chinese Mainland and Hong Kong do not recognise the conduct of lending by professional (unlicensed) money lenders. Both jurisdictions hold negative attitudes towards the legal effect of the conduct of lending by professional (unlicensed) money lender, and stipulate corresponding adverse legal consequences.	
	Difference	1. Different in legal consequences of lending money by professional (unlicensed) money lenders.	
		The laws in the Chinese Mainland expressly regulate that the legal effect of loan contract concluded by a professional money lender is null and void and that the borrower shall return the principal and pay the fund possession fees to the lender. The amount of fund possession fees is normally determined by reference to the Annual LPR.	In Hong Kong the *Money Lenders Ordinance* provides that the loan contract entered into by an unlicensed money lender is unenforceable.
		2. Different in adoption of approaches to deal with the conduct of lending by professional (unlicensed) money lenders.	
		As the laws unequivocally stipulate that a loan contract entered into by a professional-money lender is void, the courts in the Chinese Mainland are unable to exercise discretion to give any effect to the loan contracts entered into by professional money lenders.	The courts in Hong Kong can exercise discretion to give limited protection to unlicensed money lenders in consideration of the equitable principles. However, the court is very cautious when exercising such discretions.

Continue

Comparison of Legal Rules on Principal and Interest			
Key Points	**Comparison**	**Chinese Mainland**	**Hong Kong**
Principal and Interest	Similarity	1. Legislation in the Chinese Mainland and Hong Kong both adopt the same conservative and restrictive approach in the determination of principal amount in private lending cases. Only the amount actually lent will be deemed as principal. 2. Deductions such as retained interests will be deducted from the principal amount in judicial practice of both the Chinese Mainland and Hong Kong.	
	Difference	1. Different in the scope of interest.	
		The laws in the Chinese Mainland distinguish interest from liquidated damages as well as any other fees and stipulate that the total amount of all fees including interest, liquidated damages and others cannot exceed the statutory cap of four times Annual LPR.	The laws in Hong Kong distinguish interest from stamp duty as well as other similar duty and stipulate that any amount (by whatever name called) in excess of the principal is deemed as interest.
		2. Different in deductions in the calculation of interest.	
		Sums deducted from the principal amount will not be included into the interest amount in the Chinese Mainland	Sums deducted from the principal amount are likely to be included into the interest amount in Hong Kong.
		3. Different in judicial restrictions on refinancing loans.	
		The laws in the Chinese Mainland require the total amount of principal and interest of the last loan not to exceed the amount of principal and interest calculated based on the principal of the very first loan in order to prevent interests from exceeding the statutory cap.	The laws in Hong Kong only require each refinancing loan to comply with the law.

Continue

Key Points	Comparison	Chinese Mainland	Hong Kong
Loan Interest	Difference	Different in determination of loan interest when the interest is not agreed or unclear.	
		The laws in the Chinese Mainland distinguish natural persons from other contractual parties by regulating that interest, whether without agreement or with unclear agreement, of a loan between parties who are both natural persons shall be deemed as interest-free. Only interest with unclear agreement between parties, one or both of whom are not natural persons, shall be determined based on the local or the parties' course of dealing, trading modes and customs, LPR and so forth.	The laws in Hong Kong do not distinguish natural persons from other contractual parties. Interest without agreement or with unclear agreement shall first be implied from the parties' course of dealing, trading or business customs and so forth. Only interest without agreement fails to be implied will be deemed as interest-free. Equity also provides plenty of exceptions.
Default Interest	Similarity	The laws in the Chinese Mainland and Hong Kong both respect the autonomy of will of the parties and protect default interest with explicit agreement in contract under the statutory cap.	
	Difference	1. Different in the nature of default interest.	
		The laws in the Chinese Mainland prioritise the parties' agreement in identifying the nature of default interest as either liquidated damages or compensation for loss.	Common law principle in Hong Kong identifies the nature of default interest as damages for breach of contract.
		2. Different in the protection for default rate exceeding loan rate	
		The laws in the Chinese Mainland only protect the amount not exceeding statutory cap (four times Annual LPR).	The laws in Hong Kong have no explicit regulations, but a higher default rate is likely regarded as penalty and possibly rejected by court.

Continue

Key Points	Comparison	Chinese Mainland	Hong Kong
		3. Different in the calculation of default interest.	
		The laws in the Chinese Mainland regulate the calculation of default interest without agreement to be computed on the basis of the loan rate, or Annual LPR in the absence of a loan rate.	The laws in Hong Kong divide default interest without agreement into pre-judgment interest and post-judgment interest. The calculation of pre-judgment interest normally bases on Prime Rate (5.625% at present) + 1% and post-judgment interest on judgment rate (8.875% at present).
Comparison of Legal Rules on the Statutory Interest Rate Cap			
Key Points	**Comparison**	**Chinese Mainland**	**Hong Kong**
Statutory Interest Rate Cap	Similarity	Specific legal rules on the interest rate cap of loan transactions are stipulated in the statute in both Chinese Mainland and Hong Kong, and both have lowered the interest rate cap through law amendments.	
	Difference	Different in rules on the loan interest rate cap, with the protection limit for interest rates being higher in Hong Kong.	
		The interest rate cap of private lending in the Chinese Mainland is four times Annual LPR (as of July 22, 2024, four times Annual LPR is 13.4%), which is fluctuating instead of fixed.	The laws in Hong Kong provide that, except for exemptions, lending money at an effective rate of interest which exceeds 48% per annum is deemed as an offence, and exceeds 36% per annum is presumed to be extortionate.
Legal Consequences of Exceeding Statutory Interest Rate Cap	Similarity	In the Chinese Mainland and Hong Kong, the lender shall bear the corresponding adverse legal consequences if the interest rate of lending transactions exceeds the statutory cap.	
	Difference	Different in legal consequences of the loan transaction that exceeds the statutory interest rate cap.	

Continue

Key Points	Comparison	Chinese Mainland	Hong Kong
		The laws in the Chinese Mainland stipulate that the interest exceeding the cap is not protected (as of July 22, 2024, four times Annual LPR is 13.4%), but the court supports the principal, interest and fees within the scope of judicial protection.	The laws in Hong Kong stipulate that loan transactions exceeding the statutory cap of 48% shall not be enforced, that is, the court will not support the recovery of principal and interest. If the interest rate exceeds the extortionate rate of 36% and the transaction is presumed to be extortionate, the transaction may be reopened by the court. The court also has discretion to enforce the loan agreement if it exceeds the extortionate interest rate of 36% and if it is satisfied that the transaction is not extortionate.
Comparison of Legal Rules on Unclear Contractual Terms			
Key Points	**Comparison**	**Chinese Mainland**	**Hong Kong**
Repayment Order of Not Priority Specified or Unclear	Similarity	The repayment appropriation order of principal and interest between the Chinese Mainland and Hong Kong is essentially identical. If there is an agreement, it will be followed. If there is no agreement and neither party has specified the ratio of repayment appropriation, the interest will be presumed to be repaid first, followed by the principal.	
	Difference	Different in the repayment appropriation by designation.	
		The laws in the Chinese Mainland stipulate that in the absence of an agreement between the parties, repayment shall follow the order of the costs related to realising the claim, interest and principal debt.	The laws in Hong Kong allow the borrower to specify the repayment appropriation order between the principal and interest if there is no agreement. If the borrower does not specify, the lender may appropriate the repayment, but is not allowed to discharge a debt under an illegal contract or inequitable

Continue

Key Points	Comparison	Chinese Mainland	Hong Kong
			demand. If neither party specifies, the repayment follows the order of "interest prevails principal".
Loan Term Not Specified or Unclear	Similarity	In the circumstance where the loan term is not specified or unclear, the handling approach is similar between the Chinese Mainland and Hong Kong. The lender can negotiate to fix a repayment date with the borrower. If failed on renegotiation, the loan term maybe implied in fact or by trade customs. If no loan term is so fixed or implied, the lender can demand repayment from the borrower at any time within a reasonable time.	
	Difference	Different in defining the reasonable time allowed for the borrower.	
		In the Chinese Mainland, however, the determination of reasonable time shall take into account relevant factors such as the identity of the lender and the solvency of the borrower. The purpose of the reasonable time is not limited strictly to payment mechanics. The court is left with more discretion comparing to Hong Kong.	In Hong Kong, it is limited to the time necessary for the mechanics of payment.
Comparison of Legal Rules on Security Contracts			
Key Points	**Comparison**	**Mainland**	**Hong Kong**
Validity of Security Contracts When the Loan Contract is Invalid	Similarity	1. In the vast majority of circumstances, the laws in the Chinese Mainland and Hong Kong both consider that security is accessory in nature. The laws in the Chinese Mainland expressly provide in statutes that the security contract is secondary in nature and cannot stand alone the loan contract. The laws in Hong Kong provide that the creation of guarantees, mortgages, charges, and pledges is contingent on the conclusion of the loan contract and that the extent to which the surety is liable under the security contract depends on the scope of obligations under the principal loan contract.	

Continue

<table>
<tr><th>Key Points</th><th>Comparison</th><th>Chinese Mainland</th><th>Hong Kong</th></tr>
<tr><td rowspan="5"></td><td></td><td colspan="2">2. Generally speaking, when a loan contract is determined as void (or unenforceable), the laws in the Chinese Mainland and Hong Kong both negate the validity and enforceability of security contracts. The laws in the Chinese Mainland clearly stipulate that if the loan contract is invalid, the security contract will be void by its invalidity. The laws in Hong Kong provide that if a loan contract is determined unenforceable by reasons of lack of money lender's licences or charging interest at excessive interest rates, the security to the loan contract is unenforceable as well. Additionally, if a loan contract is deemed invalid or unenforceable for reasons other than those prescribed by the Money Lenders Ordinance, the guarantees, mortgages, charges, or pledges created by the surety will also be unenforceable.</td></tr>
<tr><td rowspan="4">Difference</td><td colspan="2">1. Different in exceptions to the general principle that the invalidity of a loan contract will cause the security contract void.</td></tr>
<tr><td>The laws in the Chinese Mainland require strict compliance of the secondary nature of security contracts and no statutory exception is stipulated regarding the general principle.</td><td>In Hong Kong, there are statutory exceptions to the co-extensiveness principle. Moreover, if the security is created in the form of indemnity, by virtue of its peculiar characteristic of independence, the legal effect of indemnity contract will not be affected by the invalidity of the loan contract.</td></tr>
<tr><td colspan="2">2. Different in exceptions to the surety's liability, when a security contract is determined void (or unenforceable) due to the invalidity of the loan contract.</td></tr>
<tr><td>The laws in the Chinese Mainland provide that when the invalidity of the loan contract causes the security contract void, the surety will be liable only if the surety is at fault, and the liability borne by the</td><td>In accordance with the laws in Hong Kong, if the surety creates security by the form of indemnity and if the indemnity contract is validly concluded and the conditions agreed upon are</td></tr>
</table>

Continue

Key Points	Comparison	Chinese Mainland	Hong Kong
		surety is limited to one-third of the proportion that the debtor is unable to repay.	fulfilled, the lender can demand the indemnifier to perform his obligations under the indemnity contract.
Validity of Assignment Guarantee	Similarity	1. There is a practice of assignment guarantee (or creating security by transactions) in both Chinese Mainland and Hong Kong and their manifestation forms are basically the same. Moreover, the laws in the Chinese Mainland and Hong Kong both recognise that assignment guarantee (or creating security by transactions) can perform function as security. In lending activities, it is common for the borrower to transfer the ownership of the secured property to the lender or to enter into a separate sales contract to create security for loan contract previously or subsequently concluded. The laws in the Chinese Mainland and Hong Kong both recognise security function can be created and performed by means of transferring the ownership of property or entering into a separate sales contract. 2. There are similarities in handling disputes regarding post-assignment guarantee. When resolving post-assignment guarantee disputes, the laws in the Chinese Mainland and Hong Kong both consider it is essential to ascertain the substance of the transaction of entering into a sales contract between the lender and the borrower, namely whether the parties have the true intention to engage in sales. If parties' true intention to the transaction is deemed to genuinely concluding a sales contract, the court will generally support the lender's claim requiring the borrower to continue performing his obligations under the sales contract. Laws in the Chinese Mainland expressly stipulate that if the evidence adduced by the parties proves the existence of the sales contract, but it is unable to prove that of private lending, the courts will tend to find that the conclusion of sales contract is the parties' true intention and to adjudicate on the basis of the legal relationship of sales contract. The case laws in Hong Kong clearly point out that the nature of a transaction should be ascertained in light of its substance rather than its form, which requires the court, based on case facts, to determine whether the sales contract between the lender and the borrower is intended to provide security for the loan contract previously concluded, and not to be confused by its external form.	

Continue

<table>
<tr><th>Key Points</th><th>Comparison</th><th>Chinese Mainland</th><th>Hong Kong</th></tr>
<tr><td rowspan="2"></td><td rowspan="2">Difference</td><td colspan="2">Different in the classification of assignment guarantee in judicial practice.</td></tr>
<tr><td>In the Chinese Mainland, assignment guarantee is specifically subdivided into " assignment guarantee" and "post-assignment guarantee" based on the sequence of the transfer of ownership. Under this categorisation, " assignment guarantee" can be further divided into trading-based assignment guarantee and transferring-based assignment guarantee.</td><td>The laws in Hong Kong make no specific distinctions or classification regarding this security created by means of transaction in lending activities. The laws instead focus on the determination of true nature of the transaction in light of peculiar case facts. The timing of conclusion of loan contracts and that of property transfer are generally not considered as decisive factors for the determination of true legal nature.</td></tr>
<tr><th colspan="4">Comparison of Legal Rules on Marital Debts</th></tr>
<tr><th>Key Points</th><th>Comparison</th><th>Chinese Mainland</th><th>Hong Kong</th></tr>
<tr><td rowspan="3">Marital Debts</td><td>Similarity</td><td colspan="2">1. The laws in the Chinese Mainland and Hong Kong both stipulate that debts incurred through mutual consent of the spouses shall be repaid by both of them.
2. The laws in the Chinese Mainland and Hong Kong both stipulate that debts incurred by one of the spouses in his or her own name which exceed the daily needs of the family do not generally fall within the scope of community debts.</td></tr>
<tr><td rowspan="2">Difference</td><td colspan="2">1. Different in matrimonial property regimes.</td></tr>
<tr><td>The default matrimonial property regime in the Chinese Mainland is the community of acquisition regime, with contractual property regime as an option.</td><td>Hong Kong, however, implements a separate property regime and only in exceptional cases matrimonial property is determined to be held jointly.</td></tr>
</table>

Continue

Key Points	Comparison	Chinese Mainland	Hong Kong
		2. Different in matrimonial debt regimes.	
		In the Chinese Mainland, debts incurred through mutual consent of the spouses and debts incurred by one of the spouses in his or her own name for the family's daily life both fall within the scope of community debts. Debts exceeding the daily needs of the family shall not be deemed as community debts, unless the creditor can prove that such debt is used for the married life, production and business operation by the spouses, or that such debt is incurred by the spouses through mutual consent.	There is no such concept and even description of community debt in Hong Kong laws. There is no statutory agency for daily family affairs between spouses in Hong Kong neither. Debts incurred by one of the spouses in his or her own name are generally determined as personal debts.
Comparison of Legal Rules on Limitations			
Key Points	**Comparison**	**Chinese Mainland**	**Hong Kong**
Limitation	Similarity	1. The legal effects of expiration of limitation period are similar between the Chinese Mainland and Hong Kong. Both bar the remedy by action but leave the right otherwise untouched. 2. Statutes in the Chinese Mainland and Hong Kong both provide that the defence of the limitation period must be specifically pleaded.	
	Difference	1. Different in the limitation periods.	
		In the Chinese Mainland, it is provided that a three-year limitation period is generally applicable. There is no specifically applicable limitation period for guarantee (mortgage or suretyship) in the Chinese Mainland.	The statutes in Hong Kong, however, specify different limitation periods applicable to different classes of action. The applicable limitation period to lending disputes is six years in Hong Kong. There is specific limitation period for actions to recover money secured

Continue

Key Points	Comparison	Chinese Mainland	Hong Kong
			by a mortgage or charge (for principal sum is 12 years, for interest is 6 years) in Hong Kong.
		2. Different in the rules for commencement of limitation period due to different rules on the accrue of the cause of action.	
		For loan contract without a repayment date, the laws in the Chinese Mainland provide for a reasonable period for repayment and the limitation period starts running on the expiration of the reasonable period.	In Hong Kong, for loan contract without a repayment date, the cause of action for repayment of the loan will accrue once the loan was made and the limitation period starts running then.
		3. Different in the rules for breaking the original limitation period.	
		In the Chinese Mainland, the rules for suspension and interruption of limitation period are generally applicable, while the rule of extension only applies to calculation of the maximum length of time with no specific scenario prescribed, and empowers the court to extend the maximum limitation period in exceptional cases.	In Hong Kong, there are no generally applicable rules of suspension and interruption of limitation period, but specific scenarios are prescribed for the application of extension or postponement of limitation period.
		4. Different in the maximum length of time for limitation period.	
		The maximum length of time for limitation period is generally applicable in the Chinese Mainland	There is no such rule in Hong Kong.

目　录

第一章　民间借贷的相关概念比较

第二章　职业放贷人的法律规则比较

第三章 本金与利息的法律规则比较

第四章 利率司法保护上限的法律规则比较

第五章　合同条款约定不明的法律规则比较

第六章　与担保合同关系的法律规则比较

第七章　夫妻债务制度的法律规则比较

第八章 诉讼时效的法律规则比较

结 语

CONTENTS

Chapter Ⅷ Comparison of Legal Rules on Limitations

Epilogue

第一章　民间借贷的相关概念比较

第一节　内地的法律规定

“民间借贷”原本并非一个法律概念，而是生活中约定俗成的一个称谓，一般区别于金融机构借款，即泛指在金融监管机关监督管理之外，由非金融机构参与实施的借贷行为，国外部分法系采用“非正式金融”概念。民间借贷在我国最初多指发生在基于血缘、地缘关系的同乡、同行、亲朋好友等自然人之间的借贷。随着借贷主体呈现出多元化和广泛性的特点，其内涵也随着社会经济的发展而不断演变。民间借贷的主体逐渐扩展到了大量担保公司、合会、典当行、投资公司、小贷公司、财务咨询公司等法人、非法人组织等，甚至还有为数不少的非法放贷主体，如地下钱庄或者带有黑社会性质的职业放贷人。随着民间借贷数量的高速增长，民间借贷法律问题需要进一步予以规范并解决。

最高人民法院于 1991 年发布的《关于人民法院审理借贷案件的若干意见》（已废止）第 6 条首次通过司法解释的形式将民间借贷上升为法律概念，民间借贷开始逐步被纳入法律规范的范畴。随着社会经济发展水平逐步提高、民间借贷市场日益活跃，民间借贷案件于 2015 年首次成为各类民事案件中数量排名第一的案件类型，成为各级法院反馈问题最为突出的案件类型。为统一裁判尺度，最高人民法院于 2015 年发布了《民间借贷司法解释》，并于 2020 年 8 月 18 日、2020 年 12 月 23 日进行过两次修正。民间借贷的内涵与外延是本次法律比较首先需要厘清的概念。

一、借款合同的类型

《民法典》第三编（合同编）第二分编规定的有名合同中有借款合同的专门规定。《民法典》第 667 条规定：“借款合同是借款人向贷款人借款，到期返还借款并支付利息的合同。”实践中借款合同的种类繁多，《民事案件案由规定》将借款合同纠纷作为三级案由，项下包括：金融借款合同纠纷、同业拆借纠纷、民间借贷纠纷、小额借款合同纠纷、金融不良债权转让合同纠纷、金融不良债权追偿纠纷。此外，同为三级案由的银行卡纠纷等同样具有借款合同纠纷属性。由此可见，民间借贷合同仅是借款合同的其中一种类型。

借款合同的类型复杂且适用不同的法律规定，司法实践中按照出借主体是否为依法注册的金融机构，借款可以分为金融机构借款与非金融机构借款。其中，金融机构借款可细分为银行业金融机构借款和非银行业金融机构借款。

（一）金融机构借款

根据《金融违法行为处罚办法》第 2 条第 2 款的规定，“金融机构，是指在中华人民共和国境内依法设立和经营金融业务的机构，包括银行、信用合作社、财务公司、信托投资公司、金融租赁公司等”。金融机构包括所有由金融监管部门批准设立并负责监管的金融机构。金融机构在从事金融活动中可能涉及借款业务。

1. 银行业金融机构

根据《银行业监督管理法》第 2 条第 2、3 款和《银行业金融机构反洗钱和反恐怖融资管理办法》第 3 条第 1 款的规定，银行业金融机构是指在中华人民共和国境内设立的商业银行、农村信用合作社等吸收公众存款的金融机构以及政策性银行和国家开发银行。银行业金融机构与非银行业金融机构的主要区别是，该金融机构是否能够从事吸收公众存款的业务并辅以其所从事业务领域。

2. 非银行业金融机构

非银行业金融机构，是指除中央银行、商业银行和专业银行以外的所有金融机构，主要包括公募基金、私募基金、信托、证券、保险、融资租赁等机构以及财务公司等，但我国对非银行业金融机构的范围有所限定。根据国家金融监督管理总局于 2023 年 10 月 17 日颁布的《非银行金融机构行政许可事项实施办法》第 2 条的规定，非银行金融机构包括：经国家金融监督管理总局批准设立的金融资产管理公司、企业集团财务公司、金融租赁公司、汽车金融公司、货币经纪公司、消费金融公司、境外非银行金融机构驻华代表处等机构。

《中共中央、国务院关于服务实体经济防控金融风险深化金融改革的若干意见》（中发〔2017〕23 号）已经明确规定，地方金融监管部门批准设立的小额贷款公司、融资担保公司、区域性股权市场、典当行、融资租赁公司、商业保理公司、地方资产管理公司等上述七类地方金融机构，由中央金融监管部门制定规则，地方金融监管部门实施监管。《国务院办公厅关于全面推进金融业综合统计工作的意见》（国办发〔2018〕18 号）也将上述七类地方金融组织纳入金融业综合统计范围。地方金融监管部门批准设立的上述七类地方金融机构也属于非银行业金融机构。

（二）非金融机构借款

非金融机构借款主要指自然人、法人和非法人组织的资金在社会各个领域内的融通行为，即出借主体没有经过中央或地方的金融监管部门批准设立，借款行为不在金融监管之内的私人资金融通活动。在市场主体无法从正规金融机构获取金融服务的情况下，为应对正规金融服务的缺失，大量的私人资本基于逐利性进入金融市场作为补充，非金融机构借款应运而生，填补了正规金融服务无法触及的部分。非金融机构借款在一定程度上促进了经济的发展，但其逐利性也衍生出了高利贷、套路贷等不良社会现象。

二、民间借贷的法律内涵

《民间借贷司法解释》第 1 条对民间借贷的法律概念进行了明确规定，从立法技术层面来说，其采取了正面规定和例外排除的立法方式。民间借贷的法律概念为司法实践准确适用《民间借贷司法解释》提供了较好的指引，为法院审理案件明确了司法规则。

（一）非金融机构借款一般为民间借贷

《民间借贷司法解释》第 1 条明确规定："本规定所称的民间借贷，是指自然人、法人和非法人组织之间进行资金融通的行为。"从立法背景来看，民间借贷主要是指私人资金在社会各个领域内的融通过程，是没有经过官方金融机构注册的，游离于金融监管之外的私人资金融通活动。此类资金融通行为具有非官方、非正规性的特点，具有典型的民间特性[1]。非金融机构借款属于典型的民间借贷，司法实践中对此基本达成共识。

（二）金融机构借款也可能为民间借贷

需要特别强调的是，在法律适用时容易产生一个误区，即认为民间借贷就是非金融机构借款。《民间借贷司法解释》第 1 条第 2 款明确规定："经金融监管部门批准设立的从事贷款业务的金融机构及其分支机构，因发放贷款等相关金融业务引发的纠纷，不适用本规定。"金融机构借款是否为民间借贷取决于发放贷款的金融机构是否具备金融监管部门批准从事贷款业务的资质。

1. 银行业金融机构依法从事的贷款业务不属于民间借贷

银行业金融机构因从事贷款业务而产生的纠纷被称为金融借款合同纠纷。其与民间借贷纠纷最大的区别在于，出借人的营业范围包括金融监管部门特许其从事的贷款业务，即出借人可以经常从事贷款业务，甚至以之为主营业务。营业范围意义上的贷款业务受到高度管制，是金融监管部门的行政许可事项，只有获得金融许可证的特定金融机构方可开展。如果非金融机构没有放贷资质而从事贷款业务，则会被认定为涉嫌从事"非法金融业务活动"，从而导致借款合同无效，甚至可能承担非法经营等刑事责任。

2. 非银行业金融机构依法从事的贷款业务需要区别对待

由于金融行业实行分业经营、区别监管，银保监会所批准成立的从事证券或保险及其衍生业务的金融机构，如证券公司、保险公司、期货公司、公募基金、私募基金等，通常都没有得到从事贷款业务的许可。除证券公司的融资融券，保险公司的保单质押贷款等极少数特殊情况以外，上

---

[1] 参见最高人民法院民事审判第一庭编著：《最高人民法院新民间借贷司法解释理解与适用》，人民法院出版社 2021 年版，第 48 页。

述金融机构参与的借贷活动应当被认定为民间借贷。银保监会所批准成立的信托公司、企业集团财务公司、金融租赁公司、汽车金融公司、货币经纪公司、消费金融公司的经营范围如包括发放贷款，其参与的借贷活动则属于金融借款；否则，则属于民间借贷。

值得注意的是，非银行业金融机构包含地方金融监管部门监管的地方金融机构，包括小额贷款公司、融资担保公司、区域性股权市场、典当行、融资租赁公司、商业保理公司、地方资产管理公司等七类。其中，小额贷款公司和典当行主要从事贷款业务；融资担保公司、商业保理公司、融资租赁公司、地方资产管理公司、区域性股权市场在经营过程中也可能涉及提供融资服务。上述七类地方金融机构从事贷款业务引发的纠纷不是民间借贷纠纷。[1]

第二节　香港特区的法律规定

香港特区法律中并没有民间借贷的概念，其借贷政策随着香港特区金融行业政策的变化而不断改变，从自由放任、积极不干涉、最低限度干涉的政策逐步发展到现在的“审慎干涉”政策。香港特区对“贷款”的规管主要体现在《放债人条例》及相关司法判例中。现行的《放债人条例》于1980年公布实施，旨在“对放债人及放债交易进行管制和规定，明确经营放债人业务的领牌事宜，为对付过高的贷款利率及敲诈性的贷款规定而提供保障和济助”。香港特区放贷行为总体包括以下三类情形。

一、放债人的放贷

《放债人条例》主要规范放债人的放贷行为。放债人是指“经营贷款业务（无论他是否亦经营其他业务）的人，或宣传、宣布或以任何方式显

〔1〕 详见《最高人民法院关于新民间借贷司法解释适用范围问题的批复》（法释〔2020〕27号）。

示自己是经营该业务的人”。截至2019年12月31日，香港特区已经有超过2300家持牌放债人，为个人和公司提供替代性融资渠道。

为防止放债人高利、非法放贷，损害借款人利益，《放债人条例》对放债人进行了非常严格的监管，除所有贷款都要遵循的最高利率要求以外，对放债人的牌照申领、放债的协议形式、签订协议地点、非法协议内容等均有严格且细致的规定。

（一）放债人牌照申领

《放债人条例》第9条、第10条及相关条款规定，公司和年满21周岁的个人均可以申领放债人牌照。申领放债人牌照须同时向注册处处长和香港特区警务处处长提出申请，警务处处长可安排就相关申请进行调查，以决定是否有理由反对该宗申请。在接获申请后的一定期限内，注册处处长向牌照法庭提交申请，由牌照法庭对相关申请做出聆讯及裁定。牌照法庭在进行聆讯后，可决定发出或拒绝发出牌照。牌照一经发出，其有效期为12个月，持牌人可在牌照期满前3个月申请将牌照延期。

（二）放债人放债的地点

《放债人条例》第7条规定，放债人不得在其放债人牌照所指明的处所以外的任何地方经营放债人业务。同时根据《放债人条例》第29条的规定，放债人在牌照所指明的处所以外的任何地方经营放债人业务属于犯罪。

（三）放债人放债的协议形式要求

《放债人条例》第18条规定，贷款协议订立后7日内，放债人必须按照该条例规定制备协议摘记或备忘录，由借款人亲自签署，并在签署时将该摘记或备忘录的副本给予借款人，否则关于放债人所贷出款项的还款协议或该款项的利息支付协议不得强制执行，而且相应的担保也不得强制执行。借款人有权获得关于贷款的书面协议，从而明晰各项贷款要素。

（四）放债人放债的协议内容要求

（1）《放债人条例》第 21 条和第 22 条规定，放债人的放债应当保障借款人以分期方式提早偿还或分期偿还贷款。（2）《放债人条例》第 22 条规定，禁止借款合同约定支付复利，亦禁止在借款合同中约定拖欠到期借款而提高利率或提高利息数额。（3）《放债人条例》第 27 条规定，放债人如果要求借款人承担与贷款的洽商或批给有关的成本、费用或开支，或放债人及其雇员、代理人因与贷款相关的事务向借款人收取报酬或酬金，均属不合法。（4）《放债人规例》第 12 条规定，放债人不得要求或接受任何以下对象作为贷款保证：身份证、护照或证明持有人身份或国籍的其他文件；银行储蓄存款或定期存款的存折；借款人、保证人、借款人家庭成员或保证人家庭成员的照片（无论是否已经显影）。

（五）对放债广告的限制

《放债人条例》第 26 条规定，放债人发出或刊登关于放债业务的广告，必须清楚展示“Money Lender’s Licence No.”（放债人牌照号码）字样，并紧随其后展示其放债人牌照号码。如广告中提及贷款利息，必须以年息百分率表示，广告中放债人姓名、贷款利率须以醒目方式展示。

（六）放债人放债利率上限

《放债人条例》第 24 条规定，放债人超过年息 48% 的实际利率贷出款项或邀约贷出款项，即属犯罪，一经定罪，最高可罚款 500 万港元及监禁 10 年。[1]《放债人条例》第 25（3）条规定，放债人超过年息 36% 的实际利率贷出款项即推定属敲诈性，法院有权重启交易。需要特别强调的是，根据《放债人条例》第 24 条和第 25 条的规定，实际利率的限额适用于所

---

〔1〕《放债人条例》于 2022 年 10 月 26 日正式修改，于 2022 年 12 月 30 日正式生效。该条例修改前的过高利率的入刑标准为年利率 60%，敲诈性交易的推定标准为年利率 48%。本书引用的案例均适用修改前的《放债人条例》所规定的利率。

有类型的借贷，而无论出借人是否为放债人。

（七）放债人向借款人、保证人提供资料的责任

《放债人条例》第19、20条规定，在借款人提出书面请求时，放债人应向借款人提供其借出款项的结算书，结算书中应列明借款本金，利息，借款人已偿还款项、未偿还款项的金额及到期日等信息。如该笔贷款订有保证协议，保证人提出书面请求时，放债人也应提供上述结算书。

二、受豁免的人

《放债人条例》附表1第1部特定主体的放贷行为不受《放债人条例》规管。该部分所规定的出借主体在放贷行为、放贷对象、放贷频率等因素上具有独特性，区别于放债人的放贷，其往往由专门的法例或者行业规范进行规管。例如，根据《香港银行业条例》（第155章）受香港金融监管机构监管的银行及接受存款的公司，需要遵守该条例及《银行营运守则》等。附表1第1部列明以下主体的放贷不适用《放债人条例》。

1.《银行业条例》（第155章）所指的认可机构的附属公司。

2. 根据《合作社条例》（第33章）注册的合作社。

3. 根据《储蓄互助社条例》（第119章）注册的储蓄互助社及根据该条例第Ⅺ部成立的香港储蓄互助社协会。

4. 根据《职工会条例》（第332章）登记的职工会。

5.《保险业条例》（第41章）所指的保险人，而该保险人是根据该条例获授权经营该条例附表1第2部所指明的某类别或某等类别的保险业务的。（由2015年第12号第107条修订。）

6.（由1991年第140号法律公告废除。）

7. 大学教育资助委员会。（由1995年第35号法律公告修订。）

8. 以下银行——（a）在香港以外地方成立为法团或设立的银行；（b）获《银行业条例》（第155章）第2（9）条所指的有关银行业监管当局承认为银行的银行，而该监管当局是已获根据

《外汇基金条例》（第 66 章）第 5A 条委任的金融管理专员以书面宣布为银行业监管当局，且专员认为该监管当局为本段的施行而行使充分审慎的监管者；及（由 1995 年第 49 号第 53 条代替）（c）在该银行业监管当局的所在地经营银行业务的银行。（由 1995 年第 49 号第 53 条代替。）

9. 以下机构——（a）信用保险业国际总会#会员机构；或（b）注册处处长已以书面宣布他信纳是由一个或超过一个国家政府设立的机构，而其目标是资助或担保资助任何国家的货品输出或服务输出者。

10. 根据《证券及期货条例》（第 571 章）第 V 部获发牌经营证券保证金融资业务的法团。（由 2002 年第 5 号第 407 条代替。）

11. 根据《证券及期货条例》（第 571 章）第 V 部获发牌经营证券交易业务的法团或获注册经营该业务的认可财务机构，而该法团或机构同时从事证券保证金融资以利便该法团或机构为其客户取得或持有证券。（由 2002 年第 5 号第 407 条代替。）

三、受豁免的贷款

《放债人条例》附表 1 第 2 部以贷款类型为划分依据，明确以下类型的贷款不适用《放债人条例》。《放债人条例》中规定的须申领放债人牌照、按照牌照内所列条件经营放债业务、以特定协议形式放债等专门适用于放债人的规定不适用于上述受豁免的人作出的贷款和受豁免的贷款。

1. 雇主向其雇员真诚作出的贷款。

2. 向公司作出的贷款，并以按揭、押记、留置权或其他产权负担作保证，而且该等按揭、押记、留置权或其他产权负担是——(a) 已经或将会根据《公司条例》（第 622 章）登记者；（由 2012 年第 28 号第 912 条及第 920 条代替）；（ab）已经或将会根据在《公司条例》（第 622 章）附表 9 第 2 条的生效日期（2014 年 3 月 3 日）之前不时有效的《公司条例》（第 32 章）中根据《公司条例》（第 622 章）附

表11而持续有效的条文登记者；(由2012年第28号第912条及第920条增补)；(ac) 已经根据《公司条例》(第622章) 第2 (1) 条所界定的《旧有公司条例》登记者；或 (由2012年第28号第912条及第920条增补)；(b) ［就第2 (1) 条公司 (company) 定义中 (b) 或 (c) 段所提述的公司而言］在——(由2012年第28号第912条及第920条修订)。(i)《公司条例》(第622章) 附表9第2条的生效日期 (2014年3月3日) 之前设定，并且符合以下说明者：假若该公司是根据该条例第2 (1) 条所界定的《旧有公司条例》成立为法团的，该等按揭、押记、留置权或其他产权负担便会能根据该《旧有公司条例》登记；或 (ii) 该生效日期 (2014年3月3日) 当日或之后设定，并且符合以下说明者：假若该公司是根据《公司条例》(第622章) 成立为法团的，该等按揭、押记、留置权或其他产权负担便会能根据该条例登记。(由2012年第28号第912条及第920条修订。)

3. 任何公司根据其真诚施行的信用卡计划而向根据该计划获发给信用卡的持有人作出的贷款。

4. 为购买不动产并以该不动产的按揭作为保证而真诚作出的贷款，以及再资助该项按揭而真诚作出的贷款。

5. 任何公司、商号或个别人士，而其日常业务基本上或主要并不涉及贷款者，在其通常业务运作中作出的贷款。

6. 持牌当押商根据《当押商条例》(第166章) 作出的贷款，而该条例又适用于该宗贷款者。

7. 任何法定团体根据法律为此目的而赋予的权力所作出的贷款。

8. 由以下资金来源作出的贷款——(a) 由立法会藉决议设立的基金，或由任何条例或根据任何条例设立的基金 (由1999年第23号第3条修订)；(b) 任何离职金或公积金。

9. 根据《银会经营 (禁止) 条例》(第262章) 经营的银会作出的贷款。

10. (a) 控权公司向其附属公司作出的贷款，或附属公司向其控权公司或向该控权公司属下的另一附属公司作出的贷款。(b)《公司条例》（第 622 章）第 13—15 条适用于本段的释义，犹如其适用于该条例的释义一样。（由 2012 年第 28 号第 912 条及第 920 条修订。）

11. 向公司作出的贷款，而该笔贷款——（a）成为涉及货品或服务输入香港或由香港输出的交易的一部分；及（b）是为方便该等货品或服务的输入或输出的目的而作出的。

12. （a）向拥有缴足款股本不少于 $1,000,000 或相等款额的其他认可货币的公司作出的贷款。（b）为施行本段，认可货币（approved currency）指——（i）可自由兑换港元的货币；或（ii）注册处处长为施行本段而以书面认可的货币。

13. 以某些条款作出的贷款，该等条款涉及由公司发行债权证或其他证券，而该等债权证或其他证券的招股章程是已根据《公司（清盘及杂项条文）条例》（第 32 章）注册者。（由 2012 年第 28 号第 912 条及第 920 条修订。）

14. 向某公司作出的贷款，而该公司的股份或债权证是在以下地方上市者——（a）《证券及期货条例》（第 571 章）附表 1 第 1 部第 1 条所界定的认可证券市场；或（由 2002 年第 5 号第 407 条代替）；（b）由《证券及期货条例》（第 571 章）第 3（1）条提述的证券及期货事务监察委员会为施行本段而以书面宣布为已予认可的任何其他证券市场。（由 1989 年第 10 号第 65 条修订；由 2002 年第 5 号第 407 条修订。）

15. 向第 14 段所提述的公司的附属公司作出的贷款。（1988 年第 69 号第 33 条代替。）

第三节　厘定民间借贷案件的比较范围

由于内地与香港特区在立法体例、法律体系、法律文化等各方面存在较大差异，民间借贷作为内地法律下的法律概念，在香港特区无法找到准确对应的法律概念。经对比《民间借贷司法解释》和《放债人条例》的法律规定，内地民间借贷的概念与《放债人条例》部分豁免贷款存在重合。

一、两地概念相似部分

第一，内地小额贷款公司与香港特区放债人内涵具有较高重合性。从出借主体划分的角度来看，内地的民间借贷概念与香港法下放债人的放债行为是不一致的。香港特区的放债人与内地地方金融监管机构批准设立的小额贷款公司在法律内涵上有较高的重合，均是指向经法定程序设立，可以专门从事放债业务的法律主体，其放债行为需要接受批准设立机关的监督和管理。但内地的小额贷款公司属于法人，自然人无法独立取得发放贷款的资质；而香港特区则允许自然人申领放债人牌照。

第二，内地民间借贷与《放债人条例》附表 1 中所豁免的人和豁免的贷款存在重合。其中，与《放债人条例》附表 1 第 2 部第 5 项的内涵具有较高重合性。从提取法律概念最大重合的角度出发，两地立法中的两个条文需要特别注意。(1)《民间借贷司法解释》第 1 条明确规定："本规定所称的民间借贷，是指自然人、法人和非法人组织之间进行资金融通的行为。"(2)《放债人条例》附表 1 第 2 部豁免的贷款中第 5 项规定："任何公司、商号或个别人士，而其日常业务基本上或主要并不涉及贷款者，在其通常业务运作中作出的贷款。"从上述规定来看，民间借贷的概念内涵与《放债人条例》附表 1 第 2 部第 5 项在文字表述上高度一致，均是指不以经营贷款为主要业务的个人、企业、其他组织，在日常生产、生活过程中偶发性的借贷活动。但是从法律规定的内涵和外延来看，《放债人条例》附表 1 第 2 部第 5 项所指向的贷款仅是内地民间借贷概念的一部分，而非全部。

二、本书比较的范围

通过对比两地关于放贷的法律规则，内地的民间借贷的范围不仅包括香港特区《放债人条例》附表 1 第 2 部第 5 项，还包括香港特区《放债人条例》附表 1 中的部分放债行为。本书的目的是解决内地与香港特区借款合同中的一般性问题，不专注于特殊案件的规则比较，以确保法律规则比较的指导性和实用性。经统计，司法实践中绝大多数的民间借贷案件均指向：不以经营贷款为主要业务的个人、企业、其他组织，在日常生产、生活过程中偶发性的借贷活动。由此，本书主要将内地民间借贷行为与《放债人条例》附表 1 第 2 部第 5 项规定的贷款行为进行比较。

关于本书的写作法律用语问题。需要特别说明的是，本次内地与香港特区关于民间借贷合同的比较，涉及两个完全不同法律体系法律规则的比较，不可能在法律用语方面做到完全精准统一，故本书编撰体例、比较要素点仍以内地法律规定的要素点为基准。本书的语言风格以内地法律语言风格为主。

第二章　职业放贷人的法律规则比较

第一节　职业放贷人的认定标准

一、内地的司法实践

（一）相关背景

随着改革开放的持续深入以及经济社会的飞速发展，民间借贷的“紧箍咒”被逐步放松，但是内地法律一直对职业放贷行为持反对态度。

2015 年最高人民法院在制定《民间借贷司法解释》时未将职业放贷纳入法律规制，其中的缘由在于：第一，职业放贷行为在审判实践中比较难以界定，不同地区经济发展水平不平衡，导致法院对职业放贷问题的认定产生较大分歧；第二，中国人民银行已经草拟了《放贷人条例》草案，该草案规定自然人、法人等放贷人应持牌照分类经营，并根据利率、贷款对象、用途等设置了不同监管要求。但自该草案完成至今，正式条例仍未出台，职业放贷现象近年来却愈演愈烈，严重扰乱了经济金融秩序和社会秩序，因此对规范和管制职业放贷行为的司法需求更加强烈。

（二）全国与地方层面的探索

1. 全国层面的规定

最高人民法院与最高人民检察院等机构针对职业放贷行为在刑事和民事方面都进行了探索，以求遏制民间借贷活动中的乱象，震慑非法职业放贷行为。

在刑事方面，2019 年 7 月，最高人民法院与最高人民检察院、公安部、司法部联合制定了《关于办理非法放贷刑事案件若干问题的意见》，其中第 1 条规定：“违反国家规定，未经监管部门批准，或者超越经营范围，以营利为目的，经常性地向社会不特定对象发放贷款，扰乱金融市场秩序，情节严重的，依照刑法第二百二十五条第（四）项的规定，以非法经营罪定罪处罚。前款规定中的‘经常性地向社会不特定对象发放贷款’，是指 2 年内向不特定多人（包括单位和个人）以借款或其他名义出借资金 10 次以上。贷款到期后延长还款期限的，发放贷款次数按照 1 次计算。”《关于办理非法放贷刑事案件若干问题的意见》是对职业放贷行为从刑事方面进行规制，其因对职业放贷人的认定制定了较为严格的标准，对于民商事方面的规范管理有一定的借鉴意义。

在民事方面，2019 年 11 月，最高人民法院印发的《九民纪要》首次明确了职业放贷行为的法律效力，并简要定义了职业放贷人。其中第 53 条规定：“未依法取得放贷资格的以民间借贷为业的法人，以及以民间借贷为业的非法人组织或者自然人从事的民间借贷行为，应当依法认定无效。同一出借人在一定期间内多次反复从事有偿民间借贷行为的，一般可以认定为是职业放贷人。民间借贷比较活跃的地方的高级人民法院或者经其授权的中级人民法院，可以根据本地区的实际情况制定具体的认定标准。”该条文一方面规定职业放贷人的范围不局限于自然人，也包括法人以及非法人组织；另一方面规定出借人在某段时间内存在的反复有偿向他人出借资金从而获利的行为，即属于职业放贷行为。但是，最高人民法院在该条文中并未规定职业放贷人的具体认定标准，对于民间借贷行为发生的具体时间段、该时间段内出借次数等内容，最高人民法院将认定标准的制定权授权给下级法院。

2. 地方层面的探索

基于最高人民法院的授权，各地区的法院根据本地的民间借贷司法实践情况以及地区经济发展水平制定职业放贷人的认定标准。部分省市法院分别在刑事和民事方面对职业放贷人作出规定，但也有部分省市法院出台统一规定对职业放贷人进行法律规管。以下简要列明我国部分省市法院如何对职业放贷人进行认定。

（1）浙江省高级人民法院、浙江省人民检察院、浙江省公安厅、浙江省司法厅、国家税务总局浙江省税务局、浙江省地方金融监督管理局联合出台《关于依法严厉打击与民间借贷相关的刑事犯罪强化民间借贷协同治理的会议纪要》，其中第 2 条规定：针对当前职业放贷高发等实际情况，人民法院要根据同一原告或关联原告在一段时间内所涉的民间借贷案件数量、利率、合同格式化程度等特征，结合各地实际，建立“职业放贷人名录”，进行重点管理，并每季度向公安、检察机关等协同治理单位通报情况。纳入“职业放贷人名录”，一般应当符合以下条件：①以连续 3 年收结案数为标准，同一或关联原告在同一基层法院民事诉讼中涉及 20 件以上民间借贷案件（含诉前调解，以下各项同），或者在同一中级法院及辖区各基层法院民事诉讼中涉及 30 件以上民间借贷案件的。②在同一年度内，同一或关联原告在同一基层法院民事诉讼中涉及 10 件以上民间借贷案件，或者在同一中级法院及辖区各基层法院民事诉讼中涉及 15 件以上民间借贷案件的。③在同一年度内，同一或关联原告在同一中级法院及辖区各基层法院涉及民间借贷案件 5 件以上且累计金额达 100 万元以上，或者涉及民间借贷案件 3 件以上且累计金额达 1000 万元以上的。④符合下列条件两项以上，案件数达到第①、②项规定一半以上的，也可认定为职业放贷人：（a）借条为统一格式的；（b）被告抗辩原告并非实际出借人或者原告要求将本金、利息支付给第三人的；（c）借款本金诉称以现金方式交付又无其他证据佐证的；（d）交付本金时预扣借款利息或者被告实际支付的利息明显高于约定的利息的；（e）原告本人无正当理由拒不到庭应诉或到庭应诉时对案件事实进行虚假陈述的。

（2）江苏省高级人民法院制定的《关于建立疑似职业放贷人名录制度的意见（试行）》第 2 条规定：各基层人民法院要根据自身实际，建立疑似职业放贷人名录制度。审理民间借贷案件首先要进行关联案件查询，同一出借人及其实际控制的关联关系人作为原告一年内在全省各级人民法院起诉民间借贷案件 5 件以上的，该出借人应当纳入疑似职业放贷人名录。通过案件审理或者其他途径可以初步确定为职业放贷人的，不受上述案件数量的限制。

（3）天津市高级人民法院制定的《天津法院民间借贷案件审理指南（试行）》第 21 条规定：出借人未依法取得放贷资格，在一定期间内多次反复从事有偿民间借贷的，一般可以认定构成职业放贷行为。因职业放贷行为形成的民间借贷合同无效。职业放贷行为具有营业性和营利性。审理民间借贷案件中，可以根据出借人在一定期间内放贷次数、同一原告或关联原告提起民间借贷案件数量、借贷合同约定格式化程度以及出借人是否公开推介、宣传或明示出借意愿、借款金额和利息等因素综合认定出借人是否具有营业性。同一原告或者关联原告在2年内向全市法院提起民间借贷案件5件以上，或者出借人在两年内向社会不特定人出借资金3次以上的，一般可以认定出借人的放贷行为具有营业性。借贷合同约定利息、服务费、咨询费、管理费、违约金等相关费用的，或者借款人已实际支付上述费用的，应认定出借人以营利为目的出借款项。主要业务或日常业务不涉及放贷的出借人偶尔出借款项，或者出借人基于人情往来不以营利为目的出借款项，不构成职业放贷行为。

（4）河南省高级人民法院制定的《关于加强职业放贷人审查工作的指导意见（试行）》第2条规定：未经有权机关依法批准，法人、非法人组织或者自然人在一定期间内多次从事与发放贷款业务相同或类似的民间借贷行为的，一般应认定为职业放贷人。对虽非同一出借人起诉的案件，如果该出借人与其他出借人之间具有关联关系，且符合上述行为特征，也应认定为职业放贷人。

（5）广西壮族自治区高级人民法院制定的《关于审理涉及新冠肺炎疫情民商事案件的指导意见》第8条第3款规定：加大对职业放贷行为的审查。原则上，出借人未依法取得放贷资格，在2年内向不特定多人（包括单位和个人）以借款或其他名义出借资金10次以上，可以认定构成职业放贷行为。因职业放贷行为形成的民间借贷合同无效，借款人应当返还借款本金和占用期间利息损失（按照同期全国银行间同业拆借中心公布的贷款市场报价利率计算）。

（6）新疆维吾尔自治区高级人民法院制定的《关于加强职业放贷人审查工作的指导意见（试行）》第4条规定：纳入“职业放贷人名录”，应当符合以下条件：①在同一年度内，同一出借人及其实际控制的关联关系人作为原告在同一法院涉及6件以上民间借贷案件，或者在同一中级法院及所属辖区法院累计涉及6件以上民间借贷案件的；②连续两年，同一出借人及其实际控制的关联关系人作为原告在同一法院涉及10件以上民间借贷案件，或者在同一中级法院及所属辖区法院累计涉及10件以上民间借贷案件的。以上案件数量包含涉及民间借贷申请执行的仲裁裁决、公证债权文书案件和诉前调解案件。

部分省市法院针对职业放贷行为的认定标准也进行了相关调研。例如，北京市高级人民法院民事审判第二庭、北京市第一中级人民法院民事审判第三庭联合课题组在调研北京各法院的倾向性意见后，总结职业放贷人的认定标准如下：①以连续3年收结案数为标准，在同一法院民事诉讼中涉及10件以上，或者在全市各级法院民事诉讼中涉及20件以上的；②在同一年度内，在同一法院民事诉讼中涉及5件以上，或者在全市各级法院民事诉讼中涉及10件以上的；③在同一年度内，在同一法院涉及3件以上且累计金额达1500万元以上，或者在全市各级法院涉及6件以上且累计金额达3000万元以上的。[1]

（三）上升为国家法律

2020年8月和12月，承袭司法解释和司法政策性文件关于职业放贷人的规定，最高人民法院两次修正《民间借贷司法解释》。其中第13条第3项规定，未依法取得放贷资格的出借人，以营利为目的向社会不特定对象提供借款的，人民法院应当认定民间借贷合同无效。该规定首次通过司法解释的形式对职业放贷行为进行了法律界定，并明确规定职业放贷合同属于无效合同。但是，该司法解释并未涵盖关于职业放贷人的具体认定标准，对该问题的认定未作统一规定。

（四）内地认定职业放贷人的考量因素

综合司法解释和地方司法文件相关规定，职业放贷人是指未依法取得放贷资格，以营利为目的向社会不特定对象提供借款的出借人。综合上述各地区法院制定的职业放贷人认定标准，职业放贷人的认定应当从出借人、借款人以及出借行为方面进行考量。

---

〔1〕参见北京市高级人民法院民二庭、北京市第一中级人民法院民三庭联合课题组：《职业放贷人的认定标准》，载《北京审判》2022年第2期。

1. 出借人

司法实践在考量出借人这一因素时，通常从放贷资质和关联出借人两个方面进行认定。

（1）出借人是否具有放贷资质。职业放贷人的主体可以包括法人、非法人组织和自然人。判断出借人是否具备放贷资格，一般应查验出借人是否取得金融许可证等从事贷款业务的相应资质。

（2）出借人是否存在通过关联出借人进行放贷的情形。司法实践中存在出借人借用他人名义对外放贷，或者通过关联公司对外放贷等情形，甚至部分职业放贷人为了规避法律规定，故意通过关联出借人放贷。因此在认定关联出借人时，一般着重审查：第一，是否存在同一单位的实际控制人、法定代表人、股东、工作人员或者具有其他关联关系的人；第二，是否存在亲属、朋友或者其他密切关系的人；第三，出借资金是否来源于同一自然人、法人或非法人组织；第四，是否通过债权转让的方式掩盖同一出借人的事实。然而，值得注意的是，在判断过程中不能机械性适用上述判断指标，根据（2020）最高法民申 1193 号民事裁定，法院认定不同民事主体之间可能会由于生产经营等存在资金往来，单纯以此事实不能认定双方存在关联关系。除此以外，在（2020）京民申 2875 号民事判决中，北京市高级人民法院认定亲属关系等特殊关系并非认定关联出借人的充分条件。

2. 借款人

借款人的不特定性是认定职业放贷人的重要因素之一。职业放贷人的放贷对象是社会不特定对象，这应当结合案件事实予以认定，因为生产经营活动也可能产生与不特定对象的资金往来。一般来说，出借人在一段时间内多次向不特定的对象出借款项并收取利息或变相收取利息等行为即可认定为职业放贷行为。

3. 出借行为

相较于一般的民间借贷行为，职业放贷人的出借行为一般具有营利性、营业性、反复性和经常性的特征。

（1）借贷行为是否具有营利性。认定借贷行为是否以营利为目的门槛相对较低，通常只要出借人收取利息、服务费、咨询费、管理费、违约金或资金占用费等即可认定借贷行为具有营利性。收取利息的高低并不作为认定营利性的标准，但是出借人收取不合理的高额利息，则可以辅助认定出借人的借贷行为具有营利性。

（2）借贷行为是否具有营业性。第一，经营性可以从借贷合同约定格式化程度进行判断，因为以放贷为业的出借人在客观行为上大多使用制作较为完备的借款合同和担保合同，其一般具有较为规范的合同格式、合同编号，以及较为完善的风险防控合同条款（例如，存在明确约定借款人违约时应承担公证费、诉讼费、律师费等各项费用的条款）。第二，可以从出借人是否具有公开推介、宣传或明示出借意愿等行为进行判断，因为一般的民间借贷具有偶发性、临时性和互助性等特点，而公开推介和宣传出借意愿的行为明显违反一般民间借贷的特性，显示出其不具备的商业宣传性质。

（3）借贷行为是否具有反复性和经常性。出借人在一定期间内放贷次数，以及同一出借人在某一段时间提起民间借贷案件数量应当成为重点审查对象。在出借次数的认定上，最高人民法院在（2019）最高法民申4952号民事裁定中认为，三次出借行为尚不足以认定被告从事经常性的贷款业务或者从事职业放贷行为。在民间借贷案件的诉讼次数的审查上，各地区法院的认定标准存在差异，一般以一年在两级法院提起5件民间借贷案件为基础认定标准，但是经济发达地区法院认定标准的下限更高。

二、香港特区的认定规则

香港特区在充分借鉴英国《放债人法案》（*Money Lenders Act* 1900）条款的基础上，于1911年公布并实施了《放债人条例》。该条例未对实际贷款利率进行规定，因此在借款人以借款合同存在苛刻且不合情理的条款为由向法院申请撤销合同时，法院只能对高利贷行为进行有限的法律管控。由于高利贷行为在香港特区十分猖獗并造成严重的社会问题，立法会于1980年对《放债人条例》进行修订，此次修订主要体现在两个方面：第一，《放债人条例》加入实际利率的规定，从而扩大法院对高利贷行为的规管，增加对借款人的保护。第二，《放债人条例》将注册制改为许可证发放制，明确细化放债交易和贷款业务的监管规定，增加受《放债人条例》豁免的人以及贷款的规定，并且赋予法院在合适情况下可以重开放债交易的权力。1980年修订后的《放债人条例》进一步防止高利贷和敲诈性放债行为，发挥放债人对商业活动的促进作用，成为目前香港特区规范职业放债行为的核心成文法。

香港特区法律没有职业放贷人这一法律概念，但《放债人条例》对不持有放债人牌照但经营放债业务的人进行严格的规管。一般来说，如果出借人根据《放债人条例》第2部分的申领要求获得放债人牌照，并按照《放债人条例》第3部分的要求严格进行放贷交易，几乎不产生借贷争议。但在纷繁复杂的商业活动中，出借人未获得放债人牌照却实施放债行为的情形时常存在，香港特区法院审理案件的争议焦点之一时常是认定出借人是否为无牌放债人〔1〕。

《放债人条例》第2条中将放债人明确规定为："放债人指经营贷款业务（不论他是否亦经营其他业务）的人，或宣传、宣布或以任何方式显示自己是经营该业务的人，但不包括（a）附表一第一部所指明的人；或（b）（就附表一第二部所指明的贷款而言），作出该类贷款的人。"根据上述规定，无牌放债人也存在两种类型：第一种是无放债人牌照但经营贷款业务的人；第二种是无放债人牌照但宣传、宣布或显示是经营贷款业务的人。借款人如对出借人是否为放债人存在争议，则应当由借款人承担举证责任，证明出借人是在经营贷款业务，或存在对外宣传或宣布自己在经营贷款业务。〔2〕

香港高等法院原讼法庭在Chan Miu Chu Zoe v. Choi Chiu Yuk〔3〕案中对如何认定放债人这一问题进行了总结：第一，这是由法院进行判定的事实争议，不可能给出任何描述和定义，更不用说判定这个争议的固定公

---

〔1〕 即不持有放债人牌照但经营贷款业务的人，本书为表述简洁，均简称为"无牌放债人"。

〔2〕 Billion Silver Development Ltd. v. All Wide Investments Ltd. ［2000］2 HKC 262（CA），p. 270.

〔3〕 ［2014］HKCU 477.

式。每个案件对放债人的认定都必须取决于自身的事实。第二，出借人进行交易的数量不是决定性因素。法院必须审查案件所有相关事实，如果有证据证明出借人在交易时是放债人，那么即使只有一笔交易也可能就足够认定了。第三，法院判定出借人是否为《放债人条例》所指的放债人这一争议的正确方法是审查证据。如果是，则无须考虑更多；如果没有此类证据，则法院应寻找其他证据，例如，出借人是否曾宣传或声称自己是放债人。第四，即使出借人以有偿利率和适当担保方式提供贷款，这也可能不是放债人的标志。[1] 根据 Chan Miu Chu Zoe v. Choi Chiu Yuk 案所总结的衡量因素，下文将进一步阐明每个判定因素该如何进行适用。

（一）是否为经营贷款业务的人

判定出借人是否为放债人的核心在于认定出借人是否经营贷款业务。《放债人条例》没有对何为经营贷款业务作出规定，相关认定标准被囊括在判例法之中。由于判断出借人是否经营贷款业务属于事实判断问题，对该问题的判断应当取决于每个案件所独有的事实。[2]

1. 放债行为是否具有重复性、连续性和系统性

（1）重复性

普通放债行为的出借次数一般以单次为主，偶尔会出现多次出借的情形，但这种情况并不常见。如果出借人多次、重复地向借款人发放借款，出借次数超出普通放债行为的范畴，则可以认定出借人在经营贷款业务。

Edgelow v. MacElwee[3]案明确表明重复性是认定经营贷款业务的重要标志之一。该案的原告是一名律师，但是长期用签发令状的方式向自己的“客户”发放贷款。对于该案，法院认定：第一，原告自 1912 年就多次向他人发放贷款，仅在 1915 年至 1917 年间原告就曾出借 17 笔贷款。第二，即使原告声称自己是向“客户”提供签发令状法律服务，但是原告既

---

〔1〕 Chan Miu Chu Zoe v. Choi Chiu Yuk［2014］HKCU 477，para. 21.

〔2〕 Newton v. Pyke［1908］25 TLR 127，p. 128.

〔3〕［1918］1 KB 205.

不能提供记载借款人姓名、垫付金额及收取利息的账簿，也不能提供相应的诉讼费用单来证明自己的主张。[1] 有鉴于此，法院最终认定原告属于无牌放债人，原告系以提供法律服务的名义经营贷款业务。

（2）连续性

连续性这一特征集中体现在出借人存在多次发放贷款的行为。在认定这一问题上，法院一般从出借人发放贷款的数量，或者借款协议签订的数量等方面进行认定。然而，如出借人与借款人仅存在一份借款协议，即使出借人多次向借款人发放贷款，法院也应以借款协议签订的数量为核心认定标准。

在 Supreme Design Fashion Ltd. & Hung Lai Chu v. Michael Hope International Ltd.[2] 案中，原告 Supreme Design Fashion Ltd. 与被告签订了一份关于处理建筑施工材料和设备代理的协议。根据原告的指示，被告没有为设备和材料下订单，而是为原告开具总额不超过 300 万美元的信用证。原、被告双方约定，原告需要在设备和材料交付后的 8 个月内向被告清偿这笔款项，并支付 35% 的代理佣金。根据该协议，被告向原告以及不同的香港公司开具信用证，但原告仅按照协议部分清偿款项。原告向法院起诉被告是无牌放债人，被告出借的款项因违反《放债人条例》第 23 条而无法收回。原告向香港高等法院原讼法庭主张其与被告签订的代理协议实际是贷款协议，被告所出具的信用证是向原告提供的一系列贷款。

经过审理，原讼法庭首先认定原告与被告之间的代理协议实质是贷款协议。第一，被告在该案中并没有充当采购代理，不存在订购、安排货物运输或交付的行为。第二，被告使用信贷透支额度来为他人支付订购货物货款，并企图在货物交付后的 8 个月内获得 35% 的回报的行为，符合放贷行为的特征。双方的代理协议实质上就是贷款协议，被告所获得的代理佣金事实上就是利息。[3] 在进一步判断被告是否为无牌放债人时，原讼法庭

〔1〕 Edgelow v. MacElwee [1918] 1 KB 205, p. 209.

〔2〕 [1999] HKCU 572.

〔3〕 Supreme Design Fashion Ltd. & Hung Lai Chu v. Michael Hope International Ltd. [1999] HKCU 572, para. 25 – 27.

认为要证明一个人从事放债业务，必须证明出借人的放贷交易具有一定的系统性和连续性。[1] 结合双方提交的证据，原讼法庭认定被告仅存在一次发放贷款行为。第一，该案不存在关于被告发放其他贷款的书面证据，也没有相关的贷款业务的书面广告。虽然被告的财务报表显示有大量的利息收入，但是原告无法提供充分证据证明该利息来源于放贷。[2] 第二，基于证人提供的证词，被告之前不存在以这种交易方式为他人开立信用证的行为。[3] 第三，原、被告之间只存在一份贷款合同。虽然被告多次分期向原告出借款项，但是贷款合同约定了一个固定的出借总额和相同的还款条件。[4] 综合上述理由，法院最终判定，被告没有经营贷款业务，不属于无牌放债人。

Supreme Design Fashion Ltd. & Hung Lai Chu v. Michael Hope International Ltd. 案确立了以下法律规则，出借次数不受实际分期发放贷款次数的影响，出借次数的认定应当以双方签订的借款合同为依据。其后，该法律规则被 Cheung Ping Kwong v. Chan Kin Sun[5]案继续遵循。该案的法院认定，原告与被告虽有多次保证金交易行为，但由于双方之间只签订了一份借款协议，因此法院不能认定原告的交易行为具有连续性。

总而言之，出借人的出借次数是衡量出借行为是否具有连续性的重要指标。除非出借次数超出一般借贷行为的范畴，达到商业标准或者属于规模化放贷，否则不能简单将出借次数与经营贷款业务行为画等号。出借人多次支付借款的行为并不意味着出借人进行连续或重复放贷行为，因为可能存在出借人与借款人仅订立一份贷款合同，但是该合同却约定出借人分

---

〔1〕 Supreme Design Fashion Ltd. & Hung Lai Chu v. Michael Hope International Ltd. [1999] HKCU 572, para. 37.

〔2〕 Supreme Design Fashion Ltd. & Hung Lai Chu v. Michael Hope International Ltd. [1999] HKCU 572, para. 28.

〔3〕 Supreme Design Fashion Ltd. & Hung Lai Chu v. Michael Hope International Ltd. [1999] HKCU 572, para. 30 – 31、35.

〔4〕 Supreme Design Fashion Ltd. & Hung Lai Chu v. Michael Hope International Ltd. [1999] HKCU 572, para. 38.

〔5〕 [2013] 3 HKC 319; [2012] HKCU 2456.

期支付出借款项的情形。

（3）系统性

放贷行为的系统性一般体现在模式化的贷款管理，流程化的贷款发放程序，以及完备化的贷款协议等方面。当出借人发放贷款的行为明显具有上述特征时，法院会倾向于认定出借人在经营贷款业务。然而，放贷行为的系统性虽是衡量出借人是否经营贷款业务的重要因素，却不是决定性因素。香港高等法院对Chow Wun Sing Winston v. Yiu Chun Luk〔1〕案曾作出判决，认为即使原告发放贷款的行为具有一定的系统性，但结合具体案件情形，最终认定原告并未经营贷款业务。

该案中，被告为了周转生意向周生生财务公司的 Alex Lee 寻求贷款。在 Alex Lee 的努力下，原告同意与被告签订第一份贷款协议，Alex Lee 帮助原告办理了被告的贷款和担保。由于被告在第一份贷款协议到期后无法按期偿还贷款本金和利息，被告向原告请求延期还款。原告同意被告的请求后，双方重新签订了贷款协议，但被告自 2001 年 10 月起开始拖欠利息，原告因此提起诉讼要求被告清偿债务。在一审中，被告提出抗辩称，原告在未持有放债人牌照的情况下经营贷款业务，并说明以下理由：第一，原告拥有一套复杂的贷款管理系统。第二，原告与被告签署贷款协议时，使用精心制作且准备充分的贷款协议和担保文件。第三，原告对利息的支付做了精确的记录，甚至有电脑生成的还款时间表。上述系统化的管理，足以说明原告在经营贷款业务。对于被告的抗辩，香港高等法院原讼法庭认为，虽然原告使用了专业以及商业化的方式向被告发放贷款，使其放贷行为具有系统性的特征，但是系统性并非认定经营贷款业务的决定性因素。原讼法庭认为出借人是否经营贷款业务，需要结合整个案情来认定。基于以下情形，原讼法庭判定原告并没有以经营贷款为业，原告向被告出借款项行为属于个人借贷行为，具体理由如下：第一，被告的贷款由具有专业抵押和贷款方面经验的 Alex Lee 办理，这可以合理解释原告为何有完备的

〔1〕［2006］HKCU 1247，［2008］HKCU 358.

贷款文件、计算机记载利息支付记录和自动生成还款时间表。[1] 第二，原告向被告发出的通知和信件的内容和格式都未采用标准格式。[2] 第三，在使用软件自动生成还款时间表时，原告忘记更改借款人的名字，而这种疏忽绝不会出现在正式的业务经营中。[3] 第四，原告在向被告提供借款期间仅向一人提供过贷款，不存在重复以及连续的放贷行为。[4]

虽然被告继续向高等法院上诉法庭提出上诉，但上诉法庭支持原讼法庭作出的判决，并在判词中再次肯定，判定某人是否从事放债业务，交易的系统性和连续性是一个相关因素，但不是决定性因素。[5] 同时上诉法庭也谨慎地指出，该案原告稀少的贷款次数与其举证相一致，因而最终被认定没有经营贷款业务，但是放贷次数少不意味着没有经营贷款业务。[6]

2. 以有偿方式提供贷款

经营贷款业务的一个重要特征是出借人常以收取利息或者以接受担保等有偿的方式向借款人发放贷款。但是，以有偿的方式提供贷款并不意味着出借人自动成为放债人。香港高等法院在 Chow Wun Sing Winston v. Yiu Chun Luk[7]案中认定，即使出借人以收取利息的方式或要求借款人提供相应担保的方式发放贷款，并不能直接证明出借人是放债人。其后的 Chan Miu Chu Zoe v. Choi Chiu Yuk[8]案肯定了 Chow Wun Sing Winston v. Yiu Chun Luk 案确立的以有偿方式提供借款不一定是认定放债人标志的法律规则。

3. 贷款业务占主要业务的比例

根据《放债人条例》对放债人定义的规定，经营贷款业务并未要求贷款业务是主要经营业务，贷款业务所占比例的高低不影响经营贷款行为的

---

〔1〕 Chow Wun Sing Winston v. Yiu Chun Luk [2006] HKCU 1247, para. 72 – 74.

〔2〕 Chow Wun Sing Winston v. Yiu Chun Luk [2006] HKCU 1247, para. 70.

〔3〕 Chow Wun Sing Winston v. Yiu Chun Luk [2006] HKCU 1247, para. 75.

〔4〕 Chow Wun Sing Winston v. Yiu Chun Luk [2006] HKCU 1247, para. 70.

〔5〕 Chow Wun Sing Winston v. Yiu Chun Luk [2008] HKCU 358, para. 16.

〔6〕 Chow Wun Sing Winston v. Yiu Chun Luk [2008] HKCU 358, para. 22.

〔7〕 [2008] HKCU 358.

〔8〕 [2014] HKCU 477, para. 21.

认定。在 North Central Wagon Finance Co. Ltd. v. Brailsford[1]案中，原告是一家经营多种金融业务的金融公司，其贷款业务仅占全部经营业务的0.5%。该案的法院认为，经营贷款业务的人并不因其经营规模更大的其他业务而否定其是放债人。[2] 因此，虽然原告的贷款业务所占比例极小，但并不影响法院最终认定原告是放债人。

值得注意的是，某些特定种类业务的经营与交易可能包含或隐含放贷交易活动，以至于此类交易行为容易从交易的表征上被认定为放贷活动。例如，Litchfield v. Dreyfus[3]案中的原告所经营的艺术品生意包含长期赊账服务，采用的赊账手段是客户支付货款的票据，而原告则将票据贴现或者重新续借。法院最终判定，原告将票据贴现的行为是为其持股企业以及有生意来往的朋友提供资金，属于艺术品生意的附属行为，而非放贷行为。[4]

类似的情形也发生在股票交易活动中，特别是在保证金交易中。投资人在股票经纪人处开户后，在投资人的指示下，股票经纪人使用自有资金或银行授信的信贷额度帮助投资者购买相应的股票。购买股票后，股票经纪人将从被告的保证金账户扣除股票成本、印花税、交易佣金以及手续费。从投资人和股票经纪人的交易模式来看，表面上是股票经纪人向投资人发放借款供其购买股票，而这正是 Harvester Stock Investment Co. v. Kwan Siu May[5]案中被告的抗辩理由，被告称原告对其保证金账户的管理方式在法律上等同于放贷；由于原告并非持牌放债人，因此无权售出被告保证金账户的股票，亦无权向被告追偿任何款项。香港高等法院认为，原告在法律上没有经营贷款业务，保证金业务是其股票经纪业务的组成部分之一，并非一项独立的业务。保证金交易的核心以及目的，是向客户提供信贷类别的股票经纪业务，投资人和股票经纪人都没有从事贷款业务的

〔1〕［1962］1 WLR 1288.

〔2〕North Central Wagon Finance Co. Ltd. v. Brailsford［1962］1 WLR 1288，pp. 508 – 509.

〔3〕［1906］1 KB 584.

〔4〕Litchfield v. Dreyfus［1906］1 KB 584，p. 509.

〔5〕［1987］1 HKC 271.

动机以及意图。[1] Cheung Ping Kwong v. Chan Kin Sun[2]案中适用了相同的法律规则。因此，保证金交易行为虽然包含一部分的借贷交易活动，但是并不属于《放债人条例》所规管的放贷行为。

4. 借款人的类别

（1）亲密关系之间的借款

借款人类别及其与出借人的关系是认定出借人是否为放债人的重要因素。经营贷款业务的商业性质决定借款人具有不确定性，放债人随时可向符合其放贷条件的借款人发放贷款，这些借款人一般与放债人不具有朋友关系、亲戚关系等亲密联系。

在 Litchfield v. Dreyfus[3]案中，原告曾是一名古董商人，在退休后转行做艺术品价值顾问。原告借钱给自己持股的公司和自己的古董生意朋友。在原告起诉被告要求其清偿借款时，被告抗辩原告是无牌放债人。法院认为，真正经营贷款业务的出借人的借款对象应当是不特定对象。由于该案原告的借款对象只限于古董朋友和生意朋友，不属于不特定对象，因而法院最终判定原告没有经营贷款业务，原告的行为属于朋友间友谊行为。如果出借人的借款对象局限于亲属、朋友等特定人群，则不足以认定出借人在经营贷款业务。Newton v. Pyke[4]案遵循了同样的法律规则。该案法院判定，虽然原告长期向他人出借款项，但由于借款金额数目较小且出借对象大部分是原告的朋友或亲戚，且原告从未宣传、宣布或对外表明自己是放债人，因此原告不能被认定为经营贷款业务的人。[5]

香港特区法律采纳了类似的认定标准，如果出借人与借款人之间存在朋友关系或亲属关系，则法院倾向于认定出借人的放贷行为不属于经营贷款业务。在 Chan Yuk Bun v. Tsoi Yan Yee Lily and Another[6]案中，香港

〔1〕 Harvester Stock Investment Co. v. Kwan Siu May [1987] 1 HKC 271, p. 280.

〔2〕 [2013] 3 HKC 319.

〔3〕 [1906] 1 KB 584.

〔4〕 [1908] 25 TLR 127.

〔5〕 Newton v. Pyke [1908] 25 TLR 127, p. 128.

〔6〕 [2017] HKCU 2071.

高等法院原讼法庭引用了 *Chitty on Contracts*, *Hong Kong Specific Contracts* (*5th edition*) 第9－048段的内容：法院在认定出借人是否为放债人时，借款人的身份以及借贷双方的关系是相关的考量因素。在 Cheung Chow v. Cheung Ng Sheong Steven[1]案中，原、被告是兄弟关系，原告借款给被告。该案的法院认为《放债人条例》的适用应当考虑借贷双方的关系以及借贷行为发生时的相关情形。因此，如果出借人向朋友或者亲人出借款项时不收取任何利息，也不接受任何担保，那么出借人不应被认定为放债人。[2] 原讼法庭审理后认定，原告是基于双方之间的友谊关系借钱给被告，因此最终判定原告的行为不属于经营贷款业务。[3]

（2）特定人群之间的借款

借款人的随机性、不确定性是认定经营贷款业务的重要因素，但是如果出借人的借款对象限于某一特定人群，法院仍可能认定出借人在经营贷款业务。例如，在 Premor Ltd. v. Shaw Brothers (A Firm)[4]案中，即使出借对象已限缩至摩托车经销商这一特定人群，法院仍可综合整个案情认定出借人事实上在经营贷款业务。该案的原告是一家融资租赁公司，以“库存交易”的方式向摩托经销商这一特定群体提供贷款。所谓的“库存交易”是原、被告之间签订融资租赁协议，原告为被告提供贷款用以购买特定的摩托车，然后由摩托车经销商将摩托车出租或出售。因被告未支付两笔购车款，原告提起诉讼要求被告清偿购车款，而被告则抗辩称原告是无牌放债人。面对被告的抗辩，原告主张其向被告以及其他摩托车经销商提供贷款是为了促成更多的融资租赁交易，从而促进融资租赁业务，因而原告的行为满足英国当时的《放债人法案》的豁免条款的规定，不应当被认定为无牌放债人。

该案法院拒绝了原告的主张，认为原告向摩托车经销商这一特定群体提供贷款的行为不属于融资租赁业务的一部分，且其提供贷款的根本目的

---

〔1〕［1993］HKCU 428.

〔2〕Chan Yuk Bun v. Tsoi Yan Yee Lily and Another［2017］HKCU 2071, para. 14.

〔3〕Chan Yuk Bun v. Tsoi Yan Yee Lily and Another［2017］HKCU 2071, para. 20.

〔4〕［1964］1 WLR 978.

并非促进融资租赁业务。原、被告进行的多笔“库存交易”中，其中部分交易以摩托车作为融资租赁交易的租赁物，但部分交易并未附明任何的租赁物。原、被告之间的融资租赁交易文件所约定的车辆购买价格、首期款以及仓储费都是虚构的。基于此，法院判定原、被告之间的交易与摩托车融资租赁交易毫无关系，原告向摩托车经销商这一特定群体发放贷款的根本目的并非促进其融资租赁业务，而是获取贷款利润。因此，虽然出借人向特定或固定人群发放贷款，但法院有可能因其发放贷款的目的是单纯获取贷款利润进而认定出借人属于无牌放债人。

（二）是否为宣传、宣布或显示经营贷款业务的人

宣传、宣布或显示经营贷款业务的人的认定较为简单。借款人仅需举证出借人存在宣传、宣布或显示经营贷款业务的行为，则足以向法院证明出借人是放债人，无须考虑其他因素。

在 Conroy v. Kenny[1]案中，原告经营一家 Lancashire Acceptances 的合伙企业，该合伙企业仅在 1966 年至 1967 年间持有放债人牌照。Lancashire Acceptances 在 1971 年向被告出借 6000 英镑，但截至还款日被告仅支付了利息，因原告是 Lancashire Acceptances 的合伙人，故原告向法院起诉被告要求其清偿本金。

该案的争议焦点为，原告是否为无牌放债人。对于该问题，因被告未能证明 Lancashire Acceptances 存在向他人提供规模化有息贷款的行为，一审法院驳回被告的抗辩，被告提出上诉。

上诉法院认为，一审法院在认定原告是否为无牌放债人的问题上存在错误，该案需认定的事实应为 1971 年 1 月 6 日 Lancashire Acceptances 向被告借款的行为是否属于放债行为；如果该问题的答案是否定的，则需要考虑 Lancashire Acceptances 向被告借款时是否宣传、宣布或显示自己是放债人。根据原、被告双方提供的证据，上诉法院认为原告具有显示经营贷款业务的行为：第一，案外人 Southam 律师曾为原、被告提供过法律服务，

---

〔1〕［1999］1 WLR 1345.

当被告询问案外人是否有提供贷款业务的客户时，案外人向被告推荐了Lancashire Acceptances。第二，从原告仅与案外人信件联系两次后，就与被告迅速签署借款合同的行为可以看出，原告发放贷款的行为十分熟练。[1] 第三，曾有买家想向原告购买被告抵押的房屋，买家律师询问原告其是否为放债人时，原告并未给出明确的答复。从原告回避该问题的行为，上诉法院认为原告至少自1966年就明白何为放债人，以及如果Lancashire Acceptances不是放债人，原告为何不给出否定答案。[2] 基于上述情形，上诉法院判定Lancashire Acceptances在当时确实具有显示经营贷款业务的行为，故原告属于无牌放债人。因此，如果有证据证明贷款交易时出借人声称自己是放债人，即使有且只有一笔放贷交易行为，也足以证明出借人是放债人。

三、小结

（一）相同点

第一，内地与香港特区均不认可未持有相关金融资质（放债人牌照）的放贷行为，在法律上均对其予以否定性的评价。

第二，内地与香港特区对于职业放贷人（无牌放债人）的认定均没有统一的衡量标准。内地对于职业放债人的认定仍处于探索阶段，各地法院根据本地的经济发展情况制定职业放贷人认定标准。香港特区对无牌放债人的认定散见于判例法之中，暂无统一的成文法认定标准。

第三，内地与香港特区都从出借人、借款人、出借行为三个维度对职业放贷人（无牌放债人）进行认定。在认定的方法上，均采取结合个案证据及具体案情作出综合性判断的方法进行认定。

（二）不同点

在认定职业放贷人（无牌放债人）时，内地与香港特区对于出借行为

---

〔1〕 Conroy v. Kenny［1999］1 WLR 1345，pp. 1349 – 1350.

〔2〕 Conroy v. Kenny［1999］1 WLR 1345，p. 1350.

的认定的侧重点存在差异。内地多以法院受理的民间借贷案件数量作为重要考量因素，而香港特区则以出借人实际放贷次数作为核心考量因素。

第二节　职业放贷人的法律后果

一、内地的法律规定

职业放贷人的放贷行为属于无效法律行为。根据《民间借贷司法解释（2020 第二次修正）》第 13 条的规定，未依法取得放贷资格的出借人，以营利为目的向社会不特定对象提供借款的民间借贷合同无效。民间借贷合同无效导致的法律后果一般体现在本金的偿还和资金占用费的支付两个方面。

（一）无效合同的法律后果

民间借贷合同无效意味着出借人的放贷行为自始无效。根据《民法典》第 157 条的规定，民事法律行为无效，行为人因该行为取得的财产，应当予以返还；不能返还或者没有必要返还的，应当折价赔偿。有过错的一方应当赔偿对方由此受到的损失；各方都有过错的，应当各自承担相应的责任。因此，对于尚未履行完毕的民间借贷合同，出借人和借款人无须继续履行合同义务；对于已经履行的部分，借款人依合同所取得的财产应当返还出借人，即借款人需向出借人返还本金。

假设出借人甲在未取得放贷金融资质的情况下，向借款人乙提供 100 万元的借款，双方约定借款利息按年利率 10% 的标准给付，借款期限为 1 年。乙在借款期限届满后，仅支付部分利息但拒绝偿还本金，甲向法院起诉要求乙清偿债务。由于甲未获得放贷资质，法院认定甲属于职业放贷人，以赚取利润为目的向乙提供借款，甲乙之间的借款合同无效，甲不得向法院请求乙继续履行合同义务。但甲可向法院请求要求乙返还 100 万元的借款本金。

（二）资金占用费的支付

对于民间借贷合同被认定无效后是否应当支付资金占用费的问题，法院一般以平衡出借人和借款人以及金融秩序稳定之间的利益为准绳。《九民纪要》第 34 条规定："双务合同不成立、无效或者被撤销时，标的物返还与价款返还互为对待给付，双方应当同时返还。关于应否支付利息问题，只要一方对标的物有使用情形的，一般应当支付使用费，该费用可与占有价款一方应当支付的资金占用费相互抵销，故在一方返还原物前，另一方仅须支付本金，而无须支付利息。"即使民间借贷合同无效，由于借款人使用了借款，因此原则上应当支付资金占用费。

对于资金占用费的支付标准，民商事司法实践一般按照全国银行间同业拆借中心公布的一年期贷款市场报价利率（以下简称一年期 LPR）确定。实践中，法院还会综合考虑出借人的借款来源、行为违法程度以及借款人的借款用途、履行情况等酌情调整资金占用费的支付金额。

以上述案件情形为例，如乙要求甲返还其已支付的利息，由于乙使用了甲的借款，基于平衡出借人和借款人双方利益的考量，法院会判决乙应当向甲支付使用期间的资金占用费，驳回其请求。假使甲与乙之间约定的借款利息过高，如双方约定的借款利息为年利率 20%，在未出现特殊情形的情况下，法院将按照一年期 LPR 的标准调整资金占用费。

二、香港特区的法律规定

（一）借款合同不可被强制执行（Unenforceable Contract）

香港特区法律原则上不保护无牌放债人的放债行为。《放债人条例》第 23（1）条规定："除非放债人交出牌照或以其他方法令法庭信纳在贷款之日、订立协议之日或取得担保之日，他领有牌照，否则无权向法庭追讨他贷出的款项及利息，亦无权强制执行其所订立的协议及相关担保协议。"这意味着，经营贷款业务的人只有向法院证明其持有放债人牌照，否则无权向法院申请强制执行借款合同及相关担保协议，即经营贷款业务的人无法通过法律手段收回已经出借的本金和收取相应的利息。值得注意的是，第23（1）条并没有直接列明借款合同以及担保合同是否有效，而是规定借款合同以及担保合同无法被强制执行。

内地和香港特区法律关于合同效力的规定极为相似，两地都将合同的效力分为三种类型，即有效合同、无效合同和可撤销合同。不可强制执行合同不归属于合同效力的范畴，而应当被定性为一种法律效果或法律结果。不可强制执行合同的法律效果是合同无法通过直接的法律程序来得以强制执行。不可强制执行的对象既可能包括所有的合同当事人，也可能包括其中部分当事人；不可强制执行的时效既可能是永久性的，也可能是暂时性的；不可强制执行的合同既可以是无效合同，也可以是有效合同。[1]当不可强制执行合同被认定为无效合同时，由于无效合同自始不具有任何的法律效力，讨论无效合同的执行问题并无意义，无效合同当然不可被强制执行。当不可强制执行合同被认定为有效合同时，该合同有可能间接被强制执行，或通过弥补和纠正合同的缺陷的方式[2]被直接强制执行。[3]《放债人条例》第23条仅规定出借人和借款人之间的合同不可被强制执行，但对于合同的效力，该条例并未作出相应的规定。在检索有关《放债人条例》第23条的判例的过程中，虽然存在被告请求法院判定双方签署的借款合同因原告违反该条例第23条的规定而无效且不可被强制执行的案例，然而，在相关案例中法院并未对违反该条例第23条规定的合同的法律效力作出认定[4]，香港特区司法实践对该问题的观点存在一定分歧。

（二）例外情况：法院基于公平行使自由裁量权

虽然香港特区法律对出借人未持有牌照经营贷款业务的行为一般不予

---

〔1〕 See *Halsbury's Laws of Hong Kong*, Lexis Nexis Hong Kong, [115.009] Imperfect Contracts.

〔2〕 合同的缺陷包括：合同没有遵守必要的法律手续，如有关土地的合同需以书面形式签署；或者合同没有履行必要的法律程序，如尚未进行印花税评定或者未缴纳印花税。

〔3〕 See *Halsbury's Laws of Hong Kong*, Lexis Nexis Hong Kong, [115.009] Imperfect Contracts.

〔4〕 香港高等法院原讼法庭在Chow Wun Sing Winston v. Yiu Chun Luk [2006] HKCU 1247案中以被告提供的证据不足为由驳回其诉讼请求。

保护，但是《放债人条例》第23（2）条的但书允许法院在例外情况下给予有限的保护。该条规定："但如该法庭信纳，放债人由于未能令该法庭信纳他在有关时间领有牌照，以致无权追讨该笔款项或利息，或无权强制执行该协议或保证，在所有情况下均不公平者，则该法庭可命令该放债人有权追讨该笔款项或利息，或强制执行该协议或保证，但范围以该法庭认为公平者为限，并受该法庭认为公平的修改或例外规定所规限。"法院基于公平原则的考量，可以对无牌放债人的放债行为提供例外保护。但正如高等法院上诉法庭在 Universe Link Industries Ltd. & Anor v. Liggars Ltd.[1] 案中提出，《放债人条例》第23条但书的适用完全取决于法官的仁慈，否则未获得放债人牌照或不受豁免的出借人难以收回借款的本金和利息。但是，在香港特区的司法实践中，法官鲜少根据该条款行使自由裁量权。

三、小结

（一）相同点

内地和香港特区都不认可职业放贷人（无牌放债人）的放贷行为，都对其持有否定性的法律评价并通过成文法明确规定相应的不利法律后果。

（二）不同点

第一，内地与香港特区对职业放贷人（无牌放债人）的放贷行为的否定性评价结果不同。内地法律明确规定属于职业放贷行为的民间借贷合同无效，借款人一般需要向出借人返还本金以及支付相应的资金占用费。资金占用费的金额的认定一般参照一年期 LPR。香港特区的《放债人条例》规定无牌放债人订立的借款合同不可被强制执行。

第二，内地与香港特区对职业放贷人（无牌放债人）的放贷行为的处理路径不同。由于内地法律明文规定职业放贷人的借款合同属于无效合

〔1〕［1999］2 HKLRD 383，［1999］HKCU 1688.

同，因此内地法院对职业放贷人的借款合同的处置没有自由裁量权。香港特区的法院可以基于公平原则行使自由裁量权，对无牌放债人的借款合同予以有限的保护。但是，香港特区法院对该自由裁量权的行使十分谨慎。

第三章　本金与利息的法律规则比较

第一节　本金与利息的内涵

在借贷行为中，本金指的是借款的原始金额，即借款人从出借人手中借入的资金额；利息指的是出借人因出借资金而从借款人手中获得的报酬，即借款人支配和使用资金所支付的代价。

一、内地的法律规定

《民间借贷司法解释（2020 第二次修正）》第 26 条对借款本金的规定如下："借据、收据、欠条等债权凭证载明的借款金额，一般认定为本金。"但无论是《民法典》还是《民间借贷司法解释（2020 第二次修正）》对利息这一概念的认定均没有明确解释和规定。一般来看，利息是以借款本金为基础按约定利率计算的孳息。借款本金是借款人创造经济效益的资金条件，利息则是借款人转移给出借人的就使用该借款本金所创造的经济效益的一部分。另外，《民间借贷司法解释（2020 第二次修正）》第 29 条规定，出借人与借款人既约定了逾期利率，又约定了违约金或者其他费用，出借人可以选择主张逾期利息、违约金或者其他费用，也可以一并主张。由此可见，利息与违约金、其他费用属于借款合同项下不同的费用，相互之间独立存在。《民间借贷司法解释（2020 第二次修正）》第 29 条仅是对各项费用总计设置了一年期 LPR 四倍的最高限制。

（一）相关法律概念

1. 借据

所谓借据，一般是指由借款人书写并签字盖章的凭证，表明借款人向出借人借款，内容一般记载借款人、出借人、借款金额、借款时间、借期、利息等。借据通常在出借人交付借款时，由借款人出具，表明收到借款，如借据上记载"今借到某某……元"；但有的时候，借款人在实际收到借款之前就向出借人出具了借据，如"××拟向××借××元，××于

××××年××月××日前支付”，这种情形下借据的性质更接近于借款合同。借据要根据具体记载的内容来判断其证明力。

2. 收据

所谓收据，包括收条，是指表明收到他人交来的款项的凭证。一般自然人之间会以收条的方式表明收到款项，法人则一般会出具收据。收据或收条的内容通常载明付款人、收款人、收到款项的数额、时间等，如“××××年××月××日收到××交来××元”。与借据不同，收据或收条更强调款项的实际给付而不是借款合意，故收据或收条上很有可能只写收到款项，不记载款项性质、利率等。在民间借贷司法实践中，出借人和借款人都有可能出具收据，即出借人向借款人交付借款时，借款人会出具收据；借款人向出借人偿还借款时，出借人也可能会出具收据。故对于收据，应当结合其他证据对款项性质、款项支付基于的基础法律关系、利率等作出认定。

3. 欠条

所谓欠条，是指债务人向债权人出具，用以表明尚欠款项金额、还款期限等内容的凭证，如“今欠××元，于××××年××月××日前还清”。与借据不同，欠条所表明的欠款内容可能并不仅由借款关系形成，当事人基于买卖、建设工程等其他基础法律关系形成的债权债务，经双方对账、清算后，也可能形成欠条，表明尚欠的金额。民间借贷司法实践中，借款人出具的欠条有可能会记载借款本金金额、利息金额、已还金额、尚欠金额等，也有可能只记载尚欠金额，而不区分本金和利息。

（二）预先扣除款项的法律规则

在民间借贷司法实践中，债权凭证记载的金额与实际的本金数额不一致所引发的争议一直都是司法实践的难题。其中最普遍、最常见的导致本金数额存在争议的情况之一就是预先在借款本金中扣除借款利息，即所谓的“砍头息”。

1. “砍头息”的概念和性质

“砍头息”指的是出借人在向借款人交付借款本金时被预先扣除的利

息。表面上看，预先扣除借款本金的应付利息，其利息金额并未发生实际变化，并且在还款时也不用再支付利息，一举两得。但实际来说，利息是以本金为基数按约定利率计算的孳息，应当是借款人完全支配和使用本金所承担的成本，支付利息是借款人将使用该本金所创造效益的一部分转移给出借人。如果事先从本金中扣除利息，那么借款人实际上并没有完全使用本金，其所创造经济效益的资金条件受到明显制约，这对于借款人来说是不公平的。

假设甲与乙在借款合同中约定借款金额为 10 万元，借期 1 年，借期内利息按年利率 10% 标准计算共 1 万元；但在实际交付借款时，乙先把借款期限届满时甲应付的 1 万元利息预先扣掉，只交付给甲 9 万元，甲在 1 年之后仍要还 10 万元。此时，甲的实际可支配和使用的资金仅为 9 万元，实际借款利率为 1 万元 ÷9 万元 = 年利率 11. 11% 。由上文可知，预先在本金中扣除利息，其实是出借人隐蔽地收取利息或者提高利率、规避法律规定上限的一种做法。

2. “砍头息”的相关法律规定

内地法律对预先扣除利息的行为采取禁止态度。《民法典》第 670 条规定：“借款的利息不得预先在本金中扣除。利息预先在本金中扣除的，应当按照实际借款数额返还借款并计算利息。”同时，《民间借贷司法解释（2020 第二次修正）》第 26 条也规定：“预先在本金中扣除利息的，人民法院应当将实际出借的金额认定为本金。”由上述法律规定可知，将预先扣除的利息刨除掉后借款人实际从出借人处拿到的资金额为法律意义上的借款本金。如果事先从借款本金中扣除利息，借款人只需按照实际借款数额返还借款并计算利息。砍头息的做法使出借人的利息得以提前收回，减少了出借资金的风险，但却损害了借款人的合法利益，使借款人实际上得到的资金额少于合同约定的借款数额，影响其资金的正常使用，加重了借款人的负担。上述法律规定体现了合同公平的原则，能够防止出借人利用优势地位作出不平等的合同内容。

（三）借新还旧的法律规则

1. 借新还旧的概念和性质

所谓借新还旧，指的是借款人在借款期限届满时未能足额偿还本金与利息，在与出借人协商一致后，双方对到期的借款合同进行本金与利息的结算，并将剩余欠付的利息计入新签订借款合同的借款本金当中，开始履行新的借款合同的还款义务。该种行为在《民间借贷司法解释（2020第二次修正）》第27条中，被表述为“借贷双方对前期借款本息结算后将利息计入后期借款本金并重新出具债权凭证”[1]。在内地司法实践中，更常见反复、多次结算后将欠息纳入本金利滚利连续形成多份新的借条、借款协议的情况，后期借款本金是否包含前期借款利息是内地民间借贷常见的争议纠纷之一。

对于重新出具的债权凭证的性质，存在两种不同的看法：一种观点认为，重新出具的债权凭证相当于对之前形成的本金和利息进行新的借用，从而消灭了原有的借贷关系，形成了新的借贷关系，与任何普通正常的借贷关系没有实质区别，新债权凭证载明的金额就是新的借款本金；另一种观点则认为，无论重新出具多少次债权凭证，出借人始终出借的都是最初的本金，并不会因新债权凭证而形成新的借贷关系，新债权凭证载明的金额包含了本金和复利。

2. 借新还旧的相关法律规定

《民间借贷司法解释（2020第二次修正）》第27条规定：“借贷双方对前期借款本息结算后将利息计入后期借款本金并重新出具债权凭证，如果前期利率没有超过合同成立时一年期贷款市场报价利率四倍，重新出具的债权凭证载明的金额可认定为后期借款本金。超过部分的利息，不应认定为后期借款本金。按前款计算，借款人在借款期间届满后应当支付的本息之和，超过以最初借款本金与以最初借款本金为基数、以合同成立时一

---

[1] 《民间借贷司法解释（2020第二次修正）》第27条中规定，借贷双方对前期借款本息结算后将利息计入后期借款本金并重新出具债权凭证。

年期贷款市场报价利率四倍计算的整个借款期间的利息之和的，人民法院不予支持。”

由上述法律规定可知：第一，内地法律对新出具债权凭证的性质认定采用了一种更为折中的观点，一方面，充分尊重当事人的意思自治，新债权凭证是合同双方自愿重新达成的，系真实意思表示，借款人应对其本人签名确认的内容负责，这也是民事法律行为中诚信原则的体现，因此对新的本金数额会尽量按照债权凭证载明的事项认定；另一方面，如果可以查明载明的金额确由前期借款本息结算后而来，则认定前期和后期借款之间存在相承关系，相关利息计算应当符合民间借贷中关于利率保护上限的规定。第二，虽然内地法律会尽量按照新债权凭证载明的金额认定借款本金，但在连续多次重新出具新债权凭证的情形下，借期届满时本金和利息的认定同时还需满足以下两点要求：（1）每一份新债权凭证载明的借款本金中所包含的上一期利息的利率计算标准均不能超过合同成立时一年期 LPR 四倍。如不超过，则上一期利息可直接计入新一期本金，即债权凭证载明的金额可被认定为后期借款本金；如超过，则超出部分不予保护，不能计入后期本金。（2）最后一份债权凭证履行期届满时，即借期届满之时，所载明的后期借款本金与计算后的相应借款利息之和不能超过以最初借款本金为基数计算的本息和，超出的部分法院不予支持。

二、香港特区的法律规定

香港特区《放债人条例》第 2 条就本金和利息的概念作出如下定义：“本金就任何贷款而言，指实际贷出的款额。”“利、利息不包括因为印花税或其他相类税项而合法地协定按照本条例支付的任何税项，但除此之外，包括因任何贷款或在其他方面就任何贷款而已予支付、将予支付或须予支付的超逾本金的款项，而不论该款项以何名目称之。”根据上述规定，出借人实际出借的资金额为借款人的借款本金。借款人在借贷行为中除本金及税项以外所支出的全部费用，无论出借人是以什么名义收取的，均称为利息。

（一）相关法律概念

（1）贷款（Loan），包括预支款项、贴现、为任何人支付或因任何人而支付或代任何人支付或应任何人的要求而支付的金钱、或不论因任何理由而作出的延期偿付欠款，及实质上或效力上是贷款的各项协议（不论其条款或形式为何），以及为确保任何该等贷款得以偿还而达成的协议。

（2）贷（Lend）、贷款人（Lender）的定义根据上述贷款定义解释。

（3）印花税（Stamp Duty），是指根据香港法例第117章《印花税条例》（*Stamp Duty Ordinance*）可予征收的印花税，并包括附加印花税（Additional）、买家印花税（Buyer's）及额外印花税（Special）。

（二）预先扣除和预先约定扣除款项的法律规则

在香港特区借贷类案件司法实践中，常有当事人主张借款数额与案涉借款协议载明的金额不一致的情况，出借人在出借借款时预先扣除全部或部分利息以及扣除分门别类各种费用的情况同样屡见不鲜。

1. 预先扣除款项

主要为预先扣除的全部或部分借款利息。预先扣除的利息，英文为“Retained Interest”，中文直译为“留存利息”，粤语中俗称“抽头息”。抽头息通常并不会实际交付借款人，而是由出借人直接从借款中予以扣除；或者要求借款人在收到借款后的极短时间内支付给出借人，一般为收到借款当场或当日。

除抽头息之外，一些其他费用有时也会被预先扣除，常见的名目有：手续费（Handing Fee）、处理费（Set-Up Charge）、服务费（Service Fee）、预付费（Upfront Fee）、法律费用（Legal Fee）等。

2. 预先约定扣除款项

出借人与借款人通过借款协议或者另行签订的补充协议、还款保证协议等方式，附加条件约定借款人必须在某个约定的时间向出借人支付某些费用后，才可获得借款协议中约定的借款，否则就无法正常获得借款。手续费、处理费、法律费用等上述各色名目的费用往往通过这种形式体现在借款中。这些费用即便没有预先从借款中予以扣除，借款人也往往会在如约收到借款后的短时间内支付给出借人。被冠以上述名目的各类费用不受借款人的自由支配，而是可以预见的按约退还出借人，实为出借人为规避借款利息法律规定而巧立名目的牟利。

3. 对预先扣除和预先约定扣除款项的法律规则

《放债人条例》第 2 条明确规定了只有实际贷出的款额才称为借款本金，无论以任何名义收取的任何超过本金的款项都囊括在利息的范畴内[1]。第 27 条则规定了各类名目的费用可视情况被追讨或抵偿借款本金[2]。在司法判例中，对预先扣除和预先约定扣除款项的处理，尤其是在计算借款协议的实际利率时，主要是将该款项数额从借款本金数额中予以扣除，并纳入借款利息数额中，再进一步计算实际借款利率。

香港高等法院上诉法庭审理的 Gain Wealth Global Credit & Investment Limited v. Chan Suk Fong[3]案中，原、被告双方签订借款合同，原告向被告出借 100 万港元，借期 1 年，年利率 30%。其中，双方对三笔数额（分别为 3.7 万港元、10 万港元和 11 万港元）的款项存在争议。

关于案涉借款本金数额的认定。上诉法庭最终确认为 86.3 万港元（100 万 - 3.7 万 - 10 万 = 86.3 万港元），各类款项的认定理由如下：第一，关于 3.7 万港元从借款本金中予以扣除，因该笔款项系“预付费”，

---

〔1〕《放债人条例》第 2 条规定，本金就任何贷款而言，指实际贷出的款额。利、利息不包括因为印花税或其他相类税项而合法地协定按照本条例支付的任何税项，但除此之外，包括因任何贷款或在其他方面就任何贷款而已予支付、将予支付或须予支付的超逾本金的款项，而不论该款项以何名目称之。

〔2〕《放债人条例》第 27（4）条规定，如违反本条的规定而直接或间接向任何人支付或容许向任何人支付任何款项或金钱的价值，或任何人违反本条的规定而直接或间接收受任何款项或金钱的等值，则即使有相反的协议存在，借款人仍可向该人追讨上述款项或金钱的等值，但仅以违反本条而支付或收受的款额或价值为限；如该人是放债人或其合伙人、雇主、雇员、委托人或代理人，或在任何方面代放债人行事或与放债人共谋，则该款额或价值可用作抵偿实际贷出的款额（而该贷款额须被当作据此而缩减），或可由借款人向该人或向放债人追讨。

〔3〕［2021］HKCA 1219.

并未真正支付给被告，并非“实际贷出”的款额〔1〕。第二，关于10万港元从借款本金中予以扣除，因原告未能举证证明该笔款项系在被告的授意下支付给第三方中间人，亦未能证明该笔款项系源自借款合同本身的款项安排进行放款，而该笔款项的流转过程是原告出具现金支票后由被告持票在银行柜台直接承兑现金并支付予第三方中间人，该笔款项实际上并未流转至被告手中。基于第三方中间人在交易过程中的参与度以及对借款双方的推动作用，推定该笔款项是给予第三方中间人的以期顺利推动双方借款进程的报酬，故不能认定为借款本金，应予以扣除〔2〕。第三，关于11万港元在借款本金中予以保留，虽该笔款项与前述的10万港元情况类似，但该笔11万港元的流转过程却是原告出具标注有“仅限存入受款人账户”的划线支票后由被告持票在银行柜台承兑款项并存入自己名下的银行账户内，之后再通过取现、转账等其他方式支付给第三方中间人的。该笔款项实际上已经流转至被告手中，且后续支付第三方也经过被告法律行为确认，故无法作出前述推定，应被认定为借款本金并予以保留〔3〕。

关于案涉利息数额的认定。上诉法庭最终确认为33.7万港元（30万+3.7万=33.7万港元），各类款项的认定理由如下：第一，关于借款合同约定的利息。经核算，为30万港元（100万×30%×1年）。第二，关于3.7万港元“预付费”纳入借款利息中。《放债人条例》第2（1）条规定，利息包括任何超逾借款本金的款项，因此从利息与本金的角度考量，将3.7万港元从借款本金中扣除并纳入利息符合法律规定，并不构成“重复计算”（Double Counting）〔4〕。第三，关于10万港元未纳入借款利息。根据《放债人条例》第2（1）条关于利息认定的立法精神，利息非必须支付给出借人或其代理人，只要是鉴于或以其他方式涉及借款本身

〔1〕 Gain Wealth Global Credit & Investment Limited v. Chan Suk Fong ［2021］ HKCA 1219, para. 57、62.

〔2〕 Gain Wealth Global Credit & Investment Limited v. Chan Suk Fong ［2021］ HKCA 1219, para. 66－67.

〔3〕 Gain Wealth Global Credit & Investment Limited v. Chan Suk Fong ［2021］ HKCA 1219, para. 66－67.

〔4〕 Gain Wealth Global Credit & Investment Limited v. Chan Suk Fong ［2021］ HKCA 1219, para. 62－63.

的，也可支付给其他人[1]，然该案现有证据无法证明第三方中间人是原告的贷款业务代理人[2]，也无法证明原告参与了该笔款项数额的决策，亦无法证明该笔款项与原告放款行为之间的直接联系，因此该笔款项无法被认定为利息[3]。

同样，在 Skyline Credit Limited v. Leung Hing Chung[4]案中，香港高等法院上诉法庭对于预先扣除和预先约定扣除款项也采用了相同的司法处理方式。该案中，被告向原告借款 180 万港元，约定借期 1 年、年利率 27.6%。现双方就 4 笔款项（数额分别为 49,680 港元、18,000 港元、8000 港元以及 762,320 港元）存在争议。

关于案涉借款本金数额的认定。上诉法庭最终确认为 1,724,320 港元（180 万 – 49,680 – 18,000 – 8000 = 1,724,320 港元），各类款项的认定理由如下：第一，关于 49,680 港元从借款本金中予以扣除。该笔款项系借款前 3 个月的部分抽头息，由原告在放款时直接扣除，并未实际交付给被告。第二，关于 18,000 港元从借款本金中予以扣除。该笔款项名目为“手续费”，原告在放款前要求被告签字同意支付该笔款项，否则将影响正常放款，故该笔款项为预先约定扣除款项，依法应从本金中扣除。第三，关于 8000 港元从借款本金中予以扣除。该笔款项名目为“法律费用”，由原告在放款时直接扣除，并未实际交付给被告。第四，关于 762,320 港元在借款本金中予以保留。该笔款项名为“保险费”，其流转过程为在原告出具一张面额为 872,000 港元并标注有“仅限存入受款人账户”[5]的支票后由被告持票在银行柜台承兑并将等额款项存入自己名下账户内，而后再通过

---

[1] Gain Wealth Global Credit & Investment Limited v. Chan Suk Fong [2021] HKCA 1219, para. 43.

[2] Gain Wealth Global Credit & Investment Limited v. Chan Suk Fong [2021] HKCA 1219, para. 48.

[3] Gain Wealth Global Credit & Investment Limited v. Chan Suk Fong [2021] HKCA 1219, para. 55.

[4] [2022] HKCA 1241.

[5] Skyline Credit Limited v. Leung Hing Chung [2022] HKCA 1241, para. 48.

取现的方式将762,320港元以现金形式交付给第三方中间人[1]。现有证据无法证明原告与第三方当事人之间存在业务代理关系或者串通欺诈的情况[2]，而该笔款项实际上已经流转至被告手中，且后续支付第三方也经过被告法律行为确认，故依法应认定为借款本金并予以保留。

关于利息数额的认定。上诉法庭最终确认为572,480港元（496,800 + 49,680 + 18,000 + 8000 = 572,480港元），各类款项的认定理由如下：第一，关于借款合同约定的利息。经核算，为496,800港元（180万港元 × 27.6% ×1年）。第二，关于49,680港元、18,000港元、8000港元纳入借款利息。《放债人条例》第2（1）条规定，利息包括任何超逾借款本金的款项，因此从利息与本金的角度考量[3]，将该3笔款项纳入利息符合法律规定，《放债人条例》第2条对于利息的定义涵盖了最广泛的可能性，以便可以承接借款人被要求向出借人支付的冠以任何名目或标签的金钱款项，法庭凭其实质而非形式予以认定[4]。

（三）借新还旧的法律规则

1. 借新还旧的概念

香港特区的借贷类案件司法实践中，经常会出现固定的出借人与借款人在一段时间内连续签订多份除借款金额不同外其他条件均相似的借款协议。法院在审理该类案件时，会区分案涉借款协议是单一借款协议（Single Loan）还是系列借款协议（Series of Loans）。

单一借款协议是指连续签订的多份借款协议中，后签订的借款协议承接了前一期，并对借款人前期借款欠付的本息进行了足额清偿。借款人用后一份借款协议所获得的借款完成了对前一份借款协议的履行，前期借款协议效力终结，后期借款协议随即生效，借款人与出借人之间的债权债务关系转移（Roll Over）至后期借款协议中。由此可见，香港特区的单一借

---

[1] Skyline Credit Limited v. Leung Hing Chung [2022] HKCA 1241, para. 13.

[2] Skyline Credit Limited v. Leung Hing Chung [2022] HKCA 1241, para. 48.

[3] Skyline Credit Limited v. Leung Hing Chung [2022] HKCA 1241, para. 51 – 53.

[4] Skyline Credit Limited v. Leung Hing Chung [2022] HKCA 1241, para. 125.

款协议更类似于内地的借新还旧。系列借款协议是指连续签订的多份借款协议中，每份借款协议均独立存在，有单独法律效力。多份借款协议代表了借款人与出借人之间的多重债权债务关系，各借款协议之间并不存在前后承接关系。

2. 借新还旧的普通法规则及判例

香港特区成文法条例对涉及借新还旧的借款协议的法律效力没有明确作出判定的法律规定。司法实践中的处理规则通常为针对个案的不同事实与情况作出判定，相关的普通法规则散见于不同的判例当中。

New Japan Securities International（Hong Kong）Limited v. Lim Yiong Lin〔1〕案中，原告作为放债人与被告前后一共连续签订5份借款协议，借期均为3个月，单利计息，被告在每次借款逾期时均通过后一份借款协议获得借款进行前期偿还。香港高等法院上诉法庭在该案的判词中认定，大家的共识就是每期借款都在承接前一期借款并且协议条款基本相同，当被告不能如期履约时，就通过这种方式获得原告新发放的借款来足额清偿前一期的借款本息〔2〕。随后判词中引述了英国BS Lyle Ltd. v. Chappell〔3〕案中大法官的观点：如果一个资金交易意味着出借款项给借款人并且借款人用这些款项清偿了以前的借款欠款，那么法庭不能再把这个资金交易仅仅视为一个借款的展期；通过从出借人那里获得新的借款清偿前期欠款的行为效果等同于借款人从其他人那里获得新的借款清偿对出借人的前期欠款〔4〕。最近的Honip Credit Limited v. Leung Tak Sing Paul〔5〕案中，香港高等法院上诉法庭认为，原告与被告前后连续签订7份条款内容基本相同的借款协议属于“再融资贷款”（Refinancing Loan），并援引了前述的New Japan Securities International（Hong Kong）Limited v. Lim Yiong Lin案，认为该

〔1〕［1987］HKCU 194.

〔2〕New Japan Securities International（Hong Kong）Limited v. Lim Yiong Lin［1987］HKCU 194, para. 2.

〔3〕［1932］1 KB 691.

〔4〕New Japan Securities International（Hong Kong）Limited v. Lim Yiong Lin［1987］HKCU 194, para. 7.

〔5〕［2020］HKCA 879.

案原告与被告签订的第 7 份借款协议的性质是一笔新的借款（as the New Loan），因此无须考虑是否存在复利的问题[1]。

综上所述，借新还旧借款协议通常会被视为一份新的借款协议，包含上一份借款协议未清偿的本金及利息。新协议的利息计算也不需要考量前序借款协议的利率标准，没有复利的顾虑。

三、小结

（一）相同点

第一，内地与香港特区对民间借贷借款本金的认定均采用了保守性和限制性立法视角，限定只有实际出借的款项才可被视为借款本金。

第二，内地与香港特区对于“砍头息”等预先扣除款在认定借款本金时会从本金数额中予以扣除。

（二）不同点

第一，内地与香港特区的利息内涵不同。内地法律下利息、违约金、其他费用等总计不能超过一年期 LPR 四倍的法定限额，但利息与违约金、其他费用等属于不同的法律概念。香港特区法律规定放债行为中除了本金及税项以外，超出本金的款项（无论以何种名目）均认定为利息。

第二，内地与香港特区对“砍头息”等预先扣除款在认定借款利息时的计算方式不同。内地法律未规定将“砍头息”从本金数额扣除后再纳入利息数额中。香港特区法律则规定将预先扣除款或预先约定扣除款从本金数额中扣除后，还可能再次将其纳入利息数额中。

第三，内地与香港特区对借新还旧合同的司法限制不同。内地法律要求每一期借新还旧合同均须符合法律规定，且最后一期合同期限届满之时的本金与利息总额之和不得超过以最初本金为基数计算的本金与利息总额

---

〔1〕 Honip Credit Limited v. Leung Tak Sing Paul［2020］HKCA 879，para. 4. 31.

之和，以防止出现超出司法限额征收利息的情况。香港特区法律仅要求每一期借新还旧合同均须符合法律规定，除此之外在其他方面未有明确要求。

第二节　借期内利息的法律规则

一、内地的法律规定

由于货币资本的逐利性，利息和利率作为资本相关概念，被视为货币作为一种商品的价格，对金融机构而言，除法律特别规定外，借款合同一般有利息[1]。但民间借贷不同于金融借款，民间借贷的主体既包括企业，也包括自然人，借款目的既包括生产经营的资金周转，也包括生活所需的临时用资。与金融借款相比，民间借贷在形式和内容上更趋多样化，体现在民间借贷合同中，就会呈现为有的约定利息、有的不约定利息、有的虽约定了利息但利率不明确等。司法实践中，比较常见的就是对借期内利息未作约定和对借期内利息约定不明两种情况。

对此，《民间借贷司法解释（2020第二次修正）》第24条规定："借贷双方没有约定利息，出借人主张支付利息的，人民法院不予支持。自然人之间借贷对利息约定不明，出借人主张支付利息的，人民法院不予支持。除自然人之间借贷的外，借贷双方对借贷利息约定不明，出借人主张利息的，人民法院应当结合民间借贷合同的内容，并根据当地或者当事人的交易方式、交易习惯、市场报价利率等因素确定利息。"《民法典》第680条的规定与上述规定基本一致。

据上述法律规定可知，内地法律对借款利息采取的基本态度为：在不超过利率司法保护上限的前提下，有约定的从约定；无约定的视为无息；约定不明的，自然人之间的借款视为无息，除自然人之间借款以外的借款

---

〔1〕《商业银行法》第38条规定，商业银行应当按照中国人民银行规定的贷款利率的上下限，确定贷款利率。

则应根据当地或当事人的交易方式、交易习惯、市场报价利率等因素确定利息。

（一）对借期内利息未作约定的处理规则

1. 自然人之间的借款对利息未作约定

案例：自然人甲向自然人乙借款 10 万元，双方未约定利息，甲逾期未还款，乙起诉至法院，要求甲返还借款本金 10 万元并按照银行同期贷款利率支付利息。法院一般支持乙关于甲返还本金的诉讼请求，不支持乙关于利息的诉讼请求。

2. 除自然人之间借款以外的借款对利息未作约定

案例：甲公司向乙公司借款 10 万元用于资金周转，甲公司与乙公司素有多年业务往来，双方未约定利息。甲公司逾期未还款，乙公司起诉至法院，要求甲公司返还借款本金 10 万元并按照银行同期贷款利率支付利息。法院一般支持乙公司关于甲公司返还本金的诉讼请求，不支持乙公司关于利息的诉讼请求。

虽然公司作为商事主体进行资金融通多为获取利益，但不可完全排除部分商事主体之间为临时救急而互通有无、互相扶携。与自然人相比，公司为非金融机构法人，其从事民商事行为能力、风险防范能力和对于市场预期判断能力普遍较高，也是自身利益的最佳判定者。如为获取利益，本应在借款合同中明确约定，未约定的则视为其本身没有追求利益的本意或者借款双方未达成支付利息的合意。

（二）对借期内利息约定不明的处理规则

1. 自然人之间的借款对利息约定不明

案例：自然人甲向自然人乙借款 10 万元，双方约定支付利息，但未约定利息支付标准。甲逾期未还款，乙起诉至法院，要求甲返还借款本金 10 万元并按照银行同期贷款利率支付利息。法院一般支持乙关于甲返还本金的诉讼请求，不支持乙关于利息的诉讼请求。

传统的民间借贷主体多为自然人，借款人和出借人双方一般具有亲属、同事或朋友关系，借款用途多用于子女婚嫁、教育支出、购买自用房屋以及大病医疗等突发性支出，借款目的多为无偿的互帮互助，除非当事人有明确约定，才应当支付利息。这样的规定是因为自然人之间的借贷有着互通有无的作用，能够方便生产生活，促进邻里和睦安宁，形成互帮互助、友好相处的和谐氛围。

2. 除自然人之间借款以外的借款对利息约定不明

案例：甲公司向自然人乙借款10万元用于工程建设集资，双方约定应支付利息，但未约定利息支付标准。甲公司在集资时向乙出示了《公司集资计划书》，内容载明“公司决定对××工程建设集资100万元，时间为两年，年息10%”。甲公司逾期未还款，乙起诉至法院，要求甲公司返还借款本金10万元并按照一年期LPR四倍的标准支付利息。法院判决甲公司返还本金并按照年利率10%支付利息。

对于约定不明利息的确定，实质为合同漏洞补充。合同漏洞是指合同应对某事项加以规定却未予规定，即合同欠缺条款。漏洞补充旨在补充合同的不完备，而非在为当事人创造合同，故应采用最少介入原则，避免侵害当事人的意思自治。基于这种考虑，对于除自然人之间借款之外的借款利息约定不明的情况，通常按照以下顺序和标准进行判定：

（1）结合借款合同的内容确定利息。非金融机构法人与非法人组织作为主体的民间借贷合同，多以书面形式订立，表达和传递当事人合同意图所使用的语言文字，在合同的整个内容中是有组织的，可从这种有组织的排列中找出欠缺的利息条款或洞察当事人关于利率或利息的真实本意。如上述案件中，法院审理后认为，虽双方未明确约定利息计算标准，但借款已说明用途为“工程建设”，与《公司集资计划书》中提及的内部集资款用途一致，且《公司集资计划书》中明确了内部集资的期限为2年、年息10%，故法院最终判定双方借款利息按年利率10%计算。

（2）按合同履行地或者当事人的交易方式、交易习惯确定利息。一般认为，在不违反法律、行政法规强制性规定的前提下，以下两类情形可认定为“交易习惯”：一是在交易行为当地或者某一领域、某一行业通常采用并为交易对方订立合同时知道或者应当知道的做法；二是双方当事人经常使用的习惯性做法。

（3）按订立合同时履行地的市场报价利率确定利息。《民法典》第511条规定："当事人就有关合同内容约定不明确，依据前条规定仍不能确定的，适用下列规定：……（二）价款或者报酬不明确的，按照订立合同时履行地的市场价格履行；依法应当执行政府定价或者政府指导价的，依照规定履行。"

二、香港特区的法律规定

Chitty on Contracts（*35th edition*）论述到，利息在有明确合同约定的情况下是当然要支付的；这样的约定也可以从合同双方当事人的交易过程中推断出来，例如，通过几个相似的银行账户频繁地进行收款和付款但各方当事人均无异议。同样，特定贸易或业务的习惯或做法也可被视为需要支付合同利息。[1] 对于没有约定利息的情况，该书进一步论述到，普通法的一般规则是在没有明确的合同约定或者无法通过交易过程与习惯推断出合同约定的情况下，债务或贷款的利息是不需要支付的。因此，除非证明合同涉嫌欺诈，否则在未有明示条款约定的情况下，拖欠的货款、出借的资金、待履行的金钱债务、保证款、未结算的工程款以及任何应付欠款的利息，都是不需要支付的[2]。

（一）借期内利息未作约定的法律规则

在 Lam Ching Sheung（林征嫦）v. The Personal Representative of The Estate of Tam Shui, Deceased［谭瑞（已故）遗产的管理人］& Ors.[3] 案中，香港高等法院原讼法庭采用的判定标准与前述 *Chitty on Contracts*（*35th edition*）的论述基本一致。该案中，原、被告双方口头约定借款，

---

〔1〕 See Hugh Beale, Richard Hooley, Louise Merrett, Graham Virgo, *Chitty on Contracts*, 35th Edition, Sweet & Maxwell, para. 42 – 298.

〔2〕 See Hugh Beale, Richard Hooley, Louise Merrett, Graham Virgo, *Chitty on Contracts*, 35th Edition, Sweet & Maxwell, para. 42 – 297.

〔3〕［2013］HKCU 476.

未签订书面借款协议，亦未约定利息。在结合原、被告双方的陈述和证人证言后，原讼法庭判决被告无须支付借款利息，并在判词中解释道：双方订立借款协议（该协议未约定借期内利息）的最初意图便是原告给予被告无息贷款。[1]

（二）借期内利息约定不明的法律规则

在 Chun Yip Engineering Co.（a firm）v. Silvercord Limited[2]案中，香港高等法院对于如何“从当事人交易过程（Course of Dealing）推断”作出如下阐释：在合约成立的前提下推定一个默示条款时，法庭必须谨记，该默示条款不仅要具备“合理性”（Reasonable），还要具备赋予该合约之商业效力的“必要性”（Necessary）。该案原告主张通过双方当事人交易过程可推断出原告与被告之间已达成关于利息的默示约定，高等法院审理后认为该交易过程所体现的默示约定虽可印证原告向被告征收利息是合理的，但对于实现达成约定的效力却并不必要[3]。

值得一提的是，普通法体系下的衡平法对香港特区法律体系也产生了深远的影响，其中，衡平法就规定了一些必须给付的利息，例如，无论是否有合同约定或惯例，担保人代债务人清偿欠款后向债务人追偿产生的利息须被支付[4]。

因此，据上述普通法规则及司法判例可推断，香港特区法律对借款利息的认定规则为：在不超过法定限额（即实际利率[5]不违反《放债人条例》规定）的前提下，合同有约定的从其约定；未作约定但可以通过交易过程或者特定贸易、业务习惯做法推断出来的，视为有利息；未作约定且不能推断出来的，一般视为没有利息。衡平法规定的一些特殊利息，无论

---

[1] Lam Ching Sheung（林征嫦）v. The Personal Representative of The Estate of Tam Shui, Deceased［谭瑞（已故）遗产的管理人］& Ors. ［2013］HKCU 476, para. 66.

[2] ［1997］HKCU 1.

[3] Chun Yip Engineering Co.（a firm）v. Silvercord Limited［1997］HKCU 1, para. 22.

[4] See Hugh Beale, Richard Hooley, Louise Merrett, Graham Virgo, *Chitty on Contracts*, 35th Edition, Sweet & Maxwell, para. 42 – 300.

[5] 实际利率，指按照香港特区《放债人条例》附表 2 计算的真正百分比年利率。

合同是否有约定，均视为有利息。

三、小结

关于不同点，当利息未作约定或约定不明时，内地与香港特区确定利息的方式不同。内地法律对借款主体是否为自然人加以区分，规定自然人之间的借款无论对利息未作约定还是约定不明均视为没有利息，只有除自然人之间借款以外的借款对利息约定不明时才会按当地或当事人的交易方式、交易习惯、市场报价利率等确定利息。香港特区法律对借款主体是否为自然人不作区分，对利息约定不明时均适用通过交易过程、贸易习惯等进行推断，只有对利息未作约定且无法推断时才视为无息，并且还存在衡平法规定的特殊情形。

第三节　逾期利息的法律规则

一、内地的法律规定

《民法典》第676条规定："借款人未按照约定的期限返还借款的，应当按照约定或者国家有关规定支付逾期利息。"借款人的主要义务是还本付息，未按期返还借款是一种严重的违约行为，借款人应当对其违约行为承担相应的法律责任。

（一）逾期利息的性质

逾期利息，即所谓的逾期还款利息。在借款合同中，借款人逾期未清偿欠款所承担违约责任的方式包括返还借款本金、支付借期内利息以及支付借款逾期部分的利息。其中，本金、借期内利息属于合同继续履行[1]

---

〔1〕 继续履行也称强制实际履行，是指违约方根据对方当事人的请求继续履行合同规定的义务的违约责任形式。对于金钱债务，由于其只存在迟延履行，不存在履行不能，因此，应无条件适用继续履行的责任形式。

的范畴，而逾期利息则具有以下特点：

1. 逾期利息不是法定孳息

金钱债权存在法定孳息，其基础法律关系指向的是款项支付本身。对于债权人而言，延迟支付所导致的结果为本应获得的资金、利息无法获得，因此将其认定为法定孳息是具有合理性的。但逾期还款的基础法律关系为借款合同，区别在于借款合同是出借人让渡一定时间的资金使用而获得利息收入、借款人为取得一定时间的资金使用而支付一定利息的合同。因此资金的时间价值是合同履行的重要内容，利息就是资金的时间价值，是双方对资金使用的约定价格。将逾期还款利息认定为孳息与双方对资金利息的支付本意不符。

2. 逾期利息的性质取决于当事人的合同约定

（1）借款合同违约

逾期利息因借款人未按时清偿借款而产生，是借款合同违约的一种后果。《民法典》第 577 条规定："当事人一方不履行合同义务或者履行合同义务不符合约定的，应当承担继续履行、采取补救措施或者赔偿损失等违约责任。"第 179 条规定："承担民事责任的方式主要有：（一）停止侵害；（二）排除妨碍；（三）消除危险；（四）返还财产；（五）恢复原状；（六）修理、重作、更换；（七）继续履行；（八）赔偿损失；（九）支付违约金；（十）消除影响、恢复名誉；（十一）赔礼道歉。"根据上述法条，主流观点认为，可适用于借款合同的违约责任形式有继续履行、赔偿损失〔1〕和违约金〔2〕三种。其中，赔偿损失可分为法定损害赔偿〔3〕和约定损害赔偿〔4〕。依据不同标准，违约金又可分为法定违约金和约定违约金，或者惩罚性违约金和赔偿性违约金。逾期利息体现为违约责任的哪一

---

〔1〕赔偿损失，在合同法上也称违约损害赔偿，是指违约方以支付金钱的方式弥补受害方因违约行为所减少的财产或者所丧失的利益的责任形式。

〔2〕违约金，是指当事人一方违反合同时应当向对方支付的一定数量的金钱或财物。

〔3〕法定损害赔偿是指由法律规定的，由违约方对守约方因其违约行为而遭受的损失承担的赔偿责任。

〔4〕约定损害赔偿，是指当事人在订立合同时，预先约定一方违约时应当向对方支付一定数额的赔偿金或约定损害赔偿额的计算方法。

种形式，需要依据借款合同的不同约定加以区别。

（2）借款合同约定

契约自由原则和当事人意思自治原则是合同的基础，逾期利息的性质同样取决于合同约定。如果合同中对逾期还款违约责任的形式进行了约定，则无论违约金的金额是否明确，逾期利息的性质均属于违约金；如果合同中对逾期还款违约责任的形式没有约定或者只约定了损失赔偿的计算方式，则逾期利息的性质为损害赔偿。

《民法典》对于违约金的性质倾向于补偿性为主、有限度的惩罚性为辅模式，即强调违约金的补偿性理念，同时有限地承认违约金的惩罚性。如果将逾期利息通过合同约定为违约金形式，那么参照不高于借期内利率的标准计算逾期利息，一方面体现了“违约金数额系根据违约情况而确定”，另一方面体现了违约金对实际损失的补偿性特征，将违约金作为一项违约救济措施，既保护了债权人的利益，又激励了当事人积极从事交易活动以及促进经济流转。

如果将逾期利息通过合同约定为损失赔偿计算方式，那么参照借期内利率的标准计算逾期利息则更加直观的体现了“根据违约情况确定损失赔偿数额”这一典型的赔偿性特征。因此，无论借款双方约定违约金还是损失赔偿，对逾期利息的判定都应以赔偿出借人的损失为主，以惩罚借款人为辅。对逾期利息计算标准未约定或者约定不明的情况适用借期内利率可以最大限度保护出借人的利益。

（二）逾期利息的计算标准

《民间借贷司法解释（2020 第二次修正）》第 28 条规定：“借贷双方对逾期利率有约定的，从其约定，但是以不超过合同成立时一年期贷款市场报价利率四倍为限。未约定逾期利率或者约定不明的，人民法院可以区分不同情况处理：（一）既未约定借期内利率，也未约定逾期利率，出借人主张借款人自逾期还款之日起参照当时一年期贷款市场报价利率标准计算的利息承担逾期还款违约责任的，人民法院应予支持；（二）约定了借期内利率但是未约定逾期利率，出借人主张借款人自逾期还款之日起按照借期内利率支付资金占用期间利息的，人民法院应予支持。”据上述法律规定可知，内地对逾期利息计算标准的认定大致遵循以下原则：第一，借款合同对逾期利息有约定的，从其约定，但不得超过合同成立时一年期LPR四倍的法定上限标准。第二，借款合同对逾期利息没有约定或约定不明，但约定了借期内利率的，可参照借期内利率计算逾期利息。第三，借款合同对逾期利息没有约定或约定不明，并且没有约定借期内利率的，可参照当时的一年期LPR标准计算逾期利息。

二、香港特区的法律规定

（一）逾期利息的性质

逾期利息，普通法下英文为“Default Interest”，是指因借款人逾期偿还借款而被要求支付的利息〔1〕。从历史上说，普通法并不鼓励获偿利息〔2〕。

1. 逾期利息不是借款合同代价

合同代价（Consideration），又称约因、对价，法律内涵上指的是一方为换取另一方做事的承诺而向另一方支付的金钱代价或得到该种承诺的承诺。普通法下，早在1893年，英国上议院在London，Chantham & Dover Railway Co. v. South Eastern Railway Co.〔3〕案中就曾确认“对延期偿还债务所主张的利息的赔偿不能获得法院支持”这一原则〔4〕，即逾期还款案件中不应就合同约定利息之外的利息进行判罚，虽然这一原则在近年的司法判例中已被推翻〔5〕，但足以证明普通法体系一直以来对债务利息持

〔1〕 See Hugh Beale, Richard Hooley, Louise Merrett, Graham Virgo, *Chitty on Contracts*, 35th Edition, Sweet & Maxwell, para. 42 – 307.

〔2〕 Charles T. McCoemick, *Interest as Damages*, Article 1, No. 3, Volume 9, North Carolina Law Review.

〔3〕 [1893] AC 429.

〔4〕 London, Chantham & Dover Railway Co. v. South Eastern Railway Co. [1893] AC 429.

〔5〕 英国上议院即终审法院（House of Lords）于2007年在Sempra Metals Ltd. v. Her Majesty's Commissioners of Inland Revenue and Another [2007] UKHL 34案中推翻了“延期支付的利息不能获得赔偿”这一司法原则。

保守态度。按照借款合同，一方出借资金，一方支付利息，资金的出借和本息的偿付已经构成借款合同代价。因此，逾期利息的属性并不是合同代价。

2. 逾期利息不是对侵权行为的司法救济

合同法下的不当行为可以是侵权性质的，也可以是违约性质的。当事人可就侵权行为或合同违约造成的损失进行索赔，是英国法下的一项基本原则[1]。通常对侵权行为造成损害的救济是返还型救济（Restitutionary Remedy），例如，在 Sempra Metals Limited v. Her Majesty's Commissioners of Inland Revenue and Another[2]案中，英国上议院认为，款项误付行为导致了损失，被侵权人不仅可以要求返还其应得却未得到的应付款项，还可要求一并返还应付款项在误付期间所产生的其应得却未得到的孳息。由此可见，普通法下以侵权行为为由主张偿还应得却未得到资金的孳息更偏重于强调侵权人因占用资金而窃取了"非正义的利益"（Unjust Enrichment）[3]，即所谓的不当得利。显然，就借款合同而言，借款人的逾期还款行为和出借人主张的逾期利息与不当得利这一概念并不吻合，因此，在普通法体系下逾期利息不能被视为对侵权行为的司法救济。

3. 逾期利息是对违约行为造成损害的赔偿

借款人的逾期还款行为，除了造成出借人无法获得作为借款合同对价的借款本金和利息以外，还造成了出借人因无法按时获得偿付的资金款项而间接引起的金钱损失（需要出借人自行证明），实则为一种合同违约行为。通常对违约行为造成损害的救济是赔偿型救济（Compensatory Remedy）。例如，在 Union Base Ltd. v. Tsang Shek Tong trading as Hawaii Engineering Company[4]案中，香港高等法院上诉法庭指出，违约方未按时履约付款使

---

[1] See Hugh Beale, Richard Hooley, Louise Merrett, Graham Virgo, *Chitty on Contracts*, 35th Edition, Sweet & Maxwell, para. 42 – 283.

[2] [2007] UKHL 34.

[3] Sempra Metals Ltd. v. Her Majesty's Commissioners of Inland Revenue and Another [2007] UKHL 34, para. 132.

[4] [1998] 2 HKC 349.

守约方丧失了可通过及时得到应得款项而获取的收益[1]（如投资盈利等）或守约方被迫付出了未及时得到应得款项的代价（如另行借款支出利息等），守约方对此可以主张包含无法如期使用应得款项损失的收益在内的全部赔偿[2]，这种通过征收利息的方式对损失的收益的赔偿被称为利息的赔偿（Interest as Damages）[3]。显然，借款合同逾期利息的性质更加符合这一普通法共识。

但是，要求支付逾期利息的前提是出借人必须证明延期还款造成的实际损失，这种损失应当是已经发生的，且与约定的借期内利息没有关系。不能仅仅因为约定了借款利率就认为出借人已经因借款人的逾期还款行为而遭受了损失[4]。借期内约定的利息，不能扩展到借款期限届满之后。

（二）逾期利息的计算标准

Chitty on Contracts（*35th edition*）论述到，如果借款合同双方就支付本金作出契约（Covenant）并且基于该契约经司法程序获得了法庭判决，那么该支付本金契约所附带的支付利息的义务就会与法庭判决的支付利息的义务相合并；然而，如果借款合同双方在独立于支付本金契约之外，另行就支付利息也作出契约，那么该支付利息契约就不能与法庭判决的支付利息义务相合并。[5] 简言之，当借款合同对逾期利息有单独约定时，按约定计算逾期利息；没有单独约定时，按法庭判决计算逾期利息。

1. 借款合同对逾期利息有约定

香港特区法律充分尊重合同自由和当事人意思自治原则，如果借款合

---

〔1〕 Union Base Ltd. v. Tsang Shek Tong trading as Hawaii Engineering Company [1998] 2 HKC 349, para. 11.

〔2〕 Sempra Metals Ltd. v. Her Majesty's Commissioners of Inland Revenue and Another [2007] UKHL 34, para. 132.

〔3〕 Charles T. McCoemick, *Interest as Damages*, Article 1, No. 3, Volume 9, North Carolina Law Review.

〔4〕 See Hugh Beale, Richard Hooley, Louise Merrett, Graham Virgo, *Chitty on Contracts*, 35th Edition, Sweet & Maxwell, para. 42 – 299.

〔5〕 See Hugh Beale, Richard Hooley, Louise Merrett, Graham Virgo, *Chitty on Contracts*, 35th Edition, Sweet & Maxwell, para. 28 – 009.

同中包含的条款，或独立于借款合同之外的补充、从属协议中，对逾期利息有单独约定，可以从其约定[1]。

（1）约定的逾期利率不高于借期利率

在 Honip Credit Ltd. v. Asia China Tea Export Company Ltd. & Siu Mei Yam[2]案中，对于在借款合同中约定的不超过借期利率标准的逾期利息，香港高等法院上诉法庭作出以下判定：合约双方可以约定，支付方须根据合约的条款（包括有关利率的条款），在判决后继续以合约利率支付利息[3]。该案中，原、被告双方在借款合同中约定借期利率为 24.96%，同时，合同第 6 条明确约定：借款人同意无论是在法院判决之前或以后，应付的金额的利率仍然以年利率 24.96% 计算。换言之，在法院判决之后，应付金额之利率仍然是以年利率 24.96% 计算，直至支付一切所欠金额为止。上诉法庭认为，本案借款合同第 6 条对借款人支付利息的责任有清楚的规定，而根据该条款规定，被告在本案判决后继续以合同约定的 24.96% 年利率支付利息是正确的[4]。

同样，在 Freeway Finance Company Limited（亨运财务有限公司）v. Tam Chuen On Raymond[5]案中，香港高等法院原讼法庭采用了类似的判定标准。该案中，原、被告双方于 2009 年 11 月 28 日签订借款金额为 500 万港元的借款合同，合同第 1 条约定：借款人支付给出借人的利息参照相当于实际利率月息 4%（即年息 48%）的标准以借款本金为基数按借款期限予以计算。合同第 2 条约定：借款本金及利息按等额本息的方式均分 120 期，按月还款 142,500 港元……若利息或本金或任意一期还款发生逾期，则借款人需偿还的利息无论是在诉讼程序开始后还是在法院就借款本

[1] See Hugh Beale, Richard Hooley, Louise Merrett, Graham Virgo, *Chitty on Contracts*, 35th Edition, Sweet & Maxwell, para. 42 – 310.

[2] [2016] HKCU 1333.

[3] Honip Credit Limited v. Asia China Tea Export Company Ltd. & Siu Mei Yam [2016] HKCU 1333, para. 21.

[4] Honip Credit Limited v. Asia China Tea Export Company Ltd. & Siu Mei Yam [2016] HKCU 1333, para. 22.

[5] [2010] HKCU 1462.

金及利息作出判决后，仍将按照合同第 1 条规定的利率标准进行计算，直至足额清偿为止。原讼法庭认为，该借款合同第 2 条关于逾期利息的规定可被视为一项独立的契约（Covenant），因此应当持续有效，并适用于判决后的利息计算，即判决后的利息也应遵照约定按年利率 48% 的标准进行计算。

（2）约定的逾期利率高于借期利率

《放债人条例》第 22 条规定："如根据协议须向放债人支付的款项，不论是本金或是利息，到期而有所拖欠……放债人有权就该笔款项收取单利，由拖欠之日起计至该笔款项付清为止，其实际利率不得超逾在没有拖欠的情况下就该本金收取的实际利率。"根据《放债人条例》的规定，借款人发生逾期还款行为后，对于逾期利息的计算标准一般不得超过借款合同约定的借期内利息的实际利率，但由于本条立法针对的是放债人群体，而非普通群体之间的借贷活动，故只可以此立法倾向作为指向性参考。

值得注意的是，*Chitty on Contracts*（*35th edition*）论述到，如果该过高的逾期利率只适用于自违约之日起的利息计算而对违约前的利息计算不具追溯性，且该逾期利率条款的主要目的并非威吓震慑债务人，且因债务人违约导致信贷风险增加而使逾期利率相比借期内利率所有增高的幅度是适度的又商业性合理的，那么该逾期利率就不会被视为惩罚性赔偿。[1] 换言之，合同约定过高的逾期利率很可能会被认定为惩罚性条款而不发生预期的法律效力。

从普通法体系的发展演变历程来讲，逾期利息的相关法律规定历经了一概不予保护、部分有限度的保护到如今的被动补偿性保护，香港特区的立法也受其影响。现有的司法判例中，合同双方对于逾期利息的约定高于借期内利率的情况并不常见，由此可以推知，香港特区法律并不鼓励当事人双方约定过高逾期利息的法律行为。

---

[1] See Hugh Beale, Richard Hooley, Louise Merrett, Graham Virgo, *Chitty on Contracts*, 35th Edition, Sweet & Maxwell, para. 42 – 305.

2. 借款合同对逾期利息未作约定

在没有合同约定的情形下，出借人请求逾期利息的前提是必须证明借款人逾期还款的行为已给出借人造成了实际损失。[1] *Chitty on Contracts*（*35th edition*）论述到，出借人就借款合同项下到期金额（包括利息）经司法程序获得法庭判决后，合同双方的权利义务便与法庭判决的权利义务相合并，出借人自此须以法庭裁判的金额及法定利息寻求出借人支付欠款，直至清偿为止。[2]

在香港特区的司法裁判中，逾期利息通常被分为以下两部分：判决前逾期利息（Pre－judgment Interest）和判决后逾期利息（Post－judgment Interest）。

（1）判决前逾期利息

判决前逾期利息通常指，自还款期限届满之日起至判决签发日前一日止的因逾期还款而产生的利息。根据普通法基本原则，债权人在合理有效证明其相应损失的前提下，可以就因债务人违反合同延迟付款产生的己方利息损失主张损害赔偿。香港特区法官通常会行使其酌情权（自由裁量权），参照“港元最优惠利率（Prime Rate）+1%”的利率标准，进行判决前逾期利息的计算和判罚[3]。截至2024年9月20日，港元最优惠利率为5.625%[4]，即判决前逾期利率可计为6.625%。在 Waddington Ltd. v. Chan Chun Hoo Thomas & Ors.[5] 案中，香港高等法院上诉法庭再次重申，在香港特区的司法审判中，应采用港元最优惠利率上浮1%的标准计算判

---

〔1〕 See Hugh Beale, Richard Hooley, Louise Merrett, Graham Virgo, *Chitty on Contracts*, 35th Edition, Sweet & Maxwell, para. 42－283.

〔2〕 See Hugh Beale, Richard Hooley, Louise Merrett, Graham Virgo, *Chitty on Contracts*, 35th Edition, Sweet & Maxwell, para. 28－007.

〔3〕 采用最优惠利率上浮1%的标准，始于1982年香港高等法院上诉法庭 Komala Deccof v. Pertamina［1984］HKCU 47案，该案中阐明最优惠利率上浮1%系当时主审法官的酌情权，并建议延续这一标准作为补偿一方被排除在损害赔偿之外的损失计算标准。尽管后续偶有偏离，但大部分案件依旧承袭这一计算标准。

〔4〕 最新一期港元最优惠利率为5.625%，生效日期为2024年9月20日。

〔5〕 ［2016］HKCU 1192.

决前逾期利息[1]。

如果当事人双方在审判过程中达成附带条款和解提议（Sanctioned Offer），且该提议所载内容相较法院判决来说，会部分牺牲原告的利益，则法官有权在“判定利率（Judgment Rate）+10%”的利率司法保护限额内，进行判决前逾期利息的计算和判罚。[2] 在 Golden Eagle International（Group）Limited v. GR Investment Holdings Limited[3]案中，香港高等法院原讼法庭采用了上述规定，该案原、被告双方在附带条款和解提议中达成合意，同意按判定利率标准计算判决前逾期利息，此标准高于常见的港元最优惠利率+1%计算标准。原讼法庭审查后认为该标准不超过“判定利率+10%”的利率司法保护上限，因此在尊重双方当事人意思自治的基础上，予以法律上确认[4]。

（2）判决后逾期利息

判决后逾期利息通常指，自判决签发之日起至清偿之日止的因逾期还款而产生的利息。根据《高等法院规则》第 49（1）条[5]及《区域法院规则》第 50（1）条[6]的规定，判定债项的全部或尚未清偿的部分款额须按法院所命令的利率或在无命令的情况下由终审法院首席法官借命令所决定的利率，即判定利率（Judgment Rate），来计算单利。截至 2024 年 10

---

〔1〕 Waddington Ltd. v. Chan Chun Hoo Thomas & Ors. [2016] HKCU 1192，para. 172－185.

〔2〕《高等法院规则》第 22 号命令第 24 条规定，（1）凡——（a）被告人被判须负的法律责任，高于原告人的附带条件和解提议所载的建议；或（b）与原告人的附带条款和解提议所载的建议比较，针对被告人的判决对原告更有利，则本条规则适用。（2）法庭可就判给原告人的任何款项的全数或部分（利息除外）衍生利息作出命令，该利息按不高于判定利率 10%的利率，就被告人本可无须法庭许可而接受有关提议的最后日期后的某段时间或整段期间计算。

〔3〕 [2010] 3 HKLRD 273.

〔4〕 Golden Eagle International（Group）Limited v. GR Investment Holdings Limited [2010] 3 HKLRD 273，para. 11.

〔5〕《高等法院规则》第 49（1）条规定，判定债项的总额或判定债项当其时尚未清偿的部分须带有单利——（a）利率按原讼法庭所命令者计算；或（b）如无该项命令时，利率则按终审法院首席法官不时藉命令所决定者计算，由有关判决的日期起计，直至清偿为止。

〔6〕《区域法院规则》第 50（1）条规定，判定债项的全部款额或判定债项当其时尚未清偿的部分款额——（a）区域法院所命令的利率计算的单利或（b）在无命令的情况下由终审法院首席法官藉命令所决定的利率计算的单利，计息期由该判决日期起至清偿为止。

月1日，终审法院首席法官颁令的最新一期判定利率为8.875%。

三、小结

（一）相同点

内地与香港特区均尊重当事人意思自治，对借款合同中明确约定的逾期利息，在不超过法定限额的情况下一般予以司法保护。

（二）不同点

第一，内地与香港特区对逾期利息的性质认定不同。内地法律优先考虑当事人合同约定，逾期利息的性质根据合同约定可以是违约金，也可以是损害赔偿。香港特区根据普通法原则认定逾期利息的性质为违约损害赔偿。

第二，内地与香港特区对逾期利率高于借期利率的司法保护不同。内地法律对逾期利率高于借期利率的情况，在不超过司法保护限额（一年期LPR四倍）的前提下，予以保护。香港特区法律对此没有明确规定，过高的逾期利率在司法实践中有可能被认定为惩罚性赔偿而不能获得法律保护。

第三，内地与香港特区对未约定逾期利息时的计算标准不同。内地法律规定借款合同中对逾期利息未作约定时，逾期利率可参照借期内利率；对借期内利率也未作约定时，则按照一年期LPR的标准计算逾期利息。香港特区法律将未约定情况下逾期利息的计算标准划分为判决前和判决后，判决前逾期利息通常按港元最优惠利率（目前为5.625%）+1的标准进行计算，判决后逾期利息则按判定利率（目前为8.875%）标准进行计算。

第四章　利率司法保护上限的法律规则比较

第一节 利率司法保护限额

一、内地的法律规定

利率是规范民间借贷的核心问题。从司法解释的规定来看，民间借贷的合法性与借贷利率水平紧密相关，对民间借贷利率的规制程度决定了民间借贷市场的开放程度以及对民间借贷的保护程度，也关系借贷双方的权益。司法解释规定了民间借贷利率司法保护上限，其目的不是干预借贷双方在法律限度内对利率的自由协商权，而是防止出借人乘人之危或利用优势地位损害借款人的正当利益。[1]

（一）《民间借贷司法解释（2020 修正）》下调利率上限的背景

最高人民法院在发布修正后《民间借贷司法解释（2020 修正）》时对此进行了专门介绍。简言之，基于以下五点理由：一是经济社会发展的客观要求。降低中小微企业的融资成本，引导整体市场利率下行，是当前恢复经济和保市场主体的重要举措。二是规范民间借贷活动的客观需要。大幅度降低民间借贷利率的司法保护上限，对于引导、规范民间借贷行为具有重要意义。三是确保民间借贷平稳健康发展的需要。从长远来看，大幅度降低民间借贷利率的司法保护上限，有利于互联网金融与民间借贷的平稳健康发展。四是推动利率市场化改革的必然要求。过高的利率保护上限不利于营造利率市场化改革的外部环境，也不符合利率市场化改革的方向。五是统一司法裁判标准的现实需求。有必要顺应经济发展的趋势，适时对民间借贷司法解释进行修订，给民间借贷纠纷提供更为具体明确的裁判标准和救济渠道。

---

〔1〕 参见岳彩申：《民间借贷规制的重点及立法建议》，载《中国法学》2011 年第 5 期。

（二）司法利率保护上限

1. 司法解释修正前的利率保护上限

《民间借贷司法解释》第26条规定：“借贷双方约定的利率未超过年利率24%，出借人请求借款人按照约定的利率支付利息的，人民法院应予支持。借贷双方约定的利率超过年利率36%，超过部分的利息约定无效。借款人请求出借人返还已支付的超过年利率36%部分的利息的，人民法院应予支持。”根据该规定，利率保护上限可分成三个层次进行理解：一是年利率24%以下的民间借贷利率认定为有效；二是超过年利率36%的部分认定为无效；三是年利率在24%至36%的部分认定为自然之债，已经支付的不能要求返还，未支付的亦不能要求支持。此即所谓的“两线三区”规定。

2. 司法解释修正后的利率保护上限

现行《民间借贷司法解释（2020第二次修正）》第25条规定：“出借人请求借款人按照合同约定利率支付利息的，人民法院应予支持，但是双方约定的利率超过合同成立时一年期贷款市场报价利率四倍的除外。前款所称‘一年期贷款市场报价利率’，是指中国人民银行授权全国银行间同业拆借中心自2019年8月20日起每月发布的一年期贷款市场报价利率。”根据新的规定，利率保护上限同样可分成三个层次进行理解：一是民间借贷的利率保护限额调低至一年期LPR四倍。二是一年期LPR的数值是浮动的而不是固定的，从中国人民银行公布的一年期LPR基准（截至2024年7月22日）来看，一年期LPR四倍最高达年利率17%，最低至年利率13.4%。三是一年期LPR四倍的限额可以以合同签订时所公布一年期LPR四倍的标准计算限额。

（三）新旧法律规定的衔接

《民间借贷司法解释（2020第二次修正）》第31条第2款规定：“2020年8月20日之后新受理的一审民间借贷案件，借贷合同成立于2020年8月20日之前，当事人请求适用当时的司法解释计算自合同成立到

2020 年 8 月 19 日的利息部分的，人民法院应予支持；对于自 2020 年 8 月 20 日到借款返还之日的利息部分，适用起诉时本规定的利率保护标准计算。”上述规定充分体现了法不溯及既往原则与司法解释裁判规范引导原则的有机统一。根据上述规定，对于成立于 2020 年 8 月 20 日之后的民间借贷合同，利率保护限额当然适用合同成立时 LPR 四倍的上限；但对于成立于 2020 年 8 月 20 日之前的民间借贷合同，利率标准采用“分段原则”，即 2020 年 8 月 19 日前的利率限额按照“两线三区”规定处理、2020 年 8 月 20 日之后的利率限额按照一年期 LPR 四倍处理。

例如，2019 年 8 月 19 日，出借人与借款人约定：借款 100 万元、借款期限为 2 年、月利率 3%、月利息按月支付、本金到期后一次性支付。出借人如期向借款人出借了 100 万元，借款人分别于 2019 年 9 月 19 日还款 3 万元、2019 年 10 月 19 日还款 2.5 万元、2019 年 11 月 19 日还款 2.2 万元、2019 年 12 月 19 日还款 1.5 万元，此后未再支付过任何款项。借款到期后，出借人起诉至法院。按照《民间借贷司法解释（2020 第二次修正）》之规定，2019 年 9 月至 11 月偿还的 3 个月的利息在年利率 24% - 36% 之间且已经支付，应当予以确认；2019 年 12 月 19 日应还利息为 2 万元，借款人仅付 1.5 万元，尚欠 0.5 万元；2019 年 12 月 20 日至 2020 年 8 月 19 日的应还利息为 16 万元。综上，出借人应当向借款人偿还本金 100 万元及利息（截至 2020 年 8 月 19 日利息为 16.5 万元；自 2020 年 8 月 20 日起至实际清偿之日止，以借款本金 100 万元为基数按年利率一年期 LPR 四倍的标准计付）。

二、香港特区的法律规定

（一）《放债人条例》下调利率上限的背景

香港财经事务及库务局局长许正宇表示：“近年来，社会各界对放债人利率的水平表示关注，认为利率偏高会对借款人，尤其是对低收入者造成伤害，并引起其他社会问题。我们在经参考消费委员会的建议、本地放债行业现时采用的实际利率、海外地区的贷款利率上限及其他数据后，提出下调法定贷款利率上限。"[1] 由此可见，香港特区与内地下调利率保护上限所面临的情况基本一样。香港特区的法定利率保护上限由《放债人条例》进行规定。香港立法会经过充分调研与论证后，于2022年10月26日正式修改《放债人条例》，过高利率（Excessive Interest Rates）的入刑标准由年利率60%调整至年利率48%，敲诈性交易的推定标准由年利率48%调整至年利率36%。该修订已于2022年12月30日正式生效。

（二）利率保护的上限

1. 法定贷款利率上限

《放债人条例》第24（1）条明确规定："任何人（不论是否放债人）以超过年息百分之四十八的实际利率贷出款项或要约贷出款项，即属犯罪。"第24（4）条规定："任何人犯本条所订罪行——（a）一经循简易程序定罪，可处罚款＄500,000及监禁2年；（b）一经循公诉程序定罪可处罚款＄5,000,000及监禁10年。"从该规定来看，《放债人条例》所规定的法定贷款利率上限适用各类型的贷款，如果约定利率超过了年利率48%，将构成犯罪并要承担相应的刑事责任。对此施以严格的刑事责任，是香港特区打击高利贷违法行为的重要手段。

法定贷款利率上限存在例外情形。根据《放债人条例》第24（5）条的豁免规定，向拥有缴足股本不少于100万港元或相等款额的其他认可货币的公司作出的贷款，以及作出该笔贷款的人，不适用于《放债人条例》第24条规定，即贷款实际利率不受年利率48%的上限以及相应法律后果的限制。

2. 敲诈性交易的推定标准

《放债人条例》第25（3）条明确规定："关于任何贷款的还款协议或关于任何贷款利息的付息协议，如其所订的实际利率超逾年息百分之三十六，则为本条的施行，单凭该事实即可推定该宗交易属敲诈性；但除非该

---

〔1〕《政府欢迎立会通过修订放债人条例》，载政府新闻网，https：//sc.news.gov.hk/TuniS/www.news.gov.hk/chi/2022/10/20221026/20221026_170442_560.html。

利率超逾第24（1）条所指明的利率，否则法庭在顾及与该协议有关的所有情况后，如信纳该利率并非不合理亦非不公平，则可宣布为本条的施行该协议并不属敲诈性。”关于敲诈性交易的认定，除单凭贷款实际利率超过年利率36%这一事实可推定属于敲诈性外，如该宗交易的债务人或其亲属须支付严重过高的款项或者在其他方面严重违反公平交易的一般原则，法院还可根据《放债人条例》第25（2）条的规定裁定该宗交易属于敲诈性[1]交易。

（三）新旧法律规定的衔接

《放债人条例》法定贷款利率上限的修订于2022年12月30日正式生效。为此，香港特区政府于2022年12月29日专门发布新闻公报提醒，“上述修订获立法会于今年十月通过，并适用于由明日及之后起生效的贷款还款协议及贷款利息的付息协议”。[2] 香港特区与内地一样，均采取法不溯及既往的原则。新修订的法定贷款利率上限仅适用于2022年12月30日之后生效的借款协议。

三、小结

（一）相同点

内地与香港特区对借贷交易的利率限额均通过成文法的形式进行了明确的法律规定，且两地通过修订法律的形式下调了贷款利率保护的上限。

（二）不同点

内地与香港特区对借贷交易的贷款利率保护上限规定不同，香港特区

---

〔1〕根据《放债人条例》第25（4）（5）（6）条的规定，法庭在裁定任何交易是否属于敲诈性时，须顾及的因素包括：作出贷款时的通行利率；债务人的年龄、经验、做事能力和健康状况；在达成交易时债务人所受财务压力的程度和该压力的性质；在顾及所提供的保证的性质和价值后，贷款人接受的风险程度；以及贷款人与债务人的关系等。

〔2〕《法定贷款利率上线修订明日开始生效》，载香港特别行政区政府新闻公报网，https://www.info.gov.hk/gia/general/202212/29/P2022122800407.htm。

的利率保护上限明显高于内地。内地的民间借贷利率司法保护上限为一年期 LPR 四倍，且 LPR 数值是浮动而非固定的。香港特区利率司法保护规则为：除豁免情形外，超过年利率 48%，即属犯罪；超过年利率 36%，可以推定交易属于敲诈性。

第二节 超过利率司法保护上限的法律后果

一、内地的法律规定

（一）超过利率司法保护上限后合同效力问题

《民法典》第 680 条第 1 款规定："禁止高利放贷，借款的利率不得违反国家有关规定。"至于违反法律规定后的借款合同效力问题，《民法典》没有进一步予以规定。关于该问题，《民间借贷司法解释》第 26 条表述为"超过部分的利息约定无效"；修正后现行的《民间借贷司法解释（2020 第二次修正）》第 25 条表述"双方约定的利率超过合同成立时一年期贷款市场报价利率四倍的除外"。从立法沿革来看，内地立法机关对此类合同持"部分无效"的意见。《民法典》第 156 条规定："民事法律行为部分无效，不影响其他部分效力的，其他部分仍然有效。"因此，民间借贷合同约定的利率超过司法保护上限并不必然导致合同无效，但是超出利率司法保护上限的利息不受法律保护。

（二）约定利率超过限额且部分履行后的剩余利息认定

出借人与借款人签订借款合同并约定：2021 年 1 月 1 日，出借人向借款人借出 100 万元，借款利率为年利率 20%，借款期限为 3 年（自 2021 年 1 月 1 日起至 2023 年 12 月 31 日止），每年付息一次。后出借人如约于 2021 年 1 月 1 日（当时中国人民银行公布的一年期 LPR 为年利率 3.85%）向借款人出借 100 万元，借款人如约于 2022 年 1 月 1 日和 2023 年 1 月 1 日分别支付利息 20 万元；2023 年 12 月 31 日借款合同到期后借款人未能如期还本付息，借款人所欠本金和利息计算如下（见下表）：

表　本金和利息计算

单位：元

序号	日期	本金	还款金额	应付利息	尚欠本金
1	2021. 1. 1	1, 000, 000			
2	2022. 1. 1	1, 000, 000	200, 000	154, 000	954, 000
3	2023. 1. 1	954, 000	200, 000	146, 916	900, 916
4	2023. 12. 31	900, 916		138, 741. 06	

备注：1. 应付利息 = 本金 × 年利率 15. 4%；
2. 尚欠本金 = 本金 -（还款金额 - 应付利息）。

根据法律规定，上述民间借贷案件的最高利率保护上限为合同订立时一年期 LPR 的四倍，即年利率 15. 4%（即 3. 85% ×4 倍），司法实践中一般将已付利息中超过年利率 15. 4% 的部分予以抵扣本金。根据上述计算方式，借款人应当向出借人支付本金 900, 916 元及利息（截至 2023 年 12 月 31 日利息为 138, 741. 06 元；自 2024 年 1 月 1 日起至实际清偿之日止，以借款本金 900, 916 元为基数按年利率 15. 4% 计付）。

需要特别注意的是，司法实践中部分出借人提出另一种计算方式。以上述案件为例：第一步计算出 2021 年 1 月 1 日至 2023 年 12 月 31 日总计利息 46. 2 万元（100 万元 × 年利率 15. 4% ×3 年）；第二步计算欠付利息 6. 2 万元（46. 2 万元 - 40 万元）；第三步得出出借人应付本金 100 万元及利息（截至 2023 年 12 月 31 日利息为 6. 2 万元；自 2024 年 1 月 1 日起至实际清偿之日止，以借款本金 100 万元为基数按年利率 15. 4% 计付）。从两种计算模式可以看出，后一种计算方式借款人用资成本较高，所需偿还的本息之和更多。后一种计算方式看似比较简单，但是没有考量到借款人实际的用资本金，变相提高了借款利率，故相较而言第一种计算方式更为公正。

二、香港特区的法律规定

（一）年利率超过48%的法律后果

1. 刑事法律后果

根据《放债人条例》第24（1）条的规定，以实际利率超过年利率48%贷出款项即属犯罪。出借人可能被检控，根据简易程序或公诉程序，结合实际情节，被判处不同刑期的监禁或/和不同金额的罚款。

2. 民事法律后果

除了向拥有缴足股本不少于100万港元或相等款额的其他认可货币的公司作出的贷款以及作出该笔贷款的人可以受到豁免以外，《放债人条例》第24（2）条规定："关于任何贷款的还款协议或关于任何贷款利息的付息协议，以及就该等协议或贷款而提供的保证，如其实际利率超逾第（1）款所指明的利率（即年利率48%），则不得予以强制执行。"与第二章职业放贷人的认定一样，该类合同起诉到法庭后，法庭对出借人主张的所有本金利息均不予支持。

需要特别注意的是，对于实际利率超过年利率48%（在2022年12月30日前为年利率60%）的借贷交易是否可以由法院依据《放债人条例》第25（1）条规定判决重新商议交易并确定应执行的利率，香港特区的不同案例中作出不同解释。在高等法院上诉法庭Wong Kwai Fun v. Li Fung[1]案、区域法院Lee Leo v. Cheong Oi Sum Ader[2]案等判例中，法院认为对于实际利率超过60%的借贷交易，法院有权依据自由裁量权重新商议交易。然而，在Wong Ming Wai v. Tsui Kam Ming trading as Tung Tai Construction Co.[3]案中，高等法院上诉法庭则认为实际利率超过年利率60%的借款交易既不得强制执行也不得重新商议。该案亦被高等法院原讼法庭

---

〔1〕［1994］1 HKC 549，para. 84.

〔2〕［1993］2 HKC 736，para. 9.

〔3〕［1999］HKCU 1288，para. 8.

在 Kwok Ying Lung v. Ko Chi Hung Maxwell Mabel Straube[1]、Morales Elisa Galleto v. Corriente Nenete Manejero[2]等案件判决中遵循。近年来，香港特区司法实践中大多认可超过法定贷款利率上限后，法庭没有权利重启交易。

（二）年利率在36％－48％之间的法律后果

《放债人条例》第25（3）条规定："关于任何贷款的还款协议或关于任何贷款利息的付息协议，如果其所订的实际利率超逾年息百分之三十六，则为本条的施行，单凭该事实即可推定该宗交易属敲诈性。"借款协议约定的年利率在36％至48％之间，则可推定该交易为敲诈性，但其法律后果不能一概而论，要结合案件的具体情况进一步判定，具体包括以下情形。

1. 不属于敲诈性交易，正常执行借款协议

《放债人条例》第25（3）条规定："但除非该利率超逾第24（1）条所指明的利率，否则法庭在顾及该协议有关的所有情况，如信纳该利率并非不合理亦非不公平，则可宣布为本条的施行该协议并不属敲诈性。"

2. 属于敲诈性交易，法庭重新商议交易

《放债人条例》第25（1）条规定："法庭在顾及所有情况后，可重新商议该宗交易，使交易双方均获公平对待，并可为该目的而就该宗交易的条款或交易双方的权利，作出其认为适当的命令，或给予其认为适当的指示。"

3. 属于敲诈性交易，不予强制执行

《放债人条例》第25（1）条赋予了法院的酌情权，即法院审查后认为属于敲诈性交易的，法院有酌情权决定是否重启交易。重启交易并非必然发生，如法院在顾及与该协议有关的所有情况后信纳该超过36％的实际

---

〔1〕［2000］HKCU 358，para. 23.

〔2〕［2016］HKCU 69，第13段直接引用 Wong Ming Wai v. Tsui Kam Ming trading as Tung Tai Construction Co. 案的判词。

利率不合理亦不公平，则借款协议可不予强制执行。

三、小结

（一）相同点

借贷交易利率超过利率司法保护上限的，内地与香港特区均规定出借人应承担相应的不利法律后果。

（二）不同点

内地与香港特区对超过利率司法保护上限的借贷交易的法律后果规定不同。内地法律规定不保护超出上限部分的利息，但法院对于借款本金以及司法保护范围内的利息与费用予以支持。香港特区法律规定，超过年利率48%的借贷交易即属犯罪，不得强制执行，即法院对本金、利息等均不予支持。对于超过年利率36%的借贷交易，如法院推定其为敲诈性交易，可不予强制执行或重新商议并确定应执行的利率；如法院行使酌情权信纳其不属敲诈性，则借款协议可正常执行。

第五章　合同条款约定不明的法律规则比较

第一节 清偿顺序无约定或约定不明

一、内地的法律规定

《民法典》第 561 条规定："债务人在履行主债务外还应当支付利息和实现债权的有关费用，其给付不足以清偿全部债务的，除当事人另有约定外，应当按照下列顺序履行：（一）实现债权的有关费用；（二）利息；（三）主债务。"

（一）清偿抵充的定义

清偿抵充，是指债务人对于同一债权人负担数项同种类债务，债务人的给付不足以清偿其全额债务时，确定该给付抵充这些债务中的某项或者某几项债务；或者债务人在履行主债务外还应当支付利息和实现债权的有关费用，其给付不足以清偿全部债务的，确定该给付抵充该项债务中的某个或者某几个部分。

据此可知，清偿抵充包括两种情形：一是数项债务的清偿抵充；二是一项债务中主债务与利息、实现债权的费用的清偿抵充。本节主要讨论第二种情形。

（二）清偿抵充的顺序

清偿抵充可以分为意定抵充和法定抵充，其中意定抵充又包括约定抵充和指定抵充两种情形。

1. 约定抵充

约定抵充即合同双方已约定了清偿抵充顺序。当事人就清偿顺序协商达成一致，系意思自治原则的具体体现，法律应予尊重和保护。《民法典》第 561 条的"除当事人另有约定外"明确了约定抵充的优先适用性。约定抵充可以发生在债务清偿前或清偿时，在清偿后约定抵充或者变更约定抵充的，当事人之间仍然发生效力，但不能影响担保人等有利害关系的第三人利益。

除明示约定外，约定抵充可以是合同默示约定。例如，债权人请求清偿特定某项债务而债务人并未表示反对并且予以支付；或者债务人明确给付行为系为清偿某项特定债务而债权人未表示反对并且受领。对于默示约定抵充，在司法实践中，应根据案件的具体事实进一步准确探求当事人的真实意思表示，判断在待决纠纷中，究竟是债务人与债权人之间达成了默示的约定抵充合意，还是仅系债务人的单方面主张。

2. 指定抵充

指定抵充即在合同双方无约定的情况下，由债务人在清偿时指定其履行的债务。在数项债务清偿抵充情形下，法律侧重保护债务人利益，规定可以适用指定抵充[1]；在一项债务中主债务与利息、实现债权的费用清偿抵充情形下，法律更侧重保护债权人利益，排除了指定抵充的适用，本节在此不再赘述。

3. 法定抵充

法定抵充即在合同双方无约定的情况下，法律规定的清偿抵充顺序，意在补充当事人意思之不完备。法定抵充清偿的顺序如下：

（1）实现债权的有关费用。债权人为实现债权而支出的必要费用属于额外的支出，故债务人应当优先清偿这些费用。费用发生的原因既可以是自力实现债权，也可以是借助国家公权力实现债权。司法实践中较为常见的费用主要有：保全费、诉讼费、拍卖费、登记费、公证费、执行费用等。

（2）利息。利息是债权人预期应有的收益，是资金占用的成本，应当先于主债务或者本金获得清偿。利息包括约定利息和法定利息，约定的利息不得超过法定限额，超过法定限额并发生抵充的，超出部分应自动转为对下一顺位（即主债务）的清偿抵充。

---

〔1〕《民法典》第560条第1款规定，债务人对同一债权人负担的数项债务种类相同，债务人的给付不足以清偿全部债务的，除当事人另有约定外，由债务人在清偿时指定其履行的债务。

（3）主债务。主债务是债的关系中固有的、必备的，并且用以决定债的关系类型的基本义务。将主债务置于尾端参与清偿抵充，体现了法律侧重保护债权人利益的立法取向，只要主债务存在，就会不断地产生利息或者实现债权的费用，督促债务人尽快完整地履行债务，促进交易完成。

综上所述，内地法律对借款人在借款存续期间偿还款项的清偿顺序规定如下：双方当事人有约定的从其约定；无约定且事后无法协商一致的，则按照实现债权的有关费用、利息、主债务的先后顺序予以抵充。在司法实践中，对此一般称为“先息后本”。

二、香港特区的法律规定

普通法下的债务清偿顺序规则同样对多笔债务的清偿和一笔债务下本金与利息的清偿作出规定。

Chitty on Contracts（*35th edition*）论述到，当存在多笔到期债务时，债务人有权指定其所还款项对各债务的分配比例；如果债务人不作指定，则债权人有权就债务人所还款项在多笔债务之间指定分配比例。[1] 债务人在指定分配比例时，须通过明示或默示的沟通确保债权人知晓债务人行使该权利的意思表示。债务人指定分配比例不一定发生在还款时，也可以发生在其他能清楚表示债务人指定分配比例意图的时刻，但必须确保债权人也知晓该意图。[2] 当债务人未指定还款分配比例时，就轮到债权人进行指定。债权人可以在“最后一刻”之前的任意时间指定分配比例。债权人指定分配比例是一种“依条件附带发生”的权利，只有在债务人未指定的情况下才赋予债权人该权利。同样，当债权人指定分配比例时，也需要通过明确的沟通确定债务人知晓该分配。[3] 债权人指定的分配比例不得用于抵

---

〔1〕 See Hugh Beale, Richard Hooley, Louise Merrett, Graham Virgo, *Chitty on Contracts* , 35th Edition, Sweet & Maxwell, para. 25 – 058.

〔2〕 See Hugh Beale, Richard Hooley, Louise Merrett, Graham Virgo, *Chitty on Contracts* , 35th Edition, Sweet & Maxwell, para. 25 – 059.

〔3〕 See Hugh Beale, Richard Hooley, Louise Merrett, Graham Virgo, *Chitty on Contracts*, 35th Edition, Sweet & Maxwell, para. 25 – 060.

充非法合同或不公平请求下的债务。[1]

Chitty on Contracts（*35th edition*）接着论述到，对于债务本金与利息之间的比例分配，当债务人和债权人均未对包含利息的债务指定分配比例时，法律原则上（除非有相反的意思表示）会将债务人所还款项先用于清偿所有到期的利息，再用于抵充最早到期的本金。[2]

在 Bank of China（Hong Kong）Ltd. v. Eddy Technology Co. Ltd. & Ors.[3] 案中，香港高等法院上诉法庭亦明确引述上述原则：作为法律问题，除合同条款有明确规定外，债务人有权就其所还款项在利息与本金的分配比例上作出指示。在缺少债务人有效指示的情况下，债权人可以对该款项在本金与利息之间自由进行比例分配。此外，如果债务人和债权人均没有指定分配比例，法律原则上（除非有相反的意思表示）会将债务人所还款项先用于清偿所有到期的利息，再用于抵充最早到期的本金。[4] 上诉法庭进一步指出：分配比例的权利是法律赋予的，除非本案被告受到合同条款的约束，否则他可以就每笔还款行使分配比例的权利。[5]

综上所述，香港特区关于借款人还款本息清偿顺序的认定规则为：双方当事人有约定的，从其约定；双方当事人未约定的，借款人有权就其还款指定本金与利息的分配比例；借款人未作指定的，由出借人决定分配比例（但不得抵充非法合同或不公平请求下的债务）；双方当事人均未指定分配比例的，则借款人的还款应当先用来清偿已到期的利息，再抵充本金，即“先息后本”。

---

〔1〕 See Hugh Beale, Richard Hooley, Louise Merrett, Graham Virgo, *Chitty on Contracts*, 35th Edition, Sweet & Maxwell, para. 25－061.

〔2〕 See Hugh Beale, Richard Hooley, Louise Merrett, Graham Virgo, *Chitty on Contracts*, 35th Edition, Sweet & Maxwell, para. 25－066.

〔3〕 [2019] HKCA 339.

〔4〕 Bank of China (Hong Kong) Ltd. v. Eddy Technology Co. Ltd. & Ors. [2019] HKCA 339, para. 15－16.

〔5〕 Bank of China (Hong Kong) Ltd. v. Eddy Technology Co. Ltd. & Ors. [2019] HKCA 339, para. 19.

三、小结

（一）相同点

内地与香港特区对借款人还款的本息清偿顺序规定基本一致，均为有约定的从约定，无约定且双方均未指定还款分配比例的情况下，推定为先偿还利息后偿还本金。

（二）不同点

当事人的指定抵充权有所不同。内地法律规定，只要当事人双方无约定，还款即按照实现债权的有关费用、利息、主债务的先后顺序予以清偿抵充。香港特区法律则规定，如果当事人双方无约定，则借款人有权先指定还款的本金与利息分配比例；如果借款人也未作指定，则出借人有权决定分配比例（但不得抵扣非法合同或不公平请求下的债务）；只有在当事人双方均未指定分配比例时，才按照“先息后本”顺序清偿。

第二节　借款期限无约定或约定不明

一、内地的法律规定

借款合同中借款人的主给付义务是偿还借款本金，在有息借款中借款人还须支付利息。借款人何时需要履行上述义务，取决于借款合同中约定的借款期限。因此，借款期限的确定具有重要的法律意义：一是期限本身也是一种利益。借款合同中借款人的借款期限越长，意味着借款人可以使用资金的期限越长，这对借款人而言是重要的经济利益，因此出借人原则上无权要求借款人提前偿还借款。二是借款期限是判断借款人是否构成迟延履行的时间节点。如果借款人在借款期限届满时仍未偿还借款，就要承担逾期还款的违约责任，并可能需要支付逾期利息。

（一）无约定或约定不明的具体情形

按照合同约定的期限返还借款是借款人的一项主要义务。在当事人对借款期限没有约定或者约定不明的情况下，借款人何时返还借款在实践中容易产生纠纷。

1. 借款期限无约定

司法实践中，借款期限无约定的情形较为明确，一般均为当事人在借款合同、借条中没有约定借款期限，或者无法举证证明双方之间存在口头约定、交易习惯等。例如，广东省汕尾市中级人民法院在（2022）粤15民终1538号案中认定，上诉人李某出具的《借款单》未约定借款期限，李某亦未举证证明其与被上诉人张某双方就借款期限达成补充协议或有交易习惯供参照，属于未约定借款期限的情形。广西壮族自治区高级人民法院在（2019）桂民申3095号案中认定，案涉两张借条均没有借款期限、还款日期、利息和利率的书面约定，而一审原告高某在起诉状中主张案涉两张借条分别约定了“半个月”和“几日”的借款期限，其后又在庭审中主张双方口头约定一周后还款，因此案涉借条的借款期限和还款日期既无书面约定，也无法按照高某的主张予以确定，故该案借款属于对借款期限和利率没有约定的民间借贷。

2. 借款期限约定不明

司法实践中，借款期限约定不明的情形各不相同。最高人民法院在（2017）最高法民申5133号案中提到，在美某公司与晟某公司签订的《借款协议》中，借款期限暂定为1年，但美某公司并未请求还款，而是延长借款期限，但延长至何时并未明确，应视为双方对借款期限约定不明。吉林省高级人民法院在（2019）吉民申774号案中提到，全某律、金某根、全某哲三人约定的借款期限为“10年左右”，但由于借款人金某根已去世，无法确定具体约定，该案属于借款期限约定不明。

（二）法定处理路径

根据《民法典》第510条和第675条的规定，如果借款合同中对借款期限没有约定或约定不明，应当遵循以下顺序确定借款期限：第一，按照《民法典》第 510 条的规定确定借款期限，即当事人可以就借款期限进行协议补充；不能达成补充协议的，按照合同相关条款或者交易习惯确定。第二，按照上述方式仍不能确定借款期限的，根据《民法典》第 675 条的规定，借款人可以随时返还借款，出借人可以催告借款人在合理期限内返还。此时，借款人就可以自主决定何时返还借款。出借人若要求借款人返还借款，则必须给借款人一段合理的期限。期限是否合理，要根据借款的数额、用途等，并结合案件的具体情况进行判断。

（三）难点考量因素的认定

司法实践中，认定借款期限无约定或约定不明时主要有三个难点：一是如何依照相关条款确定，二是如何依照交易习惯确定，三是如何判断催告还款的合理期限。

1. 依照相关条款确定

关于如何依照相关条款确定，实质上为合同解释的问题。合同各条款是当事人协商一致的结果，体现了当事人的真实意愿。合同的各项条款之间往往存在一定的关联，因此当合同欠缺有关内容或者对有关内容约定不明时，可以首先结合相关条款探寻当事人真实的意图，进而补充所欠缺的内容或者确定约定不明的内容。

例如，有时虽然借款合同中没有明确约定借款期限，但合同中的其他条款可能会指向借款人可以使用借款的期限，如借款合同中的借款用途等条款可能会间接反映出借款期限的长短，此时就要结合“合同相关条款”来确定借款期限。

2. 依照交易习惯确定

《最高人民法院关于适用〈中华人民共和国民法典〉合同编通则若干问题的解释》第 2 条规定了两种可以认定为《民法典》所称的“交易习惯”的类型：一是当事人之间在交易活动中的惯常做法，二是在交易行为当地或者某一领域、某一行业通常采用并为交易对方订立合同时所知道或者应当知道的做法。

对于交易习惯的认定实际上也是当事人意思自治原则的体现。对于地域性或者行业性的交易习惯，一般是合同当事人双方在订立合同时所知道或者应当知道的，彼此“心照不宣”，所以没有以书面形式体现在合同内容中。对于当事人之间在交易活动中的惯常做法，双方主观上对此一般均有意思联络。

需要注意的是，适用上述两类情形时不得违反法律、行政法规的强制性规定。

3. 催告还款的合理期限

法律对催告借款人还款的“合理期限”未作出明确的规定，实践中需要考虑出借人的身份，如是金融机构或者自然人，以及借款人的偿付能力等因素。该合理期限由出借人根据具体情况确定。在发生纠纷时，法院可以根据具体情况判定该期限是否合理。

当出借人直接以提起诉讼的方式主张借款人还款时，考虑到应给予借款人合理的准备时间，法院常以开庭之日作为催告还款的合理期限届满日，并以该时间节点作出判决。例如，北京市第一中级人民法院在（2018）京01民终2785号案中维持了北京市海淀区人民法院以立案时间起算至开庭时间的“合理准备时间”。

在当事人截至诉讼前仍保持交流的情况下，法院则需认定“催告”的时点，并根据借贷双方及借款数额等具体情形来酌定还款的合理期限。例如，在（2022）苏12民终3909号案中，上诉人滕某于2018年3月10日通过银行转账的方式向被上诉人姜某出借6万元。双方未约定借款期限。2020年9月23日，滕某向姜某要求偿还欠款，而姜某未偿还。江苏省泰州市中级人民法院就该案酌定了1个月的还款合理期限。

二、香港特区的法律规定

Chitty on Contracts（*35th edition*）论述到，如果借款时未约定借款期限，则所产生的当前债务通常是可以立即偿还的（Repayable at Once），无须任何事先追偿。借贷双方也可以再行约定还款时间，或者约定仅需在收到追偿要求后偿还。在某些适当的情况下，亦可得出合同中有关于借款期

限默示条款的结论。当借款属于经追偿才需偿还（Repayable on Demand）的情形时，债务到期的先决条件是提出有效的追偿请求。根据过往判例，在判定是否构成有效的追偿请求时，必须有明确的要求付款的意思表示，但对于具体的措辞则并无要求，只要其可传达出绝对且无其他附加条件的意思表示即可。[1]

由此可见，根据普通法的规则，当事人在借款合同中未约定借款期限的，出借人可以要求借款人立即偿还款项。双方也可以对借款期限进行二次协商或者约定。在特定情形下，亦可从合同中得出包含某些关于借款期限默示条款的结论。

（一）立即偿还时是否有合理期限

根据普通法的规则，应立即偿还的欠款将会被给予一定的合理期限，用于支付流程。*Chitty on Contracts*（*35th edition*）指出，见索即付的款项应在收到追偿请求时立即偿还。借款人仅可被给予动用支付机制清偿债务以防止逾期的时间，但并不会被给予筹措还款资金的合理期限。[2] 由此可见，立即支付可以在合理期限内，但该期限并非是筹措资金的合理期限，而是支付款项所需要花费的期限。

这一规则在英国 Bank of Baroda v. Panessar and Others[3] 案中得到了较为生动的阐述。该案涉及一份 80 余万英镑公司债券的偿还。1981 年 9 月，两家公司就所欠款项向一家银行签发了一份公司债券。该债券约定“见索即付”，如果不履行，银行有权指定一名接管人。1983 年 11 月，银行根据该债券向公司发出了追偿通知。在发出通知大约一小时后，银行就任命了一位接管人接管这两家公司。该案的争议焦点之一即是银行在指定接管人之前是否给公司预留了足够的时间。法院在对这一争议焦点进行论

---

〔1〕 See Hugh Beale, Richard Hooley, Louise Merrett, Graham Virgo, *Chitty on Contracts*, 35th Edition, Sweet & Maxwell, para. 42 – 280.

〔2〕 See Hugh Beale, Richard Hooley, Louise Merrett, Graham Virgo, *Chitty on Contracts*, 35th Edition, Sweet & Maxwell, para. 42 – 280.

〔3〕 [1986] 3 All ER 751.

述时强调：见索即付的款项应在被追偿时立即偿还；然而，在大多数情况下，一个人实际上不可能把清偿债务所需的钱随身携带。他可能把钱放在床底下的箱子里，也可能放在银行或交给受托人保管。因此，在债务人有合理的机会为清偿债务而采取合理的付款机制之前，并不算拖欠债务。当然，这仅限于付款机制所需的时间，并不包括在没有钱的情况下筹集资金的时间。在该案中，法院最终认定银行所预留的一小时是足够的。

在 Lok Wai Yee v. Man Koon Hung〔1〕案中，香港高等法院原讼法庭亦认定，在没有明确的借款期限下，按要求付款是指在要求后的合理时间内付款。〔2〕在 Kensland Realty Ltd. v. Whale View Investment Ltd. and Another〔3〕案中，香港终审法院认定，就该案房产买卖所需分解付款（Split Payment）的4600万余港元的余款而言，所预留的1小时47分钟是不合理的。

值得注意的是，对于合理期限的认定具有很强的个案性质，受到支付方式、参与人员、金额大小等多种因素的影响。前述英国案例已是近40年前的案例，当时通用的通信方式尚为电报、传真等较为传统的途径。前述香港终审法院案例发生的时间距今也有24年，且属于金额巨大的房产交易，涉及分期付款、抵押贷款以及银行、律师多方人员的参与。在各类电子支付方式如此便利的今天，这一规则下所能被预留的时间可能更短。

（二）如何确定合同中的默示条款

就认定默示条款的规定而言，在香港法下法院会为下列目的来认定合同中存在某些默示条款：一是为实现当事人的预期意图，使合同变得具有可行性的默示条款；二是为特定的政策目标（Policy Objectives）而依法在合同中确定默示条款；三是基于交易习惯而认定合同包含特定的默示条款。对应上述三类目的，合同默示条款的认定依据也包含三类，即依据相

---

〔1〕［2020］HKCU 3470.

〔2〕Lok Wai Yee v. Man Koon Hung［2020］HKCU 3470, para. 70.

〔3〕［2002］HKCU 77.

关事实、有关法律规定以及交易习惯。

1. 依据事实确定的默示条款

香港法下，法院可以在合同不完整（Incomplete）的情况下，根据当事人的预期意图认定合同包含默示条款。法院在认定时通常会采取较为谨慎的态度。Liverpool City Council v. Irwin[1]案为普通法下认定合同默示条款的经典案例。法院在该案中指出：法院在为合同加入条款时，如仅主张该条款是合理的，该条款的存在会使合同变得更好或更公平，这是不够的；法院必须认为，加入该条款是必要的（Necessary）。同时，被认定的条款应是“双方均心知肚明，且在被问及时，会毫不犹豫地同意其作为合同的一部分而存在”。在 Hughes v. Greenwich London Borough Council[2]案中，法院认为，只在有“令人信服的理由”，如“必不可少”（Essential）的情况下，才可以根据双方合同关系的实际情况确定默示条款的存在。在 Equitable Life Assurance Society v. Hyman[3]案中，法院将依据事实认定的默示条款描述为具有“严格的必要性”，需要“保守且谨慎”地进行认定。

依据事实认定默示条款有两类测试。

一是“商业效率测试”（the“Business Efficacy”Test）。商业效率测试源自 The Moorcock[4]案，法院在判词中指出，法律从“显然为合同双方的意图”中得出默示条款时，系以赋予该交易以效力为目的。二是“多管闲事的旁观者测试”（the“Officious Bystander”Test）。旁观者测试源于 Shirlaw v. Southern Foundries（1926）Ltd.[5]案。法院在该案判词中指出，从表面上看，在任何合同中，只需默示而无须明示的内容都是不言而喻的，它们的显然程度可达到，若合同双方在进行协商时，一个多管闲事的旁观者建议他们在合同中对此作出明文规定，他们会用一句“哦！当然！”来阻止这位旁观者。在 Twinkle Step Investment Ltd. v. Smart International

---

〔1〕［1977］AC 239.

〔2〕［1994］1 AC 170.

〔3〕［2002］1 AC 408.

〔4〕（1889）LR 14 PD 64.

〔5〕［1939］2 KB 206.

Industrial Ltd.[1] 案中，香港终审法院认为，这一问题的重点在于，在双方没有充分说明合同条款的情况下，被主张的默示条款是否为法院为确定合同内容而必须认定的条款。

2. 依据法律确定的默示条款

依据法律确定的默示条款属于法律施加给合同双方的条款，与合同双方的意图无关。此类条款的存在系法律拟对某些类别的合同予以规范，以保护合同当事人的利益。

3. 依据交易习惯确定的默示条款

在依据交易习惯确定默示条款时，需要注意拟认定的默示条款不得与合同中已有的明示条款相冲突。[2] 同时，并非所有交易习惯均可被作为默示条款纳入合同中。在 Eggar，Forrester Offshore Ltd. v. Hong Kong United Dockyards Ltd.[3] 案中，法院指出，为使一项交易习惯成为可被纳入合同中的默示条款，必须证明该交易习惯是“众所周知的、确定的和合理的”（Notorious，Certain and Reasonable）。

三、小结

（一）相同点

对于借款期限无约定或者约定不明的情况，内地与香港特区的处理方式基本一致：首先可由出借人与借款人协商确定；无法协商一致的，可以通过对合同的解释、交易习惯等确定；仍无法确定借款期限的，出借人可以要求借款人在合理期限内立即返还借款。

（二）不同点

内地与香港特区对于出借人立即偿还借款的“合理期限”的定义有所不同。香港法下的“合理期限”主要是指支付款项所需要的合理时间，内

---

〔1〕［1999］2 HKCFAR 255.

〔2〕 Palgrave, Brown and Son Ltd. v. Owners of SS Turid［1922］1 AC 397.

〔3〕［1987］1 HKC 318.

地法下的“合理期限”在司法实践中需要综合考量出借人的性质、借款人的偿付能力等因素进行综合性判定，在考量时并不严格限制这一期限的用途，法官有较大的自由裁量权。

第六章　与担保合同关系的法律规则比较

第一节　借款合同无效时担保合同的效力

一、内地的法律规定

在民间借贷关系中，出借人在订立借款合同时，通常会与借款人订立担保合同，如抵押合同、质押合同、保证合同以及其他具有担保功能的合同〔1〕，以此保证借款人到期无法按约定清偿债务时，出借人可以执行担保财产从而优先获得清偿。由于借款合同可能因存在高利转贷、借款合同目的违法、非法吸收存款放贷或属于职业放贷等情形而被认定合同无效，此时担保合同的效力成为出借人和借款人关注的焦点问题。

（一）担保合同的内涵、类别以及属性

1．担保合同的内涵与类别

担保合同存在狭义与广义之分。《民法典》第 388 条所规定狭义上的担保合同包括抵押合同、质押合同和其他具有担保功能的合同。抵押合同和质押合同顾名思义是设立抵押权和质押权的合同。其他具有担保功能的合同是不以指向《民法典》规定的担保物权为内容的具有担保功能的合同，主要包括让与担保、所有权保留、融资租赁以及保理等合同。让与担保、所有权保留等方式本身并不属于《民法典》明文规定的担保物权的范畴，但由于这些担保方式通过转移所有权或金钱给付请求权等方式发挥担保作用，因而具有事实上的担保功能。内地法律认可这些担保方式所具有的担保效力，但只有经过登记等方式进行公示，其对抗效力才能在法律上被予以认可。广义上的担保合同还包括以设立保证为目的的保证合同。由于在民间借贷司法实践中，借款人通过设立担保物权、保证或以其他方式

〔1〕 内地与香港特区关于担保的法律制度存在较大差异。在两地各自的法律制度下，同一个英语法律术语可能具有截然不同的法律内涵。由于术语表达的局限性，读者需要注意担保在不同法律制度下的具体内涵。

提供担保的行为十分普遍，因此本书所指的担保合同泛指广义上的担保合同。

内地担保制度规定的担保类型分为典型担保和非典型担保。典型担保主要包括抵押〔1〕、质押〔2〕、留置〔3〕以及保证〔4〕，而非典型担保方式主要包括让与担保〔5〕、融资租赁〔6〕、所有权保留〔7〕等。根据《民法典》第388条的规定，设立担保物权，应当依照《民法典》和其他法律的规定订立担保合同。这意味着，除法定担保物权直接依据法律规定设立以外，担保合同的成立是设立其他担保物权的一般成立要件。根据《民法典》第400条第1款、第427条第1款、第736条第2款的规定，当事人应当采用书面抵押合同或质押合同设立抵押权或质权；融资租赁合同要求采用书面形式。除订立书面的担保合同以外，《民法典》对不同类型的担保物权的设立规定了具体的法定形式要求，如不动产抵押权自登记时设立，动产质权自交付质押财产时设立，权利质权自交付权利凭证或办理权利质押登记时设立。〔8〕由此可见，登记是不动产抵押权、某些权利质权设立的生效要件。此外，登记还发挥对抗善意第三人的作用，例如，动产的抵押自抵押合同生效时设立，但未经登记不得对抗善意第三人。〔9〕因此，担保物权的

〔1〕抵押，是指为担保债务的履行，债务人或者第三人不转移财产的占有，将该财产抵押给债权人的，债务人不履行到期债务或者发生当事人约定的实现抵押权的情形，债权人有权就该财产优先受偿。

〔2〕质押，是指为担保债务的履行，债务人或者第三人将其动产出质给债权人占有的，债务人不履行到期债务或者发生当事人约定的实现质权的情形，债权人有权就该动产优先受偿。

〔3〕留置，是指当条债务人不履行到期债务，债权人可以留置已经合法占有的债务人的动产，并有权就该动产优先受偿。

〔4〕保证，是指为保障债权的实现，保证人和债权人约定，当债务人不履行到期债务或者发生当事人约定的情形时，保证人履行债务或者承担责任的担保方式。

〔5〕第六章第二节详细介绍让与担保的内容。

〔6〕融资租赁，是指出租人根据承租人对出卖人、租赁物的选择，向出卖人购买租赁物，提供给承租人使用，承租人支付租金的一种贸易与信贷、融资与融物相结合的非典型担保方式。

〔7〕所有权保留，是指在分期付款或延期付款的买卖合同中，双方约定出卖人在价款付清之前对标的物保留所有权。如在买受人未能按约付清款项，则出卖人有权取回标的物。

〔8〕《民法典》第402条、第429条、第441条、第443条第1款、第444条第1款、第445条第1款。

〔9〕《民法典》第403条。

设立不仅需要满足一般成立要件，还要求当事人完成法定的形式要件。

2. 担保合同的从属性

借款合同与担保合同是主从合同关系。《民法典》第388条以及第682条明文规定，从属性是担保合同的根本性质，因此该从属性是法定的；除非法律存在例外规定，当事人不能通过约定排除担保的从属性。担保合同的从属性具体表现在发生、效力、变更以及消灭四个方面。

（1）担保合同在发生上具有从属性。担保合同不能独立存在，需以借款合同的存在和生效为前提。

（2）担保合同在效力上具有从属性，其主要体现在以下几个方面：第一，担保合同的效力随借款合同的效力而定，若借款合同无效，则担保合同亦无效。借款合同无效后，担保合同以及借款合同中的担保条款均无效。当事人无法通过自行约定对抗担保合同的效力从属性。第二，担保合同的范围和强度不得大于或强于借款合同的债务范围和强度，担保人只有在债务人负有清偿责任的情况下才承担担保责任。因此，当担保人被要求承担担保责任时，担保人享有债务人对债权人的抗辩权、撤销权和抵销权，并且可以在债务人享有撤销权和抵销权的范围内拒绝承担担保责任。

（3）担保合同在变更上具有从属性。借款合同的变更会对担保合同的效力产生影响，其主要体现在：第一，当债权人和债务人在未得到担保人书面同意的情况下变更借款合同，如借款合同变更后加重担保人的责任，则担保人对加重部分不承担担保责任；如借款合同变更后减轻担保人的担保责任，则担保人只需对减轻后的债务承担担保责任。第二，借款合同全部或者部分债权发生转让时，如未通知担保人，则该债权转让不对担保人发生效力；当借款合同全部或者部分债务发生转移时，除非另有约定，担保人对未经其同意转移的债务不再承担担保责任。第三，担保合同不能被单独转让。借款合同发生转移，担保合同原则上也相应地发生转移。

（4）担保合同在消灭上具有从属性。借款合同因清偿、提存、免除、混同、抵销等原因消灭时，担保合同也应当随之消灭。

（二）借款合同无效导致担保合同无效的法律后果

当借款合同无效导致担保合同无效时，担保人是否承担责任取决于其是否具有过错。根据《民法典》第 388 条第 2 款以及第 682 条第 2 款的规定，担保合同被确认无效后，债务人、担保人、债权人有过错的，应当根据其过错各自承担相应的民事责任。具体的责任认定标准以及责任份额的承担规定在《担保制度司法解释》第 17 条之中。根据该条第 2 款规定，主合同无效导致第三人提供的担保合同无效，担保人无过错的，不承担赔偿责任；担保人有过错的，其承担的赔偿责任不应超过债务人不能清偿部分的三分之一。

当担保人无过错时，担保人不承担民事责任。担保人无过错是指担保人对于借款合同无效不知道或者不应当知道，或者未促成借款合同的成立。值得注意的是，担保人的过错并非对于借款合同无效上具有过错，因为基于合同的相对性原理，借款合同的当事人是出借人和借款人，担保人并非借款合同的主体。担保人具有过错的情形，是指担保人明知借款合同无效仍为之提供担保，或者担保人明知借款合同无效仍作为中介促成合同的订立等情形，均属于担保人应当承担民事责任的事由。[1] 例如，甲与乙签订借款合同，约定甲向乙提供 100 万元的借款。甲向乙提供借款后，为担保乙按约履行清偿借款本息的义务，甲与丙签订担保合同，由丙承担担保责任。乙未能在借款期限届满后清偿借款本息，甲起诉要求乙清偿债务，丙承担相应的担保责任。如法院经审理后发现，甲实为职业放贷人，在未获得放贷资质的情况下以营利为目的向多人提供借款，丙明知甲实为职业放贷人的事实，仍为其提供担保，则丙应当承担相应的民事责任。

在认定损害责任如何分配的问题上，法院不仅应当考虑担保人的过错，同时应当将借款合同的当事人的过错考虑在内。这是因为担保合同无效是由于借款合同无效而导致，借款合同当事人原则上也具有过错。

---

〔1〕 参见最高人民法院民事审判第二庭编著：《最高人民法院民法典担保制度司法解释理解与适用》，人民法院出版社 2021 年版，第 210 页。

因此对于出借人的损失，应当以出借人、借款人、担保人三方均分计算为标准，担保人对于出借人的损失赔偿责任应限定在借款人不能清偿部分的1/3。

二、香港特区的法律规定

（一）担保方式与担保合同

1. 担保的类别

香港特区担保制度下的担保方式相较于内地的担保方式更为多样和丰富。在利用个人信用提供担保时，借款人或担保人可以采用保证（Guarantee）、弥偿（Indemnity）、安慰信（Letter of Comfort）[1]、备用信用证（Standby Letter of Credit）[2]、履约保证（Performance Bond）[3]等方式提供担保。在采用提供不动产、动产以及权利等财产作为担保时，借款人或担保人可以采取按揭（Mortgage）、押记（Charge）、质押（Pledge）等方式设定担保物权。

2. 担保合同

在香港特区的担保制度下，担保合同不是设立担保的必要条件，不同担保方式的选择决定担保人需要完成不同的形式设立担保物权。一般而言，设立担保物权的形式要件包括订立书面担保合同和交付担保财产或财产凭证。

---

〔1〕 Geraldine Andrews, Richard Millett, *Law of Guarantees*, 7th Edition, Sweet & Maxwell, para. 14 - 010. 安慰信，是指在第三方不能或者不愿为债务人的债务提供担保时，决定为债权人提供书面保证，保证债务人将愿意继续与债权人交易，且有能力按期偿还债务。一般多见于母公司为子公司借贷行为出具安慰信。

〔2〕 备用信用证是指开证人（一般指银行）应支付人的请求开给受益人，保证在受益人出示特定单据或文件，开证人在单据相符的条件下必须付给受益人一笔规定的款项或承兑汇票的一种书面凭证。

〔3〕 Geraldine Andrews, Richard Millett, *Law of Guarantees*, 7th Edition, Sweet & Maxwell, para. 16 - 001. 履约保证（有时称为履约担保，或者见索即付保证），是指在受益人出示某些特定的文件之后，无条件地向指定的受益人支付特定的金额。

（1）以书面形式设立担保物权

当采取以信用作为担保的方式，担保人必须与出借人订立书面的担保合同。

当选择以土地[1]作为担保财产，担保人可以选择法定押记（或法定按揭[2]）、衡平法按揭或衡平法押记等形式设立担保物权。法定押记要求担保人需要根据《物业转易及财产条例》第44（1）条的规定，采用契据（Deed）形式设立。衡平法按揭和衡平法押记要求担保人采用书面合同的形式设立担保，并且书面合同需在条款中明确表达设立担保的意图。

当选择以动产作为担保财产，担保人若以法定按揭的方式设立担保，必须采用卖据（Bill of Sale）的形式设立并根据《卖据条例》进行注册登记。担保人若以衡平法按揭或衡平法押记的形式设立担保，既可以采用书面形式设立，也可以采用口头协议的方式设立。担保人若以质押的方式设立担保，必须采用书面形式。

（2）以交付形式设立担保物权

当担保人选择在土地上设立衡平法按揭，可以采用交存地契的方式设立担保物权。当担保人选择在动产或权利财产上设立衡平法按揭或衡平法押记，可以采用交付动产或财产凭证的方式设立担保物权，例如，可以采用交存股票凭证的方式在股票上设立衡平法按揭。

（二）借款合同因违反《放债人条例》不可被强制执行对担保合同的法律后果

如前文所述，借款合同无法被强制执行的两种常见情形是：一是由于出借人不具有放债人牌照而无法被强制执行，二是因为借款款合同约定过高利率而无法被强制执行。当借款合同被认定无法强制执行时，出借人能

---

〔1〕《物业转易及财产条例》第2条规定，土地包括：（a）有水淹盖的土地；（b）土地或其上的任何产业权、权利、权益或地役权；（bb）土地的不分割份数的全部或部分，以及土地或其上的任何产业权、权利、权益或地役权；及（c）附连在土地的物件或牢固于任何此类物件上的东西。

〔2〕香港特区的担保法律制度对法定按揭和法定押记不作区分，两者经常被交替使用。

否通过执行担保合同从而获得清偿并且减少损失，成为出借人最为关心的问题。

1. 因未获放债人牌照而无法被强制执行

《放债人条例》第23（1）条规定："除非放债人交出牌照或以其他方法令法庭信纳在贷款之日、订立协议之日或取得保证之日（视属何情况而定），他领有牌照，否则他无权在任何法庭追讨由他贷出的款项或该笔款项的利息，亦无权强制执行他所订立的协议或强制执行就其贷出款项而取得的保证。"该条款严格规定出借人应当获取放债人牌照后才能实施放债行为，否则当借款人拒绝向还本付息并向法院提出出借人为无牌放债人的抗辩时，未持有放债人牌照的出借人将难以获得法律救济，其与借款人订立的借款合同以及担保合同都无法被强制执行。一般情况下，当借款合同因放债人未持有牌照而被认定不可强制执行时，法院会同时认定担保合同亦无法被强制执行。

Re Kwai Chung Town Lot No. 358[1]案体现了香港特区法院严格否定违反《放债人条例》强制性规定的借款合同及其担保合同的执行效力。本案的上诉人是澳大利亚昆士兰官方破产管理人，被上诉人是 SH Lock（Hong Kong）Ltd.。第三人 Antonios Stamatellos 被澳大利亚法院宣告破产，为了获得债务清偿，第三人的其他承按人（Mortgagees）出售第三人的担保财产，并将清偿后剩余出售价款（the Surplus of the Proceeds）支付至香港特区法院。被上诉人曾向第三人提供贷款，并获得第三人提供的法定按揭和保证。此外，在另一宗诉讼中，被上诉人因其为案涉汇票的出票人，代替第三人向判决债权人付清汇票金额，因此获得相关的债权请求权。被上诉人基于其汇票持有人的顺位以及第三人提供的担保，向法院请求获得剩余出售价款。在一审中，被上诉人获得胜诉判决。上诉人不服一审判决提出上诉，其上诉理由是，被上诉人在未持有放债人牌照的情况下向债务人发放贷款，其行为违反《放债人条例》第23条的规定，因此上诉人不能收回贷款以及执行担保。香港高等法院经审理后认定，被上诉人未持有放债

[1]　[1987] 2 HKC 434.

人牌照，故第三人与被上诉人订立的法定按揭因非法性而不能被强制执行，所以被上诉人向法院获得出售剩余所得的诉讼请求不能得到法院支持。[1]

2. 因约定过高利率而无法被强制执行

《放债人条例》明确禁止出借人在借款合同中约定过高的利率，如果实际借款利率高于年利率48%，则被认定为是犯罪行为。《放债人条例》第24（2）条规定："于任何贷款的还款协议或关于任何贷款利息的付息协议，以及就该等协议或贷款而提供的保证，如其实际利率超逾第一款所指明的利率（即超逾年息百分之四十八），则不得予以强制执行。"该条款明确规定，违反《放债人条例》关于过高利率的禁止性规定，会直接且当然导致借款协议及其担保不可被强制执行。

在 Wong Kwai Fun v. Li Fung[2]案中，被告因财务困难向原告借款，原告于1986年4月2日借给被告15万港元，但在扣除法律服务费后，被告仅收到14.885万港元。在向原告借款时，被告签订了一份授权委托书，授权 Ho Sum Wah 可以代表被告出售房子。1986年4月17日，被告无法按照约定向原告偿还款项，被告于次日（4月18日）与 Wong Kwai Wing 签订一份房屋买卖协议，被告同意以60万港元的价格出售房屋，双方约定只要被告在交易日1986年7月3日之前向 Wong Kwai Wing 付清24.5万港元，则被告有权取消该协议。但在交易日到来之前，被告及其家人遭受各种催债的威胁和恐吓。1986年8月6日 Wong Kwai Wing 与原告再签订了一份房屋买卖协议，被告将以49万港元的价格出售房屋。Wong Kwai Wing 和 Ho Sum Wah 于1986年9月8日将被告的房产转让过户给原告，原告据此对被告的房屋提起占有诉讼（Action for Possession）。香港高等法院经审理后首先认定，被告不具有向 Wong Kwai Wing 出售房屋的真实意图，被告签署的授权委托书和房屋买卖协议的目的是为偿还借款本金和利息而提供担保。[3] 高等法院认定原告发放贷款的实际利率高达年利率

---

〔1〕 Re Kwai Chung Town Lot No. 358 [1987] 2 HKC 434, p. 428.

〔2〕 [1994] 1 HKC 549.

〔3〕 Wong Kwai Fun v. Li Fung [1994] 1 HKC 549, p. 569.

400%，严重超过《放债人条例》所允许的贷款实际利率。原告向被告发放的贷款及其担保都因违反《放债人条例》第 24 条而被认定为是非法的且不可被强制执行，因此被告提供的担保，即签署的授权委托书和房屋买卖协议也是非法的、不可强制执行的和无效的。[1]

（三）借款合同因其他情形无效对担保合同的法律后果

除因上述两种法定原因无法被强制执行外，借款合同还可能因为其他原因而被认定为无效并因此无法被强制执行。例如，借款合同可能因当事人存在欺诈行为（Fraud）、对借款合同的标的存在错误认识（Mistake）、存在虚假陈述（Misrepresentation）、在胁迫（Duress）下签订借款合同、因受到不当影响（Undue Influence）订立借款合同、缺乏行为能力（Lack of Capacity）等原因而无效。当借款合同因上述原因而无效时，出借人能否继续执行担保合同从而获得清偿，取决于其所采取的担保形式。

1. 以按揭、押记、质押等方式提供担保

按揭、押记以及质押的设立都附属于借款合同。当借款人通过按揭[2]、押记[3]以及质押[4]的方式提供担保时，借款合同无效会导致出借人无法继续强制执行担保。

以按揭为例，*Halsbury's Laws of Hong Kong* 说明按揭的附属性质：按揭由两个部分组成，第一部分是清偿债务的个人合同，第二部分是为清偿债务而设立在按揭人的财产及权益上的按揭，在衡平法上属于对按揭人财产及权益作出处置，但该处置的范围仅限于担保。每一按揭都暗含两项债

---

〔1〕 Wong Kwai Fun v. Li Fung [1994] 1 HKC 549，p. 572.

〔2〕 按揭（Mortgage）是债务人（按揭人）以财产处置的方式设立担保，以此保证债务人向债权人清偿借款或履行其他合同义务。

〔3〕 押记（Charge）是债务人（押记人）以分派不动产或动产的方式设立担保，以此保证债务人向债权人清偿借款或履行其他合同义务。

〔4〕 质押（Pledge）是通过订立合同约定债务人（质押人）向债权人（承押人）交付动产或所有权凭证，并由债权人持有担保物直至债务清偿完毕的方式设立担保。

务，即个人合同下债务和按揭人需清偿的个人债务。[1] 借款合同是按揭设立和存在的前提，并且按揭的效力范围受限于借款合同的效力范围。正如高等法院上诉法庭在 Easy Fortune Property Ltd. v. Yung Chun Him[2]案中提及，在考虑继续执行担保是否违反公平原则这一问题时，需要进一步考虑案件的特定事实。如果允许原告向被告追讨已减少的借款本金是公平的，那么在该有限的范围内允许原告继续执行担保也是公平的。[3] 因此，按揭的执行效力范围完全取决于借款合同被允许继续执行的范围。与按揭一样，押记和质押附属于借款合同。当法院认定借款合同因无效而无法被强制执行时，一般会同时认定保证借款合同履行的按揭、押记或质押也无法被强制执行。

2. 以保证的方式提供担保

保证（Guarantee）是为了担保债权的实现，由保证人与债权人约定，当债务人不履行义务时，由保证人代替债务人承担责任的一种担保形式。

保证合同是主合同的从合同，保证人所承担的合同义务属于附属性义务（Secondary Obligation）。这意味着，保证人承担保证义务需以主债务人存在违约行为为前提。只有当借款人存在违约行为，不履行借款合同约定的还本付息义务，保证人才承担担保责任。保证合同的承担遵循责任共存原则（the Co－Extensiveness Principle），保证人承担保证义务的范围与主债务人需要承担责任的范围大致相当，即在清偿金额、履行期限以及承担义务的条件等方面保证人承担与主债务人几乎相同的合同义务。[4] 保证合同依赖于主合同的存在而存在。因而当借款合同无效，保证合同也随之

---

〔1〕 See *Halsbury's Laws of Hong Kong*, Lexis Nexis Hong Kong, [230.632] Characteristics of A Mortgage.

〔2〕 [2019] HKCU 3671, [2019] HKCA 1055, [2020] 4 HKC 1.

〔3〕 Easy Fortune Property Ltd. v. Yung Chun Him [2020] 4 HKC 1, para. 67.

〔4〕 Geraldine Andrews, Richard Millett, *Law of Guarantees*, 7th Edition, Sweet & Maxwell, para. 6－002.

无效。[1]

当借款合同无效导致保证合同无效时，原则上保证人不再承担担保责任。但是，香港特区的成文法规定了例外情形，即使借款人无须履行合同义务和承担合同责任，保证人也应当履行保证责任。例如，保证人无法以债务人在订立合同时尚未成年为由拒绝履行保证责任[2]，或董事对超越其权限签订的合同仍需承担保证责任。[3]

值得注意的是，虽然实践中存在当事人在保证合同中约定保证责任独立条款从而保留保证责任的做法[4]，但不适用于主合同是借款合同的情形。由于保证合同的对价是出借人订立借款合同或履行借款合同的义务，即使存在保证责任独立条款，保证责任也不会被保留。[5] 因此，当保证合同的主合同为借款合同时，当事人无法通过约定保证责任独立条款突破主合同无效从合同亦无效的一般性原则。

3. 以弥偿的方式提供担保

弥偿（Indemnity）是弥偿人（Indemnitor 或 Indemnifier）为了保障债权人免受损失（Hold Harmless）而采取的一种担保方式。[6] 弥偿人所承担的合同义务是主要义务（Primary Obligation），弥偿责任的承担无须以主

---

〔1〕 Geraldine Andrews, Richard Millett, *Law of Guarantees*, 7th Edition, Sweet & Maxwell, para. 6－020. Canara Bank v. Excel Triumph Ltd. & Anor［2021］HKCU 6123,［2021］HKCFI 3747（CFI）, para. 27.

〔2〕《成年岁数（有关条文）条例》第 3 条规定，当债务人订立主合同时尚未成年，债权人无法要求其强制履行。

〔3〕《公司条例》第 120 条规定了无假定的知悉原则（No Constructive Notice），即使章程、申报表或决议内容已在登记处备存，也不应当假定外部人了解公司的章程、申报表或决议内容，因此，外部人与公司达成的合约不会因公司声称代理人无权签署而作废。

〔4〕 例如，债权人可以通过在保证合同中加入保护性条款或者分隔性条款，约定在主合同无效、可撤销或者不可强制执行的情况下，保证人无论主合同的效力如何，都应当承担保证责任。此种保证责任独立条款能在主合同存在效力瑕疵时保留保证人的保证责任，一般基于下述两种原因：第一，保证合同被认定为是弥偿合同；第二，基于不容反悔原则（Estoppel），保证人不能以主合同存在缺陷为由拒绝承担保证责任。

〔5〕 Geraldine Andrews, Richard Millett, *Law of Guarantees*, 7th Edition, Sweet & Maxwell, para. 6－028.

〔6〕 See Halsbury's Laws of Hong Kong, Lexis Nexis Hong Kong,［200.191］Nature and Definition of Indemnity.

合同违约行为的发生作为前提。[1] 当弥偿合同所约定条件满足时，债权人可以直接要求弥偿人承担责任。因此，当通过弥偿的方式提供担保时，借款合同的效力瑕疵一般不影响弥偿合同的效力，弥偿合同不因借款合同无效而当然无效。

一般而言，弥偿合同的合同效力及其执行效力不受借款合同效力的影响。当弥偿合同有效成立且合同约定的弥偿条件已成就时，债权人可要求弥偿人向其承担弥偿责任。在 Kwung Tung Hui Li Investment Ltd. v. Wong Man Pan[2]案中，原告起诉被告要求其履行名为“不可撤销担保契据”(Deed of Irrevocable Guarantee)。被告抗辩称，借款合同的约定利率违反当时的内地法律规定，所以该借款合同是无效合同，不可撤销担保契据作为从合同因借款合同无效而无效。对于被告的抗辩，香港高等法院原讼法庭首先认定“不可撤销担保契据”的性质为弥偿合同，而非保证合同，其认定理由如下：在认定当事人签订的合同的性质时，法院不应根据合同的名称决定，而是应当根据合同条款的具体内涵决定。虽然本案担保合同的名称是“不可撤销担保契据”，但是双方合同条款所约定内容实质反映弥偿的性质特征：第 1 条约定，该合同是不可撤销的以及当事人应当无条件履行；第 2 条约定，被告对原告承担连带责任；第 11 条约定，即使借款合同全部或部分内容不合法、无效或者不可被执行，担保合同的合法性和有效性不受其影响，故原讼法庭认定“不可撤销担保契据”的实质是弥偿合同。[3] 其次，在认定作为主合同的借款合同无效是否对弥偿合同的效力产生影响的问题上，原讼法庭认为即使借款合同因违反内地法律而无效，除非在香港法下存在影响弥偿合同有效性和可执行性的原因，否则弥偿合同应被认定为有效和可被执行的，不受借款合同无效的影响。[4]

由于弥偿合同存在独立性，其不受借款合同效力存在瑕疵与否的影响，因而产生出借人能否利用弥偿这一担保方式规避和逃脱《放债人条

---

〔1〕 Moschi v. Lep Air Services Ltd. [1972] 2 All ER 393, [1973] AC 331.

〔2〕 [2003] HKCU 1352.

〔3〕 Kwung Tung Hui Li Investment Ltd. v. Wong Man Pan [2003] HKCU 1352, para. 15 – 16.

〔4〕 Kwung Tung Hui Li Investment Ltd. v. Wong Man Pan [2003] HKCU 1352, para. 17 – 18.

例》规管的担忧。对于该种担忧，一方面，《放债人条例》明文禁止强制执行的担保包括弥偿在内的任何担保。例如，除非法院基于公平行使自由裁量权作出可强制执行的判决，违反《放债人条例》第 18 条、第 22 条、第 23 条以及第 25 条的借款协议及其担保都不可被强制执行。另一方面，当借款合同因违法性或违反公共政策而无效时，弥偿合同可能因非法性污染原则（Doctrine of Tainting）而被认定为无效或不可被强制执行。[1]

三、小结

（一）相同点

第一，在绝大多数情形下，内地和香港特区的法律都认为担保具有从属性。内地法律明确规定担保合同具有从属性，担保合同不能独立于借款合同的存在而存在。香港特区法律规定，保证、按揭、押记以及质押等担保的设立都从属于借款合同，担保责任的范围取决于借款合同所限定的责任范围。

第二，一般而言，当借款合同被认定无效（不可被强制执行）时，内地与香港特区均否定担保合同的效力及其可执行性。内地法律明确规定，借款合同无效，担保合同亦随之无效。香港特区法律规定，借款合同因出借人无牌放债或约定过高利率而被认定无法强制执行，担保合同亦无法被强制执行。借款合同因《放债人条例》之外的原因而被认定为无效或无法被强制执行，担保人所提供的保证、按揭、押记或质押亦无法被强制执行。

（二）不同点

第一，内地与香港特区对借款合同无效、担保合同亦无效的例外规定不一致。内地法律要求担保合同严格遵循从属性，未对借款合同无效、担

---

〔1〕 See Hugh Beale, Richard Hooley, Louise Merrett, Graham Virgo, *Chitty on Contracts*, 35th Edition, Sweet & Maxwell, para. 19 – 053.

保合同亦无效的法律规则作出例外规定。香港特区法律对保证所遵循的责任共存原则存在法定例外规定。当以弥偿的方式提供担保，由于弥偿具有独立性，弥偿合同的效力不受借款合同无效的影响。

第二，当担保合同因借款合同无效而被认定为无效（不可被强制执行）时，内地和香港特区对担保人需要承担责任的例外情形规定不一致。内地法律规定，当借款合同导致担保合同无效时，担保人只有在有过错的情况下才承担赔偿责任，且其所承担的责任不应超过借款人不能清偿部分的1/3。根据香港特区法律，当担保人以弥偿的方式提供担保，当弥偿合同有效成立且合同约定的弥偿条件已成就时，出借人可以继续要求弥偿人向其承担弥偿责任。

第二节　让与担保的效力问题

一、内地的法律规定

在民间借贷活动中，除了采用传统的抵押、质押或第三人保证等方式向出借人提供担保以外，出借人在与借款人订立借款合同时，通常还采取另行订立买卖合同，或将担保物的所有权转至出借人名下的方式提供担保，以此增加出借人实现债权的可能性。此种非典型的担保方式，根据标的物所有权转移的先后顺序，可以分为让与担保和后让与担保两种形式。

（一）让与担保

让与担保属于非典型担保的一种。债务人或第三人与债权人签订合同，约定在债权人无须支付对价的情况下，债务人或第三人将财产转移至债权人名下，当债务人在清偿期届满后无法清偿债务时，债权人可以就转让财产受偿。

1. 让与担保的表现形式及特征

让与担保主要有两种表现形式，包括买卖式担保和所有权转让式担保。买卖式担保，是指债务人以买卖的方式移转标的物的所有权，实际上以买卖价款的名义向债权人提供担保，并且双方约定日后买回该标的物的担保形式。所有权转让式担保，是指债务人为担保债务清偿，将担保标的物所有权移转给债权人，当债务人清偿债务后，债权人将标的物的所有权归还给担保人；如债务人在履行期限届满后不能清偿债务，债权人有权就担保物受偿。

虽然表现形式不一，但让与担保一般具有以下基本特征：第一，通过让与担保的形式设立担保时，担保人需要将标的物所有权暂时转移至债权人名下，债权人成为标的物形式上的所有人；第二，为了使担保人继续对担保标的物享有使用权，债权人通常会与担保人签订关于标的物的借用合同或者租赁合同，由担保人继续使用标的物；第三，当债务人按照合同约定履行债务后，债权人应当返还标的物的所有权；第四，债务人与债权人约定，当债务人无法在债务履行期限届满时清偿债务，担保标的物的所有权由债权人享有。[1]

实践中常见的一种让与担保情形是当事人约定回购条款。债务人与债权人约定将标的物转移至债权人名下，在一定期限后再由债务人或者其指定的第三人以本金加上溢价款回购，如债务人到期不回购的，则标的物的所有权直接归债权人所有。例如，信托投资公司通过收购房地产开发项目等特定资产的方式向资产转让方发放借款。双方约定，信托投资公司作为受让方持有特定资产并向资产转让方支付收购价款，履行期限届满后由资产转让方向信托投资公司回购，回购款为收购价款本金和固定比例的溢价款。此种情形下，虽然信托投资公司与资产转让方未明确表明提供担保的意思表示，双方的交易行为事实上符合让与担保的基本特征。双方约定回购条款的目的并非取得财产的所有权，而是获得对借款的担保。从双方交易模式的构造来看，双方约定的回购期间对应主债务的履行期限，回购价款采取本金加上溢价款实质对应债务本金及利息。

---

〔1〕参见最高人民法院民事审判第二庭编著：《最高人民法院民法典担保制度司法解释理解与适用》，人民法院出版社 2021 年版，第 635 页。

2. 让与担保的法律效力

《民法典》虽然没有对让与担保作出专门规定，但是《民法典》明确规定了当事人可以签订其他具有担保功能的合同设立担保物权，其中就包括可以签订让与担保合同。目前，实务界和理论界都倾向于认可让与担保合同的法律效力，具体理由如下：

第一，基于物权法定原则与物债两分原则认可让与担保合同的效力。物权法定原则的内涵是物权的种类、内容、效力以及公示方法由法律规定，原则上不能由法律之外的规范性文件进行规定，也不允许当事人自由创设。根据物债两分原则，物权法定原则本身对合同效力不产生影响，且让与担保合同的效力并不因其是特殊的非典型担保而被区分对待，让与担保合同的效力仍然应当依据《民法典》关于合同一般生效要件规则进行判断。

第二，让与担保合同符合合同生效的一般要件。一方面，让与担保合同本身不违反法律、行政法规的强制性规定，也不违反公序良俗。[1] 另一方面，让与担保是集担保和让与性于一体的行为，让与担保当事人进行所有权转让的行为是其真意所为。[2] 让与担保中关于债务人不履行到期债务时财产归债权人所有的约定，实质是债权人支配担保财产的交换价值，其最终目的是获得债务清偿，而非取得财产的所有权。因此，当事人转让有权的真实意思是为了实现担保的目的，因此该意思表示不属于通谋虚假，不能以虚假意思表示为由认定让与担保无效。[3]

第三，流押、流质的禁止性规定不影响让与担保合同的效力。《民法典》第401条和第428条规定，即使债权人与债务人约定债务人不履行到期债务时担保财产归债权人所有，但该约定不发生法律效力，债权人对担保财产仅享有优先受偿权。该条款仅明确反对流押、流质条款会导致发生物权变动，但并未否定双方基于缔约自由所产生的合同效力。让与担保关

---

〔1〕《民法典》第153条。

〔2〕参见最高人民法院民事审判第二庭编著：《最高人民法院民法典担保制度司法解释理解与适用》，人民法院出版社2021年版，第635页。

〔3〕参见谢在全：《民法物权论》（下册），中国政法大学出版社2011年版，第1105页。

于无法清偿债务情况下财产归属的条款，应当被认定为无效条款，而这不影响当事人提供担保的真实意思表示，也不影响让与担保合同的整体效力。[1]

3. 让与担保的实现

《民法典》第401条和第428条的禁止性规定，不认可让与担保合同中关于债务人在债务履行期限届满时不能清偿债务，债权人可以不经过任何清算过程即可获得财产的所有权的约定。该禁止性条款的立法原意是，防止债权人乘债务人之急而滥用优势地位，通过压低担保价值的方式谋取暴利。基于此，《担保制度司法解释》第68条对让与担保的实现进行明确的法律规定。

让与担保的担保效力的实现需要经过法定程序。一方面，法院应当对债务人或第三人与债权人的约定进行审查。由于《民法典》明令禁止流押、流质条款，法院着重审查决定担保财产所有权归属或关于优先受偿权的合同条款。另一方面，权利公示是赋予债权人优先受偿权的核心要素，因此让与担保合同的当事人应当完成财产权利变动的公示，即动产应当完成交付、不动产或者股权等权利应当完成变更登记。让与担保合同当事人一般存在以下三种合同约定情形：

第一，当约定内容为债务人或第三人财产将在形式上转移至债权人名下，如债务人不履行到期债务，债权人有权对财产折价或者以拍卖、变卖该财产所得价款偿还债务，法院一般认定该约定有效。如果当事人已经完成财产权利变动的公示，债权人有权在债务人不履行到期债务时，向法院请求参照民法典关于担保物权的有关规定就该财产优先受偿。

第二，当约定内容为债务人或第三人财产将在形式上转移至债权人名下，如债务人不履行到期债务，财产归债权人所有，法院一般认定该约定无效，但当事人有关提供担保的意思表示的效力不受影响。如果当事人已经完成财产权利变动的公示，当债务人不履行到期债务，债权人不能向法

[1] 参见陈永强：《〈民法典〉禁止流质之规定的新发展及其新解释》，载《财经法学》2022年第5期。

院请求对该财产享有所有权，但是有权请求参照《民法典》关于担保物权的规定对财产折价或者以拍卖、变卖该财产所得的价款优先受偿。当债务人因无法清偿债务，向法院请求对财产折价或者以拍卖、变卖所得的价款清偿债务，法院一般支持债务人的请求。当债务人清偿债务后，债权人应当返还财产。

第三，当约定内容为债务人或第三人财产将在形式上转移至债权人名下，在一定期间后再由债务人或者其指定的第三人以交易本金加上溢价款回购，如债务人到期不履行回购义务，财产归债权人所有，法院一般认定该约定无效。如果回购的对象自始不存在，法院一般按照实际构成的法律关系进行处理。

（二）后让与担保

1. 后让与担保表现形式及性质

后让与担保在交易中的表现形式是，债权人和债务人在订立借款合同的同时订立买卖合同，约定当债务人不能到期偿还借款本息时债务人应当履行买卖合同，以买卖合同标的物抵债。[1] 因此，后让与担保可被视为买卖式让与担保的变种形式。

（1）后让与担保与让与担保的相同点

后让与担保与让与担保在权利转移的性质、价值、功能以及归属定位等方面并无本质区别。两种担保方式转移标的物所有权都是为了担保另一债权的履行，而不是为了最终取得标的物的所有权。这一点区别于典型的财产权转让行为，因为在典型的财产权转让行为中，买受人的主要义务是支付转让款，主要权利是买受人取得财产权后，对财产权有完整的所有权。因此，在后让与担保和让与担保下，合同标的物的受让人通常无须支付转让款，在债务履行期限届满前，受让人对标的物并无处分权，对标的物不享有完整的所有权。

---

〔1〕 参见杨立新：《后让与担保：一个正在形成的习惯法担保物权》，载《中国法学》2013 年第 3 期。

（2）后让与担保与让与担保的不同点

后让与担保与让与担保的区别仅在于所有权转移的先后顺序。让与担保是在担保设定之初就将标的物的所有权转移至债权人名下，而后让与担保是在债务人未依照合同约定履行债务后才转移标的物的所有权。[1] 进言之，让与担保的债权人由于所有权已先行转移，从而取得标的物的所有权，对标的物所享有的权利处于既得状态；后让与担保的债权人只有在债务人违约时才能取得标的物的所有权，因而取得的是期待权而非现实物权。

2. 后让与担保纠纷的处理方式

《民法典》认可后让与担保作为非典型担保所具有的担保功能，但是采用此种担保方式往往会产生更多的纠纷。例如，当借款人提供后让与担保，如借款人到期不能清偿借款本息，出借人（买受人）通常主张履行买卖合同，要求借款人（出卖人）办理房屋过户登记，以直接取得买卖合同标的物的方式获得债务的清偿。对此，借款人则往往以房屋价值和借款金额差距较大，或与市场价格严重不符，或买卖合同是无效合同为由进行抗辩，不同意履行房屋买卖合同。针对此种情形，《民间借贷司法解释（2020第二次修正）》第23条特别规定了后让与担保纠纷的处理方式。

（1）坚持基础法律关系审理的原则

在面对民间借贷合同和买卖合同互相缠绕不清的情形时，法院应当坚持基础法律关系审理的原则，厘清当事人的真实意思表示究竟是通过订立买卖合同为民间借贷合同设定担保，还是通过支付对价以获得买卖合同标的物的所有权。

当双方当事人对同一笔款项产生争议，其中出借人主张为购房款，而借款人主张为借款，法院应当依据案件的证据决定该笔争议款项的性质。在司法实践中，一般会存在以下三种判定情形：

第一，如当事人能证明民间借款合同和买卖合同同时存在，且买卖合同是为民间借贷合同提供担保的，法院一般认定担保事实，按照民间借贷

[1] 参见杨立新：《司法实践的后让与担保与法律适用》，载《人民法治》2015年第9期。

法律关系审理。

第二，如当事人所提交证据可证明买卖合同存在，但不足以证明民间借贷事实存在的，法院一般认定双方订立的买卖合同是其真实的意思表示，按照买卖合同法律关系审理。

第三，如当事人所提交证据可证明民间借贷合同和买卖合同均存在，但是不能证明买卖合同是为民间借贷合同提供担保的，一般根据案件具体情况确定合同的性质。例如，借款合同约定的借款期限届满或借款人不能偿还借款时，出借人与借款人签订房屋买卖合同偿还借款。在这种情形下，如双方买卖合同约定的购房款价格合理，一般应认定买卖合同有效。因为买卖合同签订实质是民间借贷债权债务关系的转化，或者是当事人另行增加的一种清偿借款的履行方式，而非预先约定的对借款关系的担保。

（2）对于当事人有关履行买卖合同诉讼请求的处理

当法院认定应当按照民间借贷关系处理案件，但当事人主张双方之间是买卖合同关系，从而导致当事人主张与法院认定不一致时，法院一般将双方当事人之间争议的法律关系究竟是民间借贷法律关系还是买卖合同关系作为焦点问题进行审理，以保障当事人能够充分行使辩论权。当事人可以根据法院审理情况变更诉讼请求，将主张履行买卖合同的诉讼请求变更为要求债务人清偿借款本金和利息。当事人也可以坚持原来的主张不予变更。如果当事人坚持原来的主张，法院一般不要求当事人必须变更诉讼请求，而是根据当事人的诉讼请求作出相应的裁判，但这并不妨碍当事人今后再以法院认定的法律关系为基础另行起诉。[1]

3. 后让与担保的实现

在法院认定出借人和借款人之间签订的买卖合同实质是作为民间借贷

---

〔1〕《最高人民法院关于民事诉讼证据的若干规定》第53条规定，诉讼过程中，当事人主张的法律关系性质或者民事行为效力与人民法院根据案件事实作出的认定不一致的，人民法院应当将法律关系性质或者民事行为效力作为焦点问题进行审理。但法律关系性质对裁判理由及结果没有影响，或者有关问题已经当事人充分辩论的除外。存在前述情形，当事人根据法庭审理情况变更诉讼请求的，人民法院应当准许并可以根据案件的具体情况重新指定举证期限。

合同的担保时，出借人只有在获得按照民间借贷法律关系审理的生效判决，且借款人不履行生效判决确定的金钱债务后，出借人才可申请拍卖买卖合同标的物，从而获得债务清偿。[1] 对于拍卖所得的价款与应偿还借款本息之间的差额，出借人或者借款人有权主张返还或者补偿。如果拍卖所得价款超过应偿还借款本息，差额应当返还给借款人；如果拍卖所得价款不足以偿还借款本息，就不足的部分，出借人仍可以向借款人主张补偿，如申请执行借款人的其他财产等。[2]

虽然出借人在获得生效判决且借款人不履行判决确定的义务时，可以向法院申请拍卖买卖合同标的物从而获得清偿，但是这不意味着出借人对拍卖买卖合同标的物所得的价款理所应当地享有优先受偿权。如果双方当事人仅签订了买卖合同，但是对买卖合同标的物本身并未设立抵押、质押，也未进行所有权转移，这对第三人不产生公示效果。由于未对权利变动进行公示，第三人无法以此为依据判断是否和借款人进行交易，在此种情形下，如果出借人仍对价款享有优先受偿权，这将对借款人的其他债权人有失公平，并且影响交易安全。如果双方不仅签订了买卖合同，而且已经进行了权利转移，如动产已经交付、不动产已经办理所有权转移登记，对第三人已经具有了公示的效果，在此种情形下认定出借人对价款享有优先受偿权具有合理性。

二、香港特区的法律规定

在香港特区的借贷活动中，借款人也通过提供类似于让与担保的担保方式从而获得借款。由于急于筹集资金或其财务状况出现恶化，借款人可能选择在借款合同签订前将自己的财产转让至出借人名下，或在借款合同签订后与出借人另行订立一份买卖合同的方式提供担保。对于此种以交易行为作为借款合同的担保，香港特区的担保法律没有特别命名。在认定交

[1] 《民间借贷司法解释（2020 第二次修正）》第 23 条第 2 款。

[2] 参见最高人民法院民事审判第一庭编著：《最高人民法院民法典民间借贷司法解释理解与适用》，人民法院出版社 2021 年版，第 350 页。

易行为是否能发挥担保的作用的问题上，香港特区法院采取与内地法院相似的态度，认可借款合同签订前后所进行的交易行为可以作为借贷行为的担保。

（一）借款合同签订前进行的交易行为

借款人采用在借款合同订立前将其财产转让至出借人名下的方式提供担保，其目的在于增加出借人对其清偿债务的信心。对于以财产转让交易行为提供担保，香港特区法院采取整体考量的方式认定其是否能发挥担保的功能和作用。在考量整个借款和财产转让交易过程后，如发现该交易过程的主要特征满足借款行为以及担保行为的一般交易特征，香港特区法院一般承认该财产转让行为事实上是为其后进行的借款行为提供担保。

在 Ding Huirong v. China Times Securities Ltd. and Another[1]案中，原告于 2017 年 4 月将其持有的一家上市公司的股票作为筹措资金的担保。原告在被告一处开户，并于 2017 年 5 月 8 日将作为担保的股票转入被告一的账户中，被告一根据其与原告签订的担保代理协议保管股票。原告与被告二于 2017 年 6 月 1 日签订借款合同和质押协议，被告二于 2017 年 6 月 3 日向原告发送筹措资金通知并发放了第一期借款。期后，被告二并未按照借款合同发放剩余的借款，而是向原告发出通知，告知原告已存在违约行为，被告二基于借款合同获得处置股票的权利。故原告提起诉讼，主张被告二向原告发放借款时存在欺诈和欺骗行为，违反了《证券及期货条例》和《放债人条例》；基于衡平法赎回权（Equity of Redemption），原告还要求赎回作为担保的股票。

在一审中，高等法院原讼法庭认定发生在借款合同订立前的股票转让行为属于担保行为，因此原告拥有衡平法回赎权。并且，原讼法庭还认定原告与被告二之间的借款合同条款构成对原告行使赎回权的非法阻碍。两被告不服一审判决提出上诉，其上诉理由之一是一审判决对股票转让行为的定性是错误的，并且判决中关于借款合同条款构成行使赎回权非法阻碍

---

〔1〕［2021］HKCU 1328，［2021］HKCA 419.

的结论也是错误的。

对于两被告提出的上诉理由，上诉法庭经审理后认为，原讼法庭将股票转让行为认定是对其后借款发放行为的担保，该法律定性是正确的。在认定一项交易真正的法律性质时，上诉法庭认为应当着重关注双方所签订的合同框架，并应当将合同视为一个整体对待，以此探究这项交易的实质效果。上诉法庭最终认定原告在签订借款合同前将股票转让至被告一账户的行为是为借款合同提供担保，理由如下：第一，借款合同的序言以及前言部分的描述都表明原被告之间的关系是借贷关系，其中对被告二所享有权益的描述表明股票转让行为事实上是一种担保安排。[1] 第二，借款合同的主体条款明确体现借款行为和担保行为的实质交易特征。借款合同中存在关于保证债务人适当履行义务的担保利益条款、追加担保金额条款以及担保变更保障条款，这使原被告之间的股票转让交易与股票销售、回购行为的一般特征明显不相符。[2] 第三，原告具有支付利息的义务，并且合同中包含旨在保护被告二利息的违约条款和救济条款，进一步说明双方之间的交易应为借款行为。[3]

因此，若从整体的角度审视，出借人与借款人之间的财产转让行为满足借贷行为的实质特征，那么即使财产转让行为发生的时间点在借款合同签订之前，法院会倾向于认定该财产转让行为实质是为后续订立的借款合同提供担保，而非真正的买卖行为或自愿转让行为。

（二）借款合同签订后进行的交易行为

另一种常见的以交易行为作为担保的方式是，在出借人与借款人签订借款合同后，出借人要求或借款人主动另行订立买卖合同；双方在合同中约定，如借款人未能在约定的还款日向出借人清偿借款本息，出借人可以要求借款人继续履行买卖合同。然而，此种以借款人继续履行合同作为担

---

〔1〕 Ding Huirong v. China Times Securities Ltd. and Another [2021] HKCU 1328, para. 29 – 30.

〔2〕 Ding Huirong v. China Times Securities Ltd. and Another [2021] HKCU 1328, para. 31 – 32.

〔3〕 Ding Huirong v. China Times Securities Ltd. and Another [2021] HKCU 1328, para. 33.

保的方式能否为之前签订的借款合同提供担保，时常成为出借人和借款人的争议焦点。对于该问题，香港特区法院一般根据案件的具体交易情形来认定双方订立的买卖合同的真正性质。

在 Lee Leo v. Cheong Oi Sum Ader[1]案中，区域法院认定，借款合同订立后发生的公寓转让行为实质是借款人向出借人提供担保，并且双方之间的交易应受《放债人条例》规管。本案中，被告向原告借款 11 万港元，但实际只收到 75,665 港元。还款期限届满后，被告因无力偿还借款，将自己的公寓以远低于其实际价值的价格过户转让给原告，原告于次年出售该公寓并获利颇丰。在先前的诉讼中，区域法院认定原被告之间的借款的实际贷款利率为年利率 216%，该借款因违反《放债人条例》第 24 条而不可被强制执行。原告继而请求法院依据该条例第 25（1）条行使重开交易的自由裁量权。

对于原告的诉讼请求，区域法院总结本案的焦点问题为，被告转让公寓的行为是否落入《放债人条例》第 25 条所规定的“交易”范围之内，从而使法院可以行使自由裁量权决定是否可以重启交易。对于该问题，原告主张转让公寓的行为与双方之间的借款无关，第 25 条所规定的交易必须仅限于原始的借款或借款时所提供的担保，不应当扩展至其后的交易。然而，法院不认可原告的主张，并认定第 25 条所使用的“交易”不局限于法条字面意义所规定的借款合同及其担保，双方的公寓转让行为属于第 25 条所规定的“交易”[2]，即属于为借款提供担保的行为，认定理由如下：第一，由于《放债人条例》是救济性法律，因而在认定第 25 条使用的“交易”（Transaction）一词所囊括范围大小的问题上，法院应当谨慎采用限缩解释的方式解释法律。[3] 第二，在认定公寓转让行为是否属于“交易”时，法院应当关注交易的实质而不应仅停留在其采用的形式上，故在综合考虑本案的案情后，区域法院最终确信原被告都具有将转让公寓作为

[1] [1993] 2 HKC 736.

[2] Lee Leo v. Cheong Oi Sum Ader [1993] 2 HKC 736, p. 741.

[3] Lee Leo v. Cheong Oi Sum Ader [1993] 2 HKC 736, p. 740.

清偿借款或提供借款担保的意图。首先，案涉公寓的转让未经原被告自由协商或以公平的价格进行交易，原告也没有向被告支付相应的定金；其次，原告可在未支付剩余房款的情况下，直接获得公寓的所有权和空置占有权；再次，虽然原告给予了被告回购公寓的选择，但是原告明知被告处于财务困境不可能进行回购；最后，原被告在讨论借款事宜时，被告曾提出以其公寓作为担保，且原告也曾在发放借款之前向土地局问询和核实过公寓的情况。[1] 由此可见，《放债人条例》中认定的担保的类型不局限于借款合同及其担保，也包括出借人和借款人在签订借款合同后订立的买卖合同。

在面对出借人和借款人订立借款合同后，再另行订立买卖合同的情形，香港特区法院会倾向于认定双方后续订立的合同是为借款合同提供担保。但是，这一倾向并不具有普适性，且不意味着所有在借款合同之后签订的买卖合同都理应被认定为担保。

在 Cheung Bing Sum Juana v. Leo Lee[2]案中，被上诉人 Leo Lee 曾向上诉人 Cheung Bing Sum Juana 提供 1.5 万港元的借款，但上诉人无法偿还该笔债务。因陷入经济困境，上诉人提出以 38 万港元的价格将其公寓卖给被上诉人。被上诉人接受了要约，并支付了 2.5 万港元作为定金，并且表示将从购房余款扣除上诉人的欠款。上诉人向被上诉人出具收据并载明公寓的详细信息。因上诉人没有按照买卖合同完成交易，被上诉人向法院提起具体履行（Specific Performance）的诉讼。

由于一审判决驳回上诉人提出的被上诉人所支付的 2.5 万港元是借款的抗辩，上诉人随后向香港高等法院提起上诉，并抗辩称被上诉人向其发放的借款违反《放债人条例》第 24（1）条的规定，买卖合同作为借款的担保也因第 24（2）条的规定而不可被强制执行。上诉法庭驳回该抗辩，并认定双方之间的借贷行为与签订公寓买卖合同的行为是两项独立的交

[1] Lee Leo v. Cheong Oi Sum Ader [1993] 2 HKC 736, p. 741.
[2] [1996] 4 HKC 130.

易[1]，上诉人因此上诉至英国枢密院[2]。

枢密院司法委员会认同香港高等法院上诉法庭作出的判决，认定签订公寓买卖合同的行为是一项独立的交易，该合同订立的目的并非为借款提供担保，其认定理由如下：第一，本案缺乏足够的证据证明被上诉人曾说服上诉人将公寓卖给他，也缺乏证据证明上诉人以低价出售该公寓，以及双方订立买卖合同的目的实质是上诉人向被上诉人提供偿还借款的担保。第二，双方的借款与公寓买卖两者之间唯一的联系是，被上诉人同意在购买公寓后，不要求上诉人立即向其支付借款，而是从应付购房款余额中抵扣上诉人未还的借款。假使从最极端的角度看待本案，在不考虑被上诉人购买公寓动机的情况下，双方的买卖合同有可能被认定为担保的原因在于，被上诉人购买公寓的权利与抵销上诉人未还借款的权利紧密相连。第三，本案的被上诉人的诉讼请求并非要求执行该担保，即不要求进行债务抵销，而是愿意按照买卖合同的约定支付扣除定金后的全部购房余款。基于此，司法委员会认为，考虑在极端情况下才存在的担保是否因为《放债人条例》第24（2）条而不能执行这一问题，没有继续讨论的必要。[3]

总而言之，在认定买卖合同是否实质为之前订立的借款合同提供担保时，一方面，法院应当依据出借人和借款人签订的借款合同的情况来确定，例如，借款合同的实际借款利率是否约定过高、借款合同是否按照《放债人条例》第18条的要求拟定等。另一方面，法院应当根据出借人和借款人在交易过程中发生的具体情形来确定，如买卖合同的销售价格是否按照市场价格确定、出借人作为买家是否支付买卖合同的定金、是否存在出借人或借款人向对方明示订立买卖合同的目的是提供担保的意思表示，以及出借人的诉讼请求是要求强制执行担保还是要求继续履行买卖合同

---

[1] Cheung Bing Sum Juana v. Leo Lee [1994] 3 HKC 132, para. 138A.

[2] 由于该案件发生在香港回归之前，因此案件可上诉至英国枢密院（Privy Council）。枢密院司法委员会于1833年成立，由枢密院的上议院主席，上议院首席大法官，前任上议院主席，上议院法官及英国枢密院的其他会员组成。司法委员会具有司法权，可对由任何殖民地法庭提出的上诉进行聆讯。在1997年7月1日之前，枢密院司法委员会可接收和聆讯来自香港最高法院和香港上诉法庭的上诉。

[3] Cheung Bing Sum Juana v. Leo Lee [1996] 4 HKC 130, p. 134.

等。如出借人和借款人的借款合同约定较高借款利率，存在借款人向出借人表明在无法清偿债务时，将出售自己的财产作为借款的担保的情形，且后续签订的买卖合同中约定的出售价格远低于市场价格以及出借人没有向借款人支付定金，法院倾向于认定双方签订的买卖合同实质是为借款合同提供担保。

三、小结

（一）相同点

第一，内地与香港特区都存在让与担保（以交易行为提供担保）的实践，其表现形式基本一致。并且，两地的法律都承认让与担保（以交易行为提供担保）具有担保效力。在两地的借贷活动中，借款人采取将担保物的所有权转至出借人名下，或另行订立买卖合同的方式，为先前或后续签订的借款合同提供担保。两地的法律都认可此种财产转让交易行为或签订买卖合同的方式，能够发挥担保的功能和效力。

第二，内地与香港特区在处理后让与担保纠纷方面存在相似之处。在解决后让与担保纠纷时，两地的法律都认为应当对出借人与借款人订立买卖合同这一交易的实质进行认定，即出借人和借款人是否具有进行买卖行为的真实意思表示。如认定出借人与借款人订立买卖合同是双方的真实意思表示，则出借人要求借款人继续履行买卖合同的主张一般会得到法院支持。内地法律明确规定，如当事人所提交证据可证明买卖合同存在，但不足以证明民间借贷事实存在的，法院一般认定双方订立的买卖合同是其真实的意思表示，按照买卖合同法律关系审理。香港特区的判例法明确指出，交易性质的认定应当关注交易的实质而非其形式，即应当根据案件事实认定出借人和借款人之间的买卖合同是否为成立在先的借款合同提供担保，而不应当被买卖合同的外在表现形式所迷惑。

（二）不同点

内地与香港特区在司法实践中对让与担保的分类存在不同。内地司法实践中根据合同标的物所有权转让的先后顺序，将让与担保的类型具体细分为让与担保和后让与担保两种方式，其中让与担保还可被进一步细分为买卖式担保和所有权转让式担保。香港特区法律对借贷活动中出现的以交易行为作为担保的行为不作具体的类型区分，而是注重根据案件的具体情形断定交易行为的真正性质，一般未将借款合同订立的时间点以及财产转让的时间点作为判断的决定性因素。

第七章　夫妻债务制度的法律规则比较

第一节　内地的法律规定

一、条文演变

（一）原《婚姻法》及司法解释

2001年修正的原《婚姻法》第41条规定，离婚时原为夫妻共同生活所负的债务，应当共同偿还。2003年公布的《最高人民法院关于适用〈中华人民共和国婚姻法〉若干问题的解释（二）》第24条规定，在婚姻关系存续期间，夫妻一方以个人名义所负的债务，一般按照夫妻共同债务处理，但夫妻一方能够证明债权人与债务人明确约定为个人债务，或者能够证明属于《婚姻法》第19条第3款规定情形[1]的除外。上述规定将举证责任课以夫妻一方，由夫妻一方举证证明所借债务非用于夫妻共同生活，如举证不足，则夫妻双方应共同承担偿还责任。

（二）原2018年《夫妻债务司法解释》

随着经济社会的发展，我国城乡居民家庭财产结构、类型、数量、形态以及理财模式等发生了巨大变化。夫妻一方因创业、投资，甚至与债权人恶意串通等情形而大额举债，造成夫妻另一方在毫不知情的情况下背上沉重债务负担的问题日益凸显，引发了进一步规范和细化夫妻共同债务认定标准的呼声。

为合理分配举证责任，平衡保护债权人利益和夫妻中未举债一方的利益，最高人民法院于2018年出台了《夫妻债务司法解释》，明确了夫妻共同债务的认定标准和规则。对于夫妻一方以个人名义对外所负的债务，尤其是超出了家庭日常生活所需的范围时，需由债权人证明债务用于夫妻共

[1] 夫妻对婚姻关系存续期间所得的财产约定归各自所有的，夫或妻一方对外所负的债务，第三人知道该约定的，以夫或妻一方所有的财产清偿。

同生活或者共同生产经营，或者债务的负担系基于夫妻双方共同的意思表示；如果债权人不能证明的，则不能认定为夫妻共同债务。自此，夫妻共同债务的举证责任由夫妻一方转移至债权人一方。

（三）现行《民法典》的有关规定

1. 夫妻共同债务制度

（1）夫妻共同债务的类别

《民法典》吸收了《夫妻债务司法解释》相关内容的精神，为解决实践中争议较大的夫妻债务问题提供了较为明确的法律依据。《民法典》第1064条规定了三类夫妻共同债务。一是基于共同意思表示所负的夫妻共同债务，即夫妻双方共同签名或者夫妻一方事后追认等共同意思表示所负的债务。二是为家庭日常生活需要所负的夫妻共同债务，即夫妻一方在婚姻关系存续期间以个人名义为家庭日常生活需要所负的债务。三是债权人能够证明的夫妻共同债务，即夫妻一方在婚姻关系存续期间以个人名义超出家庭日常生活需要所负，但债权人能够证明系用于夫妻共同生活、共同生产经营或者基于夫妻双方共同意思表示的债务。

（2）夫妻共同债务的偿还

根据《民法典》第1089条的规定，夫妻共同债务由夫妻共同偿还，共同财产不足清偿或者财产归各自所有的，由双方协议清偿。

2. 夫妻共同财产制度

内地的夫妻财产制度系以共同财产制为原则，同时辅以约定财产制。根据《民法典》第1062条的规定，在婚姻关系存续期间所取得的以下五类财产为夫妻共同财产：一是工资、奖金、劳务报酬；二是生产、经营、投资的收益；三是知识产权的收益；四是继承或者受赠的财产（遗嘱或者赠与合同中确定只归一方的财产除外）；五是其他应当归共同所有的财产。同时，《民法典》第1065条提供了约定财产制的选择。男女双方可以以书面形式约定婚姻关系存续期间所得的财产以及婚前财产归各自所有、共同所有或者部分各自所有、部分共同所有。

二、夫妻共同债务的认定规则

（一）基于共同意思表示所负的夫妻共同债务

“共同意思表示所负的债务”通常表现为夫妻双方事前共同签字，或者是夫妻一方事后追认的债务，即俗称的“共债共签”。“共债共签”规则下的夫妻共同债务，属于多个民事主体基于共同签字等共同意思表示所形成的债务，是民法意思自治原则和合同相对性原理的体现。

这一制度安排一方面考虑了在债务形成之时，债权人往往处于优势地位，课以其一定的风险控制义务，可以有效避免债权人因事后无法举证证明债务属于夫妻共同债务而遭受不必要的损失，有利于保障交易安全。另一方面也能够在家庭重大财产利益的处分上保护夫妻另一方的利益，尊重其知情权和同意权，从债务形成源头上尽可能杜绝夫妻一方“被负债”现象发生，对于最大限度地减少纠纷具有积极意义。

应当注意的是，事后追认的方式不限于书面合同形式，电话录音、短信、微信、邮件等能够承载相关内容的通信方式均可能作为事后追认的具体形式加以参考。

（二）为日常家庭生活需要所负的夫妻共同债务

1. 日常家事代理权下夫妻共同债务的类型

夫妻日常家事代理权，是指夫妻一方因家庭日常生活需要而与第三方为一定民事法律行为时互为代理的权利。夫妻一方在日常家庭事务范围内，与第三方所实施的一定民事法律行为，视为依夫妻双方的意思表示所为的民事法律行为，产生的法律后果由夫妻双方共同承担。

因夫妻日常家事代理权产生的常见夫妻共同债务的类型一般包括正常的吃穿用度、子女抚养教育经费、老人赡养费、家庭成员的医疗费等。在（2021）京01民终9731号民间借贷纠纷案中，北京市第一中级人民法院认定，案涉借款虽为被告配偶所借，但根据证据显示，被告配偶为家庭收入的主导方，其收入为家庭主要收入来源，且所借款项用于未成年子女出国留学，故该债务为夫妻共同债务。在（2019）苏 01 民终 3461 号民间借贷纠纷案中，江苏省南京市中级人民法院认定，原审被告汪某在夫妻关系存续期间以个人名义向被上诉人所借款项用于孩子的奶粉、尿不湿、衣服、玩具及其他用品和家里生活，该款项系上诉人与原审被告的夫妻共同债务。

需要强调的是，家庭日常生活需要的支出是指通常情况下必要的家庭日常消费，立足点在于“必要”。随着经济社会的发展、家庭财富的累积以及生活方式的变化，其认定标准也应顺时更新。

2. 日常家事代理权的法律后果

依据《民法典》第 1060 条的规定，夫妻一方因家庭日常生活需要而实施的民事法律行为，对夫妻双方发生效力，即该民事法律行为所产生的法律效果归属于夫妻双方，取得的权利由夫妻双方共同享有，产生的义务包括债务等由夫妻双方共同承担。

在前述（2021）京 01 民终 9731 号案件中，虽然案涉借款为被告配偶所借，但因其被认定为夫妻共同债务，被告应在配偶死亡后承担清偿义务。在（2019）苏 01 民终 3461 号案件中，案涉借款系上诉人与原审被告的夫妻共同债务，上诉人应当与原审被告共同偿还。

（三）债权人能够证明的夫妻共同债务

1. 需要债权人证明的夫妻共同债务类型

婚姻关系存续期间，夫妻除因行使日常家事代理权形成日常家事债务外，还会与第三人形成其他债权债务关系，如大额借贷、赠与、不动产买卖等。根据《民法典》的规定，夫妻一方在婚姻关系存续期间以个人名义所负的债务，超出家庭日常生活需要的，原则上不认定为夫妻共同债务。

同时，为平衡各方当事人利益，《民法典》通过为债权人设置举证责任的形式，保留了将前述债务认定为夫妻共同债务的可能性。债权人能够证明“该债务用于夫妻共同生活、共同生产经营或者基于夫妻双方共同意思表示”的，该债务将被认定为夫妻共同债务。债权人举证不能的，该债务将由举债一方个人承担。

将举证责任课以债权人，一方面，可以倒逼债权人在成立债权债务关系时尽到审慎的注意义务，要求举债人的配偶签字同意，确保债务的形成为夫妻双方的共同意思表示，通过事前防范减少事后纠纷；另一方面，是在最大限度避免夫妻一方与债权人恶意串通损害另一方合法权益的基础上，切实保障债权人的合法权益。

2. 债权人举证责任的理解维度

（1）债权人能够举证证明该部分债务是用于夫妻共同生活的，可以认定为夫妻共同债务

夫妻共同生活包括但不限于家庭日常生活，此处需要债权人举证证明的范围，是超出家庭日常生活所需的部分，如大额借款用于购买房产、投资创业等。这些支出系夫妻双方共同消费支配，或者用于形成夫妻共同财产，或者基于夫妻共同利益管理共同财产产生的支出，性质上均应属于夫妻共同生活的范围。

（2）债权人能够举证证明该部分债务是用于夫妻共同生产经营的，也可以认定为夫妻共同债务

夫妻共同生产经营的情形非常复杂，主要是指由夫妻双方共同决定生产经营事项，或者虽由一方决定但另一方进行了授权的情形。因此，判断生产经营活动是否属于夫妻共同生产经营，要根据经营活动的性质以及夫妻双方在其中的地位作用等综合认定。夫妻共同生产经营所负的债务一般包括双方共同从事工商业、共同投资以及购买生产资料等所负的债务。

在（2019）粤民再 373 号买卖合同纠纷案中，广东省高级人民法院认为，虽然被告何某系被告立某公司的股东、法定代表人，但不能认定公司收益与其个人收益一致，案涉货款收益也不能认定为被告何某的个人收益，更不能认定为被告何某与被告李某（何某之妻）的共同收益并用于其共同生活。即使被告李某在被告立某公司负责财务工作，也并非公司股东或者高管人员，不符合夫妻共同生产经营的情形，故案涉货款收益也不能认定为用于被告何某与被告李某的夫妻共同生产经营。在（2022）浙 07

民终2755号买卖合同纠纷案中，浙江省金华市中级人民法院认定，上诉人主张案涉的砂石款49万余元及9万元利息系被上诉人祝某与被上诉人叶某的夫妻共同债务，但其未能举证证明存在二被上诉人共同经营本案欠款涉及的工程的情况，且上诉人与被上诉人叶某的微信聊天记录、通话录音亦无法表明其具有明确的债务加入的意思表示，故该笔债务为被上诉人祝某的个人债务。

（3）债权人能够举证证明该部分债务系基于夫妻双方共同意思表示的，亦可认定为夫妻共同债务

在（2021）粤06民终9425号民间借贷纠纷案中，广东省佛山市中级人民法院适用原《夫妻债务司法解释》，就案涉金额300余万元、严重超出家庭日常生活所需的债务作出了非夫妻共同债务的认定，裁判理由为债权人未举证证明案涉款项用于债务人夫妻共同生活、共同生产经营，且债务人夫妻一方亦未明确对案涉债务为夫妻共同债务进行追认或明确表示愿意承担。

强调债权人的举证证明责任，能够促进债权人尽到谨慎注意义务，引导相关主体对于大额债权债务实行“共债共签”，体现从源头控制纠纷、更加注重交易安全的价值取向，也有利于强化公众的市场风险意识，从而平衡保护债权人和未举债夫妻一方的利益。

第二节　香港特区的法律规定

香港特区实行与内地截然不同的夫妻财产制度。香港特区的夫妻财产制度分布于《婚姻条例》（第181章）、《已婚者地位条例》（第182章）、《婚姻法律程序与财产条例》（第192章）等法例中。其中，最常被提及的为《已婚者地位条例》中的相关条款。需要注意的是，《已婚者地位条例》对离婚程序中财产分割的问题不适用。目前，学界与实务界均认为，分别财产制为香港特区夫妻财产制度的原则性规定。

一、分别财产制

（一）已婚女性地位独立

《已婚者地位条例》第3条“已婚女性的能力”规定：（1）除本条例另有规定外，已婚女性在以下各方面，犹如未婚时一样——（a）有取得、持有及处置财产的能力；（b）就侵权行为、合约、债务或义务而言，有自我承担责任及被委以责任的能力；（c）在侵权行为、合约或其他方面，有起诉及被起诉的能力；及（d）受有关破产的法律及受判决与命令的执行所规限。（2）已婚女性在各方面均可担任受托人或遗产代理人，犹如未婚时一样。第4条“已婚女性的财产”规定：除本条例另有规定外，凡——（a）于1936年3月20日以前，属已婚女性的专有财产或根据衡平法代其持有作其专用的财产；或（b）于该日以后结婚的女性，在结婚时已拥有或正拥有的财产；或（c）于该日以后，已婚女性已取得或正取得的财产，或已转予或正转予该已婚女性的财产，须全归该女性所拥有，犹如未婚时一样，该财产并可据此而予以处置。无论在本条例生效日期（1971年10月7日）之前或之后，女性在享有财产方面的预用权或让与权如受到限制，而该等限制不可能加诸对该财产的男性享有者，则该等限制概无效力。

综上，香港特区的法律明确规定已婚女性有独立的财产权利和财产义务，有取得、持有及处置财产的能力。对于侵权行为、契约、债务或义务而言，已婚女性有自我承担责任及被委以责任的能力，可担任受托人或遗产代理人。女性对于已拥有或正拥有的财产权利，不因其已婚而发生变化。

（二）夫妻各自承担责任

《已婚者地位条例》第10条“免除丈夫负起妻子在侵权行为、合约、债务及义务上的责任”规定：除本条例另有规定外，某女性的丈夫无须纯粹因身为该女性的丈夫而就以下事宜负责——（a）该女性婚前或婚后所犯的侵权行为，或其婚前所订立的合约，或所负的债务或义务；或（b）在上述侵权行为、合约、债务或义务的法律程序中被起诉或成为法律程序的一方。

由前述规定可知，除非另有规定，香港特区夫妻结婚后各自独立承担财产责任，其中即包含独立承担各自的债务。丈夫无须仅因丈夫的身份对其妻子婚前或婚后所犯的侵权行为、婚前所订立的契约、所负的债务和义务承担责任。

（三）夫妻之间无必要代理权

作为成文法例，《已婚者地位条例》免除了“妻子的必要代理权”。该条例第 11 条规定：任何法律规则或衡平法，若授予妻子权限，使其能作为丈夫的必要代理人而以其丈夫的信用做担保或以其信用借款者，现均予以撤销。在普通法下，“必要代理权”（Agency of Necessity）为类似内地“日常家事代理权”的体现方式。[1] 基于该条规定，可见香港特区不存在夫妻之间日常家事代理权的适用。需要注意的是，《已婚者地位条例》虽然免除了必要代理权，但并不影响夫妻之间构成其他于法律上有效的代理关系。

（四）配偶对于财产增值部分的权利

《已婚者地位条例》第 9 条规定了配偶对于财产增值部分的权利持有问题。该条规定：现宣布若丈夫或妻子以金钱或有价事物分担改善土地财产或非土地财产的状况，而其分担亦有相当实质，且该土地财产或非土地财产或其变卖所得的款项是由夫妻双方或任何一方拥有实益权益的，则除非夫妻之间有明订或默示的相反协议，否则曾分担的丈夫或妻子须被视为因分担而取得一份或一份加大的实益权益，份额于当时可能已由双方协议决定，若无此协议，则在丈夫或妻子的实益权益是否存在或份额多寡的问

---

〔1〕 参见冉克平：《论因“家庭日常生活需要”引起的夫妻共同债务》，载《江汉论坛》2018 年第 7 期。

题产生时（无论是产生于夫妻之间的法律程序还是其他法律程序中），由聆讯法庭以其认为在一切情况下均属公正者为准。

上述规定意味着，香港特区的分别财产制并非“一刀切”的绝对化分割，也并非登记在谁名下即为谁的财产。根据该条规定，如出现配偶对某一财产的增值存在“贡献”（法例英文原词为“Contributions”，中文法例中称为“分担”）时，作出贡献一方将就该财产取得一份或一份加大的实益权益。也即，作出贡献的一方可能就其原本并不拥有的财产取得一份实益权益，或者夫妻二人针对同一财产的实益权益份额比例因其中一方对财产增值作出了贡献而产生变化。

（五）对债权人的保护

《已婚者地位条例》第 12 条“为欺诈债权人而作的馈赠”规定：本条例内任何规定均不得解释为使以下事项有效——（a）为针对丈夫的债权人，丈夫对妻子作出的任何财产馈赠，但赠后该财产仍继续由丈夫掌管、处置或具有表面所有权；或由妻子或以妻子名义用丈夫的金钱作出的储存或其他投资，藉以欺诈丈夫的债权人；或（b）为针对妻子的债权人，妻子对丈夫作出的任何财产馈赠，但赠后该财产仍继续由妻子掌管、处置或具有表面所有权；或由丈夫或以丈夫名义用妻子的金钱作出的储存或其他投资，藉以欺诈妻子的债权人，凡作上述储存或投资的金钱均可予以追回，犹如本条例尚未通过一样。

由前述规定可见，在保护交易安全、维护债权人利益方面，夫妻双方为逃避债务、为欺诈债权人而作出的夫妻双方之间的赠与无效且可予以追回。该条规定杜绝了不法人士利用夫妻分别财产制“假赠与真转移”，从而侵害债权人利益的可能性。

（六）分别财产制在借贷类纠纷中的体现

在香港特区，鉴于夫妻分别财产制的存在，以及“夫妻共同债务”“夫妻必要代理权”等概念和制度的“缺失”，一般而言，除非夫妻双方在借款时已完成“共债共签”，即夫妻双方从借款伊始就作为共同借款人，否则债权人只能对实际签字借款的一方进行追讨，实践中一般不会直接将借款人的配偶列为共同被告。在缺乏特别的诉因（Cause of Action）的情况下，如故意隐匿财产、恶意转移资产或者共同持有家庭房屋等，即使债权人将非借款一方列为被告，也将承担被法院剔除（Strike Out）的风险。除此之外，在极特殊情况下，法院亦可能通过分析借款合同成立的过程，将非签字一方认定为共同借款人。[1]

二、关于财产归属的争议解决

（一）成文法途径

根据《已婚者地位条例》第 6 条、第 7 条的规定，当夫妻之间就财产所有权或管有权产生争议时，包括认为自己曾经在对方管有或控制的金钱、财产或权益中拥有实益权的，可向法官提出申请要求裁决。法官经审理后，可作出要求夫妻一方付给另一方适当款项的裁决。

（二）衡平法途径

香港特区也存在通过衡平法推定信托的方式认定夫妻共同持有某项财产的途径。在（2016）沪 01 民终 2239 号所有权确认纠纷案中，上海市第一中级人民法院根据香港特区的衡平法确认案涉房产的归属问题。该案中，上诉人徐某与被上诉人张某均为香港特区永久性居民，双方于 1987 年在香港特区结婚。在婚姻关系存续期间，徐某在上海购入案涉房屋，并支付了购房款及银行贷款。案涉房屋登记在徐某一人名下。徐某与张某对婚内财产无特别约定。现张某主张确认对案涉房屋享有 50% 的产权份额。

上海市第一中级人民法院认为，双方就案涉房屋产权归属发生的纠纷，从形式上看是对不动产权属的确认之诉，但张某是基于与徐某的婚姻关系而要求确认系争房屋权属归两人共有，其实质是因婚姻关系所产生的

---

〔1〕 Chow Yu Heung Elsa v. Li Muk Ming［2006］HKCU 1664.

财产争议，应当适用《涉外民事关系法律适用法》第24条[1]之规定来决定案件准据法。因张某与徐某没有协议选择共同适用的法律，根据《最高人民法院关于适用〈中华人民共和国涉外民事关系法律适用法〉若干问题的解释（一）》（当时生效）第15条[2]之规定，应以张某与徐某形成婚姻关系的时间作为确认双方经常居所地的时间节点，故应认定香港特区为张某与徐某争议中的指引实体法适用的经常居所地，本案就案涉房屋权属产生的纠纷，应适用香港特区法律。

张某与徐某均对香港特区法律中关于夫妻财产法律关系的规定进行了确认，即香港成文法中规定实行夫妻分别财产制，但在衡平法或判例法中，如存在财产推定信托，则可认定登记在夫妻一方名下的不动产为夫妻共有。案涉房屋产权取得于徐某与张某婚姻关系存续期间，但产权仅登记在徐某一方名下，徐某与张某也不存在关于案涉房屋产权归属的书面协议，故从香港成文法的规定来看，案涉房屋应属徐某一人所有。从香港衡平法的角度来看，就案涉房屋产权归属，徐某与张某间是否存在财产推定信托系双方争议的主要焦点。

该案中香港特区律师出具的法律意见书中载明：夫妻婚后财产的处分，除双方有明确的协议外或存在推定信托外，应适用夫妻分别财产制。如有推定信托的情况，则需要有明示或推定建立推定信托的合意，即必须要有共享该财产的共同合意，以及主张推定信托的一方因任何协议、安排等合意而令其在该财产上享有权益。推定信托，是指虽然甲方与乙方并没有为财产明确设立任何信托协议（包括口头或书面协议），但基于衡平法的原则，有关财产可能属于信托财产，其中一方为受托人，而另一方或双方同时为实益人。故即使其中一方是财产的法定拥有人，但未必是财产的

[1] 夫妻财产关系，当事人可以协议选择适用一方当事人经常居所地法律、国籍国法律或者主要财产所在地法律。当事人没有选择的，适用共同经常居所地法律；没有共同经常居所地的，适用共同国籍国法律。

[2] 自然人在涉外民事关系产生或者变更、终止时已经连续居住1年以上且作为其生活中心的地方，人民法院可以认定为涉外民事关系法律适用法规定的自然人的经常居所地，但就医、劳务派遣、公务等情形除外。

唯一实际权益拥有人或拥有全部实际权益，而是以受托人的身份代实益人持有全部或部分法定权益。共同意图推定信托较适用于夫妻关系，通常构成共同意图推定信托存在两项条件：第一，甲方与乙方在购买财产时（或在例外情况下，购买财产后），双方均有意图共同拥有财产权益；第二，其中一方依据该共同意图，作出令其个人利益受损的行为，如甲方付出购买该财产的金额或缴付（因购买该财产而产生的）按揭贷款额。那么，即使甲方与乙方之间缺乏任何书面协议，共同意图推定信托亦有可能成立。

在该案中，上海市第一中级人民法院通过论述和评判徐某和张某之间是否存在共有系争房屋的合意、张某是否为取得系争房屋作出贡献或存在使自己利益受损的行为两个要件，最后认定案涉房屋仅为徐某一方所有。

第三节　小　　结

一、相同点

第一，内地与香港特区均规定，夫妻双方通过共同签字等共同意思表示所负担的债务由夫妻双方共同承担。

第二，内地与香港特区均规定，夫妻一方以个人名义超出家庭日常生活需要对外所借款项一般不认定为夫妻共同债务。

二、不同点

第一，内地与香港特区在夫妻财产制度上存在区别。内地以夫妻共同财产制为原则，以约定财产制为例外。香港特区则以分别财产制为原则，仅在特殊情况下可认定夫妻共同持有某一项财产。

第二，内地与香港特区在夫妻债务制度上存在区别。内地对夫妻双方共同意思表示所负的债务及夫妻一方以个人名义因家庭日常生活需要所负的债务一般认定为夫妻共同债务；超出家庭日常生活需要所负的债务一般不认定为夫妻共同债务，除非债权人有证据证明该债务用于夫妻共同生活、共同生产经营或者基于夫妻双方共同意思表示。香港特区法律没有单独对夫妻共同债务作出专门的定义或规定，夫妻一方对外负担的债务一般认定为个人债务，且香港特区夫妻之间无日常家事代理权。

第八章　诉讼时效的法律规则比较

第一节　内地的法律规定

《民法典》对内地的诉讼时效进行了规定，包含诉讼时效的期间，分期履行债务的诉讼时效，诉讼时效的起算，诉讼时效的中止、中断情形，诉讼时效届满的法律效果等。

现假设甲为出借人，乙为借款人，双方约定借款金额为50万元，借款期限自2023年5月20日至2024年5月20日。本节将以上述简易案例为基础对诉讼时效的各类规定进行诠释。

一、诉讼时效期间

（一）普通诉讼时效期间

根据《民法典》第188条的规定，内地的普通诉讼时效期间为3年。民间借贷纠纷适用普通诉讼时效。以本节开头的简易案例为例，如2024年5月20日还款期限届满，乙未履行还款义务，则甲对乙的诉讼时效期间自2024年5月20日起算，至2027年5月20日止。《民法典》没有对保证债务的诉讼时效作出特别规定，在借款存在担保的情况下，保证债务也适用普通诉讼时效，时效期间为3年。

（二）特别诉讼时效期间

内地的某些专门法中规定了特别诉讼时效期间，如《保险法》规定，人寿保险的被保险人或者受益人向保险人请求给付保险金的诉讼时效期间为5年。《海商法》规定，就海上旅客运输向承运人要求赔偿的请求权，时效期间为2年。专门法中关于诉讼时效期间的特殊规定，优先于《民法典》中普通时效期间的规定适用。民间借贷纠纷不适用特别诉讼时效期间的规定。

二、诉讼时效的起算

《民法典》第188条中规定，诉讼时效期间自权利人知道或者应当知道权利受到损害以及义务人之日起计算。根据该条规定，诉讼时效的起算需要满足三个条件：一是权利客观上受到侵害。二是权利人知道或应当知道权利受到侵害，所谓应当知道指的是以一般人的标准，权利人在当时的情况下应当知道权利受到侵害。三是权利人知道或应当知道具体侵害人。实践中，诉讼时效的起算要根据案件情况予以确定。在借款纠纷中，诉讼时效的起算一般以履行期限的届满作为起算时点，具体分为以下几类情况。

（一）已约定履行期限

《民法典》第675条中规定，借款人应当按照约定的期限返还借款。因此，合同中约定了履行期限的，诉讼时效期间自履行期限届满之日起算。在前述简易案例中，甲乙双方约定了借款期限自2023年5月20日至2024年5月20日，则诉讼时效自2024年5月20日起算。

（二）未约定履行期限

对于未约定履行期限的情况，《民法典》及其他相关法律法规[1]所规定的处理思路为：首先，依照《民法典》第510条的规定确定履行期限，可以确定的，诉讼时效自确定的履行期限届满之日起算。其次，对于无法确定履行期限的情况，借款人可以随时返还，出借人也可以随时请求借款人返还，但应当给予合理的准备时间，诉讼时效自出借人要求借款人履行义务的宽限期届满之日起算。最后，借款人在出借人第一次向其主张权利

---

〔1〕根据《民法典》第675条的规定，借款人应当按照约定的期限返还借款。对借款期限没有约定或者约定不明确，依据该法第510条的规定仍不能确定的，借款人可以随时返还；贷款人可以催告借款人在合理期限内返还。《诉讼时效规定》第4条中规定，诉讼时效自债权人要求债务人履行义务的宽限期届满之日起算。债务人在债权人第一次向其主张权利之时明确表示不履行义务的，诉讼时效期间从债务人明确表示不履行义务之日起计算。

之时明确表示不履行义务的，诉讼时效期间从借款人明确表示不履行义务之日起计算。

以前述简易案例为例，如甲乙未约定借款期限，且双方亦无法确定借款期限的，乙可以自 2023 年 5 月 20 日起随时向甲偿还 50 万元借款。同时，甲也可以随时要求乙偿还借款，但需要给予乙一定的宽限期。例如，甲于 2024 年 1 月 1 日要求乙偿还，并给予合理的宽限期 7 日，则诉讼时效自 2024 年 1 月 8 日起算。如乙在 2024 年 1 月 1 日即明确表示不还款的，则诉讼时效从 2024 年 1 月 1 日起算。

在实际案件中，法院会根据借款人和出借人之间的协议内容、借款行为的时间点以及双方的行为来确定诉讼时效是否起算。在（2021）鲁 02 民终 12526 号民间借贷纠纷案中，山东省青岛市中级人民法院认定，因案涉借条中未约定还款时间，且债务人亦抗辩称债权人从未向其索要过欠款，故该案诉讼时效未开始起算，对上诉人已过诉讼时效的抗辩不予支持。

（三）分期履行的债务

《民法典》第 189 条规定，当事人约定同一债务分期履行的，诉讼时效期间自最后一期履行期限届满之日起计算。以前述简易案例为例，如甲乙约定 50 万元借款在一年借款期限内分三期偿还，第一期于 2023 年 8 月 20 日前偿还，第二期于 2024 年 1 月 30 日前偿还，最后一期于 2024 年 5 月 20 日前偿还，但乙每一期均逾期未还，诉讼时效期间仍自 2024 年 5 月 20 日起算。

在处理分期履行债务的诉讼时效时，需要注意分期履行与定期履行的区别。分期履行债务的给付总额在债权债务成立时即可确定，是一个债务的分批分次履行。定期履行债务则存在多个独立的债务，给付总额在债权债务成立时一般并不确定。

（四）担保

1. 抵押担保

根据《民法典》第 419 条的规定，抵押权人应当在主债权诉讼时效期间行使抵押权。也即，抵押权期间受制于主债权诉讼时效。主债权诉讼时效发生中断、中止、延长等变化的，抵押权期间将同步发生变化。以前述简易案例为例，如乙以其名下房产为甲借出的 50 万元提供抵押，甲应在该 50 万元的诉讼时效期间内行使抵押权。

2. 保证

（1）一般保证

根据《民法典》第 694 条第 1 款的规定，一般保证的诉讼时效从保证人拒绝承担保证责任的权利消灭之日起开始计算。这一制度与一般保证人先诉抗辩权制度相吻合。以前述简易案例为例，如丙为该 50 万元借款向甲提供一般保证，保证期间 6 个月，而乙未在 2024 年 5 月 20 日前偿还借款，甲应先在 2024 年 5 月 20 日起的 6 个月内向乙提起诉讼或仲裁，并就乙的财产依法强制执行仍不能偿还借款后，才可要求丙承担保证责任。也即，甲针对丙的保证之债诉讼时效自前述情形出现之日起算。除此之外，如乙出现了《民法典》第 687 条中列明的四类情形时[1]，甲也可自该四类情形出现之日起向丙主张要求其承担保证责任。

（2）连带责任保证

根据《民法典》第 694 条第 2 款的规定，连带责任保证的债权人在保证期间届满前请求保证人承担保证责任的，从债权人请求保证人承担保证责任之日起，开始计算保证债务的诉讼时效。与一般保证不同，在连带责任保证中，保证人没有先诉抗辩权，债权人可以直接请求保证人承担保证责任。以前述简易案例为例，如丙向甲提供的是连带责任保证，保证期间 6 个月，而乙未在 2024 年 5 月 20 日前偿还借款，则甲可在 2024 年 5 月 20 日起的 6 个月内（即保证期间内）向丙主张要求其承担保证责任，保证之债的诉讼时效自甲要求丙承担保证责任之日起算。

---

〔1〕一般保证的保证人在主合同纠纷未经审判或者仲裁，并就债务人财产依法强制执行仍不能履行债务前，有权拒绝向债权人承担保证责任，但是有下列情形之一的除外：（1）债务人下落不明，且无财产可供执行；（2）人民法院已经受理债务人破产案件；（3）债权人有证据证明债务人的财产不足以履行全部债务或者丧失履行债务能力；（4）保证人书面表示放弃本款规定的权利。

三、诉讼时效的计算

（一）期间的开始

《民法典》第 201 条规定了期间的计算方法。根据该条规定，按照日、月、年计算期间的，开始的当天不算入，从下一天开始计算。以前述简易案例为例，甲对乙的诉讼时效期间自 2024 年 5 月 20 日起算，其中 5 月 20 日当日不算入，即甲最早可在 2024 年 5 月 21 日向乙提起诉讼。

（二）期间的结束

根据《民法典》第 203 条的规定，期间的最后一日是法定休假日的，以法定休假日结束的次日为期间的最后一日。例如，诉讼时效期间计算至最后一日时为周日的，则以次日即周一作为期间的最后一日。诉讼时效期间计算至最后一日为 10 月 1 日国庆假期的，则以 10 月 8 日即国庆假期结束的次日为期间的最后一日。

四、诉讼时效的中止、中断、延长与最长诉讼时效期间

（一）诉讼时效的中止

诉讼时效中止，是指在时效进行过程中，因发生一定法定事由使权利人不能行使请求权，从而暂停计算时效期间，待阻碍消灭后再继续计算时效期间的制度。《民法典》第 194 条规定了 5 种诉讼时效中止的情形：（1）不可抗力；（2）无民事行为能力人或者限制民事行为能力人没有法定代理人，或者法定代理人死亡、丧失民事行为能力、丧失代理权；（3）继承开始后未确定继承人或者遗产管理人；（4）权利人被义务人或者其他人控制；（5）其他导致权利人不能行使请求权的障碍。该五种情形需发生在诉讼时效期间的最后 6 个月内才产生中止效力。自中止时效的原因消除之日起满 6 个月，诉讼时效期间届满。在前述简易案例中，如甲对乙的诉讼时效自 2024 年 5 月 20 日起算，甲于 2027 年 3 月 20 日出现了因病成为限制民事行为能力人的情形，导致其无法进行追偿，则诉讼时效自 2027 年 3

月 20 日起中止，并将在确定了甲的法定代理人之日起继续计算 6 个月。

（二）诉讼时效的中断

诉讼时效期间的中断，是指在诉讼时效期间进行中，由于法定事由的发生而推翻了诉讼时效存在的基础，从而使已经进行的时效期间全归于无效，诉讼时效期间重新计算。《民法典》第 195 条规定了 4 种诉讼时效中断的情形：（1）权利人向义务人提出履行请求；（2）义务人同意履行义务；（3）权利人提起诉讼或者申请仲裁；（4）与提起诉讼或者申请仲裁具有同等效力的其他情形。以前述简易案例为例，甲对乙的诉讼时效自 2024 年 5 月 20 日起算，期间为 3 年。甲在 2025 年 5 月 21 日向乙提出了还款请求，产生了中断诉讼时效的效力，甲对乙债权的诉讼时效自 2025 年 5 月 21 日起重新计算 3 年。

在（2023）苏 13 民终 639 号民间借贷案中，江苏省宿迁市中级人民法院认定，案涉借条未约定还款期限，借款人经出借人首次催要借款后虽未能在合理期限内还款，但经证人证实，直至起诉前出借人每年都会到借款人家中催要借款。出借人催要借款的行为表明其一直积极行使其权利，产生了诉讼时效中断的效力，故案涉借贷关系并未过诉讼时效。

（三）诉讼时效的延长与最长诉讼时效期间

根据《民法典》第 188 条的规定，内地的最长诉讼时效为 20 年。最长诉讼时效的计算采用的是客观标准，从权利受到损害之日开始计算，不考虑权利人何时知道权利受到侵害及具体义务人，也不适用中断、中止的规定。从权利受到损害之日起超过 20 年的，除极特殊情况下的诉讼时效延长外，法院不予保护。也即，诉讼时效的延长仅适用于最长诉讼时效期间，不适用于普通诉讼时效期间。以前述简易案例为例，甲对乙的诉讼时效自 2024 年 5 月 20 日起算，即使期间发生了各种使诉讼时效中断、中止的事由，但自 2044 年 5 月 20 日起，法院就不再就甲对乙享有的债权予以保护。

在（2019）冀 06 民终 2671 号生命权、健康权、身体权纠纷案中，原告 6 岁时触电受伤，之后父亲去世、母亲改嫁，其由重度残疾的爷爷以及智力障碍的奶奶照看，成长环境对智力发展程度产生重大影响。原告起诉时 20 年期间已届满，河北省保定市中级人民法院以“本人对时效届满在主观上无过错”“家庭几经变故的特殊性”为由，认定构成延长事由。

五、诉讼时效的援引

（一）法院

根据《民法典》第 193 条的规定，法院不得主动适用诉讼时效的规定。这一规定的原因在于，诉讼时效抗辩权本质上是义务人的一项私权利，行使与否属于义务人意思自治范畴。法院不得主动适用诉讼时效的规定，包括向当事人主动援引、释明诉讼时效的规定，以及主动适用中止、中断、延长等与诉讼时效相关的全部规定。当事人缺席审理或者公告送达的，视为放弃答辩权利，法院亦不得主动适用诉讼时效的规定。以前述简易案例为例，甲对乙的诉讼时效自 2024 年 5 月 20 日起算，期间为 3 年，如甲在 2028 年 3 月 1 日才对乙提出诉讼，而乙未应诉答辩，则法院不得以诉讼时效届满为由驳回甲的诉讼请求。

（二）当事人

“因时效而直接受益”的当事人可以提出诉讼时效的抗辩，一般包括债务人与保证人。《诉讼时效规定》对于当事人在何时、何种情形下可提出诉讼时效抗辩作出了相关规定。

一是当事人应当在一审期间提出诉讼时效抗辩。当事人在二审期间提出的，除有新证据可证明对方的请求权已过诉讼时效之外，法院不予支持。当事人在一审期间未提出诉讼时效抗辩，而后又以诉讼时效期间届满为由申请再审或者提出再审抗辩的，法院亦不予支持。

二是诉讼时效期间届满后当事人又作出同意履行义务的意思表示或者自愿履行义务的，不得再以诉讼时效期间届满为由进行抗辩。

三是保证人享有主债务人的诉讼时效抗辩权。主债务诉讼时效期间届满，保证人可提出主债务诉讼时效抗辩。保证人未主张前述诉讼时效抗辩权，承担保证责任后向主债务人行使追偿权的，法院不予支持。

六、诉讼时效届满的法律效果

（一）义务人取得时效抗辩权

根据《民法典》第 192 条的规定，诉讼时效期间届满的，义务人可以提出不履行义务的抗辩。就民间借贷纠纷而言，诉讼时效届满的法律效果是借款人取得了时效抗辩权，出借人丧失胜诉权。也即，出借人仍然可以起诉，法院也应当受理。如果借款人没有提出时效抗辩，或者自愿放弃时效抗辩权，法院仍将维护出借人的利益。如果借款人提出了诉讼时效抗辩，则法院将驳回出借人的诉讼请求。

（二）义务人可以放弃时效抗辩权

如前文所述，诉讼时效抗辩权行使与否属于义务人意思自治范畴。因此，诉讼时效期间届满后，义务人虽取得时效抗辩权，但也可以选择放弃该权利。在放弃的方式上，实践中主要包含同意履行和已自愿履行两种情形。需要注意的是，根据《诉讼时效规定》第 19 条的规定，义务人放弃时效抗辩权的，不得再次援引，包括不得再次提出时效届满的抗辩，也不得要求权利人返还已自愿偿还的借款。以前述简易案例为例，甲对乙的诉讼时效自 2024 年 5 月 20 日起算，期间为 3 年，如甲在 2028 年 3 月 1 日才对乙提起诉讼，而乙在收到法院送达的诉讼材料后主动向甲还清了 50 万元借款，则不得再在诉讼中提出诉讼时效届满的抗辩，也不得请求甲返还已偿还的 50 万元。

第二节　香港特区的法律规定

《时效条例》对香港特区的诉讼时效期间作出了规定，并对不同类别诉讼的时效期间作了分类和列举。例如，根据《民事责任（分担）条例》第 3 条的规定，就任何损害向任何其他人追讨分担款项的诉讼时效期间为 2 年；简单合约或侵权行为、强制执行担保、强制执行某项裁决的诉讼时效期间为 6 年；追讨藉按揭财产或其他财产押记而获得保证的本金的诉讼时效期间为 12 年；官方收回土地的诉讼时效期间为 60 年，等等。

一、诉讼时效期间

（一）简单合同纠纷适用的诉讼时效期间

《时效条例》第 4（1）条规定，基于简单合约或侵权行为的诉讼，于诉讼因由（Cause of Action，即诉因）产生的日期起计满 6 年后，不得提出。对于合同来说，诉因自违约时产生，即针对合同违约提出的诉讼必须自违约起 6 年内提出。普通的借款合同纠纷适用 6 年的诉讼时效期间。该条规定并不适用于强制履行合约（Specific Performance）、强制令（Injunctions）或其他衡平法救济（Equitable Relief）的申索。

（二）追讨藉按揭或押记而获得保证的款项的诉讼

根据《时效条例》第 19（1）条的规定，追讨藉按揭（Mortgage）或其他财产押记（Charge）而获得保证的款项的诉讼，不得在收取有关款项的权利产生的日期起计满 12 年后提出。从该条规定可知，对于借款类纠纷而言，当案涉借款通过按揭或其他财产押记而获得保证时，追讨该借款本金的诉讼时效为 12 年。实践中，“其他财产押记”所适用的具体类型视案情由法院裁量。

（三）追讨就藉按揭或其他押记而获得保证的款项所应缴而欠缴的利息

《时效条例》第 19（5）条规定，追讨就藉按揭或其他押记而获得保证的款项所应缴而欠缴的利息，不得在利息到期应缴的日期起计 6 年届满后提出。承按人（Mortgagee）对本金的权利受时效限制的，对利息的权利也将受到限制。[1] 同时，根据相关英国判例，在满足该款规定的情况下，承按人虽然不得提出诉讼，但作为赎回或收取按揭担保物出售收益的条件，按揭人必须支付所有拖欠的利息，无论拖欠时间多长。

二、诉讼时效的起算

对基于合同的诉讼，诉讼时效自违约发生之日起算，[2] 即诉因自违约之日起产生。对于借款类合同纠纷而言，则于借款人未按照约定偿还借款之日起算。

（一）约定了履行期限

在针对借款的诉讼中，如果约定了还款时间或者还款条件，则诉讼时效从约定的期限届满或条件发生时开始计算。[3]

（二）未约定履行期限

根据普通法规则，如果借贷双方没有约定偿还借款的日期，则借款将立即到期，诉因即刻产生。这一规则同样适用于约定了需经追偿后才须偿还的情形，诉因仍自借款发放时产生。香港高等法院上诉法庭在 Lee Siu Fong Mary v. Ngai Yee Chai[4]案中适用了这一规则。在该案中，原告主张在 1994 年至 1995 年向被告提供了 8 笔借款，但被告仅部分清偿。原告于 2002 年向被告提起诉讼，被告以超过 6 年诉讼时效为由提出抗辩，认为他无须再清偿欠款。上诉法庭经查明，确认了其中的 4 笔于 1994 年发放的借款。因原被告双方未约定还款期限，上诉法庭结合前述普通法规则认定，本案中原告的诉因自 1994 年借款发放时即产生，诉讼时效由此起算。

---

〔1〕 See *Cap.* 347 *Limitation Ordinance with Annotation*, Lexis Nexis Hong Kong, para. 4. 20. Elder v. Northcott [1930] 2 Ch 422, [1930] All ER Rep 398.

〔2〕 Yeung Shu v. Alfred Lau & Co. (A Firm) (Chang Pao Ching, Third Party) [1996] 1 HKC 562 (CFI).

〔3〕 See *Halsbury's Laws of Hong Kong*, Lexis Nexis Hong Kong, [245. 042] Actions Founded on Contracts of Loan. Lim Ban Thoon v. Chintung Securities Ltd. [1991] 2 HKC 204 (CA).

〔4〕 [2006] 1 HKC 157 (CA).

（三）分期履行的债务

在分期还款的情况下，假设合同约定了如有任何一期逾期则全部欠款立即到期的，则整笔债务的诉讼时效从首次逾期起算。[1] 如果在任何一期逾期的情况下，整笔债务是“按要求”（on Demand）偿还的，则诉讼时效自出借人要求偿还时起算。[2]

（四）追讨藉按揭或押记而获得保证的款项的诉讼

根据《时效条例》第19（1）条的规定，追讨藉按揭或其他财产押记而获得保证的款项的诉讼，不得在“收取有关款项的权利产生的日期”起计满12年后提出。该条规定曾于1991年进行修订，修订前的诉讼时效为20年。

在Broada Ltd. v. Chow Cheuk Yin[3]案中，香港高等法院基于原告的申请，依照《时效条例》第19（1）条宣告一项登记设立于1957年8月26日的按揭已不再有效（No Longer of Effect）。该案中，按揭项下的本金为3000港元，应于1958年2月26日偿还。1976年，原告的前身因需要在按揭的土地上建设房屋向政府作出声明，承诺其已取得承按人（即被告）的同意，同时进一步声明，其已多年未见过被告，也无法找到被告。该声明于1976年1月23日在土地登记处办理了登记。法院基于此认定，在1976年之前的许多年以及之后，该按揭项下的欠款均未被支付过利息或本金。法院因此依照《时效条例》第19条判定，被告不得再以诉讼方式追讨藉按揭而获得保证的本金及利息，也不得提起任何止赎权诉讼。法院在判词中论述到，因该案的诉因产生于1991年7月1日以前，因此适用修正前第19（1）条所规定的20年诉讼时效期间。

需要注意的是，“收取有关款项的权利产生的日期”这一描述并不是

---

〔1〕 See *Cap.* 347 *Limitation Ordinance with Annotation*, Lexis Nexis Hong Kong, para. 4. 08.

〔2〕 See *Halsbury's Laws of Hong Kong*, Lexis Nexis Hong Kong, [245. 042] Actions Founded on Contracts of Loan.

〔3〕 [1997] 3 HKC 168.

一个固定的公式，而是一种具有较强个案性质的确定方法，需要结合具体案件中受担保债权的还款条件、受担保债权诉讼因由的产生时间等因素进行判断。在 Siu Wing Yee Angeline v. Earning Yield Ltd.[1]案中，香港高等法院原讼法庭拒绝简单地以设立押记的时间来计算诉讼时效，认为时效并不从押记设立的日期起算，而是从诉讼因由产生的日期起算。在 Alpha Star Enterprises Ltd. v. Personal Representative of Tang Mei Shin (Deceased)[2]案中，香港高等法院原讼法庭在判词中指出，原告有责任证明承按人对按揭人和/或涉诉财产进行追讨的时效已过。同时，《时效条例》第 19（3）条规定，收取藉按揭或押记而获得保证的本金的权利，以及就受按揭或押记所规限的财产的止赎权利，在该项财产仍包含任何未来权益或尚未到期或终结的人寿保险单时，并不当作产生。

（五）追讨就藉按揭或其他押记而获得保证的款项所应缴而欠缴的利息

《时效条例》第 19（5）条规定，追讨就藉按揭或其他押记而获得保证的款项所应缴而欠缴的利息，不得在“利息到期应缴的日期”起计 6 年届满后提出。这一规定的诉讼时效起算时点为，出借人依据借款协议首次可以提出诉讼追讨利息之日，而非应付利息之日。[3]

（六）期间计算

诉因产生的当日不计算在内。当期限的最后一日落在法院非工作日时，则顺延至下一个法院工作日。[4] 作为一般原则，期间一旦开始计算，则不会因后续发生的“无行为能力”或“资格丧失”而中断（Broken）。这一规则最早可见于英国 Prideaux v. Webber[5]案中，但成文法条规定了

[1] [2013] 6 HKC 281.

[2] [2002] 4 HKC 218.

[3] See *Cap. 347 Limitation Ordinance with Annotation*, Lexis Nexis Hong Kong, para. 19.13.

[4] See *Cap. 347 Limitation Ordinance with Annotation*, Lexis Nexis Hong Kong, para. 4.06.

[5] [1661] 1 Lev 31.

可推翻这一规则的特定情形。同时，如当事人未一致同意在协商期间对诉讼时效暂停计算（Suspended），诉讼时效将持续计算。[1]

三、诉讼时效的延长或延后

《时效条例》规定了三类诉讼时效的延长或延后的情况：一是当诉因产生时原告无行为能力（Under a Disability）的情况；二是被告（或被告的“前身”，或被告的代理人）以书面形式承认（Acknowledgment）或部分缴款（Part Payment）的情况；三是诉讼系基于欺诈（Fraud），或诉讼权利被故意隐瞒，或诉讼是为了摆脱（Relief）一项错误的后果。

（一）无行为能力

《时效条例》第 22（1）条规定，本条例订明时效期的诉讼权，如在该诉讼权产生的日期，在该诉讼权在其方面产生的人并无行为能力，则有关诉讼可在该人停止无行为能力或该人去世（以首先发生者为准）的日期起计 6 年内的任何时间提出，即使该时效期已届满亦然。

根据该条例第 22（3）条的规定，“无行为能力”的范围包含幼年人或精神不健全（of Unsound Mind）的人。根据《释义及通则条例》（第 1 章）第 3 条，“幼年人”是指未满 18 岁的人。关于“精神不健全”的含义，有判例意见认为应采取宽松的态度，使“精神不健全的人”不仅限于精神病患者，还应包括不能管理自己事务的人。[2] 就这一目的而言，在下列两类情况下，一个人将不可推翻地被认定为精神不健全：一是当他根据任何授权拘留精神不健全人的条例或其他成文法例被扣留（Detain）时，包括被定罪或等待审判的人；二是在他根据《精神健康条例》（第 136 章）的规定自愿接受治疗期间。

（二）承认或部分缴款

《时效条例》第 23（1）条规定，凡有收回土地的诉讼权（包括止赎

[1] Ho Cheung Electrical Engineering Co. Ltd. v. Ko Wai Sun [2017] HKCU 661.

[2] See *Cap. 347 Limitation Ordinance with Annotation*, Lexis Nexis Hong Kong, para. 22. 05.

诉讼权）产生，或者非土地财产的承按人就该财产提起止赎诉讼的权利产生，并且土地或非土地财产的占有人承认诉讼权持有者的所有权，则该权利被视为作出承认之日而非之前产生。同样，在承按人提出止赎或其他诉讼的情况下，如前述财产的占有人或负有法律责任缴付按揭债项的人就该债项缴付了款项（无论是本金还是利息），则诉讼权被视为在缴款之日而非之前产生。

从前述条款可知，该条款所适用的诉讼类型仅限于收回土地的诉讼（含止赎诉讼）与非土地财产承按人的止赎诉讼。就借款类纠纷而言，该条款可能适用的场景为：在借款人未依约偿还欠款、且该借款有按揭作为担保时，承按人对已作按揭土地或者非土地财产提起止赎诉讼。

需要注意的是，该条规定已就可适用的范围作了明确列举，不可直接延伸适用至其他承认或者部分缴款的场景。但其他场景下的承认或者部分缴款，是否会基于其他法律规定或原则而产生诉讼时效“实际上”延长的效果（例如，借款合同双方协商一致对有关还款期限或者条件进行修改），应当结合具体案例和所涉及的法律规定或原则具体分析。

（三）欺诈、隐瞒及错误

根据《时效条例》第26（1）条的规定，当有关诉讼是基于被告的欺诈行为，或者被告蓄意对原告隐瞒任何有关原告诉讼权的事实，或者该诉讼是为解除某项错误所致的结果而寻求济助，则诉讼时效在原告发觉、或经合理努力而应可发觉该欺诈行为、隐瞒或错误之前，并不开始计算。

1. 关于“欺诈”（Fraud）在该条款中的含义

“欺诈”需构成相关诉讼因由的重要（Essential）组成部分，且其定义与普通法下一般“欺诈”的定义无异，但亦有判例认为可扩大延伸至“不合理的行为”。

2. 关于“蓄意隐瞒”（Concealment）在该条款中的含义

根据《时效条例》第26（3）条的规定，在若干时间内可能不被发觉的情况下蓄意地背离责任（Duty），即构成蓄意隐瞒涉及责任背离的事实。

3. 关于“错误”（Mistake）的范围

该条款适用于在普通法下追偿因事实错误而支付款项的诉讼，或在衡平法下追偿因事实或法律错误而支付款项的类似索偿。[1]

4. 关于“经合理努力”（Reasonable Diligence）的程度

在 Peco Arts Inc. v. Hazlitt Gallery Ltd.[2]案中（该案涉及一幅艺术作品的买卖，案涉作品原被主张为真品，但其后被发现为复制品），被认定“合理努力”并不意味着尽一切可能，而是指一个通常的（Ordinary）谨慎的（Prudent）艺术品买家在同等情况下会做的事情。在 Baron v. Hartford Fire Insurance Co. & Ors.[3]案中，香港高等法院上诉法庭也适用了这一标准。此外，原告负有举证责任，证明如不采取他通常不会采取的特别措施，则不可能发现欺诈等行为。[4]

四、诉讼时效的援引

根据《高等法院规则》第 18 号命令第 8 条规则“必须特别作诉的事宜”的第（1）款，任何一方必须在继申索陈述书之后的任何状书中，特别就任何属以下情况的事宜作诉（如履行、解除、任何关于时效的法规、欺诈或任何反映不合法事情的事实）。也即，当事人要以诉讼时效提出抗辩的，必须专门提出，即使根据申索书上载明的内容可以看出诉讼时效已经届满。

五、诉讼时效届满的法律效果

一般而言，在相关时效期限届满时，《时效条例》的后果为阻却（Bar）通过诉讼程序获得救济。在前述 Lee Siu Fong Mary v. Ngai Yee Chai[5]案中，香港高等法院上诉法庭认定案涉借款于 1994 年发放，在双

---

〔1〕 Re Diplock, Diplock v. Wintle [1948] Ch 465, [1948] 2 All ER 318.

〔2〕 [1983] 1 WLR 1315, [1983] 3 All ER 193.

〔3〕 [1995] 1 HKC 149.

〔4〕 Paragon Finance Plc. v. DB Thakerar & Co. (A Firm) [1999] 1 All ER 400.

〔5〕 [2006] 1 HKC 157 (CA).

方未约定还款期限的情况下，出借人的诉因自 1994 年发放借款时即产生，诉讼时效由此开始计算。因该案所适用的诉讼时效期间为 6 年，即 2000 年诉讼时效届满，而原告于 2002 年才提起诉讼，因此上诉法庭支持了被告关于诉讼时效的抗辩理由，并驳回了原告的请求。

需要注意的是，时效届满并不导致实际权利的丧失。因此，所持债权已过诉讼时效的债权人如有除诉讼外的其他方式来实现其债权的，《时效条例》并不阻止其通过这些方式进行追偿。[1]

第三节 小　　结

一、相同点

第一，内地与香港特区的诉讼时效制度在时效届满的法律效果上大致相同，均阻却了权利人通过诉讼程序获得救济的途径，但并不否定权利的存在。

第二，内地与香港特区均通过成文法规定诉讼时效的抗辩需由当事人专门提出。

二、不同点

第一，内地与香港特区的诉讼时效期间不同。内地规定了普遍适用的 3 年普通诉讼时效期间，香港特区则对不同类别诉讼的时效期间进行了列举。对于借款纠纷而言，内地的诉讼时效为 3 年，香港特区则为 6 年。此外，内地并未针对特定的担保而专门规定不同的诉讼时效期间，而香港特区则针对藉按揭和押记而获得保证的款项规定了专门的诉讼时效期间（本金 12 年、利息 6 年）。

第二，内地与香港特区在特定情况下诉讼时效的起算时点也因关于请

〔1〕 See *Halsbury's Laws of Hong Kong*, Lexis Nexis Hong Kong, [245.031] Cases Where the Remedy is Barred and not the Right.

求权产生的规定不一致而有所不同。例如，对于没有约定期限的借款合同来说，内地法律规定了还款的合理期限，诉讼时效自合理期限届满之日起算；香港特区的诉讼时效则自借款发放之日起算。

第三，内地与香港特区关于突破原有诉讼时效期间的规定不同。内地关于诉讼时效中断、中止的规定具有普遍适用的效力，而诉讼时效的延长仅适用于最长诉讼时效，且未列举具体场景，仅赋予法院在极特殊情况下对最长诉讼时效进行延长。香港特区没有专门的诉讼时效中断、中止的规定，但对诉讼时效的延长或延后规定了具体适用的场景。

第四，内地与香港特区最长诉讼时效期间不同。内地法律对最长诉讼时效期间作出了普遍适用的规定，而香港特区则未作此类普遍适用的规定。

结　　语

法治是最好的营商环境。作为与商事主体经营活动最密切的法律制度，民间借贷的法律规定既是规范资金融通行为的指引，也是保护出借人和借款人合法权益的盾牌。本书以内地与香港特区民间借贷利率司法保护限额、本金和利息计算、职业放贷人认定、夫妻债务制度等八个关键主题为“小切口”，通过比较研究内地与香港特区的法律可以看出，两地在尊重意思自治、维护商事正义等方面秉持共同的理念，商事法律规则衔接具有深厚而坚实的基础。这不仅为探索大湾区规则衔接有益路径奠定了基础，更为未来进一步深化规则衔接树立了强有力的信心。

粤港澳大湾区法律规则衔接不是一蹴而就的任务，需要结合司法实践的需求、法律规则的修改不断更新、探索。本书以涉港商事审判中集中凸显的民间借贷类纠纷为研究对象，在法律理论和司法实践中综合展示法律规则的异同点，初步探索出一条可行的商事实体规则衔接路径，为后续的规则衔接积累方法和经验。接下来，前海法院将持续坚守“一国”之本、善用“两制”之利，立足商事审判实践，拓展跨境法律规则比较研究的深度与广度，为跨境投资者提供更全面、详实的法律规则衔接指南，推动内地与香港特区商事法律规则的“软联通”，促进内地与香港特区经济发展的“深融合”，为国家推进粤港澳一体化高质量发展贡献前海法院力量。

最后，特别感谢陈庆辉大律师、周立新大律师在本书编撰过程中提供的协助；同时特别感谢研修生齐颖、虞玉娟对本书翻译提供的协助。

Chapter I

Comparison of Relevant Concepts of Private Lending

Section One Laws in the Chinese Mainland

"Private lending" was originally not a legal concept but a conventional term. It is generally distinguished from loans provided by financial institutions, and broadly refers to lending activities carried out by non-financial institutions without the supervision and regulation of financial regulatory authorities. Some foreign jurisdictions adopt the concept of "informal finance".

In the Chinese Mainland, private lending initially referred to loans between neighbours, fellow-villagers, colleagues, friends, relatives and other related people based on kinship, geographic connections or friendships. With the increase in the diversity and scope of private lending participants, the meaning of private lending has continuously evolved with the social and economic development. The participants of private lending have gradually expanded to a large number of guarantee companies, rotating savings and credit association (ROSCA), pawnshops, investment companies, micro-credit companies, financial consulting companies and other corporate or unincorporated organisations. There are also a significant number of illegal lending entities, such as illegal private banks or professional lenders with gangland backgrounds. With the rapid growth in the volume of private lending, it has become necessary to further address and regulate legal issues associated with private lending.

In 1991, the Supreme People's Court of the People's Republic of China (hereinafter referred to as the Supreme People's Court) first defined "private lending" as a legal concept through judicial interpretation in Article 6 of the *Several Opinions on the People's Courts Trial of Lending Cases* (now repealed). This marked the beginning of the gradual incorporation of private lending into legal regulations. As the level of social and economic development gradually increased and the private lending market became increasingly active, the number of private lending cases ranked on top of all civil cases for the first time in 2015. Problems and questions arising out of private lending cases are mostly reported by courts at all levels. To unify the standard for adjudication, the Supreme People's Court issued the *Judicial Interpretations on Private Lending* in 2015, which was subsequently amended twice, on August 18, 2020 and December 23, 2020. For the purpose of this comparison, the intension and extension of the concept of "private lending" need to be clarified first.

I. Types of Loan Contracts

The *Civil Code*, in the second sub-part of Part III (Contracts), contains specific provisions on loan contracts among the named contracts. Article 667 of the *Civil Code* stipulates: "A loan contract is a contract under which a borrower borrows a loan from a lender and repays the loan with interests when the loan becomes due." In practice, there are many types of loan contracts. The *Provisions of the Supreme People's Court on the Causes of Action in Civil Cases* classifies loan contract disputes as a third-level cause of action, which includes financial loan contract disputes, interbank lending disputes, private lending disputes, small loan contract disputes, contract disputes over transfer of distressed financial claims, and disputes over recovery of distressed financial claims. In addition, bank card disputes, which are also classified as a third-level cause of action, possess the attributes of loan contract disputes. Therefore, it is evident that private lending contracts are just one type of loan contracts.

The types of loan contracts are complex and while different ones apply different legal provisions. In judicial practice, they are generally divided into financial institution loans and non-financial institution loans depending on whether the lender is a legally registered financial institution. Financial institution loans can be further subdivided into banking financial institution loans and non-banking financial institution loans.

i. Financial Institution Loans

According to Paragraph 2 of Article 2 of the *Measure for Punishment of Illegal Financial Acts*, the term "financial institution" refers to the institutions that are legally established and engage in the finance business within the territory of the People's Republic of China, including banks, credit cooperatives, financial companies, trust and investment companies, lease financing companies, etc. Financial Institutions include all financial institutions approved and supervised by financial regulatory authorities, and may involve loan business in their financial activities.

1. Banking Financial Institution

According to Paragraphs 2 and 3 of Article 2 of the *Banking Supervision Law of the People's Republic of China* and Paragraph 1 of Article 3 of the *Measures for the Administration of Combating Money Laundering and Financing of Terrorism by Banking Financial Institutions*, banking financial institution refers to commercial banks, rural credit cooperatives and other financial institutions, policy banks and the China Development Bank established within the territory of the People's Republic of China and engage in taking in deposits from the general public. The main difference between banking financial institutions and non-banking financial institutions is whether the financial institution can engage in both public deposit-taking and lending activities.

2. Non-banking Financial Institution

Non-banking financial institution refers to all financial institutions other than the central bank, commercial banks and specialised banks, mainly including institutions such as public funds, private funds, trusts, securities, insurance, financial leasing, and finance companies, among others. However, the scope of non-banking financial institutions in China is subject to certain limitations.

The *Opinions of the CPC Central Committee and the State Council on Ser-*

ving the Real Economy, and Preventing and Controlling Financial Risk, and Deepening Financial Reforms (No. 23 [2017], CPC Central Committee) clarified that seven types of local financial institutions, approved by local financial regulatory authorities, including micro-credit companies, financing guarantee companies, regional equity markets, pawnshops, financial leasing companies, commercial factoring companies, and local asset management companies, shall be regulated by rules formulated by the central financial regulatory authorities and supervised by local financial regulatory authorities. The *Opinions of the General Office of the State Council on Fully Advancing the Work of Consolidated Financial Statistics* (No. 18 [2018] of the General Office of the State Council) also included the above seven types of local financial institutions into the scope of consolidated financial statistics. The above seven types of local financial institutions approved by local financial regulatory authorities are also classified as non-banking financial institutions.

ii. Non-Financial Institution Loans

Non-financial institution loans mainly refer to the financial transactions among natural persons, legal persons and unincorporated organisations in various fields of the society. These loans are private financing activities in which the lending entities are not established with the approval of central or local financial regulatory authorities, and the lending activities are not subject to financial supervision. In a situation where market participants cannot obtain financial services from formal financial institutions, a large amount of private capital, driven by profit, floods into the financial market as a supplement. This gives rise to non-financial institution loans, filling the gap where formal financial services are unavailable. Although non-financial institution loans have, to some extent, promoted economic development, their profit-driven nature has also led to negative results such as usury and trap loan.

II. Statutory Definition of Private Lending

Article 1 of the *Provisions on Private Lending* explicitly defines the legal concept of private lending. From the perspective of legislative technique, it adopts an approach of explicit definition with excluded exceptions. The legal concept of private lending provides guidance for the accurate application of the *Provisions on Private Lending* in judicial practice, and clarifies the judicial rules for the courts to follow when hearing cases.

i. Non-Financial Institution Loans Are Generally Private Lending

Article 1 of the *Provisions of Private Lending* expressly provides that "private lending as referred to in these regulations refers to the act of financing between natural persons, legal persons and unincorporated organisations". Considering the legislative background, private lending primarily refers to the process of private capital circulating in various social fields, unregistered with official financial authorities and operating outside the scope of financial regulation. This type of financial transactions is unofficial and unregulated, embodying typical private characteristics.[1] In judicial practice, it is widely recognised that non-financial institution loans are a typical form of private lending.

ii. Financial Institution Loans May Also Be Private Lending

It is important to highlight that a common misconception in legal practice is to equate private lending solely with non-financial institution loans. Paragraph 2 of Article 1 of the *Provisions on Private Lending* clearly stipulates that "financial institutions and their branches engaged in loan business approved by finan-

---

[1] See the First Civil Division of the Supreme People's Court, *The Supreme People's Court Understanding and Application of New Judicial Interpretation on Private Lending*, People's Court Press, 2021, p. 48.

cial regulatory authorities are not subject to these regulations for disputes arising from the granting of loans and other related financial businesses". Whether a loan from a financial institution is private lending depends on whether the lender financial institution is approved by financial regulatory authorities to engage in loan business.

1. Loans Issued Legally by Banking Financial Institutions Are Not Private Lending

Disputes arising from the loan business conducted by banking financial institutions are called "financial loan contract disputes". The primary difference between these and private lending disputes is that the business scope of banking financial institutions includes the loan business authorised by the financial regulatory authorities, meaning that they as lenders can regularly engage in loan activities, or even take it as their main business. Loan business for the purpose of doing business is highly regulated and requires administrative licensing by the financial regulatory authorities. Only specific financial institutions possessing financial licences are permitted to conduct such business. If a non-financial institution conducts loan business without necessary licences, it will be deemed as engaging in "illegal financial business activities", rendering the loan contract invalid and potentially leading to criminal liability for illegal business operations.

2. Loan Business Conducted Legally by Non-Banking Financial Institutions Needs to Be Treated Differently

Due to the respective operations and differentiated supervision of the financial industry, institutions authorised by the China Banking and Insurance Regulatory Commission (CBIRC) to engage in securities, insurance or their derivative businesses—such as securities companies, insurance companies, futures companies, publicly offered funds, and private funds—generally do not have permission to conduct loan business. Except for specific cases, such as capital and securities lending by securities companies or policy mortgage loans by insurance companies, lending activities conducted by the aforementioned financial institutions should be regarded as private lending. Lending activities conducted by trust companies, finance companies of enterprise groups, financial leasing companies, auto finance companies, currency brokerage companies, and consumer finance companies, established with the CBIRC's approval and within their business scope, are considered financial loans; otherwise, they are deemed private lending.

Notably, non-banking financial institutions include local financial institutions supervised by local financial regulatory authorities, such as micro-credit companies, financing guarantee companies, regional equity markets, pawnshops, financial leasing companies, commercial factoring companies, and local asset management companies. Among these seven entities, micro-credit companies and pawnshops normally engage in loan business; while financing guarantee companies, commercial factoring companies, financial leasing companies, local asset management companies, and regional equity markets may also provide financing services. Disputes arising from the loan business conducted by the above seven local financial institutions are not considered disputes over private lending[1].

Section Two Laws in Hong Kong

There is no specific legal concept of private lending in Hong Kong laws. Lending policies in Hong Kong have been changing along with its financial policies, progressing from laissez-faire to positive non-interventionism, minimal intervention, and currently, a "prudent intervention" policy. The regulation of

---

[1] See the *Official Reply of the Supreme People's Court on the Scope of Application of New Judicial Interpretations on Private Lending*, Interpretation No. 27 [2020] of the Supreme People's Court.

"loans" in Hong Kong is mainly included in the *Money Lenders Ordinance* and its related judicial precedents. The current *Money Lenders Ordinance* was issued and came into force in 1980. It aims to "provide for the control and regulation of money lenders and money-lending transactions, the licensing of persons carrying on business as money lenders, and to provide protection and relief against excessive interest rates and extortionate stipulations in respect of loans". Lending activities in Hong Kong generally include the following three categories.

I. Lending by Money Lenders

The *Money Lenders Ordinance* primarily regulates the lending activities of money lenders. A money lender is defined as "every person whose business (whether or not he carries on any other business) is that of making loans or who advertises or announces himself or holds himself out in any way as carrying on that business". As of December 31, 2019, there are more than 2,300 licensed money lenders in Hong Kong, providing alternative financing channels for individuals and companies.

In order to prevent money lenders from engaging in high-interest, illegal lending activities that harm borrowers' interests, the *Money Lenders Ordinance* imposes very strict supervision on money lenders. In addition to the maximum interest rate requirement that applies to all loans, there are strict and detailed regulations regarding the money lender's licence application, the form of a loan agreement, the location of signing, and the content of illegal agreements, etc.

i. Application for a Money Lender's Licence

According to Section 9, 10 and related provisions of the *Money Lenders Ordinance*, companies and individuals aged 21 or above can apply for a money lender licence. Copies of application for a money lender licence must be submitted to both the Registrar and the Commissioner of Police of Hong Kong. The Commissioner of Police may cause an investigation to be carried out in respect of the relevant application to determine whether there are grounds for objecting to the application. Within a certain period after receiving the application, the Registrar shall lodge the application with the Licensing Court, which will hear and determine the application. After the hearing, the Licensing Court may decide to issue or refuse to issue the licence. Once issued, the licence is valid for 12 months, and the licensee may apply for the renewal of his licence within a period of 3 months prior to the expiration.

ii. Location of Money Lending

According to Section 7 of the *Money Lenders Ordinance*, no person shall carry on business as a money lender at any place other than the premises specified in such licence. Additionally, according to Section 29 of the *Money Lenders Ordinance*, any person who carries on business as a money lender at any place other than the premises specified in his licence commits an offence.

iii. Form of Money Lending Agreement

According to Section 18 of the *Money Lenders Ordinance*, no agreement for the repayment of money lent by a money lender or for the payment of interest on money so lent, and no security given to any money lender in respect of any such agreement or loan, shall be enforceable, unless within 7 days after the making of the agreement, a note or memorandum in writing of the agreement is made in accordance with the *Money lenders Ordinance* and signed personally by the borrower, and a copy of such note or memorandum is given to the borrower at the time of signing. The borrower is thus entitled to a written agreement outlining all loan elements.

iv. Content of Agreement by Money Lender

(1) Section 21 and 22 of the *Money Lenders Ordinance* provide that money lenders must allow borrowers to repay their loans early or in instalments.

(2) Section 22 of the *Money Lenders Ordinance* prohibits the payment of compound interest, and the rate or amount of interest being increased by reason of any default in the payment of sums due under the agreement. (3) Section 27 of the *Money Lenders Ordinance* states that it is illegal for a money lender to require a borrower to bear costs, charges or expenses incidental to or relating to the negotiations for or the granting of the loan, and it shall not be lawful for any money lender or his employer or agent to demand or receive any remuneration or reward whatsoever from a borrower. (4) Section 12 of *Money Lenders Regulations* provides that no money lender shall demand or accept as security for any loan any of the following: (i) identity card, passport or other document establishing the identity or nationality of the holder; (ii) bank savings or deposit account book; or (iii) a photograph (whether developed or not) of the borrower or surety or of any member of the family of the borrower or surety.

v. Restriction on Money-Lending Advertisements

Section 26 of the *Money Lenders Ordinance* provides that advertisements issued or published for money lending business must clearly show the words "Money Lender's Licence No." immediately followed by the number of the licence of the money lender. If the advertisement mentioned loan interest, it shall be expressed as a rate per cent per annum. Also, the name of the money lender and the loan interest rate must be mentioned in a conspicuous manner.

vi. Maximum Interest Rates for Loans by Money Lenders

Section 24 of the *Money Lenders Ordinance* provides that any person who lends or offers to lend money at an effective rate of interest which exceeds 48 per cent per annum commits an offence. If convicted, the maximum penalty is a fine of HK $ 5,000,000 and imprisonment for ten years.[1] Section 25(3) of the *Money Lenders Ordinance* also stipulates that a money lender who lends in excess of the effective interest rate of 36 per cent per annum is presumed to be extortionate and the court has the power to reopen the transaction. It is important to emphasise that, under Sections 24 and 25 of the *Money Lenders Ordinance*, the limits on effective interest rates apply to all types of lending, regardless of whether the lender is a money lender.

vii. Duty of Money Lender to Give Information to Borrower And Surety

According to Section 19 and 20 of the *Money Lenders Ordinance*, a money lender shall, on demand in writing by the borrower, supply to the borrower a statement, showing information including but not limited to the amount of the principal of the loan, the rate per cent per annum of interest charged, the amount of any payment already received by the money lender, the amount of every sum not yet paid and the date on which it became or will become due. If the loan includes a guarantee agreement, the money lender shall also supply the above statement on demand in writing by the surety.

II. Exempted Persons

The lending activities carried out by specific entities listed in Part 1 of Schedule 1 of the *Money Lenders Ordinance* are not governed by the Ordinance. These lending entities often have unique characteristics in terms of lending activities, target borrowers, and lending frequency, distinguishing them

---

[1] The *Money Lenders Ordinance* was formally amended on October 26, 2022, and came into force on December 30, 2022, as amended. The pre-amendment standard of sentencing for excessive interest rates was 60 per annum under the Ordinance, and the presumptive standard for extortionate trading was 48 per annum. The cases cited herein all apply the interest rates set forth in the pre-amendment *Money Lenders Ordinance*.

from typical money lenders. Instead, they are regulated by specialised laws or industry norms. For instance, banks and deposit-taking companies regulated by the *Hong Kong Monetary Authority under the Banking Ordinance* (Cap. 155), must comply with that ordinance and the *Code of Banking Practice*. Part 1 of Schedule 1 specifies the following entities whose lending activities are exempted.

1. Any subsidiary of an authorised institution within the meaning of the *Banking Ordinance* (Cap. 155).

2. A co-operative society registered under the *Co-operative Societies Ordinance* (Cap. 33).

3. A credit union registered under the *Credit Unions Ordinance* (Cap. 119) and the Credit Union League of Hong Kong incorporated under Part XI of that Ordinance.

4. A trade union registered under the *Trade Unions Ordinance* (Cap. 332).

5. An insurer, within the meaning of the *Insurance Ordinance* (Cap. 41), authorized under that Ordinance to carry on a class, or classes, of insurance business specified in Part 2 of Schedule 1 to that Ordinance. (Amended 12 of 2015 s. 107)

6. (Repealed L. N. 140 of 1991)

7. The University Grants Committee. (Amended L. N. 35 of 1995)

8. A bank which is—

(a) incorporated or established outside Hong Kong;

(b) recognised as a bank by the relevant banking supervisory authority within the meaning of section 2(9) of the *Banking Ordinance* (Cap. 155) which has been declared in writing by the Monetary Authority appointed under section 5A of the *Exchange Fund Ordinance* (Cap. 66) to be a banking supervisory authority in respect of which he is of the opinion that it exercises adequate prudential supervision for the purposes of this paragraph; and

(c) carrying on banking business in the place where that banking supervisory authority is located. (Replaced 49 of 1995 s. 53)

9. An organisation—

(a) which is a member of the International Union of Credit and Investment Insurers ("The Berne Union"); or

(b) in respect of which the Registrar has declared in writing that he is satisfied that it was established by one or more national governments with the object of financing, or guaranteeing the financing of, the export of a country's goods or services.

10. A corporation licensed to carry on a business in securities margin financing under Part V of the *Securities and Futures Ordinance* (Cap. 571). (Replaced 5 of 2002 s. 407)

11. A corporation licensed to carry on, or an authorised financial institution registered for carrying on, a business in dealing in securities under Part V of the *Securities and Futures Ordinance* (Cap. 571) who engages in securities margin financing in order to facilitate acquisitions or holdings of securities by the corporation or institution for its client. (Replaced 5 of 2002 s. 407)

III. Exempted Loans

Part 2 of Schedule 1 of the *Money Lenders Ordinance* classifies loans based on their types and specifies that the following types of loans are exempted. The loans made by the said exempted persons and exempted loans are not subject to the requirements of the *Money Lenders Ordinance*, including obtaining a money lender's licence, operating under the conditions specified in the licence, and specific form of agreement.

1. A loan made bona fide by an employer to his employee.

2. A loan made to a company secured by a mortgage, charge, lien or other encumbrance—

(a) registered, or to be registered, under the *Companies Ordinance* (Cap. 622); (Replaced 28 of 2012 ss. 912 & 920); (ab) registered, or to be registered, under a provision of the *Companies Ordinance* (Cap. 32) as in force from time to time before the commencement date of Section 2 of Schedule 9 to the *Companies Ordinance* (Cap. 622), having a continuing effect under the Schedule 11 to the *Companies Ordinance* (Cap. 622). (Added 28 of 2012 ss. 912 &920); (ac) registered under a former Companies Ordinance as defined by the section 2 (1) of the *Companies Ordinance* (Cap 622.); (Added 28 of 2012 ss. 912 & 920); (b) which would, in the case of a company referred to in paragraph (b) or (c) of the definition of company in section 2(1) —— (Amended 28 of 2012 ss. 912 &920). (i) where the mortgage, charge, lien or encumbrance was created before the commencement date (Mach 3, 2014) of section 2 of Schedule 9 to the *Companies Ordinance* (Cap. 622), be able to be registered under a former Companies Ordinance as defined by section 2(1) of the *Companies Ordinance* (Cap. 622) if the company were incorporated under that former Companies Ordinance; or (ii) where the mortgage, charge, lien or encumbrance is created on or after that commencement date (Mach 3, 2014), be able to be registered under the *Companies Ordinance* if the company were incorporated under that Ordinance (Cap. 622). (Amended 28 of 2012 ss. 912 &920).

3. A loan made by a company under a bona fide credit-card plan scheme operated by the company to any holder of a credit-card issued under that scheme.

4. A loan made bona fide for the purchase of immovable property on the security of a mortgage of that property, and a loan made bona fide to refinance such a mortgage.

5. A loan made by a company, or a firm or individual whose ordinary business does not primarily or mainly involve the lending of money, in the ordinary course of that business.

6. A loan made by a licensed pawnbroker under the *Pawnbrokers Ordinance* (Cap. 166), being a loan to which that Ordinance applies.

7. A loan made by any statutory body under any power conferred by law in that behalf.

8. A loan made from—a fund established by resolution of the Legislative Council or by or under an ordinance; (Amended 23 of 1999 ss. 3); any superannuation or provident fund.

9. A loan made by any chit-fund operated under the *Chit-Fund Business (Prohibition) Ordinance* (Cap. 262).

10. (a) A loan made by a holding company to its subsidiary, or by a subsidiary to its holding company or to another subsidiary a subsidiary company of the same of holding company. (b) Sections 13, 14 and 15 of the *Companies Ordinance* (Cap. 622) shall apply to the interpretation of this paragraph as it applies to the interpretation of that ordinance. (Amended 28 of 2012 xx. 912 &920)

11. A loan made to a company where the loan —

(a) forms part of a transaction involving the export from, or the import into, Hong Kong of goods or services; and (b) is for the purpose of facilitating that import or export, as the case may be, of the goods or services.

12. (a) A loan made to a company that has a paid up share capital of not less than $1,000,000 or an equivalent amount in any other approved currency. (b) For the purpose of this paragraph, approved currency means a currency—(i) freely convertible into Hong Kong dollars; or (ii) approved in writing by the Registrar for the purposes of this paragraph.

13. A loan upon terms involving the issue by a company of debentures or other securities in respect of which a prospectus has been registered under the *Companies (Winding Up and Miscellaneous Provisions) Ordinance* (Cap. 32). (Amended 28 of 2012 ss. 912 &920)

14. A loan made to a company the shares or debentures of which are listed on—(a) a recognised stock market as defined in the Section 1 of Part 1 of Schedule 1 to the *Securities and Futures Ordinance* (Cap 571); or (Replaced 5 of 2002 s. 407); (b) any other stock market declared in writing, by the Securities and Futures Commission referred to in the Section 3 (1) of the *Securities and Futures Ordinance* (Cap. 571) to be approved for the purpose of this paragraph. (Amen-

ded 10 of 1989 s. 65; 5 of 2002 s. 407)

15. A loan made to the subsidiary of the company referred to in paragraph 14. (Replaced 69 of 1988 s. 33)

Section Three Defining the Comparative Scope of Private Lending Cases

Due to the significant differences in legislative frameworks, legal systems, and legal cultures between the Chinese Mainland and Hong Kong, the concept of "private lending" in the Chinese Mainland laws finds no exact counterpart in Hong Kong laws. However, upon comparing the regulations in the *Provisions on Private Lending* and the *Money Lenders Ordinance*, there are some overlaps between the concept of "private lending" in the Chinese Mainland and certain exempted loans listed in the *Money Lenders Ordinance*.

I. Similarities Between the Concepts

Firstly, there is a significant overlap between the ranges of micro-credit companies in the Chinese Mainland and money lenders in Hong Kong. From the perspective of lenders, private lending in the Chinese Mainland is completely different from the lending activities by money lenders under Hong Kong laws. Money lenders in Hong Kong and micro-credit companies approved by local financial regulatory authorities in the Chinese Mainland share considerable similarities in their statutory definitions. They both are legal entities established through statutory procedures, specifically authorised to engage in loan business, and are subject to the supervision and management of the approving authorities. However, micro-credit companies in the Chinese Mainland are legal persons while natural persons are not allowed to acquire licences for loan business in the Chinese Mainland. Whereas in Hong Kong, it is possible for a natural person to apply for a money lenders licence.

Secondly, there is an overlap between the concept of "private lending" in the Chinese Mainland and the loans listed in Schedule 1 ("Exempted Persons" and "Exempted Loans") of the *Money Lenders Ordinance*, especially Section 5 of Part 2 in Schedule 1. To extract the maximum overlap in legal concepts, the following two provisions in the legislation need to be noted: (1) Article 1 of the *Provisions on Private Lending* provides that, for the purpose of this Provisions, "private lending" means the act of financing among natural persons, legal persons and unincorporated organisations. (2) Section 5 of Part 2 "Exempted Loans" in Schedule 1 of the *Money Lenders Ordinance* provides that, a loan made by a company, or a firm or individual whose ordinary business does not primarily or mainly involve the lending of money, in the ordinary course of that business. The above provisions indicate that the concept of "private lending" in the Chinese Mainland and the exemption in Section 5 of Part 2 in Schedule 1 of the *Money Lenders Ordinance* both refer to incidental lending activities by individuals, companies, or other organisations that do not primarily engage in lending as their main business. However, it is important to note that the loans referred to in Section 5 of Part 2 in Schedule 1 of the *Money Lenders Ordinance* only overlap with part of the concept of "private lending" in the Chinese Mainland, not the entirety.

II. Scope of Comparison in This Book

By comparing the rules of lending in both jurisdictions, it is evident that the scope of "private lending" in the Chinese Mainland overlaps with not only the loans defined in Section 5 of Part 2 in Schedule 1 of the *Money Lenders Ordinance*, but also some lending activities listed in other parts of Schedule 1. This book aims to address the rules on general issues in loan contracts between the Chinese Mainland and Hong Kong, but not the special circumstances in exceptional cases, so as to ensure that the fruit of the comparison is practical and instructive. Statistics of the judicial practice shows that most private lending cases involve occasional lending activities by individuals, companies, or other organisations that do not primarily engage in lending as their main business. Therefore, the comparison in this book is mainly between the private lending in the Chinese Mainland and the loans defined in Section 5 of Part 2 in Schedule 1 of the *Money Lenders Ordinance*.

It should be noted that this comparison of private lending contracts between the Chinese Mainland and Hong Kong involves rules from two different legal systems, which makes it impossible to be completely unified in the use of legal terminologies. Therefore, the issues compared and the compilation of this book are based on the legal elements defined by the laws and regulations in the Chinese Mainland. The language style of this book mainly follows the legal language style of the Chinese Mainland.

Chapter Ⅱ

Comparison of Legal Rules on Professional Money Lenders

Section One　Criteria for Determination of Professional Money Lenders

I. Judicial Practices in the Chinese Mainland

i. Background

The restriction on private lending has been continuously released with the rapid development of economy and the deepening of reform and opening-up policy. However, the laws in the Chinese Mainland have been consistently opposed to the practice of professional money lending.

When the Supreme People's Court enacted the *Provisions on Private Lending Cases* in 2015, no article regarding the regulation of the conduct of professional money lending was drafted and included for the following reasons. Firstly, it was considerably difficult to determine the conduct of professional money lending in adjudication practices due to the disparity in economic development in different regions, resulting in different rulings on this issue. Secondly, the People's Bank of China had drafted the *Money Lenders Regulation* which provided that money lenders including natural persons and legal persons shall carry on specific types of business pursuant to their licences, and that various supervision requirements on money lenders were established according to interest rates, the classes of borrowers, the purposes of loans and so forth. However, since the completion of the draft, the *Money Lenders Regulation* has not been officially enacted and the activities of professional money lending has become increasingly prevalent, which caused severe disruptions in economic, financial and social stability. As a result, the call within the judicial field for regulating and controlling the conduct of professional money lending becomes increasingly urgent.

ii. Exploration at the National and Local Levels

1. Regulations at the National Level

National authorities including the Supreme People's Procuratorate of the People's Republic of China (hereinafter referred to as the Supreme People's Procuratorate) and the Supreme People's Court have explored the approaches to better regulate the conduct of professional money lending in terms of criminal law and civil law so as to curb the chaos in private lending practice and deter illegal money lending business.

In respect of criminal law, the Supreme People's Procuratorate, the Supreme People's Court, the Ministry of Public Security and the Ministry of Justice collaboratively formulated the *Opinion on Several Issues concerning the Handling of Criminal Cases of Illegal Money Lending*. Article 1 of the Opinion provides: "whoever, in violation of state stipulations and without the approval of supervision authorities, or exceeding the permitted scope of business, regularly provides loans to nonspecific persons with the purpose of profit-making, thereby disrupting the stability of financial market and if the circumstances are serious, is to be convicted and punished in accordance with Item (4) of Article 225 of the *Criminal Law of the People's Republic of China*. The term of 'regularly provides loans to nonspecific persons' as mentioned in the preceding paragraph means that lending money to all and sundry including natural persons and legal persons under the guise of personal loans or otherwise more than 10 times within 2 years, and that if the loan due is to be extended, such loan shall be treated as one loan only." As this opinion regulates the conduct of professional money lending from the perspective of criminal law, the standard for determination of professional money lenders is formulated in a strict manner which can provide useful reference for civil regulation of professional money lenders.

In respect of civil law, the *Conference Minutes* issued by the Supreme People's Court in November 2019 specified the legal effect of professional money lending conducts for the first time. Article 53 of the *Conference Minutes* provides: "Private lending by legal persons, who do not obtain the qualification of money lending according to the laws, and by unincorporated organisations or natural persons engaged in private lending, shall be determined invalid in accordance with the laws. A lender who repeatedly engages in remunerative private lending for a certain period may generally be determined as a professional money lender. High people's courts in regions where private lending is relatively active or intermediate people's courts authorised by them may develop specific determination standards according to local actual circumstances." On the one hand, this article expressly stipulates the scope of professional money lenders, including not only natural persons but also legal persons and unincorporated organisations. One the other hand, this article defines the conduct of professional money lending as a lender obtaining profits by means of repeatedly lending funds to others within a certain period of time. Nevertheless, the Supreme People's Court did not specify clear and concrete criteria for determination of professional money lenders and no article was laid down regarding the period of occurrence of private lending conducts, the numbers of loans made within the relevant period and so forth. Instead, the Supreme People's Court delegated the lower courts to set out criteria for determination of professional money lenders.

2. Regulations at the Local Level

As authorised by the Supreme People's Court, the courts at all levels can formulate specific criteria for determination of professional money lenders in accordance with the judicial practices of private lending and the level of economic development in local areas. While some courts set out criminal and civil standards respectively in ascertaining professional money lenders, other courts formulate consolidated criteria to regulate the conducts of professional money lending. The following briefly illustrates how certain courts determine the issue of whether a lender is a professional money lender or not.

(1) The High People's Court of Zhejiang Province, the People's Procura-

torate of Zhejiang, Zhejiang Provincial Department of Public Security, Zhejiang Provincial Department of Justice, Zhejiang Provincial Tax Service of State Taxation Administration and Zhejiang Provincial Administration for Financial Regulation jointly formulated the *Minutes on Cracking Down Criminal Offences and Facilitating Cooperation in Management of Private Lending*. Article 2 of this Minutes provides: In response to chaotic status quo of professional money lending business, the courts should establish a directory of professional money lenders in line with the number of private lending cases involving the same plaintiff or an affiliated plaintiff over a period of time, the interest rates, the degree of formatting of loan contracts and the actual circumstances. The court should supervise professional money lenders on this directory and quarterly report to the police and procuratorial authorities. The lenders listed on the directory should satisfy either of the following requirements: ①Based on the number of cases filed and closed in three consecutive years, the same plaintiff or an affiliated plaintiff is involved in more than 20 cases (including pre-trial mediation hereinafter) in one primary court or more than 30 cases in one intermediate court and/or in multiple primary courts within its jurisdiction. ②In the same year, the same plaintiff or an affiliated plaintiff is involved in more than 10 cases in one primary court, or more than 15 cases in one intermediate court and/or in multiple primary courts within its jurisdiction. ③In the same year, the same plaintiff or an affiliated plaintiff is involved in more than 5 cases in one intermediate court and/or in multiple primary courts within its jurisdiction while the total accumulated amount exceeds ¥1 million; or is involved in more than 3 cases while the total accumulated amount exceeds ¥10 million. ④The lender may be determined as a money lender if the number of cases reaches more than half of the number stipulated in aforementioned requirement ① or ②, and two or more of the following conditions are satisfied: (a) the IOU adopts standard form; (b) the defendant raises a defence that the plaintiff is not the de facto lender, or that the plaintiff requires the defendant to pay the principal and interest to a third party; (c) the principal of the loan is claimed to be paid by cash without other evidence to support; (d) the interest is retained in the delivery of the principal, or the effective interest paid by the defendant is significantly higher than the agreed interest; (e) the plaintiff defaults without a good reason or the plaintiff appears but makes a false statement before the court.

(2) The High People's Court of Jiangsu Province formulated the *Opinion on Establishment of Directory System of Suspected Money Lenders* (*Trial*). Article 2 of this Opinion provides: Primary courts should establish a directory of suspected professional money lenders based on their actual situations. The first step taken in the trial of private lending cases is to carry out a related-case enquiry. If a lender or a related party under his control, either acting as the plaintiff, is involved in more than 5 cases in courts at all levels in the province within one year, the lender should be included in the directory of suspected professional money lenders. If a lender is determined as a professional money lender in the court hearing or by any other means, the aforementioned limit on the number of cases will not be applied.

(3) The High People's Court of Tianjin Municipality formulated the *Guidance of Hearing Private Lending Cases* (*Trial*). Article 21 of the Guidance provides: If a lender does not legally obtain the qualification for money lending and repeatedly engages in private lending activities for profit over a certain period, the lender's conduct can be determined as professional money lending conduct. The private lending contracts concluded as a result of professional money lending conducts are void. Professional money lending conduct has the nature of business and profit-making. In the trial of private lending cases, the court can determine whether a lender runs the business of money lending by comprehensively considering the factors such as the number of loans made over a certain period of time, the number of private lending cases brought by the same plaintiff or an affiliated plaintiff over a period of time, the degree of formatting of loan contracts, whether the lender has publicly promoted, advertised, or ex-

plicitly expressed the willingness to lend, the amount of the loan and the interest rates. If the same plaintiff or an affiliated plaintiff initiates more than 5 private lending cases in courts at all levels, or a lender lends money to nonspecific borrowers for more than 3 times within the period of two years, the lender's conduct may be regarded as running business. If a loan contract includes provisions on interests, service fees, consultancy fees, administration fees and liquidated damages, or if the borrowers have already paid the aforementioned fees, the lender's conduct should be deemed profit-making. If a lender runs main business or day-to-day business not involving money lending business and just occasionally lends money, or if a lender lends money for maintenance of personal relationships instead of making profits, the lender's conduct should not be determined as professional money lending.

(4) The High People's Court of Henan Province formulated the *Guidance on Strengthening the Examination of Money Lenders (Trial)*. Article 2 of the Guidance provides: The legal persons, unincorporated organisations and natural persons, who frequently engage in professional money lending activities or activities similar to money lending over a period of time without approval of authorities, should be deemed as professional money lenders. If a lender, despite initiating proceedings independently, has some relationship with other lenders, and his or her conduct satisfies the above characteristics of professional money lending, the lender should be deemed as a professional money lender as well.

(5) The High People's Court of Guangxi Zhuang Autonomous Region formulated the *Guidance on Trial of Civil and Commercial Cases During the Covid-19 Pandemic*. Item 3 of Article 8 provides: The courts should devote more efforts to scrutinise professional money lending conducts. In principle, if a lender who has no qualification for money lending lends funds to nonspecific borrowers (including legal persons and natural persons) for more than 10 times within 2 years under the guise of personal loans or otherwise, the lender's conduct may be determined as professional money lending. The private lending contracts

concluded as a result of professional money lending conducts are void. The borrower should return the principal and pay the interests for possession (calculated on the basis of annual loan prime rate released by the National Interbank Funding Centre).

(6) The High People's Court of Xinjiang Uygur Autonomous Region formulated the *Guidance on Strengthening the Examination of Money Lenders (Trial)*. Article 4 of the Guidance provides: The lenders listed in the directory of professional money lenders should satisfy the following conditions: ①In the same year, the same lender and the related party under his control are involved as plaintiffs in more than 6 private lending cases in the same primary court, or more than 6 private lending cases in the same intermediate court and/or in multiple primary courts within its jurisdiction. ②In two consecutive years, the same lender and the related party under his control are involved as plaintiffs in more than 10 private lending cases in the same primary court, or more than 10 private lending cases in the same intermediate court and/or in multiple primary courts within its jurisdiction. The aforesaid private lending cases include applications for enforcement of arbitral awards, notarised instrument of debt cases and pre-trial mediation cases.

Some provincial and municipal courts have also conducted relevant research on the criteria for determination of professional money lending conducts. For instance, a joint research group established by the Second Civil Division of the High People's Court of Beijing Municipality and the Third Civil Division of the First Intermediate People's Court of Beijing Municipality collected the opinions from courts at all levels in Beijing regarding their inclination of rulings in private lending cases and summarised the following criteria: ①Based on the number of cases filed and closed over three consecutive years, the lender is involved in more than 10 cases in the same court, or is involved in more than 20 cases in courts at all levels in Beijing. ②Within the same year, the lender is involved in more than 5 cases in the same court, or is involved in more than 10 cases in courts at all levels in Beijing. ③Within the same year, the lender is involved in more than 3 cases where the total amount of money accumulated exceeds ¥15 million in the same court, or is involved in more than 6 cases where the total amount of money accumulated exceeds ¥30 million in courts at all levels.[1]

iii. Escalating to National Laws

In August and December 2020, inheriting the previous judicial interpretations and judicial policy documents on professional money lenders, the Supreme People's Court amended the *Provisions on Private Lending Cases* twice. Item 3 of Article 13 provides that in the circumstance where a lender that has not obtained lending qualification in accordance with the laws provides a loan to unspecific borrowers in the society for profit-making purpose, the court shall determine the private lending contract as null and void. The amended *Provisions on Private Lending Cases* defines the conduct of professional money lending through the form of judicial interpretation for the first time and explicitly stipulates that professional money lending contracts are null and void. However, the amended *Provisions on Private Lending Cases* did not cover the specific criteria for determination of professional money lenders and did not set out consolidated criteria to approach this issue.

iv. The Factors for Determining Professional Money Lenders in the Chinese Mainland

By reference to related judicial interpretations and local judicial documents, a professional money lender means a lender who does not obtain legal

[1] See joint research group of the Second Civil Division of the High People's Court of Beijing Municipality and the Third Civil Division of the First Intermediate People's Court of Beijing Municipality, *The Standard for Determination of Professional Money Lenders*, Beijing Adjudication, Vol. 2 (2022).

qualification and lends money to nonspecific persons for the purpose of profit-making. Considering all the criteria for determination of professional money lenders established by courts in different regions, the determination factors can be summarised from the perspectives of lenders, borrowers and the conduct of lending.

1. Lenders

When the perspectives of lenders are taken into consideration in judicial practice, it is necessary to consider whether a legal qualification for money lending is obtained and whether there are affiliated lenders.

(1) Whether a lender is legally qualified for money lending business. The entities of professional money lenders include legal persons, unincorporated organisations and natural persons. In ascertaining whether a lender has the qualification for money lending, the court should strictly examine whether the lender has obtained financial licences that enable the lenders to carry on money lending business.

(2) Whether a lender provides loans through an affiliated lender. In judicial practice, there are lenders providing funds in the names of other persons or by way of affiliated companies. Some malicious professional money lenders even intentionally lend money through affiliated lenders so as to circumvent the laws. Therefore, when determining the issue of affiliated lenders, it is crucial to examine the following facts. Firstly, whether there is a de facto controller, legal representative, shareholder, employee or person having related relationship of the same company. Secondly, whether there is kinship, friendship or any other close relationship between the lender and the affiliated lender. Thirdly, whether the funds lent come from the same person, legal person or unincorporated organisation. Fourthly, whether the assignment of rights is utilised to conceal the fact that the lender and the affiliated lender are the same person. However, it is worth noting that the determinative indicators mentioned above cannot be mechanically applied in the legal reasoning process. According to the

case of (2020) SPC Civil Retrial Application No. 1193, the Supreme People's Court held that the mere fact that the defendant and the plaintiff had financial transactions was unable to sufficiently prove the existence of affiliation relationship, because production and operation activities may also create numerous financial transactions between different civil entities. In addition, in the judgement of (2020) Beijing Civil Retrial Application No. 2875, the High People's Court of Beijing Municipality held that a special relationship between parties such as kinship was not a sufficient condition for the determination of affiliated lenders.

2. Borrowers

Whether a borrower is nonspecific person is a significant factor in determining professional money lenders. The borrowers to whom the professional money lenders provide funds are nonspecific and this should be determined on a case-by-case basis because production and operation activities may also result in several financial transactions between the lender and nonspecific persons. Generally speaking, if a lender lends money to nonspecific persons and charges interests or fund possession fees over a certain period of time, the lender's conduct shall be regarded as professional money lending conduct.

3. Conduct of Lending

Compared to normal private lending activities, the lending activities conducted by professional money lenders exhibit typical characteristics of profitability, commerciality, repetitiveness, and continuity.

(1) Whether the conduct of lending is for profit-making. The threshold for determining whether the lending conduct is for profit is relatively low. In general, once the lender charges interest, service fees, advisory fees, management fees, fees for breach of contract or fund possession fees, his conduct of lending can be regarded as for profit. The amount of interest charged is an irrelevant factor, but if the lender unreasonably charges for high interest, the lender's conduct is highly likely to be deemed as for profit.

(2) Whether the lenders run the business of money lending. Firstly, this issue can be determined by the degree of formatting of loan contacts. This is because the lenders who run the business of money lending will use well-organised loan contracts and security contracts, which normally adopt standardised contract format, contract number as well as risk-control clauses (for instance, a clause expressly provides that in the event of default the borrowers will bear the cost and disbursement of notary fees, court costs, legal fees and so forth). Secondly, this issue can be also determined by whether the lenders publicly announce, advertise or express their willingness and intention to lend money since the normal private lending conduct is occasional, provisional and reciprocal in characteristics. Public promotion or advertisement of intention to lend money is obviously contrast to the aforesaid characteristics of normal private lending conduct and presents the nature of commercial advertisement that the private lending should never have.

(3) Whether the conduct of lending is repetitive and continuous. The number of loans provided by a lender and the number of cases brought by the same lender within a certain period of time should be the focus of examination. In terms of the number of loans, the Supreme People's Court in the case of (2019) SPC Civil Retrial Application No. 4952 held that despite only three loans made by the defendant to the plaintiff, it was insufficient to conclude that the defendant regularly engaged in lending business or carried on professional money lending business. With respect to the number of private lending cases, the courts in different regions have discrepant standards for determination. The basic standard for determination is 5 private lending cases filed in a primary court and/or an intermediate court, while the courts in economically-developed regions will hold stricter standards.

II. Criteria for Determination in Hong Kong

The *Money Lenders Ordinance* was published and put into effect in 1911, the provisions of which comprehensively followed the main provisions of the *Money Lenders Act* 1900 (*UK*). As the 1911 Ordinance failed to make provisions regarding effective interest rates, the courts only had limited power to control and regulate the conduct of lending money at usurious rates when the borrowers applied for setting aside the loan contracts on the ground that the terms were "harsh and unconscionable". Due to the rampancy of usury conducts and serious social problems caused by the loan sharks, the Legislative Council amended the Ordinance in 1980 in the following two aspects. Firstly, a provision regarding effective interest rate was purposefully added which further expended the court's power on regulation of usury and increased the protection of borrowers. Secondly, the amendment changed the registration system to a licensing system, clearly specified the regulations on loan transactions and money lending business, added extra provisions for exempted money lenders and exempted loans, and empowered the court to re-open certain money lending transactions in appropriate circumstances. After the 1980 amendment, the Ordinance not only further prevented the practice of lending money at excessive or extortionate interest rates, but also expedited the role of money lenders as facilitators of commercial activities. The Ordinance has been the core statute in regulating the conduct of money lending in Hong Kong.

While there is no legal concept of professional money lenders in Hong Kong law, the *Money Lenders Ordinance* implements stringent regulations on persons who carry on money lending business without money lender's licences. Generally speaking, if a lender obtains a money lender's licence in accordance with the application requirements in Part II of the Ordinance and carries on money lending business pursuant to Part III of the Ordinance, there will be rare disputes arisen in the money lending practice. However, in the sophisticated and complicated commercial practice, there are numerous cases where the lenders are not properly licensed but engage in money lending activities. Hence, one of the core issues that the courts have to deal with is whether the lender is an unlicensed money lender[1].

The definition of money lender is clearly set out in Section 2 of the *Money Lenders Ordinance*, which provides that "money lender means every person whose business (whether or not he carries on any other business) is that of making loans or who advertises or announces himself or holds himself out in any way as carrying on that business, but does not include (a) a person specified in Part 1 of Schedule 1; or (b) as respects a loan specified in Part 2 of Schedule 1, any person who makes such loan." According to the definition above, unlicensed money lenders can also be divided into two types. The first type is a person who has no money lender's licence but carry on money lending business and the second type is a person who has no money lender's licence but advertises, announces or holds out as carrying on money lending business. If a borrower disputes whether the lender is a money lender falling within the definition under Section 2, the burden of proof falls upon the borrower to prove that the lender was carrying on the business as a money lender, or was advertising or announcing carrying on money lending business.[2]

In the case of *Chan Miu Chu Zoe v. Choi Chiu Yuk*[3], the Court of First Instance of the High Court summarised the legal principles for determination of money lenders as follows: Firstly, the issue is a matter of fact to be determined by the court for each case. It is not possible to set out any description or definition, still less fixed formula for the determination of this issue. Each case must be reviewed according to its facts. Secondly, the number of transactions made by the lender is not the determining factor. The court has to look at all the relevant facts of the case. Even one transaction may be sufficient if there is evi-

[1] Unlicensed money lender is a person who runs the business of money lending without holding a money lender's licence. For the sake of brevity, this book refers this sort of persons as unlicensed money lenders.

[2] *Billion Silver Development Ltd. v. All Wide Investments Ltd.* [2000] 2 HKC 262 (CA), p. 270.

[3] [2014] HKCU 477.

dence to show that the lender was a money lender at the time of the transaction. Thirdly, the proper approach for the court to determine this issue is to look at the evidence to determine if the lender was a money lender within the meaning of the Ordinance, and if so, it is not necessary to consider further. If there is no such evidence, the court then should look for other evidence as whether the lender had advertised or held out as a money-lender. Fourthly, even if the lender made the loan at remunerative interest rates and with proper security, this might not be an indicium of a money lender. [1] The application of each relevant factor concluded in *Chan Miu Chu Zoe v. Choi Chiu Yuk* is illustrated and explained in detail hereinafter.

i. Carrying on the Business as Money Lenders

The core test for determining money lenders is whether the lender carries on business as a money lender. The *Money Lenders Ordinance* do not lay down any definition or description regarding the term of carrying on business as a money lender and the relevant criteria for determining this issue are set out in case laws. Whether a person carries on business as a money lender must be a question of fact in each case and thus it is crucial to resolve this issue by considering the peculiar features of each case. [2]

1. Repetition, Continuity and System of Money Lending

(1) Repetition

The number of loans advanced in the ordinary lending practice is generally one, and occasionally there are more than one which is very exceptional. If a lender repeatedly makes multiple loans to borrowers which causes the number of loans made beyond the scope of ordinary money lending, the lender can be regarded as carrying on money lending business.

---

[1] *Chan Miu Chu Zoe v. Choi Chiu Yuk* [2014] HKCU 477, para. 21.

[2] *Newton v. Pyke* [1908] 25 TLR 127, p. 128.

The case of *Edgelow v. McElwee*[1] clearly indicates that repetition is one of the important indicators for determining whether a person carries on money lending business. In this case, the plaintiff as a solicitor chronically lent money to his "clients" by means of issuing writs. The court in this case decided as follows. Firstly, the plaintiff habitually lent money from 1912 onward and advanced no less than 17 loans during 1915 – 1917. Secondly, although the plaintiff claimed that he provided the "clients" with legal service by way of issuing writs, the plaintiff not only failed to produce any book of account showing the names of the borrowers, the amounts advanced or the interest charged, but also was unable to adduced evidence of any bill of costs he ever sent to prove his claim.[2] For the reasons above, the court held that the plaintiff was an unlicensed money lender and he carried on money lending business in the disguise of his vocation as a solicitor.

(2) Continuity

The continuity is mainly reflected in the lenders' conduct that the lender makes several loans to borrowers. When determining the issue of continuity, the courts will make decisions with respect to the number of loans advanced or the number of loan agreements made by the lender. However, where the lender enters into only one loan agreement but makes multiple loans to the borrower, the court shall determine the issue of continuity by giving significant weight to the number of loan agreements sentered into by the parties.

In *Supreme Design Fashion Ltd. & Hung Lai Chu v. Michael Hope International Ltd.*[3], the plaintiff Supreme Design Fashion Ltd. entered into an agency agreement regarding the management of building and equipment and materials with the defendant. On the plaintiff's instruction, the defendant did

---

[1] [1918] 1 KB 205.

[2] *Edgelow v. MacElwee* [1918] 1 KB 205, p. 209.

[3] [1999] HKCU 572.

not place orders for the equipment and materials and simply issued letters of credit up to a total amount no exceeding three million US dollars. The parties agreed that the plaintiff should repay this amount with an agency commission of 35% within 8 months after all the equipment and materials had been delivered. Pursuant to the agreement, the defendant issued several letters of credit in favour of the plaintiff and various Hong Kong companies, but the plaintiff only made partial repayment to the defendant. The plaintiff brought an action against the defendant claiming that the defendant was an unlicensed money lender and that the loan made to the defendant was irrecoverable for violation of Section 23 of the *Money Lenders Ordinance*. The plaintiffs contended that the agency agreement executed was in fact a loan agreement and that the letters of credit represented a series of loans made by the defendant to the plaintiffs.

After the trial, the Court of First Instance determined that the agency agreement between the plaintiff and the defendant was in substance an agreement for a loan. Firstly, the defendant did not act as a purchasing agent as it did not place order or arrange for shipping or delivery. Secondly, the defendant used its own credit facilities to pay for goods ordered by another and expected to get a return of 35% on that money within 8 months after the delivery of the goods, which significantly satisfied the characteristics of money lending conduct. The agency agreement was in fact a loan agreement and the agency commissions received by the defendant were interest.[1] When further determining whether the defendant was an unlicensed money lender, the court held that to prove that a person carried on business as a money lending, it was necessary to prove some degree of system, repetition and continuity in the money lending transactions.[2] After considering evidence adduced by both parties, the court

---

[1] *Supreme Design Fashion Ltd. & Hung Lai Chu v. Michael Hope International Ltd.* [1999] HKCU 572, para. 25 - 27.

[2] *Supreme Design Fashion Ltd. & Hung Lai Chu v. Michael Hope International Ltd.* [1999] HKCU 572, para. 37.

concluded that there was only a single loan made by the defendant. Firstly, there is no documentary evidence of other loans, or of written advertisements within the trade. Though the defendant's financial returns showed considerable income from interest, the plaintiff failed to provide sufficient evidence to prove that the interest was derived from the loan.[1] Secondly, based on the evidence of the witness, the defendant did not issue letters of credit for others in the manner of this transaction in previous trading.[2] Thirdly, it was one contract entered into by the plaintiffs and the defendant. Although the defendant made a series of advances, the total of amount was fixed and the repayment followed on the fixed event of delivery.[3] For the aforementioned reasons, the court came to a conclusion that the defendant did not carry on the money lending business and thus was not an unlicensed money lender.

The case of *Supreme Design Fashion Ltd. & Hung Lai Chu v. Michael Hope International Ltd.* established the rules that the number of loans is not affected by the number of instalments but is determinative in light of the number of loan contracts concluded by parties. This proposition was later cited with approval in *Cheung Ping Kwong v. Chan Kin Sun*[4], in which the court held that in spite of several transactions between the plaintiff and the defendant, the defendant did not engage in money lending business because only one loan agreement was reached by parties.

Overall, when determining whether the conduct of lending is continuous, the number of loans advanced by the lender is one of the significant indicators. Unless the number of loans is well beyond the normal range to the extent that it

---

[1] *Supreme Design Fashion Ltd. & Hung Lai Chu v. Michael Hope International Ltd.* [1999] HKCU 572, para. 28.

[2] *Supreme Design Fashion Ltd. & Hung Lai Chu v. Michael Hope International Ltd.* [1999] HKCU 572, para. 30 - 31, 35.

[3] *Supreme Design Fashion Ltd. & Hung Lai Chu v. Michael Hope International Ltd.* [1999] HKCU 572, para. 38.

[4] [2013] 3 HKC 319.

reaches commercial standard or becomes large-scale, it is improper to roughly equate the number of advances of money with the number of loans. Multiple advances of loans do not necessarily represent that the lender continuously or repeatedly engages in the conduct of money lending because there may be circumstances where the lender only enters into one loan contract with the borrower but an instalment plan is agreed therein.

(3) System

The system of money lending normally embodies in the following aspects: standardised loan management, streamlined loan advance procedures, and completed loan agreement preparation. If the conduct of lending money satisfies these features, the court will incline to determine the lender carries on the business as a money lender. However, the degree of system is a strong indicator for determine whether a person carries on business as a money lender, but it is not determinative. In *Chow Wun Sing Winston v. Yiu Chun Luk*[1], after considering the merits of the case, the High Court made a determination that the plaintiff did not carry on business as a money lender despite certain degree of system shown in plaintiff's conduct of lending.

In this case, the defendant sought a loan from Alex Lee from Chow Sang Sang Nominee Limited in order to run business. With the effort of Alex Lee, the plaintiff agreed to enter into the first loan contract with the defendant. Alex Lee then assisted the plaintiff to manage the loan and the security. Since the defendant failed to repay the principal and interest at the expiration of the term of the loan contract, he asked the plaintiff for an extension. The plaintiff agreed and re-entered a loan contract with the defendant. But the defendant defaulted in the payment of interest since October 2001. The plaintiff then sued the defendant for repayment of debt.

At first instance, the defendant raised a defence that the plaintiff carried on

[1] [2006] HKCU 1247; [2008] HKCU 358.

business as a money lender without a money lender's licence and contended the following arguments. Firstly, the plaintiff owned a sophisticated system of management of debt. Secondly, the terms of loan agreements and the documentation of the loan were clear and properly prepared. Thirdly, the plaintiff had kept a good record of the interest payments and had computer-generated repayment schedules. These systematic management of debt sufficiently demonstrated that the plaintiff was carrying on the business of money lending.

Having regard to the defence and arguments, the Court of First Instance held that, though the plaintiff adopted professional and business-like approaches to make loans to the defendant which caused the conduct of lending by the plaintiff seemed to be systematic, the degree of system was not a determinative factor. The court maintained that the merits of the case played an essential role in determining the issue whether the plaintiff carried on money lending business. Due to the following circumstances, the court considered that the plaintiff did not carry on money lending business and that the loan made to the defendant was mere an individual loan. Firstly, the loan and security were managed by Alex Lee who had abundant experience in collateral and money lending matters which justified the utilisation of properly prepared loan documents, good record of interest payments and computer-generated repayment schedules.[1] Secondly, the contents and format of the notices and letters to the defendant were not standardised.[2] Thirdly, the plaintiff forgot to change the lender's name when adapting the computer software for the production of the repayment schedules. It was a clear omission which definitely would not occur in the business of money lending.[3] Fourthly, the plaintiff only made one loan to others during the making of loan to the defendant and thus the plaintiff did not continuously and

---

〔1〕 *Chow Wun Sing Winston v. Yiu Chun Luk* [2006] HKCU 1247, para. 72 – 74.

〔2〕 *Chow Wun Sing Winston v. Yiu Chun Luk* [2006] HKCU 1247, para. 70.

〔3〕 *Chow Wun Sing Winston v. Yiu Chun Luk* [2006] HKCU 1247, para. 75.

repetitively lend money to all and sundry.[1]

Although the defendant appealed to the Court of Appeal, the Court of Appeal sustained the decision made by the Court of First Instance and upheld that a certain degree of system and continuity was a relevant factor but not determinative.[2] Nevertheless, the Court of Appeal cautiously pointed out that although the court eventually concluded that the plaintiff was not running a business of money lending as the small number of loans was consistent with the evidence adduced by the plaintiff, the small number of loans did not mean the impossibility of carrying on money lending business.[3]

2. Providing Profit-Making Loans

In general practice of money lending, an important feature of carrying on money lending business is that the lender often makes loan to borrowers with profit such as charging interest or accepting security. However, the charging of interest or the acceptance of security for money lent does not automatically make the person a money lender. The High Court in *Chow Wun Sing Winston v. Yiu Chun Luk*[4] held that even if the lender made the loan at remunerative interest rates and with proper security, this might not be an indicium of a money lender. *Chan Miu Chu Zoe v. Choi Chiu Yuk*[5] subsequently adopted the principle established in the case of *Chow Wun Sing Winston v. Yiu Chun Luk* that the making of loans with profit is not a conclusive factor when determining the issue of money lender.

3. Proportion of Money Lending Business

According to the definition of money lender set out in the *Money Lenders Ordinance*, there is no requirement that the business of money lending must be

---

[1] *Chow Wun Sing Winston v. Yiu Chun Luk* [2006] HKCU 1247, para. 70.

[2] *Chow Wun Sing Winston v. Yiu Chun Luk* [2008] HKCU 358, para. 16.

[3] *Chow Wun Sing Winston v. Yiu Chun Luk* [2008] HKCU 358, para. 22.

[4] [2008] HKCU 358.

[5] [2014] HKCU 477.

the major business run by the lender, the proportion of which is irrelevant in the determination of money lenders. The case of *North Central Wagon Finance Co. Ltd. v. Brailsford*[1] concerned with the fact that the plaintiff was a financial company engaging in multiple sorts of financial business and the business of money lending merely took up 0.5% of the whole business. The court in this case held that a person who made a business of lending money was not any the less a money lender because he carried on some other business as well as on a much larger scale.[2] Hence, despite the trifling proportion of the money lending business, the court eventually regarded the plaintiff as a money lender.

It is remarkable that the lending of money may be incidental to certain types of business and transactions so that carrying on these types of business, on the face of it, can be easily regarded as carrying on the money lending business. For instance, in the case of *Litchfield v Dreyfus*[3], the art business carried on by the plaintiff provided long-term credit service to the customers and the usual course was for the customers to pay their purchases with their bills and the plaintiff discounted and renewed the bills. In this case the court held that the conduct of discounting and renewal of bills by the plaintiff was mere incidental to the carrying on the business of antiques sale instead of money lending. The conduct aimed to provide funds to the company where he was a shareholder, and friends with whom he had been connected in business.[4]

Similar circumstances occur in share trading, especially in the margin trading. The investor will initially open a margin account with the stock company and then, upon the instructions by the investor, the stockbroker will use his own funds or credit granted by bank to purchase shares. Upon the purchase, the

---

[1] [1962] 1 WLR 1288.

[2] *North Central Wagon Finance Co. Ltd. v. Brailsford* [1962] 1 WLR 1288, pp. 508 - 509.

[3] [1906] 1 KB 584.

[4] *Litchfield v. Dreyfus* [1906] 1 KB 584, p. 590.

stockbroker will debit the defendant's margin account for the cost of shares, stamp duty, trading commission and service fee. The trading pattern between the investor and the stockbroker is such that ostensibly the stockbroker issued loans to the investor for the purchase of shares. This is exactly the defence raised by the defendant in the case of *Harvester Stock Investment Co. v. Kwan Siu May*[1]. The defendant alleged that the plaintiff's management of her margin account was legally tantamount to money lending, and that since the plaintiff was not a licensed money lender, it had no right to sell the shares in the defendant's margin account and no right to recover any money from the defendant. The High Court held that the plaintiff did not, in law, conduct the business of money lending, and that margin trading was an integral part of its stockbroking business, not a separate business. The core and purpose of margin trading was to provide credit-type stockbroking business to customers, and neither the investors nor the stockbrokers had any motive or intention to engage in the lending business.[2] The case of *Cheung Ping Kwong v. Chan Kin Sun*[3] applied the same rule. Therefore, although the margin trading encompassed a portion of lending and borrowing activities, it is not a lending conduct regulated by the *Money Lenders Ordinance*.

4. Class of the Borrowers

(1) Loans between Intimate Relationships

It is vital to consider the class of borrowers and their relationship with the lenders when deciding whether a person carries on business as a money lender. The commercial nature of money lending business dictates that the borrowers are nonspecific or uncertain. Money lenders may, at any time, provide funds to persons who meet his lending conditions, and who generally do not have inti-

---

[1] [1987] 1 HKC 271.

[2] *Harvester Stock Investment Co. v. Kwan Siu May* [1987] 1 HKC 271, p. 280.

[3] [2013] 3 HKC 319.

mate ties with the lenders such as friendships and kinships.

In *Litchfield v. Dreyfus*[1], the plaintiff, who used to be an art dealer and became an art value advisor after retirement, lent money to the company which he was a shareholder and his friends in the antique business. When the plaintiff sued for the repayment of loan, the defendant then raised a defence the plaintiff was an unlicensed money lender. The court held that the plaintiff did not carry on money lending business because a money lender lent money to unspecific people. In this case, the plaintiff only lent money to relatives and friends who were connected in business and based on friendship. As a result, if a person only lends money to relatives, friends or persons of similar kinds, it is less likely for the court to find that the person carries on business as a money lender. A similar approach is adopted and applied in *Newton v. Pyke*[2]. In this case the court held that although the plaintiff had been engaging in lending activities for a long time, he lent small amounts to persons who were mostly his friends or relatives. Besides, the plaintiff had never advertised, announced or held himself out as a money lender.[3] Due to these circumstances, the court found that the plaintiff did not carry on business as a money lender.

Hong Kong laws adopt a similar standard for determination. If there is friendship or kinship between the lender and the borrower, the court will incline to find that the lender does not carry on business as a money lender. In *Chan Yuk Bun v. Tsoi Yan Yee Lily and Another*[4], the Court of First Instance cited the statements by the learned editors in *Chitty on Contracts*, *Hong Kong Specific Contracts* (*5th edition*) at Paragraph 9 – 048: The identity of the borrower and his relationship with the moneylender is a factor considered relevant by the courts in determining whether he is a moneylender. In *Cheung Chow v. Cheung*

---

[1] [1906] 1 KB 584.

[2] [1908] 25 TLR 127.

[3] *Newton v. Pyke* [1908] 25 TLR 127, p. 128.

[4] [2017] HKCU 2071.

Ng Sheong Steven[1], the plaintiff lent money to his brother. The court found when applying the rules in *Money Lenders Ordinance*, the relationships between the lender and the borrower, and related situation in which the loan was made, should be taken into consideration. Accordingly, one is not a money lender if he lends money to friends or relatives without charge of interest or security.[2] After trial, the Court of First Instance found that the plaintiff made the loan to the defendants entirely out of friendship and that the plaintiff did not carry on a money lending business.[3]

(2) Loans between Certain Class of Borrowers

The uncertainty and randomicity of borrowers are important factors in finding whether a lending business is being operated. However, if the lender's borrowing is limited to a particular group of people, the court may still find that the lender carries on money lending business. For example, in *Premor Ltd. v. Shaw Brothers*[4], though the borrowers were limited to a specific group of motorcar dealers, the court comprehensively considered all relevant facts and came to a decision that the lender was carrying business as a money lender. In this case, the plaintiff was a financial leasing company and conducted "stocking transactions" with only the motorcar dealers. Here is how the "stocking transactions" worked. The plaintiff and defendant entered into financial leasing agreement where the plaintiff lent money to the defendant for the purchase of specific motorcars. Then a motorcar dealer would put the motorcars for rent or on sale. While the plaintiff brought an action for repayment of two unpaid sums for the purchases, the defendant raised a defence that the plaintiff was an unlicensed money lender. In response to the defence, the plaintiff contended that the money lent to the defendant and other dealers were only for the purpose of

---

[1] [1993] HKCU 428.

[2] *Chan Yuk Bun v. Tsoi Yan Yee Lily and Another* [2017] HKCU 2071, para. 14.

[3] *Chan Yuk Bun v. Tsoi Yan Yee Lily and Another* [2017] HKCU 2071, para. 20.

[4] [1964] 1 WLR 978.

sales of motorcars and promotion for financial leasing business, and thus he fell within the exception of the then British *Money Lenders Act* and should not be regarded as an unlicensed money lender.

However, the court in this case denied the plaintiff's argument and held that the money lent to the specific group of motorcar dealers was neither in the course of nor for the purpose of promoting financial leasing business. The plaintiff and the defendant conducted several "stocking transactions", some of which specified certain motorcars as leased property and other of which included nothing as leased property. Despite the existence of financial leasing documents, these documents were entirely fictitious, regarding purchase prices of motorcars, initial payment and storage charges which had never existed. For the reasons above, the court found that there was no actual connection between the transactions conducted by the parties and the financial leasing transactions. The primary object of lending money to the motorcar dealers was to obtain profits via loan instead of facilitating financial leasing business. Therefore, when a lender made loans to particular class of borrowers, the court is likely to regard such lender as an unlicensed money lender if his mere purpose for the lending is to obtain profits via loans.

ii. Announcement, Advertisement or Appearance as Carrying on Money Lending Business

It is relatively easy to determine whether a lender advertises, announces or show himself as a money lender carrying on that business. If the borrower proves that the lender has the conduct of announcing or advertising as a money lender, the court is sufficiently satisfied that the lender is a money lender without any consideration of other factors.

In *Conroy v. Kenny* [1], the plaintiff ran a partnership business called

---

[1] [1999] 1 WLR 1345.

Lancashire Acceptances, which only held a money lender licence during 1966 to 1967. The defendant borrowed 6000 pounds from the partnership business and only repaid the interest till the due date. Since the plaintiff was a partner of Lancashire Acceptances, the plaintiff brought an action for repayment of the outstanding debt.

The critical issue of this case was whether the plaintiff was an unlicensed money lender. On this issue, as the defendant had failed to show that at the material time Lancashire Acceptances provided patterns of loans at interest to others, the court of first instance refused the defence alleged by the defendant. The defendant then sought to appeal on the decision.

The court of appeal considered that the trial judge's approach in determining whether the plaintiff was a money lender was wrong and what the trial judge should have asked in this case was whether on January 6, 1971 the business of Lancashire Acceptances was that of money lending. If that question was not answered in affirmative, then it was necessary to consider whether on that date Lancashire Acceptances advertised or announced itself or held itself out in any way as carrying on that business. By virtue of the evidence adduced by parties, the court came to a conclusion that the plaintiff did advertise itself as a money lender carrying on money lending business at the time making loan to the defendant. Firstly, Mr. Southam used to provide legal service to both the plaintiff and the defendant, and when the defendant asked him if he had any clients who were in the business of lending money, Mr. Southam gave him the name of Lancashire Acceptances. Secondly, it could be obviously interfered from the quick execution of loan contract after exchanging the letters twice between Mr. Southam and the plaintiff that the plaintiff was experienced and was treading ground he had trodden before. [1] Thirdly, there used to be a purchaser intending to purchase the mortgaged property and when the solicitor acting for the

---

[1] *Conroy v. Kenny* [1999] 1 WLR 1345, pp. 1349 – 1350.

purchaser asked whether the plaintiff were unlicensed money lenders, no clear reply was given by the plaintiff. From the silence demonstrated in the correspondence, the court was satisfied that the plaintiff knew from at least 1966 what was meant by an unlicensed money lender and if Lancashire Acceptances were not an unlicensed money lender, there should have been a negative answer given by the plaintiff. [1] For the aforementioned circumstances, the court determined that Lancashire Acceptances was at the material time holding itself out as carrying on money lending business and thus the plaintiff was an unlicensed money lender. In summary, if there is evidence that the lender advertises, announces or holds himself out in any way as carrying on money lending business and even there is only one transaction, it is adequate to prove the lender is a money lender.

III. Summary

i. Similarity

Firstly, the laws in the Chinese Mainland and Hong Kong do not endorse the conduct of lending without a financial qualification (or a money lender's licence) and both hold a negative attitude towards it.

Secondly, there is no consolidated standard for determination of a professional (unlicensed) money lender in the Chinese Mainland and Hong Kong. The Chinese Mainland is still at an exploratory stage in determination of professional money lenders and the courts at all levels formulate contextualised criteria for determination of professional money lenders in light of the level of economic developments in local area. The criteria for determination in Hong Kong are scattered in case law and no consolidated criteria is summarised and fixed by the statutes.

---

[1] *Conroy v. Kenny* [1999] 1 WLR 1345, p. 1350.

Thirdly, the laws in the Chinese Mainland and Hong Kong both determine whether a person is a professional (unlicensed) money lender from the following three aspects: the lenders, the borrowers and the conduct of lending. Both jurisdictions adopt a comprehensive approach to determine this issue by taking into account the specific evidence and peculiar features of each case.

ii. Difference

When determining the issue of professional (unlicensed) money lenders, the Chinese Mainland and Hong Kong have different emphasis on the ascertainment of lending conduct. The courts in the Chinese Mainland consider the number of private lending cases as a significant factor, while the courts in Hong Kong stress on the factor of the actual number of loans made by the lenders.

Section Two Legal Consequences of the Conduct of Professional Money Lenders

I. Laws in the Chinese Mainland

The conduct of lending by professional money lenders is void ab initio. In accordance with Article 13 of the *Provisions on Private Lending Cases (2020 Second Amendment)*, if a lender, who does not obtain qualification for money lending in accordance with the laws, provides loans to unspecific persons in the society for profit-making purpose, the people's court shall determine the private lending contract as null and void. The legal consequences of invalidity of private lending contracts are generally reflected in two aspects: the repayment of the principal and the payment of fund possession fees.

i. Nullity of the Loan Contract

The nullity of private lending contracts means that the conduct of lending is null and void at the very beginning. As provided in Article 157 of the *Civil Code*, when a civil juristic act becomes null and void, the party who acquired property as a result of such act shall return the same; if it is impossible or unnecessary to return such property, compensation shall be paid at an estimated price. The party at fault shall compensate the other party for the loss it suffers as a result of the act; if both parties are at fault, they shall bear the corresponding responsibilities respectively. Therefore, if the loan contract has not yet been fulfilled, there is no need for the lender and the borrower to continue performing the obligations under the loan contract. If the loan contract has been partially fulfilled, the borrower shall return the property obtained from the lender. Namely the borrower shall return the principal to the lender.

Assuming the Lender A made a loan of ¥1 million to Borrower B without obtaining legal qualification for money lending, both parties agreed that the interest rates were 10% per annum and the term was one year. After expiration of the term, B only paid part of interest but refused to repay the principal and thus A initiated legal actions claiming for repayment of debt. Since A obtained no legal qualification for money lending, the court determined that A was a professional lender who made the loan to B for the purpose of profit-making and the loan contract between A and B was invalid. The court would reject A's claim to require B to continue performing the obligations but would support A's claim for return of the principal of ¥1 million.

ii. Payment of Fund Possession Fees

In terms of whether the borrower should pay the fund possession fees when the loan contract is determined as void contract, it is necessary to maintain the balance between the interest of the lender and the borrower and the stability of financial order. Article 34 of the *Conference Minutes* provides: "In the case of the non-establishment, invalidity or cancellation of a bilateral contract, the restitution of the subject matter and return of payment shall be reciprocal payment and be made by the parties at the same time. For whether interest should be paid, as long as a party has used the subject matter, the payment for the use shall generally be made, and as the payment may be offset against the funding cost payable by the party in possession of the payment for the subject matter, one party shall pay only the principal, without paying the interest, before the other party returns the subject matter." Despite the nullity of the private lending contract, the borrower ought to pay the fund possession fees as long as the borrower makes use of the fund.

As for the payment standard of the fund possession fees, the amount in judicial practice is determined by annual loan prime rate released by the National Interbank Funding Centre (Hereinafter referred as Annual LPR). In practice, the courts will exercise their direction to adjust the amount of the fund possession fees by considering the following factors such as the source of the loan, the degree of violation of the laws, the use of loan and the performance of the loan contract.

Taking the aforementioned example. If B made a claim to the court requiring A to return the interest paid, the court would, on the contemplation of the balance of interests between the lender and the borrower, reject B's claim and make a decision that B should pay off fund possession fees as B had used the loan money. If the interest rate agreed upon was excessive, for example, the interest rate was 20% per annum, the court would assess the payable amount of fund possession fees in accordance with Annual LPR subject to exceptional circumstances.

II. Laws in Hong Kong

i. The Loan Contract is Unenforceable

In principle, the laws in Hong Kong do not provide any protection to the conduct of money lending by unlicensed money lenders. Pursuant to Section 23 (1) of the *Money Lenders Ordinance*: "Money lender shall be entitled to recover in any court any money lent by him or any interest in respect thereof or to enforce any agreement made or security taken in respect of any loan made by him unless he satisfies the court by the production of his licence or otherwise that at the date of the loan or the making of the agreement or the taking of the security (as the case may be) he was licensed." This means that unless the lender proves the holding of a money lender's licence, the lender is not entitled to apply to the courts to enforce the loan contract and the security taken regarding the loan. Namely the lender is unable to recover any principal lent or interest accrued thereon by legal means. It is notable that Section 23(1) does not explicitly demonstrate the legal effect of the loan contract and the security contract. It merely specifies that the loan contract and security contract are unenforceable in the circumstance where the lender does not hold a money lender's licence.

There are similarities in respect of the effect of contracts under the laws in the Chinese Mainland and Hong Kong, both of which categorise the contractual effect into three types including valid contract, void contract and voidable contract. Unenforceable contract cannot be pigeonholed in the aforesaid three types of contractual effect, and it should be characterised as certain sort of legal effect or legal consequence. The legal effect of an unenforceable contract is that the contract cannot be enforced by means of direct legal proceedings. The contract may be unenforceable by any of the parties to it, or simply by some of them; the unenforceability may be perpetual or temporary; the unenforceable contract may be void contract or valid contract. [1] If an unenforceable contract is deemed void, it makes no sense to discuss the issue of enforcement because a void contract has no legal force at all from the very beginning. Therefore, it

---

[1] See *Halsbury's Laws of Hong Kong*, Lexis Nexis Hong Kong, [115.009] Imperfect Contracts.

can be said that a void contract is certainly an unenforceable contract. If an unenforceable contract is a valid contract, it may be indirectly enforceable, or by curing contractual defects[1] become directly enforceable.[2] Section 23 of the *Money Lenders Ordinance* only regulates with regards to the unenforceability of the contract entered into by the unlicensed lender and the borrower, but no provision is made in respect of the legal effect of the contract. In the course of searching for case laws regarding Section 23 of the *Money Lenders Ordinance*, though there is a case where the defendant claimed that the loan contract entered into by parties were void and unenforceable by reason of the plaintiff's violation of Section 23, the court in this case made no ruling on whether the loan contract in breach of Section 23 was invalid or not. [3] So there are some different views on whether a loan contract unenforceable for breach of Section 23 was a valid contract or a void contract in judicial practice.

ii. Exception: The Discretion Exercised by the Courts under Equity

Although the conduct of carrying on business as a money lender without licence will not be legally protected in Hong Kong, Section 23(2) of the *Money Lenders Ordinance* allows the court to provide limited protection in exceptional circumstances. This provision stipulates: "Provided that if the court is satisfied that in all the circumstances it would be inequitable if a money lender who did not satisfy it that he was licensed at the relevant time was thereby not entitled to so recover such money or interest or to enforce such agreement or security, the court may order that the money lender is entitled to recover such money or in-

---

[1] The contractual defects include the non-compliance of legal formality such as no writing form adopted in the execution of contract concerning land, and non-performance of legal procedures such as adjudication or repayment of stamp duty not being made.

[2] See *Halsbury's Laws of Hong Kong*, Lexis Nexis Hong Kong, [115.009] Imperfect Contracts.

[3] The court in *Chow Wun Sing Winston v. Yiu Chun Luk* [2006] HKCU 1247 rejected the defendant's claim on the ground that the defendant failed to prove that the plaintiff was a money lender.

terest or to enforce such agreement or security to such extent, and subject to such modifications or exceptions, as the court considers equitable." In consideration of the principles in equity, the court can exceptionally grant relief to unlicensed money lender. As the court in the case of *Universe Link Industries Ltd. &Anor v. Liggars Ltd.* [1] points out, the application of proviso to Section 23 depends on the mercy of the judge so that the unlicensed or unexempted lender can recover some principal and interest. However, the judges rarely exercise such discretion in judicial practice.

III. Summary

i. Similarity

The Chinese Mainland and Hong Kong do not recognise the conduct of lending by professional (unlicensed) money lenders. Both jurisdictions hold negative attitudes toward the legal effect of the conduct of lending by professional (unlicensed) money lender and stipulate corresponding adverse legal consequences.

ii. Difference

Firstly, the legal consequences of lending money by professional (unlicensed) money lenders differs in the laws in the Chinese Mainland and Hong Kong. The laws in the Chinese Mainland expressly regulate that the legal effect of loan contract concluded by a professional money lender is null and void and that the borrower shall return the principal and pay the fund possession fees to the lender. The amount of fund possession fees is normally determined by reference to the Annual LPR. In Hong Kong the *Money Lenders Ordinance* provides that the loan contract entered into by an unlicensed money lender is unenforceable.

---

[1] [1999] 2 HKLRD 383; [1999] HKCU 1688.

Secondly, the Chinese Mainland and Hong Kong adopt different approaches to deal with the conduct of lending by professional (unlicensed) money lenders. As the laws unequivocally stipulate that a loan contract entered into by a professional money lender is void, the courts in the Chinese Mainland are unable to exercise discretion to give any effect to the loan contracts entered into by professional money lenders. The courts in Hong Kong can exercise discretion to give limited protection to unlicensed money lenders in consideration of the equitable principles. However, the court is very cautious when exercising such discretions.

Chapter Ⅲ

Comparison of Legal Rules on Principal and Interest

Section One Principal and Interest

Principal in a loan refers to the original amount of money borrowed by the borrower from the lender. Interest refers to the payment received by the lender for lending money, i. e. the remuneration paid to the lender by the borrower for the use of money.

I. Laws in the Chinese Mainland

Article 26 of the *Provisions on Private Lending* (2020 *Second Amendment*) defines the principal as: "The amount borrowed clearly stated in a document such as receipt, IOU, or any other certificate of indebtedness shall normally be determined as the principal." However, neither the *Civil Code* nor the *Provisions on Private Lending* (*2020 Second Amendment*) has explicitly defined and explained the concept of interest.

Generally, interest, as fructus civiles, is calculated on the basis of the loan principal and contractual rate. The principal is the foundation for the borrower to create economic benefits, while the interest is a portion of benefits transferred to the lender from the borrower as the remuneration for using the principal.

In addition, Article 29 of the *Provisions on Private Lending* (*2020 Second Amendment*) provides that where the lender and the borrower have agreed on both default interest, liquidated damages, and other expenses, the lender may claim for one or all of them. Thus, it can be seen that interest, liquidated damages and other expenses are different charges under the loan contract and exist independently of each other. Article 29 above has merely established a statutory cap of four times Annual LPR on the total charges.

i. Relevant Legal Concepts

1. Certificate of Indebtedness

Normally written, signed and sealed by the borrower, a certificate of indebtedness contains names of the borrower and the lender, the date of lending, the loan term, the principal amount, and the interest rate, etc., indicating that the borrower borrows money from the lender. A certificate of indebtedness usually is issued by the borrower upon the granting of the loan, to prove the receipt of such money. For example, the certificate may state that: "Today, [borrower's name] received [amount] from [lender's name]." While sometimes, the borrower issues the certificate before granting. For example, the certificate states "[borrower's name] intends to borrow [amount] from [lender's name] and to be repaid by [date]." Under such circumstance, the nature of the certificate is closer to that of a loan contract. Therefore, the determination of the probative force of the certificate of indebtedness shall be based on what it specifically states.

2. Receipt

A receipt, or a receipt slip, is a document serves as evidence of receiving money from another party. Usually, a natural person is likely to issue a receipt slip, while a legal person prefers a receipt. The content of a receipt typically covers names of the payer and the payee, the amount received, the date of receipt, etc. For example, a receipt states "Received [amount] from [payer's name] on [date]". Unlike the certificate of indebtedness, the receipt emphasises more on the grant of money but not the intent to borrow, thus it possibly just states the amount received without mentioning the use and rate. In judicial practice, the borrower and the lender are both likely to issue receipts to each other after receiving and repaying the loan. Therefore, the determination of the probative force of receipt shall take into account evidence regarding to the use, contractual relationship, interest rate and other elements of the loan.

3. IOU

An IOU is nicknamed from "I Owe You", refers to the document issued by the debtor to indicate the amount of money owed and time limit of repayment, etc. For example, an IOU states "[debtor's name] owes [amount] to the [creditor's name] and will pay it off on [date]." Unlike the certificate of indebtedness, an IOU may not arise from a lending-borrowing relationship. Sales, constructions and other contractual relationships may also involve the use of IOUs. Judicial practices see some IOUs issued by the borrower clearly state the principal and interest as well as the paid sums and unliquidated amount, while some merely state an unliquidated amount without mentioning whether it is principal or interest.

ii. Deductions in Advance

The discrepancy between the amount stated in the contract and the amount actually granted to the borrower has always been a key issue in disputes between the parties from private lending cases. One of the most common situations is a deduction in advance, i. e. by name of "retained interest" when granting the loan.

1. Retained Interest

As suggested by its name, retained interest literally refers to a sum of interest deducted by the lender when granting the loan to the borrower. Prima facie, it seems that such deduction of interest in advance has not changed the amount of contractual interest at all and the borrower does not need to pay interest any more when the loan is due, for whom which seems convenient. However, this is not the way to do the math. Interest, generating from the use of certain money, is a cost for the borrower and a benefit for the lender. Interest shall be calculated based on the amount of money the borrower actually occupies and a deduction of interest in advance makes the amount of money lent in fact less than what it is supposed to be, which is unfair for the borrower since the benefits created from such amount will also be less than it should be.

For instance, B borrowed ¥100,000 from A for one year with an interest rate of 10% per annum (total interest being ¥10,000). However, A deducted ¥10,000 as interest when granting B the loan and B only received ¥90,000. According to the contract, B was still required to repay the principal of ¥100,000 after one year. Under such situation, the truth is B only occupied and utilised ¥90,000 for one year but paid ¥10,000 as interest. The effective interest rate of the loan becomes 11.11% per annum (¥10,000 ÷ ¥90,000). Obviously, such deduction is in fact a trick played by the lender to avoid the control imposed by law and to collect more benefits from the borrower.

2. Rules for Retained Interest

The laws in the Chinese Mainland prohibit the deduction of interest in advance. Article 670 of the *Civil Code* states: "Loan interest shall not be deducted in advance from the principal. Where there is interest deducted in advance, the amount of money actually granted shall be deemed as the principal with interest carried correspondingly." Meanwhile, Article 26 of the *Provisions on Private Lending (2020 Second Amendment)* also stipulates that: "Where the interest is deducted in advance, the people's court shall deem the amount of money actually lent as principal." Pursuant to the provisions above, it can be acknowledged that the amount actually received by the borrower is the principal in law. If there is a deduction of interest in advance, the borrower only needs to repay the actual amount received with corresponding interest. The so-called retained interest enables the lender to recover benefits in advance and lower the risk of lending, but at the same time it jeopardises the legitimate interests of the borrower by granting less amount of money, which affects the intended use of the loan and increases the burden on the borrower. The aforesaid provisions reflect the principle of fairness in contract law and prevent the lender from making unfair contracts by taking advantage of his dominant position.

iii. Refinancing

1. Concept of Refinancing

Refinancing mainly refers to a situation where a borrower, who fails to fully repay the principal and interest of a loan within the loan term, enters into a new loan contract with the same lender in order to obtain money to fully repay the outstanding balance on the previous loan and bears new obligations on the repayment of the new loan. Article 27 of the *Provisions on Private Lending* (*2020 Second Amendment*) defines it as: "the lender and the borrower take unpaid sums of principal and interest of the previous loan into the amount of principal of the new loan".[1] Judicial practices in the Chinese Mainland often see the parties repeatedly take unpaid sums into the amount of new principal and form plenty of new contracts in a successive order. Disputes over such issue usually arise from whether the unpaid interest sum of previous loan should be taken into the principal sum of a new loan.

There are two different views towards the nature of the new loan in judicial practice in the Chinese Mainland: The first one is that the new loan contract is in fact independent like any other contracts, since it has established a new lending-borrowing relationship between the parties, and the principal sum stated in the contract is principal de facto. The other one is that the new loan contract is not independent and has not established a new relationship between the parties, and the principal sum in the new contract in fact has included the original principal and the compound interests.

2. Rules for Refinancing

Article 27 of the *Provisions on Private Lending* (*2020 Second Amend-*

---

[1] Article 27 of the *Provisions on Private Lending* (*2020 Second Amendment*) stipulates that the lender and the borrower take unpaid sums of principal and interest of the previous loan into the amount of principal of the new loan.

ment) provides that: "Where the borrower and the lender take unpaid sums of principal and interest of a previous loan into the amount of principal of a new loan, provided that the interest sum not exceeding the sum calculated based on the statutory cap (four times Annual LPR), the amount of principal shall be deemed as the new principal. The part in excess of the statutory interest sum shall not be deemed as part of the new principal. Accordingly, the total amount of the principal and interest in the last contract, if it exceeds the total amount of principal in the first contract and interest calculated based on the original principal and the statutory cap (four times Annual LPR at the time of the formation of the first contract), shall not be supported by the people's court."

It can be inferred from the above provisions that: First, the laws in the Chinese Mainland hold a moderate attitude towards the nature of the new loan contract. On the one hand, the laws fully respect the autonomy of will of the parties in contract and give as much freedom as possible in determining principal. On the other hand, the laws confirm the successor position of the new loan once its principal amount is proven to be calculated on the basis of the previous sums. Second, to determine the loan contracts to be in a successive order, the following two conditions must be satisfied: (1) Each unpaid interest sum to be taken into the amount of the new principal shall not exceed the statutory interest sum (calculated on the basis of four times Annual LPR at the time of contract formation); otherwise, the exceeding part cannot be deemed as part of the new principal. (2) The total amount of the principal and the interest in the last contract shall not exceed the total amount of the principal in the first contract and of the interest calculated based on the first principal and the statutory cap; otherwise, the exceeding part shall not be supported by laws.

II. Laws in Hong Kong

Section 2 of the *Money Lenders Ordinance* defines the principal and the interest as follows: "Principal, in relation to a loan, means the amount actually lent. " "Interest does not include any sum lawfully agreed to be paid in accordance with this Ordinance on account of stamp duty or other similar duty, but save as aforesaid includes any amount (by whatever name called) in excess of the principal, which amount has been or is to be paid or payable in consideration of or otherwise in respect of a loan. " Pursuant to the above provisions, the actual amount lent by the lender is the loan principal for the borrower. All expenses incurred, in whatever name of, in borrowing paid by the borrower, other than principal and duties, are called interest.

i. Relevant Legal Concepts

(1) Loan includes advance, discount, money paid for or on account of or on behalf of or at the request of any person, or the forbearance to require payment of money owing on any account whatsoever, and every agreement (whatever its terms or form may be) which is in substance or effect a loan of money, and also an agreement to secure the repayment of any such loan.

(2) The definitions of Lend and Lender shall be construed aforesaid accordingly.

(3) Stamp Duty means stamp duty chargeable under the *Stamp Duty Ordinance* (Cap. 117) and includes additional stamp duty, buyer's stamp duty and special stamp duty.

ii. Rules for Deductions in Advance and Pre-agreed Deductions

Judicial practices in Hong Kong often see lending cases in which the amount of loan claimed by one party is inconsistent with the amount stated in the agreement since it is common for some lenders to deduct part or even all of the interest and other fees in various names and labels when granting the loan.

1. Deduction in Advance

Deductionin advance primarily refers to part or all of the loan interest deducted in advance when lending. The deducted interest is called retained interest, translated as "留存利息" in Chinese and colloquially known as "cau tau sik" in Cantonese. Usually, the retained interest is directly deducted by the lender from the loan without ever passing through the borrower's hands, or be paid to the lender by the borrower within a rather short period of time, typically on site or on the same day, after receiving the loan.

Sometimes there are fees deducted in advance apart from the retained interest, commonly in the name of the so-called handling fee, set-up charge, service fee, upfront fee, legal fee, etc.

2. Pre-Agreed Deduction

When the parties agree on a loan to be granted on the condition that the borrower must pay certain fees to the lender at the agreed-upon time stipulated in the loan agreement, a separate supplementary agreement, or a repayment guarantee agreement, or other similar agreements. Fees mentioned above are labelled as handling fee, set-up charge, legal fee and various other names. Even if such pre-agreed fees are not deducted in advance from the loan, they are in most cases paid to the lender within a quite short period of time once the borrower received the money. Refunded to the lender as expected, these fees are actually not at the disposal of the borrower, which in fact reflects a trick played by the lender to avoid the control imposed by laws and make more illegal profits from lending.

3. Rules for Deductions in Advance and Pre-Agreed Deductions

Section 2 of the *Money Lenders Ordinance* stipulates that only the amount actually lent is the loan principal, and that any sum in excess of the principal (by whatever name called) is interest.[1] Section 27 indicates that such deduc-

---

[1] Section 2 of the *Money Lenders Ordinance*: "Principal, in relation to a loan, means the amount actually lent." "Interest does not include any sum lawfully agreed to be paid in accordance with this Ordinance on account of stamp duty or other similar duty, but save as aforesaid includes any amount (by whatever name called) in excess of the principal, which amount has been or is to be paid or payable in consideration of or otherwise in respect of a loan."

tions may be recovered by the borrower or set off against the principal.[1]

In judicial practices, courts in Hong Kong usually take away such deductions, as well as pre-agreed deductions, from the amount of principal whilst include them into the amount of interest in determining the actual principal and the effective interest rate of a loan.

In *Gain Wealth Global Credit & Investment Limited v. Chan Suk Fong*[2] heard by the Court of Appeal of the High Court, the parties signed a loan agreement of HK $ 1,000,000 for one year with an annual interest rate of 30% and were in dispute over three deductions (HK $ 37,000, HK $ 100,000 and HK $ 110,000 respectively).

In respect of the principal amount, the Court of Appeal determined the amount to be HK $ 863,000 (HK $ 1,000,000 – HK $ 37,000 – HK $ 100,000 = HK $ 863,000) with the following reasons: First, the sum of HK $ 37,000 was deducted from the principal amount since it was a "pre-paid fee" never truly granted to the defendant and thus did not constitute an amount "actually lent"[3]. Second, the sum of HK $ 100,000 was deducted from the principal amount since the plaintiff failed to prove the payment of such sum to an intermediary third party was under the instruction of the defendant, or was made according to the loan agreement. Furthermore, the sum of HK $ 100,000 was issued by the plaintiff with a cash cheque and later cashed by the defendant in a bank counter

---

[1] Section 27(4) of the *Money Lenders Ordinance*: "If any money or money's worth is directly or indirectly paid or allowed to or received by any person in contravention of this section, the amount or value thereof, to the extent of such contravention and notwithstanding any agreement to the contrary, may be recovered by the borrower from such person or, if such person is the money lender or a partner, employer, employee, principal or agent of the money lender or is in any way acting for or in collusion with him, may be set off against the amount actually lent (and that amount shall be deemed to be reduced accordingly) or may be recovered by the borrower from such person or from the money lender."

[2] [2021] HKCA 1219.

[3] *Gain Wealth Global Credit & Investment Limited v. Chan Suk Fong* [2021] HKCA 1219, para. 57,62.

and directly paid to the third party on site, which means it never in fact came into the defendant's pocket. Based on the third party's participation in the whole transaction process as well as its promotion for the loan agreement between the parties, it can be presumed that such sum of HK $ 100,000 was actually a remuneration for the third party in anticipation of a successful lend-borrowing course.[1] Therefore, it shall be deducted from the principal amount. Third, the sum of HK $ 110,000 was kept to arrive at the deemed principal since it was issued by the plaintiff with a crossed cheque marked "account payee only" and deposited by the defendant into her bank account, from which withdrawn and handed to the third party. Although similar to the aforesaid HK $ 100,000, this sum of HK $ 110,000 in fact came into the defendant's pocket and was paid to the third party with the defendant's personal confirmation[2]. Thus, the sum shall be deemed as principal.

In respect of the interest amount, the Court of Appeal determined the amount to be HK $ 337,000 (HK $ 300,000 + HK $ 37,000 = HK $ 337,000) with the following reasons: First, the contractual interest amount was HK $ 300,000 (HK $ 1,000,000 * 30% * 1). Second, the sum of HK $ 37,000 was included as interest because Section 2(1) of the *Money Lenders Ordinance* provides that interest includes any amount (by whatever name called) in excess of the principal. The court, following the *Money Lenders Ordinance*, held that the deduction of HK $ 37,000 from the principal amount whilst including it into the interest amount would not constitute "double counting".[3] Third, the sum of HK $ 100,000 was not included as interest. Although Section 2(1) of the *Money*

---

[1] *Gain Wealth Global Credit & Investment Limited v. Chan Suk Fong* [2021] HKCA 1219, para. 66 – 67.

[2] *Gain Wealth Global Credit & Investment Limited v. Chan Suk Fong* [2021] HKCA 1219, para. 66 – 67.

[3] *Gain Wealth Global Credit & Investment Limited v. Chan Suk Fong* [2021] HKCA 1219, para. 62 – 63.

Lenders Ordinance stipulates that the amount qualified as interest is not required to be paid or payable to the lender or its agent but could be paid to someone else so long as it is paid or payable in consideration of or otherwise in respect of a loan[1], the court held that all available evidence at present failed to establish an agency regarding to loan business between the plaintiff and the intermediary third party[2], nor to prove an involvement of the plaintiff in deciding on the sum of HK $ 100,000 paid to the third party[3], nor to prove the direct connection between such sum and the plaintiff's lending conduct. Hence, such sum should not be included as interest.

Similarly, in *Skyline Credit Limited v. Leung Hing Chung*[4], the Court of Appeal of the High Court gave the same treatment to deductions and pre-agreed deductions in the determination and calculation of principal and interest. The parties from a loan contract of HK $ 1,800,000 for one year with an annual interest rate of 30% were in dispute over four deductions (HK $ 49,680, HK $ 18,000, HK $ 8000 and HK $ 762,320 respectively).

In respect of the principal amount, the Court of Appeal determined the amount to be HK $ 1,724,320 (HK $ 1,800,000 – HK $ 49,680 – HK $ 180,000 – HK $ 8000 = HK $ 1,724,320) with the following reasons. First, the sum of HK $ 49,680 was deducted from the principal amount as it was retained interest never truly granted to the defendant and thus did not constitute an amount "actually lent". Second, the sum of HK $ 18,000 in the name of "handing fee" was deducted from the principal amount since it actually was a pre-agreed deduction required by the plaintiff before lending and the defendantwas forced to

[1] *Gain Wealth Global Credit & Investment Limited v. Chan Suk Fong* [2021] HKCA 1219, para. 43.

[2] *Gain Wealth Global Credit & Investment Limited v. Chan Suk Fong* [2021] HKCA 1219, para. 48.

[3] *Gain Wealth Global Credit & Investment Limited v. Chan Suk Fong* [2021] HKCA 1219, para. 55.

[4] [2022] HKCA 1241.

agree in anticipation for a successful money arrangement. Third, the sum of HK $ 8000 so-called "legal fee" was deducted from the principal amount since it in fact was a deduction never truly granted to the defendant. Fourth, the sum of HK $ 762,320 labelled as insurance fee was deemed as principal and kept to arrive at the principal amount because it was issued by the plaintiff with a crossed cheque of HK $ 872,000 marked "account payee only"[1] and deposited by the defendant into personal bank account, from where later HK $ 762,320 was withdrawn in cash and handed to the third party[2]. The court held the opinion that since all available evidence failed to prove an agency or a fraud between the plaintiff and the intermediary third party[3], the sum which truly came into the defendant's pocket and paid with the defendant's personal confirmation should be deemed as principal.

In respect of the interest amount, the Court of Appeal determined the amount to be HK $ 572,480 (HK $ 496,800 + HK $ 49,680 + HK $ 18,000 + HK $ 8000 = HK $ 572,480) with the following reasons. First, the contractual interest amount was HK $ 496,800 (HK $ 1,800,000 * 27.6% * 1). Second, the sums of HK $ 49,680, HK $ 18,000 and HK $ 8000 respectively were all included as interest because Section 2(1) of the *Money Lenders Ordinance* provided that interest includes any amount (by whatever name called) in excess of the principal.[4] The definition of interest under Section 2 was cast in the widest possible terms in order to catch any payments which borrowers were made to pay to money lenders under various names or labels and the court should look at the substance not the form.[5]

---

[1] *Skyline Credit Limited v. Leung Hing Chung* [2022] HKCA 1241, para. 48.

[2] *Skyline Credit Limited v. Leung Hing Chung* [2022] HKCA 1241, para. 13.

[3] *Skyline Credit Limited v. Leung Hing Chung* [2022] HKCA 1241, para. 48.

[4] *Skyline Credit Limited v. Leung Hing Chung* [2022] HKCA 1241, para. 51 – 53.

[5] *Skyline Credit Limited v. Leung Hing Chung* [2022] HKCA 1241, para. 125.

iii. Refinancing

1. The Concept of Refinancing

Judicial practices in Hong Kong often see the signing of several similar loan agreements with same terms but different principal sums between the same lender and the same borrower over a relatively fixed period of time. For such agreements involved in trials, the court will firstly label them as either a single loan or a series of loans.

A single loan refers to the situation where among plenty of successively signed loan agreements, each subsequent agreement derives from its previous one and the borrower has discharged unliquidated obligations by using the money obtained from the later loan to fully pay off the previous outstanding debts. With the termination of the previous loan agreement and the commencement of the subsequent one, the contractual relationship between the lender and the borrower rolls over into the newly signed agreement. Thus, it can be seen that the concept of single loan in Hong Kong is more like that of refinancing in the Mainland. Series of Loans refers to the situation where among plenty of successively signed loan agreements, each agreement does not derive from one another and thus has an equal status with an independent legal validity. Plenty of loan agreements just represent the existence of multiple contractual relationships between the lender and the borrower.

2. Common Law and Precedents of Refinancing

Legislation in Hong Kong has no provisions in respect of the validity of refinancing loan agreements. The rulings vary from case to case depending on the specific facts and circumstances of each individual case.

In *New Japan Securities International (Hong Kong) Limited v. Lim Yiong Lin*[1] heard by the Court of Appeal of the High Court, the plaintiff, as a

[1] [1987] HKCU 194.

moneylender, made five loans to the defendant which had been used to discharge the defendant's liabilities for principal and interest under earlier loans. Each of the five loans was made for a period of three months and simple interest was payable. The court found that it was common ground for both parties that these loans were the successors of earlier loans on similar terms which, as and when the defendant had defaulted on his obligations, however, had successively been rolled over in the sense that the plaintiff made fresh loans to him of sums sufficient to discharge his accrued liability for principal and interest[1]. Having referred to what Greer LJ stated in *BS Lyle Ltd. v. Chappell*[2], the court also held that if the transaction meant that the money was lent to the borrower and that the borrower with that money paid off the old loan, the court was no longer in a position to treat the transaction as a mere renewal since what had happened was that the old loans had been paid off and a new loan had been entered into, and the position was exactly the same as it would have been if the borrower had borrowed from someone else the money necessary to repay the old loan and obtained a new loan[3].

Recently, in *Honip Credit Limited v. Leung Tak Sing Paul*[4], the Court of Appeal of the High Court confirmed that seven loan agreements on similar terms signed between the parties were actually refinancing loan agreements and after referring to the abovementioned *New Japan* Case the court addressed its decisive opinion that the 7th loan agreement was in fact a new loan and as the new loan it did not levy compound interest[5].

To sum up, a refinancing loan that sufficiently discharges the borrower's

---

〔1〕 *New Japan Securities International (Hong Kong) Limited v. Lim Yiong Lin* [1987] HKCU 194, para. 2.

〔2〕 [1932] 1 KB 691.

〔3〕 *New Japan Securities International (Hong Kong) Limited v. Lim Yiong Lin* [1932] 1 KB 691, para. 7.

〔4〕 [2020] HKCA 879.

〔5〕 *Honip Credit Limited v. Leung Tak Sing Paul* [2020] HKCA 879, para. 4.31.

liability to principal and interest of earlier loans will normally be treated as a new loan. In calculating the interest of the new loan, there is no need to consider the interest of earlier loans and the possibility of compound interest.

III. Summary

i. Similarity

Firstly, legislation in the Chinese Mainland and Hong Kong both adopt the same conservative and restrictive approach in the determination of principal amount in private lending cases. Only the amount actually lent will be deemed as principal.

Secondly, deductions such as retained interests will be deducted from the principal amount in the judicial practice of both Chinese Mainland and Hong Kong.

ii. Difference

Firstly, in terms of the scope of interest, the laws in the Chinese Mainland distinguish interest from liquidated damages as well as any other fees and stipulate that the total amount of all fees including interest, liquidated damages and others cannot exceed the statutory cap of four times Annual LPR. The laws in Hong Kong distinguish interest from stamp duty as well as other similar duty and stipulate that any amount (by whatever name called) in excess of the principal is deemed as interest.

Secondly, in terms of deductions in the calculation of interest, sums deducted from the principal amount will not be included into the interest amount in the Chinese Mainland. In Hong Kong, sums deducted from the principal amount are likely to be included into the interest amount.

Thirdly, in terms of judicial restrictions on refinancing loans, the laws in the Chinese Mainland require the total amount of principal and interest of the last loan not to exceed the amount of principal and interest calculated based on the principal of the very first loan in order to prevent interest from exceeding the statutory cap. The laws in Hong Kong only require each refinancing loan to comply with the law.

Section Two Loan Interest

I. Laws in the Chinese Mainland

Due to the profit-seeking nature of money capital, interest and interest rate, both capital-related concepts, are normally seen as the price of money as a commodity. Therefore, unless otherwise provided by law, a loan contract is usually interest-bearing[1]. Private lending, however, differs from lending by financial institutions. The subjects of private lending include both enterprises and natural persons, and the purposes of borrowing are not only for business operations but also for temporary life needs. Compared to financial lending, private lending tends to be more diversified in its forms and contents. Private lending contracts, as can be seen in practice, are not always interest-bearing. Some carry interest while some not, and some carry interest but without an explicit rate. Judicial practices in the Chinese Mainland often see private lending contracts without agreement or without explicit agreement on interest.

For above situations, Article 24 of the *Provisions on Private Lending* (2020 *Second Amendment*) stipulates: "Where the contract parties have no agreement on interest and the lender claims payment of interest, the people's court shall not support such claim. Where the contract parties, both are natural

---

[1] Article 38 of the *Law of the People's Republic of China on Commercial Banks*: "Commercial banks shall determine loan interest rate in accordance with the upper and lower limits for loan interest rates prescribed by the People's Bank of China."

persons, have unclear agreement on interest and the lender claims payment of interest, the people's court shall not support such claim. Except for loans between natural persons, if the loan interest is not clearly agreed upon by the borrower and the lender, and the lender claims the payment of interest, the people's court shall determine the interest in light of the contents of the contract and in accordance with the local or the parties' trading modes, trading practices, LPR and other relevant factors." Article 680 of the *Civil Code* is basically consistent with the above provision.

Pursuant to the aforesaid legal provisions, it can be concluded that rules for the determination of loan interest in the Chinese Mainland basically are: On the premise of not exceeding the statutory cap, the people's court will support what the parties have agreed on interest. Where the parties have no agreement, the loan contract shall be deemed as interest-free. Where the parties have unclear agreement on interest, unless the parties are natural persons which will lead to the loan contract be deemed as interest-free, the loan contract shall be deemed as interest-bearing and the people's court shall determine the interest in accordance with the local or the parties' trading modes, trading practices, LPR and other relevant factors.

i. Loan Interest without Agreement

1. Both Parties Are Natural Persons

Case: A borrowed ¥100,000 from B without an agreement on interest. Later A defaulted and B sued A for the principal of ¥100,000 and interest calculated on LPR. The court supported B's claim for principal but rejected B's claim for interest.

2. One or Both Parties Are Not Natural Persons

Case: Company A borrowed ¥100,000 from Company B for cash flow without an agreement on interest since A and B had a long history of business dealings. Later A defaulted and B sued A for the principal of ¥100,000 and interest calculated on LPR. The court supported B's claim for principal but rejected B's claim for interest.

Although companies normally get involved in financial transactions for profits, it is still undeniable that sometimes they are doing these out of emergencies. Compared with natural persons, companies as non-financial institution corporations, usually are more capable of engaging in civil and commercial conducts, risk control and making judgment for market expectations, which make them better decision makers of self-interest. Interest should be explicitly stipulated in the loan contract; otherwise, the contract should be deemed as without interest.

ii. Loan Interest with Unclear Agreement

1. Both Parties Are Natural Persons

Case: A borrowed ¥100,000 from B. They agreed on interest payable but not clearly on the amount or calculation standards. Later A defaulted and B sued A for the principal of ¥100,000 and interest calculated on LPR. The court supported B's claim for principal but rejected B's claim for interest.

Traditionally, private lending primarily occurs between natural persons. The borrower, usually a relative, colleague or friend of the lender, is in need of irregular expenses for children's marriage, education, house-purchase, disease treatment and so forth. Such lending is mainly for doing a favour and thus is usually interest-free unless expressly mentioned otherwise. The purpose of the abovementioned regulation is to facilitate production and daily life and promote peace and harmony in the neighbourhood and eventually create an atmosphere of mutual help and friendly interaction.

2. One or Both Parties Are Not Natural Persons

Case: Company A borrowed ¥100,000 from Person B for engineering construction. They agreed on interest payable but not clearly on the amount or calculation standards. Before lending, A showed B its Funding Plan which stated that the company intends to raise fund of ¥1,000,000 for two years with an annual interest rate of 10%. Later A defaulted and B sued A for the principal of ¥100,000 and interest calculated on four times Annual LPR. The court supported B's claim for principal but ordered the interest to be calculated on 10% per annum.

The determination of interest with unclear agreement from the parties is in fact a supplement to the loan contract. The absence of certain clauses in a contract, also known as a loophole, refers to the situation where a contract is supposed to specify a certain matter but failed to do so. A supplement is for the purpose of completing a contract but not creating a new one between the parties, and thus it shall follow the minimal intervention principle in avoidance of infringing the autonomy of will of contractual parties. Based on the above considerations, the determination and calculation of loan interest with an unclear agreement between parties, one or both of whom are not natural persons, shall consider these factors in the following sequence:

(1) The Contents of the Contract

Loan contracts involving non-financial institution corporations and unincorporated organisations are typically concluded in writing with well-organised language to express and convey the parties' intentions to the contract, through which such absent clause or the true intention of the parties concerning loan interest can possibly be observed. In the aforesaid case where company A and person B did not reach a clear agreement on the amount or calculation of interest, the court still held that the purpose of the loan for engineering construction stipulated in the contract between the parties was consistent with the purpose of the loan stipulated in A's Funding Plan, which clearly stated the funding for two years with an annual rate of 10%, and therefore made a judgment for interest on 10% per annum.

(2) Trading Modes and Customs in the Place of Performance or between the Parties

Generally, on the premise of not violating the mandatory provisions of laws and administrative regulations, the following two situations can be identified as "trading customs": First, practices that are commonly used in the local area of the transaction, or in a certain field or industry, and which the counterparty knew or should have known at the time of contract formation; Second, customary practices that are frequently used by the two parties.

(3) The LPR in the Place of Performance at the Time of Contract Formation

Article 511 of the *Civil Code* stipulates: "Where an agreement between the parties concerning the content of their contract is unclear and such content cannot be determined according to the provisions of the preceding Article, the following provisions shall be applied: ……(2) where the price or remuneration is not clearly stipulated, the contract shall be performed in accordance with the market price in the place of performance at the time the contract is concluded. Where the government-set or government-guided price shall be applied as required by laws, the contract shall be performed on such a price."

II. Laws in Hong Kong

Chitty on Contracts (*35th edition*) states that contractual interest is, of course, payable wherever there is an express agreement to that effect. Such an agreement may also be inferred from a course of dealing between the parties, e.g., if it has been frequently charged and paid without objection in similar accounts. Similarly, an obligation to pay interest may arise from the custom or usages of a particular trade or business.[1] In cases where interest is not agreed upon in the contract, *Chitty on Contracts* (*35th edition*) further states that at common law, the general rule was that interest was not payable on a debt or loan in the absence of express agreement or some course of dealing or custom to

---

[1] See Hugh Beale, Richard Hooley, Louise Merrett, Graham Virgo, *Chitty on Contracts*, Sweet & Maxwell, 35th Edition, para. 42-298.

that effect. Therefore, unless the contract is suspected of fraud, interest payments on overdue amounts, lent funds, outstanding monetary debts, guarantees, unsettled project payments, and any payable arrears are not required in the absence of express terms.[1]

i. Loan Interest without Agreement

The Court of First Instance of the High Court made an adjudication based on criteria in consistent with the principle stated aforesaid by *Chitty on Contracts* in *Lam Ching Sheung (林徵媮) v. The Personal Representative of The Estate of Tam Shui, Deceased (譚瑞(已故)遗产的管理人) & Ors.*[2]. The parties made an oral loan contract without an agreement on interest. After taking all statements of the parties and the witnesses into consideration, the court rejected the plaintiff 's claim for interest since the court found that the intention at the very beginning of the contract was lending an interest-free loan to the defendant.[3]

ii. Loan Interest with Unclear Agreement

In *Chun Yip Engineering Co. (a firm) v. Silvercord Limited*[4], the High Court explained how to "infer an implied term from the course of dealing" as follows: "It must borne in mind that for the court to imply a term (assuming that an agreement exists), the implied term must be one which is not only reasonable but also necessary so as to give business efficacy to the agreement." The plaintiff claimed an implied agreement on interest to be inferred from the transaction process between the parties. After the hearing, the court held that it

---

[1] See Hugh Beale, Richard Hooley, Louise Merrett, Graham Virgo, *Chitty on Contracts*, Sweet & Maxwell, 35th Edition, para. 42 – 297.

[2] [2013] HKCU 476.

[3] *Lam Ching Sheung (林徵媮) v. The Personal Representative of The Estate of Tam Shui, Deceased (譚瑞(已故)遗产的管理人) & Ors.* [2013] HKCU 476, para. 66.

[4] [1997] HKCU 1.

may be reasonable that because the defendant used to charge this rate of interest, the defendant should pay the plaintiff the same rate of interest, however, such a term is not necessary for there to be a loan agreement.[1]

What is worth mentioning is that equity under the common law also has a profound influence on laws in Hong Kong. The rule in equity is that, in certain circumstances, interest is payable even in the absence of any agreement or custom to that effect. For instance, the right of a surety who has paid the creditor, to be indemnified by the principal debtor, carries a right to interest, according to the equity.[2]

In conclusion, based on common law rules and judicial practice aforesaid, the rules for the determination of loan interest in Hong Kong are as follows: On premise of not in excess of statutory cap (i. e., the effective rate[3] does not violate the *Money Lenders Ordinance*), interest with explicit agreement shall be enforced. Interest with unclear agreement but possibly implied from the course of dealing between the parties, or the customs or practices of particular trades or businesses, shall be deemed enforceable. Interest without agreement and cannot be implied shall not be supported in a normal situation. Interest under equity, whether with or without agreement, shall be enforced.

III. Summary

As for differences, the laws in the Chinese Mainland distinguish natural persons from other contractual parties by regulating that interest, whether without agreement or with unclear agreement, of a loan between parties who are both natural persons shall be deemed as interest-free. Only interest with unclear

---

[1] *Chun Yip Engineering Co. (a firm) v. Silvercord Limited* [1997] HKCU 1, para. 22.

[2] See Hugh Beale, Richard Hooley, Louise Merrett, Graham Virgo, *Chitty on Contracts*, Sweet & Maxwell, 35th Edition, para. 42 – 300.

[3] Effective Rate means the true annual percentage rate of interest calculated in accordance with Schedule 2 of the *Money Lenders Ordinance*.

agreement between parties, one or both of whom are not natural persons, shall be determined based on the local or the parties' course of dealing, trading modes and customs, LPR and so forth. However, the laws in Hong Kong do not distinguish natural persons from other contractual parties. Interest without agreement or with unclear agreement shall first be implied from the parties' course of dealing, trading or business customs and so forth. Only interest without agreement fails to be implied will be deemed as interest-free. Equity also provides plenty of exceptions.

Section Three Default Interest

I. Laws in the Chinese Mainland

Article 676 of the *Civil Code* states: "A borrower who fails to repay the loan within the agreed time limit shall pay an overdue interest in accordance with the agreement or the relevant regulations of the State." The borrower's major obligation is to repay the principal and interest. Failure in repayment on time constitutes a material breach of contract, for which the borrower shall bear corresponding legal obligations.

i. Nature of Default Interest

Default interest is known as the interest incurred on late payment. In a loan contract, the ways for the borrower to discharge his obligation for late payment include the payment of principal, contract interest and default interest. The payment of principal and contract interest is within the domain of continued performance of contract[1], while the payment of default interest is not. Default interest has the following characteristics:

1. Default Interest Is Not Fructus Civiles

Monetary claims (Certa Pecuria) generate fructus civiles. The fundamental legal rationale behind the claim for principal and contract interest is the action of the repayment of the loan. A late payment makes the principal and contract interest fail to be recovered by the creditor. Thus, it seems reasonable to treat both principal and contract interest as fructus civiles. However, the fundamental legal rationale behind the claim for default interest is the loan contract itself. Different from default interest, contract interest could be seen as an income for the lender who gives out money for a period of time and an expense for the borrower who takes use of the money for the same period of time, thus it is a cost for occupying the money, which plays an essential role in the performance of contract. Default interest is not the cost of occupying the money and therefore it cannot be deemed as fructus civiles.

2. Nature of Default Interest Depends upon Parties' Agreement

(1) Breach of Loan Contracts

Default interest derives from the borrower's failure in repayment on time and is a consequence of breach of loan contract. Article 577 of the *Civil Code* stipulates: "Where a party fails to perform his contractual obligation or his performance does not conform to the agreement, he shall bear default liability such as continuing to perform his obligations, taking remedial measures, or compensating for losses." Article 179 stipulates: "The main ways of bearing civil responsibilities include: (1) cessation of the infringement; (2) removal of the

---

[1] Continued Performance, also known as compulsory actual performance, is a method of bearing default liability in which the breaching party continues to perform its obligations under the contract at the request of the other party. The fulfilment of pecuniary obligations can only be delayed and cannot be exempted due to failure to perform, whether de jure or de facto. Therefore, the method of continued performance must be applied unconditionally.

nuisance; (3) elimination of the danger; (4) restitution; (5) restoration; (6) repair, redoing or replacement; (7) continuance of performance; (8) compensation for losses; (9) payment of liquidated damages; (10) elimination of adverse effects and rehabilitation of reputation; and (11) extension of apologies." According to these above provisions, it is generally believed remedies for breach of contract are continuance in performance, compensation for loss[1] and payment of liquidated damages[2]. Furthermore, the compensation for loss can be categorised into two types, namely the statutory compensation[3] and the contractual compensation[4]. While the liquidated damages can also be categorised as statutory damages and contractual damages, or as punitive damages and compensatory damages. In which category the default interest exists shall be decided based on the parties' agreement.

(2) Parties' Agreement in Loan Contract

The doctrine of freedom of contract and the principle of autonomy of will of the parties are both cornerstones in law. The nature of default interest is upon the parties' agreement. Therefore, where the parties specify liquidated damages, in whatever amount, as the borrower's obligation of breach of contract, the default interest shall be deemed as liquidated damages. Where the parties specify a compensation or a calculation of compensation, the default interest shall be deemed as a compensation for loss.

The *Civil Code* tends to encourage liquidated damages as compensation and

---

[1] Compensation for Loss, also known as damages for breach of contract under contract law, is a method of bearing default liability wherein the breaching party compensates the injured party through monetary payment for the loss of property or loss of benefits resulting from the breach.

[2] Liquidated Damages is a method of bearing default liability wherein the breaching party pays money or delivers property to the other party in the event of default.

[3] Statutory Compensation refers to compensation liability imposed by law, which obligates the breaching party to compensate the non-breaching party for the losses incurred due to the breach of contract.

[4] Contractual Compensation refers to the agreed compensation amount or method of calculating damages between the parties when concluding the contract.

limits it as a penalty. If the default interest is agreed by the parties in contract as liquidated damages, the statutory cap of default rate not exceeding loan rate is a reflection not only of determining damages on damage but also of a remedy with compensatory characteristic, which protect the creditor and the debtor at the same time.

If the default interest is agreed by the parties in contract as compensation for loss, the statutory cap of default rate not exceeding loan rate is a direct reflection of determining compensation amount on loss. To sum up, whether as liquidated damages or compensation, the default interest shall first be awarded to compensate the lender's loss but not to punish the borrower's misconducts. The statutory cap for default rate not exceeding loan rate is able to protect the lender's interests to the largest extent.

ii. Calculation of Default Interest

Article 28 of *Provisions on Private Lending (2020 Second Amendment)* stipulates: "Where the parties have an agreement on default rate, the rate shall apply, provided that it does not exceed four times Annual LPR at the time of signing up the contract. If the parties have no agreement or no explicit agreement on default rate, the people's court shall handle the matter in light of different situations: (1) where the parties have neither agreement on loan rate nor agreement on default rate and the lender claims default interest on Annual LPR from the day of the borrower's default in repayment, the people's court shall support it. (2) where the parties have agreement on loan rate but not on default rate and the lender claims for default interest on loan rate since the day of the borrower's default in repayment, the people's court shall support it." According to the above provision, the legal principles for the calculation of default interest in the Chinese Mainland are as follows: First, where the parties have an agreement on default rate, the rate shall apply, provided that it does not exceed four times Annual LPR at the time of contract formation. Second, where the parties have agreement on the loan rate but have not made the default rate explicit, the loan rate can be applied in calculating the default interest. Third, where the parties have neither agreement on loan rate nor agreement on default rate, the Annual LPR shall apply in calculating default interest.

II. Laws in Hong Kong

i. Nature of Default Interest

Default Interest under the common law, namely 逾期利息 in Chinese, is the payment of interest demanded after the borrower's default in the repayment of a loan.[1] Historically, the common law did not encourage the award of interest.[2]

1. Default Interest Is Not Consideration

A consideration can be defined as the giving of something of value to the other party in exchange for a promise and can be deemed as a price of the party's intention to make a legally binding contract. The House of Lords of the United Kingdom confirmed in *London, Chatham & Dover Railway Co. v. South Eastern Railway Co.*[3] that "at common law a court had no power to award interest by way of damages for the late payment of a debt"[4], which means the claim for interest, except contractual interest, occurring from late payment of a loan shall not be supported. Although this principle has been o-

---

[1] See Hugh Beale, Richard Hooley, Louise Merrett, Graham Virgo, *Chitty on Contracts*, Sweet & Maxwell, 35th Edition, para. 42 – 307.

[2] Charles T. McCoemick, *Interest As Damages*, Article 1, No. 3, Volume 9, North Carolina Law Review.

[3] [1893] AC 429.

[4] *London, Chantham & Dover Railway Co. v. South Eastern Railway Co.* [1893] AC 429, para. 437.

verturned in recent cases[1], it still indicates the traditionally conservative attitude towards default interest under common law. The payment of interest by the borrower has already constituted the consideration for the lending of loan by the lender in a loan contract. Therefore, the nature of default interest is not a consideration.

2. Default Interest Is Not a Remedy for Tort

Misconduct under the contract law can be classified as tort or breach of contract. The parties with the right to claim damages for loss caused by tort or-breach of contract is also a fundamental principle under the British laws.[2] Usually, the remedy for tort is called the Restitutionary Remedy. In *Sempra Metals Limited v. Her Majesty's Commissioners of the Inland Revenue and Another*[3], the House of Lords of the United Kingdom held that restitutionary remedy allowed by the laws of this country to a person who had made a payment under a mistake could entitle the claimant to recover not only the payment but also interest thereon that the person under the obligation to make repayment had never received or to recover the value of an assumed benefit derived from the mistaken payment that that person had never in fact enjoyed. Therefore, it could be seen that to recover the value of an assumed benefit not in fact enjoyed by tort at common law was more likely to claim an unjust enrichment obtained by the borrower through tort.[4] Obviously, default interest derived from the borrower's late repayment of loan is not consistent with unjust enrichment, which indicates the default interest shall not be deemed as remedy for tort at

[1] The Court of Final Appeal (House of Lords) of the United Kingdom overturned the judicial principle that "interest on late payments is not compensable" in *Sempra Metals Ltd. v. Her Majesty's Commissioners of Inland Revenue and Another* [2007] UKHL 34.

[2] See Hugh Beale, Richard Hooley, Louise Merrett, Graham Virgo, *Chitty on Contracts*, Sweet & Maxwell, 35th Edition, para. 42 – 283.

[3] [2007] UKHL 34.

[4] *Sempra Metals Ltd. v. Her* Majesty's *Commissioners of Inland Revenue and Another* [2007] UKHL 34, para. 132.

common law.

3. Default Interest Is Compensation for Breach of Contract

The borrower's default in payment leads to the loss of the lender in not only the principal and interest but also the assumed benefit generated from in-time payment thereafter (the lender's burden to prove), which in fact is a breach of contract. Usually, the remedy for breach of contract is called the Compensatory Remedy. In *Union Base Ltd. v. Tsang Shek Tong trading as Hawaii Engineering Company*[1], the Court of Appeal in the High Court held that the overriding principle was that interest should be awarded to the plaintiff, not as compensation for the damage done, but for being kept out of the money which ought to have been paid (e. g. investment profits, etc.) to him[2]. Moreover, if by reason of the late payment the lender had actually incurred interest charges in obtaining finance from an alternative source, such loss could be recoverable as special damage, provided that it was in the reasonable contemplation of the parties at the time the contract was made that such charges would be incurred.[3] Interest as compensation allowed by laws for the use or detention of money, or as additional damages for loss of the use of money due was interest as damages.[4] Apparently, the nature of default interest is more consistent with this concept under common law.

However, the prerequisite for the claim of default interest is that the lender must have proved the actual loss caused by the borrower's late repayment, already occurred and is not related to contract interest. A contract to pay interest up to the date of repayment of the debt does not necessarily imply an agreement

---

[1] [1998] 2 HKC 349.

[2] *Union Base Ltd. v. Tsang Shek Tong trading as Hawaii Engineering Company* [1998] 2 HKC 349, para. 11.

[3] *Sempra Metals Ltd. v. Her Majesty's Commissioners of Inland Revenue and Another* [2007] UKHL 34, para. 132.

[4] Charles T. McCoemick, *Interest As Damages*, Article 1, No. 3, Volume 9, North Carolina Law Review.

to pay interest beyond that date in the event of default in repayment.[1] Interest agreed upon within the term shall not be extended after the expiration of the term.

ii. Calculation of Default Interest

Chitty on Contracts (*35th edition*) states that where there is a covenant to pay a principal sum, and the judgment is obtained upon the covenant for that sum, any covenant to pay interest which is merely incidental to the covenant to pay the principal sum is merged in the judgment.[2] If, however, the covenant to pay interest is expressed in such a manner as to be independent of the covenant to pay the principal sum, it is not merged or extinguished in the judgment. To summarise, where there is separate agreement on default interest in a loan contract, the calculation shall follow it. If there is no such agreement, the calculation shall be based on the judgment.

1. Loan Contract with Agreement on Default Interest

The laws in Hong Kong fully respect the autonomy of will of the parties in contract. Often it is agreed that interest at the contractual rate is payable after as well as before any judgment and the validity of such a provision depends on whether the covenant for the payment of interest is an independent covenant or a covenant which is merely ancillary to the payment of the principal money.[3]

(1) Default Rate Not Exceeding Loan Rate

In *Honip Credit Ltd. v. Asia China Tea Export Company Ltd. & Siu Mei Yam*[4], the Court of Appeal in the High Court gave a judgment that, on basis

---

[1] See Hugh Beale, Richard Hooley, Louise Merrett, Graham Virgo, *Chitty on Contracts*, Sweet & Maxwell, 35th Edition, para. 42 – 299.

[2] See Hugh Beale, Richard Hooley, Louise Merrett, Graham Virgo, *Chitty on Contracts*, Sweet & Maxwell, 35th Edition, para. 28 – 009.

[3] See Hugh Beale, Richard Hooley, Louise Merrett, Graham Virgo, *Chitty on Contracts*, Sweet & Maxwell, 35th Edition, para. 42 – 310.

[4] [2016] HKCU 1333.

of a finding of fact that the agreed default interest rate by the parties did not exceed their agreed loan rate in the same contract, the paying party is required to pay interest in accordance with the terms of the contract (including those relating to the rate of interest) and not in accordance with the rate of interest on the judgment.[1] The plaintiff and the defendant had reached an agreement on interest rate of 24.96% per annum in their loan contract, of which the clause 6 stipulated as the borrower had agreed the amount of interest payable of the loan should be calculated, whether before or after any judgment of a court, on the basis of 24.96% per annum continuously. In other words, the remaining debt still carried interest on 24.96% annually after the judgment of the court until full discharge. The court held that clause 6 of the loan contract was clear enough for the borrower's obligation to pay and could be seen as a covenant of default interest, according to which the calculation should continue to be based on 24.96% per annum.[2]

Similarly, the Court of Frist Instance of the High Court held the same opinion in respect of the calculation of default interest in *Freeway Finance Company Limited (亨运财务有限公司) v. Tam Chuen On Raymond*[3]. On 28 November, 2009, the parties signed a loan contract of HK $5,000,000 with clause 1 stipulating effective interest rate of monthly 4% (48% per annum) and clause 2 concerning 120 instalments in total (repayment of HK $142,500 per month). Furthermore, clause 2 also provided that the interest payable of the borrower incurred from default in principal or interest of any instalment shall be calculated, whether before or after the commitment of legal proceedings, or the judgement of a court, according to the rate stipulated in clause 1 of this contract

[1] *Honip Credit Limited v. Asia China Tea Export Company Limited & Siu Mei Yam* [2016] HKCU 1333, para. 21.

[2] *Honip Credit Limited v. Asia China Tea Export Company Limited & Siu Mei Yam* [2016] HKCU 1333, para. 22.

[3] [2010] HKCU 1462.

until full liquidation. The court saw the provision in respect of default interest from clause 2 of the loan contract as an independent covenant and confirmed its effectiveness, and thus reassured it to be applied in the calculation of interest after the judgment, which meant the interest after judgment should also be calculated on the basis of 48% per annum accordingly.

(2) Default Rate Exceeding Loan Rate

Section 22 of the *Money Lenders Ordinance* stipulates: "Any agreement made for the loan of money by a money lender shall be illegal if it provides directly or indirectly for—(c) the rate or amount of interest being increased by reason of any default in the payment of sums due under the agreement." According to such section, rate for interest calculation after the borrower's default in repayment shall normally not exceed the effective interest rate of the loan contract. However, Section 22 is made to regulate money lenders but not ordinary people, in that way such regulation can only be regarded as a reference from the legislative orientation.

What's worthy of our attention is the statement in *Chitty on Contracts* (*35th edition*) that a clause that provides for interest to increase on default will not be held to give rise to a penalty if the increase is not retrospective but only prospective from the date of default, if the dominant contractual purpose of the clause is not to deter default, and if the increase is modest and commercially justifiable by reason of the increased credit risk represented by a debtor in default.[1] To put in another word, a contractual provision for payment of a higher rate of interest after a default in payment by the borrower is open to attack as a penalty.

Pursuant to the development of common law system, the legal regulation in respect of default interest has gone through different stages from non-protec-

---

[1] See Hugh Beale, Richard Hooley, Louise Merrett, Graham Virgo, *Chitty on Contracts*, Sweet & Maxwell, 35th Edition, para. 42 - 305.

tion, limited protection till today's compensatory protection, which also impacted the legislation in Hong Kong in a certain degree. Hardly can it be seen an agreement between the parties on a higher default rate than loan rate in current cases in Hong Kong. It accordingly can be inferred that the laws in Hong Kong is not willing to see the parties to make agreements on higher rate of default interest.

2. Loan Contract without Agreements on Default Interest

In absence of agreements on default interest in a loan contract, a creditor receiving late payment may therefore recover any lost interest, provided that the loss is pleaded and proven.[1] *Chitty on Contracts* (*35th edition*) states that where a lender obtains judgment for the amount due under a loan, then the contract merges in the judgment so that the lender no longer has a cause of action in contract for either the principal or the remaining interest and must instead seek execution of the judgment with statutory interest on the judgment until payment is made.[2]

Judicial practices in Hong Kong usually treat default interest in two parts, namely the pre-judgment interest and the post-judgment interest.

(1) Pre-Judgment Interest

Pre-judgment interest is typically defined as interest accruing on late payment from the due date to the day before judgment date. According to basic principles of the common law, a creditor may claim for damages for the loss of interest arising from the debtor's breach of contract in late payment, provided that the loss is proven. Judges in Hong Kong usually exercise their discretion in calculating and awarding pre-judgment interest on rate of "Hong Kong Dollar

---

[1] See Hugh Beale, Richard Hooley, Louise Merrett, Graham Virgo, *Chitty on Contracts*, Sweet & Maxwell, 35th Edition, para. 42 – 283.

[2] See Hugh Beale, Richard Hooley, Louise Merrett, Graham Virgo, *Chitty on Contracts*, Sweet & Maxwell, 35th Edition, para. 28 – 007.

Prime Rate + 1% "[1]. As of September 20, 2024, the Hong Kong Dollar Prime Rate is 5.625% [2], which means the pre-judgment interest rate is 6.625%. In *Waddington Ltd. v. Chan Chun Hoo Thomas & Ors.*[3], the Court of Appeal of the High Court reiterated the calculation of pre-judgment interest should be based on Prime Rate plus 1%.[4]

According to Order 22 in Rule 24 of the *Rules of the High Court*, the court may order interest on the whole or part of any sum of money (excluding interest) awarded to the plaintiff at a rate not exceeding 10% above judgment rate for some or all of the period after the latest date on which the defendant could have accepted the offer, if the defendant is held liable for more than the proposals contained in a plaintiff's sanctioned offer or the judgement against a defendant is more advantageous to the plaintiff than the proposals contained in the plaintiff's sanctioned offer.[5] In G*olden Eagle International (Group) Limited v. GR Investment Holdings Limited*[6], the Court of First Instance of the High Court adopted such rule. The parties agreed to calculate the pre-judgment interest at a rate higher than Hong Kong Dollar Prime Rate + 1%. The court confirmed the agreed rate did not exceed the "judgment rate + 10%" and thus gave

[1] The standard of 1% above the prime rate began in 1982 in *Komala Deccof v. Pertamina* [1984] HKCU 47, the Court of Appeal of the High Court clarified that 1% above the prime rate under judge's discretion should be maintained as a standard for compensating a party for damages from recovering loan. Judgments of a vast majority of lending cases have adopted such standard thereafter.

[2] The latest HKD Prime Rate is 5.625% with the effective date of September 20, 2024.

[3] [2016] HKCU 1192.

[4] *Waddington Ltd. v. Chan Chun Hoo Thomas & Ors.* [2016] HKCU 1192, para. 172 – 185.

[5] Section 24 in Order 22 of the *Rules of the High Court*: "(1) This rule applies where—(a) a defendant is held liable for more than the proposals contained in a plaintiff's sanctioned offer; or (b) the judgment against a defendant is more advantageous to the plaintiff than the proposals contained in a plaintiff's sanctioned offer. (2) The Court may order interest on the whole or part of any sum of money (excluding interest) awarded to the plaintiff at a rate not exceeding 10% above judgment rate for some or all of the period after the latest date on which the defendant could have accepted the offer without requiring the leave of the Court."

[6] [2010] 3 HKLRD 273.

respect to the autonomy of will of the parties in contract.[1]

(2) Post-Judgment Interest

Post-judgment interest is typically defined as interest accruing on late payment from judgment date to the day of a full liquidation. Under Rule 49(1) of the *High Court Ordinance*[2] and Rule 50(1) of the *District Court Ordinance*[3], simple interest shall be payable on the whole or any part of a judgment debt at such rate as the court may order or, in the absence of such order, as the Chief Justice may determine by order, that is, the judgment rate. As of Octorber 1, 2024, the latest judgment rate ordered by the Chief Justice of the Court of Final Appeal is 8.875%.

III. Summary

i. Similarity

The laws in the Chinese Mainland and Hong Kong both respect the autonomy of will of the parties and protect default interest with explicit agreement in contract under the statutory cap.

ii. Difference

Firstly, in terms of the nature of default interest, the laws in the Chinese Mainland prioritise the parties' agreement in identifying the nature of default in-

[1] *Golden Eagle International (Group) Limited v. GR Investment Holdings Limited* [2010] 3 HKLRD 273, para. 11.

[2] Section 49(1) of the *Rules of the High Court*: "Judgment debts shall carry simple interest—(a) at such rate as the Court of First Instance may order; or (b) in the absence of such order, at such rate as may be determined from time to time by the Chief Justice by order, on the aggregate amount thereof, or on such part thereof as for the time being remains unsatisfied from the date of the judgment until satisfaction."

[3] Section 50(1) of the *Rules of the District Court*: "Judgment debts are to carry simple interest—(a) at the rate the Court orders; or (b) in the absence of an order, at the rate the Chief Justice determines by order, on the total amount of the judgment debt, or on the part that for the time being remains unpaid, from the date of the judgment until payment."

terest as either liquidated damages or compensation for loss. Common law principle in Hong Kong identifies the nature of default interest as damages for breach of contract.

Secondly, in terms of the protection for default rate exceeding loan rate, the laws in the Chinese Mainland only protect the amount not exceeding statutory cap (four times Annual LPR). The laws in Hong Kong have no explicit regulations, but a higher default rate is likely regarded as penalty and possibly rejected by court.

Thirdly, in terms of the calculation of default interest, the laws in the Chinese Mainland regulate the calculation of default interest without agreement to be computed on the basis of the loan rate, or Annual LPR in the absence of a loan rate. The laws in Hong Kong divide default interest without agreement into pre-judgment interest and post-judgment interest. The calculation of pre-judgment interest normally bases on Prime Rate (5.625% at present) + 1% and post-judgment interest on judgment rate (8.875% at present).

Chapter Ⅳ

Comparison of Legal Rules on the Statutory Interest Rate Cap

Section One Statutory Interest Rate Cap

I. Laws in the Chinese Mainland

The interest rate is a core issue in private lending regulation. The provisions of judicial interpretations indicate that the legality of private lending is highly correlated with the level of the interest rate of a loan. The regulation over the interest rate decides how inclusive the sector is and how well the sector is protected, as well as affecting the rights and interests of both lenders and borrowers. The *Provisions on Private Lending (2020 Second Amendment)* specifies the statutory interest rate cap in private lending, which seeks to prevent lenders from leveraging an imbalanced power structure and jeopardising borrowers' interests, instead of restraining lenders and borrowers from negotiating the interest rate within legal limits.[1]

i. The Background of Lowering Interest Rate Cap in *Provisions on Private Lending (2020 Amendment)*

The Supreme People's Court specifically introduced the context of lowering the upper limits for interest rates after publishing the *Provisions on Private Lending (2020 Amendment)*. In general, it is based on the following five reasons. Firstly, the decision fulfils the quest for economic and social development. Reducing the overall market interest rate level to lower the financing threshold for micro, small and medium-sized enterprises (MSMEs) is essential to economic recovery and ensuring operations of market entities. Secondly, the decision meets the needs of regulating private lending activi-

---

[1] See Yue Cai Shen, *Key Points of Regulation on Private Lending and Legislative Suggestions*, Chinese Legal Science, 2011, Issue 5, 88-89.

ties. Lowering the statutory interest rate cap greatly helps the guidance and regulation of private lending. Thirdly, the decision ensures the stable and healthy growth of the internet finance and that of the private lending sector in the long term. Fourthly, the decision is the prerequisite of the interest rate liberation reform. High-interest rate cap not only hinders the creation of a favourable external environment for the interest rate liberation reform, but also does not align with the reform objectives. Fifthly, the decision responds to the demand of standardising judicial criteria. It is necessary to amend the *Provisions on Private Lending* at appropriate times to adapt to the economic development, providing more accurate judicial criteria and remedies for private lending cases.

ii. Statutory Interest Rate Cap

1. The Statutory Interest Rate Cap Before the Amendment

Article 26 of the *Provisions on Private Lending* specifies that "Where the interest rate agreed upon by the borrower and the lender does not exceed the annual interest rate of 24%, and the lender claims the payment of interest at the agreed interest rate, the people's court shall support such a claim. Where the interest rate agreed upon by the borrower and the lender exceeds the annual interest rate of 36%, the agreed interest on the excessive part shall be null and void. If the borrower claims the return of the paid interest on the part exceeding the annual interest rate of 36%, the people's court shall support such a claim." The provision can be broken down to three parts. Firstly, an annual interest rate in private lending of less than 24% is deemed as effective. Secondly, the amount exceeding the annual interest rate of 36% is deemed as ineffective. Thirdly, the amount between the annual interest rate of 24% and 36% is considered as obligatio naturalis, where the amount paid cannot be asked to return, and the amount to be paid will not be supported. This is known as the "three categories by two lines" rule.

2. The Statutory Interest Rate Cap After the Amendment

Article 25 of the current *Provisions on Private Lending* (*2020 Second Amendment*) specifies that "Where the lender claims the payment of interest at the interest rate agreed upon in the contract, the people's court shall support the claim, except the case that the interest rate agreed upon by both parties exceed four times Annual LPR when the contract is concluded. For the purpose of the preceding paragraph, the 'Annual LPR' means the LPR for one-year loan published on a monthly basis from August 20, 2019 by the National Interbank Funding Center authorised by the People's Bank of China." The provision can also be interpreted from three tiers. Firstly, the statutory interest rate cap in private lending is reduced to four times Annual LPR. Secondly, the Annual LPR is fluctuating rather than fixed. According to the benchmark of Annual LPR (as of July 22, 2024) published by People's Bank of China, the highest rate of four times Annual LPR was 17% and the lowest was 13.4%. Thirdly, the statutory interest rate cap (four times Annual LPR) can be calculated based on Annual LPR of the year when the contract was concluded.

iii. The Alignment of the New and the Old Provisions

Paragraph 2 of Article 31 of the *Provisions on Private Lending* (*2020 Second Amendment*) specifies: "For a first-instance private lending case newly accepted after August 20, 2020, if the loan contract was formed before August 20, 2020, and either party claims that the interest from the formation of the contract to August 19, 2020 be calculated according to the then *Provisions*, the people's court shall support the claim; and the interest from August 20, 2020 to the date of payment of the loan shall be calculated according to the interest rate protection standard established by these provisions at the time of bringing the lawsuit." This provision integrates both the non-retroactivity principle and the basic guiding function of judicial interpretations. It can be seen that for the case of private lending contracts concluded after the August 20, 2020, the statutory interest rate cap is four times Annual LPR; yet in the case of private lending contracts concluded before August 20, 2020, the interest rates are calculated separately. In other words, the interest occurred before the August 19, 2020 follows the "three categories by two lines" rule, while that incurred after the August 20, 2020 is then four times Annual LPR.

For example, on August 19, 2019, the lender and the borrower agreed to borrow ¥1,000,000, a loan term of two years, a monthly interest rate of 3%, interest paid monthly, and a lump-sum payment of principal at maturity. The lender lent ¥1,000,000 to the borrower as scheduled, and the borrower repaid ¥30,000 on September 19, 2019, ¥25,000 on October 19, 2019, ¥22,000 on November 19, 2019, and ¥15,000 on December 19, 2019, and no payment was made since then. When the loan was due, the lender sued the borrower. In accordance with the provisions of the *Provisions of Private Lending (2020 Second Amendment)*, the interest for the three months repaid from September to November 2019 was between 24% – 36% per annum and had been paid, and should be recognised. The interest repayable till December 19, 2019 was ¥20,000, and the borrower paid only ¥15,000, with a balance of ¥5,000 still owed. The interest repayable from December 20, 2019 to August 19, 2020 was ¥160,000. In summary, the lender should repay to the borrower the principal amount of ¥1,000,000 and interest (interest of ¥165,000 as of August 19, 2020; accrued from August 20, 2020 until the date of full discharge, based on the principal amount of the loan of ¥1,000,000 at the rate of four times Annul LPR).

II. Laws in Hong Kong

i. Background of Lowering Interest Rate Cap in the *Money Lenders Ordinance*

Mr. Christopher Hui, the Secretary for Financial Services and the Treasury Bureau, said, "In recent years, there are growing concerns about interest rates charged on lending. Excessive interest rates would harm borrowers, particularly those with low incomes, and lead to other social problems. Our plan to lower the statutory interest rate cap for lending has referred to the recommendations of the Consumer Council, the effective interest rates adopted by the local money lending sector, the interest rate cap for lending overseas, and other market statistics."[1] It shows that a parallel situation is faced by Hong Kong when deciding to lower the cap, which is stipulated in the *Money Lenders Ordinance*. The Ordinance is officially amended after thorough research and deliberation by the Legislative Council of the Hong Kong Special Administrative Region on the October 26, 2022. According to the amended Ordinance, the excessive interest rates for criminally illegal is lowered from 60% to 48% per annum, and the threshold of extortionate rate is lowered from 48% to 36% per annum. The amended Ordinance came to effect on December 30, 2022.

ii. Interest Rate Cap

1. Statutory Interest Rate Cap

Section 24 (1) of the *Money Lenders Ordinance* specifies: "Any person (whether a money lender or not) who lends or offers to lend money at an effective rate of interest which exceeds 48 per cent per annum commits an offence."

---

〔1〕 Government News Network, *The Government Welcomes the Legislative Council's Approval of the Amendment to the Moneylenders Ordinance.* https://sc.news.gov.hk/TuniS/www.news.gov.hk/chi/2022/10/20221026/20221026_170442_560.html.

Section 24 (4) provides that "Any person who commits an offence under this section shall be liable—(a) on summary conviction to a fine of HK $500,000 and to imprisonment for 2 years; (b) on conviction on indictment to a fine of HK $5,000,000 and to imprisonment for 10 years." It can be seen that the interest rate cap under the *Money Lenders Ordinance* applies to loan of all types. Lenders setting an effective rate of interest over 48% per annum commit an offence and are held criminally liable. Exerting serious criminal liability is a key measure to fight against usury in Hong Kong.

The interest rate cap does not apply to some exceptions. According to the exemptions specified in Section 24 (5), Section 24 does not apply to a loan made to a company that has a paid up share capital of not less than HK $1,000,000 or an equivalent amount in any other approved currency, and as respects such loan, any person who makes such loan. The loans made under these exemptions are not bounded by the interest rate cap of 48% per annum and the corresponding legal consequences.

2. Presumption of an Extortionate Rate

Section 25 (3) of the *Money Lenders Ordinance* specifies: "Any agreement for the repayment of a loan or for the payment of interest on a loan in respect of which the effective rate of interest exceeds 36 per cent per annum shall, having regard to that fact alone, be presumed for the purposes of this section to be a transaction which is extortionate; but except where such rate exceeds the rate specified in section 24(1), the court may declare that any such agreement is not extortionate for the purposes of this section if, having regard to all the circumstances relating to the agreement, the court is satisfied that such rate is not unreasonable or unfair." However, the presumption of an extortionate rate is not limited to the case where the effective rate of interest of a loan exceeds 36%. Courts may also determine a transaction is extortionate by Section 25 (2) if it requires the debtor or a relative of his to make payments which are grossly exorbitant, or it otherwise grossly contravenes ordinary principles of fair-dealing.[1]

iii. The Alignment of the New and the Old Ordinance

The amendments to the statutory interest rate cap stipulated in the *Money Lenders Ordinance* came to effect on December 30, 2022. The press was released by the Government of the Hong Kong Special Administrative Region on December 29, 2022: "The above amendments were passed by the Legislative Council in October this year, and will apply to loan repayment agreements and interest payment agreements coming into force from tomorrow."[2] Just like the Chinese Mainland, the non-retroactivity principle is also adopted in Hong Kong. The amended statutory interest rate cap only applies to loan contracts coming into force after December 30, 2022.

III. Summary

i. Similarity

Specific legal rules on the interest rate cap of loan transactions are stipulated in the statute in both the Chinese Mainland and Hong Kong, and both have lowered the interest rate cap through law amendments.

ii. Difference

Rules on the loan interest rate cap are different in the Chinese Mainland

---

[1] Pursuant to Section 25(4), (5) and (6) of the *Money Lenders Ordinance*, in determining whether a transaction is extortionate for the purposes of this section, regard shall be had to such evidence as is adduced concerning, interest rate prevailing at the time it was made, debtor's age, experience, business capacity and state of health; and the degree to which, at the time of entering into the transaction, lender or other person was under financial pressure, and the nature of that pressure, the degree of risk accepted by the lender, having regard to the nature and value of any security provided; lender's or other person's relationship to the debtor etc.

[2] The Government of the Hong Kong Special Administrative Region Press Releases, *Amendments to statutory interest rate cap take effect from tomorrow.* https://www.info.gov.hk/gia/general/202212/29/P2022122800407.htm

and Hong Kong, with the protection limit for interest rates being higher in Hong Kong. The interest rate cap of private lending in the Chinese Mainland is four times Annual LPR, which is fluctuating instead of fixed. While the laws in Hong Kong provide that, except for exemptions, lending money at an effective rate of interest which exceeds 48% per annum is deemed as an offence, and exceeds 36% per annum is presumed to be extortionate.

Section Two Legal Consequences of Exceeding Statutory Interest Rate Cap

I. Laws in the Chinese Mainland

i. Validity of Contracts When Exceeding Statutory Interest Rate Cap

The first paragraph of Article 680 of the *Civil Code* stipulates: "Usurious loans are prohibited, and the interest rate for lending shall not violate the relevant regulations of the State." As for the effect of borrowing in violation of state regulations, the *Civil Code* does not further provide for it. Regarding this issue, Article 26 of the *Provisions on Private Lending* states that "the interest agreement exceeding part is invalid"; Article 25 of the *Provisions on Private Lending (2020 Second Amendment)* states that "except when the interest rate agreed upon by both parties exceeds four times Annual LPR when the contract is concluded." According to the evolution of the legislation, the legislative opinion on such contracts is "partially invalid". Article 156 of the *Civil Code* states: "If invalidation of a part of a civil juristic act does not affect the validity of the other part, the other part of the act remains valid." Therefore, the interest rate agreed in the private lending contract while exceeding the statutory interest rate cap does not necessarily lead to the invalidity of the contract. However, the interest exceeding the statutory interest rate cap is not protected by laws.

ii. Determination of Remaining Interest After Partial Performance of the Agreed Interest Rate Exceeding the Cap

For example, the lender and the borrower signed a contract which provided that the lender would lend ¥1,000,000 to the borrower on January 1, 2021 at an annual interest rate of 20% over a period of three years (from January 1, 2021 to December 31, 2023) with the interest paid once a year. The lender then lent ¥1 million to the borrower as agreed on January 1, 2021 (when the Annual LPR announced by the People's Bank of China was 3.85% per annum). The borrower paid ¥200,000 in interest on January 1, 2022 and January 1, 2023 respectively. After the loan contract due on December 31, 2023, the borrower failed to repay the principal and interest as scheduled, and the principal and interest owed by the borrower are calculated as follows:

Table: Calculation of Principal and Interest

Currency: RMB

No.	Date	Principal	Repayment Amount	Interest Payable	Principal Outstanding
1	Jan. 1, 2021	1,000,000			
2	Jan. 1, 2022	1,000,000	200,000	154,000	954,000
3	Jan. 1, 2023	954,000	200,000	146,916	900,916
4	Dec 31, 2023	900,916		138,741.06	

Remarks: 1. Interest Payable = Principal ×15.4% per annum
2. Principal Outstanding = Principal − (Repayment Amount − Interest Payable)

According to the laws, the statutory interest rate cap for the aforementioned private lending cases is four times Annual LPR at the time of contract formation, 15.4% per annum (i.e., 3.85% ×4). In judicial practice, the portion of the interest paid that exceeds the annual interest rate of 15.4% is generally deducted from the principal. According to the above calculation method, the borrower should pay the lender the principal of ¥900,916 with interest (calculated up to the date on December 31, 2023 at ¥138,741.06 with further interest on the principal sum of ¥900,916 at the rate 15.4% per annum from January 1, 2024 to the date of full discharge).

It is important to note that some lenders have proposed another calculation method in judicial practice. Take the aforementioned case as an example: the first step is to calculate the total interest of ¥462,000 from January 1, 2021 to December 31, 2023 (¥1,000,000 × annual interest rate of 13.8% ×3 years); the second step is to calculate the outstanding interest of ¥62,000 (¥462,000 – ¥400,000); the third step is to conclude that the borrower shall pay the principal of ¥1,000,000 with interest of ¥62,000 (calculated up to the date on December 31, 2023; with further interest on the principal sum of ¥1,000,000 at the rate 13.8% per annum from January 1, 2024 to the date of full discharge). It can be seen from the two calculation methods that the latter one has a higher cost of capital for the borrower, requiring a greater sum of principal and interest. The latter calculation method seems to be simpler, but it does not take into account the actual use of capital by the borrower, and increases the loan interest rate in disguise, so the first calculation method is fairer.

II. Laws in Hong Kong

i. Legal Consequences of Effective Interest Rate Exceeding 48% per annum

1. Criminal Legal Consequences

As mentioned in the previous section, under Section 24 (1) of the *Money Lenders Ordinance*, it is an offence to lend money at an effective interest rate of more than 48% per annum. The lender may be prosecuted, subject to summary proceedings or prosecution, depending on the fact, and sentenced to different terms of imprisonment or fines of different amounts.

2. Civil Legal Consequences

With the exemption of a loan made to a company with a fully paid up share capital of not less than HK $ 1 million or an equivalent amount in another approved currency and the person making the loan being exempted, Section 24 (2) of the *Money Lenders Ordinance* provides that: "An agreement to repay any loan or an agreement to pay interest on any loan, and a security given in respect of such agreement or loan, shall not be enforceable if the effective rate of interest exceeds the rate specified in subsection (1), which is 48% per annum." Consistent with the legal consequences of professional (unlicensed) money lenders in Chapter 2, if an action regarding such contract is brought to the court, the court will not support the recovery of the principal and interest claimed by the lender.

In particular, it requires special attention that there has been a divergence in interpretations in different cases within Hong Kong regarding whether a court can, under Section 25(1) of the *Money Lenders Ordinance*, order a renegotiation of a loan transaction with an effective interest rate exceeding an annual rate of 48% (which was 60% before December 30, 2022), and determine the enforceable rate. In the Court of Appeal of the High Court case of *Wong Kwai Fun v. Li Fung*[1] and the District Court case of *Lee Leo v. Cheong Oi Sum Ader*[2], the courts held that they had the discretion to renegotiate transactions where the actual interest rate exceeded 60%. However, in the case of *Wong Ming Wai v. Tsui Kam Ming trading as Tung Tai Construction Co.*[3], the Court of Appeal of the High Court ruled that loan transactions with an effective interest rate exceeding an annual rate of 60% were neither enforceable nor renegotiable. This case also followed the High Court's decision in *Kwok Ying Lung*

---

[1] [1994] 1 HKC 549, para. 84.

[2] [1993] 2 HKC 736, para. 9.

[3] [1999] HKCU 1288, para. 8.

v. Ko Chi Hung Maxwell Mabel Straube [1], *Morales Elisa Galleto v. Corriente Nenete Manejero* [2]. In recent years, the judicial practices in Hong Kong have mostly recognised that the court is empowered to reopen transactions after the statutory interest rate cap is exceeded.

ii. Legal Consequences of Effective Interest Rate Between 36% and 48% per annum

Section 25 (3) of the *Money Lenders Ordinance* provides: "Any agreement for the repayment of a loan or for the payment of interest on a loan in respect of which the effective rate of interest exceeds 36 per cent per annum shall, having regard to that fact alone, be presumed for the purposes of this section to be a transaction which is extortionate." If the effective interest rate of the loan agreement is between 36% and 48% per annum, it is presumed that the transaction is extortionate, and its legal consequences vary with the specific circumstances of each case, including the following circumstances.

1. Transaction Not Extortionate and Contract Enforceable

Section 25 (3) of the *Money Lenders Ordinance* provides: "but except where such a rate exceeds the rate specified in section 24(1), the court may declare that any such agreement is not extortionate for the purposes of this section if, having regard to all the circumstances relating to the agreement, the court is satisfied that such rate is not unreasonable or unfair."

2. Transaction Extortionate but Re-opened

Section 25(1) of the *Money Lenders Ordinance* provides: "the court may reopen the transaction so as to do justice between the parties having regard to all the circumstances, and, for that purpose, make such orders and give such di-

[1] [2000] HKCU 358, para. 23.

[2] [2016] HKCU 69, in paragraph 13 the judgment of *Wong Ming Wai v. Tsui Kam Ming trading as Tung Tai Construction Co.* was directly cited.

rections in respect of the terms of the transaction or the rights of the parties thereunder as the court may think fit."

3. Transaction Extortionate and Contract Unenforceable

Section 25(1) of the *Money Lenders Ordinance* gives the court a discretion to reopen a transaction that the court, having regard to all the circumstances, considers to be an extortionate transaction. Reopening of the transaction is not necessary and the loan agreement may be unenforceable if the court is satisfied that the effective interest rate in excess of 36% is unreasonable and unfair having regard to all the circumstances surrounding the agreement.

III. Summary

i. Similarity

In the Chinese Mainland and Hong Kong, lenders shall bear the corresponding adverse legal consequences if the interest rate of lending transactions exceeds the statutory cap.

ii. Difference

For the loan transaction that exceeds the statutory interest rate cap, the laws in the Chinese Mainland stipulate that the interest exceeding the cap is not protected, but the court supports the principal, interest and fees within the scope of judicial protection. However, the laws in Hong Kong stipulates that loan transactions exceeding the statutory cap of 48% shall not be enforced, that is, the court will not support the recovery of principal and interest. If the interest rate exceeds the extortionate rate of 36% and the transaction is presumed to be extortionate, the transaction may be reopened by the court. The court also has discretion to enforce the loan agreement if it exceeds the extortionate interest rate of 36% and if it is satisfied that the transaction is not extortionate.

Chapter V

Comparison of Legal Rules on Unclear Contractual Terms

Section One Repayment Order of Priority Not Specified or Unclear

I. Laws in the Chinese Mainland

Article 561 of the *Civil Code* stipulates: "In addition to performing the principal obligation, a debtor shall pay to the creditor interests and other expenses related to the enforcement of the obligation. Where the payment is not sufficient to discharge all of the obligations, unless otherwise agreed by the parties, he shall perform the obligation in accordance with the following order: (1) the relevant expenses incurred by the creditor for enforcing his claim; (2) the interests; and (3) the principal obligation."

i. Definition of Repayment Appropriation

Repayment appropriation occurs where a debtor owes several obligations of the same type to the same creditor, and the debtor's performance for repayment is insufficient to discharge all the obligations. In such circumstance, the repayment made is appropriated to discharge one or more of those debts. Furthermore, where the debtor is obligated to pay interest and costs in addition to the principal debt and the repayment made is insufficient to settle the total amount owed, the repayment is appropriated to discharge one or more parts of the debt.

Accordingly, repayment appropriation involves two scenarios: appropriating repayment to several debts and appropriating repayment to the principal debt, interest, and the costs associated with realising the claim. This Section mainly discusses the second scenario.

ii. Order of Repayment Appropriation

Repayment appropriation can be categorised into intentional repayment appropriation or statutory repayment appropriation. Intentional appropriation can be subdivided into repayment appropriation by agreement and repayment appropriation by designation.

1. Repayment Appropriation by Agreement

Repayment appropriation by agreement is that the parties to the contract have agreed on the order of repayment appropriation. The parties' agreement on repayment appropriation reflects the principle of free will, which should be respected and safeguarded in law. The stipulation of "unless otherwise agreed by the parties" in Article 561 of the *Civil Code* emphasises the priority of the repayment appropriation by agreement. An agreement on repayment appropriation may be reached at or before the time of repayment. If the appropriation agreement is reached after repayment or if the contents of the agreement are altered, the agreement will remain valid between the parties but will not affect the rights of any third party involved, such as guarantors.

The repayment appropriation by agreement can be expressed or implied. The following examples demonstrate typical implied repayment appropriation agreements. For instance, the creditor requests discharge of a specific debt, and the debtor does not object and proceeds to make the repayment; or the debtor gives clear expression that the repayment is made for discharge of a specific debt, and the creditor does not object and accepts it. In judicial practice, the true intention of the parties regarding the implied agreement is determined based on the specific facts of the disputed case. This determination aims to ascertain whether the debtor and the creditor genuinely reach an implied agreement or whether it is merely an assertion made by one party.

2. Repayment Appropriation by Designation

If there is no agreement on repayment appropriation between the contractual parties, the debtor can designate the debt to be discharged upon repayment. In the circumstance where the repayment is appropriated for discharge of multiple debts, the law emphasises the protection of the debtor's interests, allowing the debtor to designate the repayment appropriation.[1] However, in the circumstance where repayment is appropriated for the discharge of principal debt, interest, and costs associated with realising the claim in the same debt, the law leans towards the protection of the creditor's interests, excluding the application of repayment appropriation by designation. This section will not further elaborate on this point.

3. Statutory Repayment Appropriation

Statutory repayment appropriation is that in the absence of an agreement between the contractual parties, the law specifies the order of repayment appropriation so as to fill in the incomplete intention of the parties. The order of statutory repayment appropriation provides as follows:

(1) Costs associated with the realisation of the claim. The necessary costs incurred by the creditor to realise the creditor's rights are considered additional expenditures, which should be prioritised to be repaid by the debtor. The costs may arise from either private remedy or public remedy to enforce creditor's rights. In judicial practice, the following costs are commonly incurred: costs of preservation, litigation fees, auction fees, registration fees, notary fees, and execution fees.

(2) Interest is the anticipated profits of the creditor and the costs for utilisation of the funds, which should be discharged in priority over the principal debt. Interest encompasses both contractual and statutory interest. Contractual interest must not surpass the statutory cap. If the statutory cap is exceeded and excess interest has been paid, the surplus amount shall automatically be appropriated to the repayment of the principal debt next in line.

(3) Principal debt is the fundamental element constituting the debtrelation-

---

[1] Article 560 of the *Civil Code* provides that "where a debtor owes to a creditor multiple obligations of the same kind, and the debtor's performance is not sufficient to discharge all of the obligations, upon making performance, the debtor shall designate which obligation is to be discharged, unless otherwise agreed by the parties".

ship, defining the substantial nature of the creditor-debtor relationship. Placing the principal obligation at the end of the repayment appropriation order reflects the legislative intention to prioritise the protection of the creditor's interest. As long as the principal debt has not been discharged, it continues to accrue interest or the costs of realising the claim. This encourages the debtor to perform the obligation of repayment promptly and completely, thereby facilitating the completion of the transaction.

In summary, the laws in the Chinese Mainland outlines the repayment appropriation order during the loan terms as follows: If there is an agreement between the parties, it will be adhered to; If no agreement is agreed upon or no consensus in this regard is subsequently reached, the repayment will be appropriated in accordance with the order of the costs associated with realising the claim, the interest and the principal debt. This repayment appropriation order is generally referred to as "interest prevails principal" in judicial practice.

II. Laws in Hong Kong

The rules of repayment appropriation order under common law also specify the repayment of multiple debts and the appropriation of principal and interest under a single debt.

As stated in *Chitty on Contracts (35th edition)*, where several separate debts are due from the debtor to the creditor, the debtor may, when making a payment, appropriate the money paid to a particular debt or debts, and if the creditor accepts the payment so appropriated, he must apply it in the manner directed by the debtor; if, however, the debtor makes no appropriation when making the payment, the creditor may do so.[1] It is essential that an appropriation by the debtor should take the form of a communication, express or im-

[1] See Hugh Beale, Richard Hooley, Louise Merrett, Graham Virgo, *Chitty on Contracts*, Sweet & Maxwell, 35th Edition, para. 25 - 058.

plied, to the creditor of the debtor's intention to appropriate the payment to a specified debt (or debts), so that the creditor may know that his rights of appropriation as creditor cannot arise. It is not essential that the debtor should expressly specify at the time of the payment, which debt or account he intended the payment to be applied to. His intention may be collected from other circumstances showing that he intended at the time of the payment to appropriate it to a specific debt or account. The intention of the debtor to make the appropriation must, however, be clear, as known to both parties.[1] Where the debtor has not exercised his option, and the right to appropriate has therefore devolved upon the creditor, he may exercise it at any time 'up to the very last moment' or until something happens that makes it inequitable for him to exercise it. The creditor's right is thus a 'contingent' right which arises only in the event that the debtor does not make an appropriation. The appropriation must be communicated in some form by the creditor to the debtor. This communication may take the form of an express notification given by the creditor to the debtor or it may take the form of the creditor dealing with the payment in a form that is visible to the debtor.[2] The doctrine of appropriation does not entitle a creditor who receives money on account from his debtor to apply it towards the satisfaction of a debt due under an illegal contract or to claim which does not constitute any legal or equitable demand.[3]

Chitty on Contracts (*35th edition*) further states that where there is no appropriation by either debtor or creditor in the case of a debt bearing interest, the law will (unless a contrary intention appears) apply the payment to discharge

---

[1] See Hugh Beale, Richard Hooley, Louise Merrett, Graham Virgo, *Chitty on Contracts*, Sweet & Maxwell, 35th Edition, para. 25-059.

[2] See Hugh Beale, Richard Hooley, Louise Merrett, Graham Virgo, *Chitty on Contracts*, Sweet & Maxwell, 35th Edition, para. 25-060.

[3] See Hugh Beale, Richard Hooley, Louise Merrett, Graham Virgo, *Chitty on Contracts*, Sweet & Maxwell, 35th Edition, para. 25-061.

any interest due before applying it to the earliest items of principal.[1]

In the case of *Bank of China (Hong Kong) Ltd. v. Eddy Technology Co. Ltd. & Ors.*[2], the Court of Appeal of the High Court expressly cited the above principle and held that "as a matter of law, unless there were contractual provisions stipulating otherwise, the defendants as debtor had the right to give directions on the appropriation of their payments between interests and principals. In the absence of any effective directions from the defendants, the plaintiff was at liberty to appropriate the monies paid by the 1st defendant between interests and principals. Further, where there is no appropriation by either debtor or creditor, the law (unless a contrary intention appears) applies the payment to discharge any interest due before applying it to the earliest items of principal".[3] The Court of Appeal further pointed out that "as we have seen, the right to appropriate is a right conferred by law as opposed to the term of the Letter. Unless the defendants were bound by any contractual provisions, they could exercise that right at any time in respect of each payment without the need for any indulgence from the plaintiff".[4]

In summary, the rules governing the repayment appropriation order of principal and interest in Hong Kong are as follows: If the parties have an agreement, it shall be followed; in the absence of an agreement, the borrower has the right to specify the appropriation ratio of principal and interest for repayment; If the borrower does not specify, the lender determines the appropriation ratio (without the entitlement to discharge a debt under an illegal contract or an inequitable demand); If neither party specifies the appropriation ratio, the

---

[1] See Hugh Beale, Richard Hooley, Louise Merrett, Graham Virgo, *Chitty on Contracts*, Sweet & Maxwell, 35th Edition, para. 25-066.

[2] [2019] HKCA 339.

[3] *Bank of China (Hong Kong) Ltd. v. Eddy Technology Co. Ltd. & Ors.* [2019] HKCA 339, para. 15-16.

[4] *Bank of China (Hong Kong) Ltd. v. Eddy Technology Co. Ltd. & Ors.* [2019] HKCA 339, para. 19.

borrower's repayment shall first be allocated to clear the due interest, then to repay the principal, which is consistent with " interest prevails principal ".

III. Summary

i. Similarity

The repayment appropriation order of principal and interest between the Chinese Mainland and Hong Kong is essentially identical. If there is an agreement, it will be followed; If there is no agreement and neither party has specified the ratio of repayment appropriation, the interest will be presumed to be repaid first, followed by the principal.

ii. Difference

There are differences with regard to the repayment appropriation by designation. The laws in the Chinese Mainland stipulate that in the absence of an agreement between the parties, repayment shall follow the order of the costs related to realising the claim, interest and principal debt. The laws in Hong Kong allow the borrower to specify the repayment appropriation order between the principal and interest if there is no agreement. If the borrower does not specify, the lender may appropriate the repayment, but is not allowed to discharge a debt under an illegal contract or inequitable demand. If neither party specifies, the repayment follows the order of "interest prevails principal".

Section Two Loan Term Not Specified or Unclear

I. Laws in the Chinese Mainland

The main duty of the borrower in a loan contract is to repay the principal, and in an interest-bearing loan contract is to repay with interest. The time for repayment is fixed in the loan term specified in the contract. Therefore, it is of substantial importance in law that the loan term is fixed: Firstly, the loan term itself is a kind of interest. The later the repayment date is, the longer the borrower is entitled to use the funds. This is an important economic interest for the borrower and generally the lender is unable to demand the borrower to repay the loan in advance. Secondly, the loan term is a decisive time factor in determining whether the borrower has delayed in performance. If the borrower fails to repay the loan upon expiration of the term, he is liable for breach of the loan contract and may need to pay the default interest.

i. Specific Circumstances

It is a primary obligation of the borrower to repay the loan within the agreed term. Disputes may arise with regard to the repayment date where the loan term is not specified or unclear between the parties.

1. Loan Term Not Specified

The situation is relatively crystal clear when there is no agreement on the loan term in a loan contract or IOU, or when it cannot be proved that there exist oral agreements or trade customs between the parties. In the case of (2022) Guangdong Civil Final No. 1538, the Shanwei Intermediate People's Court of Guangdong Province held that there was no loan term agreed in this case for the reason that the loan agreement provided by the appellant LI did not stipulate the loan term and LI failed to prove that there were supplemental agreements or trade customs regarding the loan term between him and the respondent ZHANG. In the case of (2019) Guangxi Civil Retrial Application No. 3095, the High People's Court of Guangxi Zhuang Autonomous Region held that no written agreement regarding the loan term, interest amount and interest rate was included in the two disputed IOUs. At first instance, the plaintiff GAO asserted in the statement of claim that the loan terms agreed was "half a month" and "a few days" respectively in the IOUs. However, GAO backtracked in the hearing that the loan term agreed was "a week". Since there was no evidence proving the existence of any written agreement on loan terms and repayment dates, the court determined that the disputed loans were made without agreements on loan terms and interest rates.

2. Unclear Loan Term

The situations where the loan term is unclear vary from case to case. In the case of (2017) SPC Civil Retrial Application No. 5133, the Supreme People's Court held that the loan term should be deemed unclear. In this case, the company MEI and the company SHENG concluded a loan contract in which the loan term agreed was "tentatively scheduled for one year". Upon the expiration of one year, the company MEI did not demand repayment but extended the loan term for an unfixed period. In the case of (2019) Jilin Civil Retrial Application No. 774, although the loan term agreed by the parties was "about ten years", the Jilin High People's Court held that the loan term was unclear and the exact repayment date was also incapable of being determined due to the demise of the debtor.

ii. Statutory Handling Approach

Pursuant to Article 510 and Article 675 of the *Civil Code*, where the loan term is not specified or unclear, the determination of the loan term shall be in the following order. Firstly, the term should be ascertained according to Article 510 of the *Civil Code* that the parties can fix a loan term through renegotiation or by reference to other clauses in the contract or trade customs. Secondly, if the parties fail to fix a repayment date, then according to Article 675 of the *Civil Code*, the borrower can repay the loan at any time, while the lender can also at any time demands repayment from the borrower within a reasonable time. Accordingly, the borrower can decide the repayment date on his own. If the lender demand repayment from the borrower, he should give the borrower a reasonable period of time. The test of reasonableness shall take into account the loan amount, the purpose of the loan and specific circumstances in each case as well.

iii. Key Factors in Determining Loan Term

In dealing with the situation where the loan term is not specified or unclear, the following three factors are vital and should be carefully thought through.

1. By Reference to the Relevant Contract Clauses

To determine the loan term by reference to the relevant contract clauses is, in essence, a question of contract interpretation. Contract clauses reflect the final result of the parties' negotiation and represent their true intention and the-clauses often interact with each other in a contract. Hence, when certain contractual content is missing or unclear, it is preferable to firstly seek the true intention of the parties by reference to relevant contract clauses, so as to complete the missing part or ascertain the uncertainty.

For example, although the loan term is sometimes not specified in the loan contract, it is necessary to determine the term by reference to the relevant contract clauses as other clauses in the contract may imply the term available for the borrower to use the fund, such as a loan purpose clause which obliquely reflects the length of the term.

2. By Reference to Trade Customs

Article 2 of the *Interpretation by the Supreme People's Court of Several Issues Concerning the Application of Title One General Provisions of Book Three Contracts of the Civil Code* provides for two types of trade customs for the purpose of the *Civil Code*. The first type is the customary practices in the course of transactions between the parties. The second is the commonly adopted practices in the local area or a certain field or industry of the transaction, which the parties know or should have known while entering into the contract.

The determination of trade customs reflects the principle of autonomy of will. The parties, while entering into the contract, often have or ought to have knowledge of trade customs commonly adopted in the local area or relevant industry, and thus come to a tacit agreement to adopt such trade customs as an implied clause instead of an express clause in the contract. With regard to the customary practices in the course of transactions, the parties are generally required to have previous dealings.

However, it should be noted that the application of aforementioned approaches to determine the loan term is subject to the mandatory provisions in laws and regulations.

3. Reasonable Time for Repayment

The laws do not specify the length for the reasonable time regarding the lender's demand for repayment but leave it to the discretion of the lender. In practice, it is necessary to take into account relevant factors such as the identity of the lender (a financial institution or a natural person) and the solvency of the borrower. In deciding whether the time given is reasonable, the court will consider all relevant circumstances in each case.

If the lender directly demands repayment from the borrower by bringing actions without any previous demand, the court considers it essential to grant the reasonable time to the borrower which is deemed to be the period between the case filing date and the hearing date. In the case of (2018) Beijing 01 Civil Final No. 2785, the Beijing First Intermediate People's Court upheld the decision of Beijing Haidian People's Court that the reasonable time should be from the case filing date to the hearing date.

In the case where the parties keep contact up till the litigation, the court needs to determine the date of demand for repayment and the length of the reasonable time particularly based on the parties' relationship and the loan amount in each case. In the case of (2022) Jiangsu 12 Civil Final No. 3909, the appellant TENG lent ¥60,000 to the respondent JIANG through bank transfer. The parties did not agree on a loan term. TENG demanded repayment from JIANG on September 23, 2020, but JIANG did not repay. Taizhou Intermediate People's Court determined that the reasonable time in this case should be one month.

II. Laws in Hong Kong

According to *Chitty on Contracts* (*35th edition*), where money is lent without stipulation as to the time of repayment, a present debt is created which is generally repayable at once without any previous demand. However, it is open to the parties to fix a time for repayment, or to agree that the loan will only be repayable on demand. Suitable implications as to such matters would readily be made in appropriate circumstances. Where the loan is repayable on demand, the making of a valid demand is a pre-condition of the debt becoming due. There are precedents stating that to constitute a valid demand there must be a clear intimation that payment is required and nothing more is necessary as long as it is of a peremptory character and unconditional. [1]

The abovementioned shows the common law position that where the loan term is not specified in the loan contract, the lender can demand repayment from the borrower once the money is lent. The parties can also renegotiate or fix a new time for repayment. Implications as to the loan term can be made in appropriate circumstances.

i. Reasonable Time for Immediate Repayment

The common law position is that where the money is repayable immediately, the borrower will be given a reasonable time to implement the mechanics of payment. According to *Chitty on Contracts* (*35th edition*), money payable on demand is repayable immediately on demand being made. The borrower is al-

[1] See Hugh Beale, Richard Hooley, Louise Merrett, Graham Virgo, *Chitty on Contracts*, Sweet & Maxwell, 35th Edition, para. 42 – 280.

lowed only such time as is necessary to implement the mechanics of payment needed to discharge the debt before being in default, but not a reasonable time to muster the resources to pay the debt.[1] That is to say, the reasonable time allowed is for the course of payment but not the raising of money.

The rule is stated vividly in the English case of *Bank of Baroda v. Panessar and Others*[2] which concerned the repayment of a debenture. In September 1981, two associated companies executed a debenture in favour of a bank in respect of moneys owed. The debenture was provided for the repayment on demand of all moneys thereby secured and, in default of compliance, for the bank to be entitled to appoint a receiver. In November 1983 the bank served on the companies a notice of repayment demand. About an hour later the bank appointed a receiver who took control of the companies. One of the issues in this case was whether the companies had been given sufficient time to pay the outstanding amount. With regard to this issue, the court emphasised: "Money payable on demand is repayable immediately on demand being made; Nevertheless, it is physically impossible in most cases for a person to keep the money required to discharge the debt about his person. He may in a simple case keep it in a box under his bed; it may be at the bank or with a bailee. The debtor is therefore not in default in making the payment demanded unless and until he has had a reasonable opportunity of implementing whatever reasonable mechanics of payment he may need to employ to discharge the debt. Of course, this is limited to the time necessary for the mechanics of payment, and it does not extend to any time to raise the money if it is not there to be paid." The court eventually determined that the one-hour time in this case was sufficient.

In *Lok Wai Yee v. Man Koon Hung*[3], the Court of First Instance of the

---

[1] See Hugh Beale, Richard Hooley, Louise Merrett, Graham Virgo, *Chitty on Contracts*, Sweet & Maxwell, 35th Edition, para. 42 – 280.

[2] [1986] 3 All ER 751.

[3] [2020] HKCU 3470.

High Court also agreed that payment on demand means payment within a reasonable time after the demand.[1] In *Kensland Realty Ltd. v. Whale View Investment Ltd. and Another*[2], the Court of Final Appeal held that for a split payment of HK $46.75 million implemented for a sale of shop premises, a period of 1 hour and 47 minutes allowed by the vendor to the purchaser in this case was not reasonable.

It should be noted that the determination of reasonable time varies case by case and is affected by a variety of factors such as the payment methods, the parties involved and the outstanding amount. The aforementioned case *Bank of Baroda v. Panessar and Others* happened nearly 40 years ago, when traditional methods such as telegrams and facsimiles were more commonly used for communication. *Kensland Realty Ltd. v. Whale View Investment Ltd. and Another* was a case 24 years ago and concerned a sale of real estate with a huge amount of money, involving part payment, mortgages and the participation of multiple parties including not only the purchaser and the vendor, but also the bank and the solicitors. With electronic payment being so convenient nowadays, time left under this rule may be shorter.

ii. Rules of Implying Terms into Contracts

The courts in Hong Kong may imply terms into a contract for the following reasons: firstly, to give effect to the perceived intentions of the parties and make the contract workable; secondly, to fulfil certain policy objectives as a matter of law; and thirdly, on the basis of trade customs. Accordingly, terms can be implied in fact, in law, or by trade customs.

1. Implying Terms in Fact

Under the laws in Hong Kong, terms may be implied in fact, based on the

---

[1] *Lok Wai Yee v. Man Koon Hung* [2020] HKCU 3470, para 73.

[2] [2002] HKCU 77.

perceived intentions of the parties but will be implied only where the contract would otherwise be incomplete. The courts are often careful on this point. In *Liverpool City Council v. Irwin*[1], which is a classic case on this issue, the court stated: "It is not enough for the court to say that the suggested term is a reasonable one the presence of which would make the contract a better or fairer one; it must be able to say that the insertion of the term is necessary. The terms implied should be what both parties know and would, if asked, unhesitatingly agree to be part of the bargain." In *Hughes v. Greenwich London Borough Council*[2], the court held that implied terms based on the particular factual circumstances of the parties' contractual relationship could only be so implied where there was a "compelling reason", i. e. where it is "essential". In *Equitable Life Assurance Society v. Hyman*[3], the court described terms implied in fact as being of "strict necessity", only being so implied "sparingly and cautiously".

There are two tests for implying terms in fact.

The first one is the "business efficacy" test, which is derived from *The Moorcock*[4]. The court in this case pointed out that the implication which the law drew from what must obviously had been the intention of the parties, the law drew with the object of giving efficacy to the transaction. The second one is the "officious bystander" test, which is derived from *Shirlaw v. Southern Foundries (1926) Ltd.*[5]. The court stated that prima facie which in any contract was left to be implied and need not be expressed was something so obvious that it went without saying so that, if, while the parties were making their bargain, an officious bystander were to suggest some express provision for it in

---

[1] [1977] AC 239.

[2] [1994] 1 AC 170.

[3] [2002] 1 AC 408.

[4] (1889) LR 14 PD 64.

[5] [1939] 2 KB 206.

their agreement, they would testily suppress him with a common "Oh, of course!". In *Twinkle Step Investment Ltd. v. Smart International Industrial Ltd.* [1], the Court of Final Appeal pointed out that the question was whether the term contended for was one which the court must imply in order to establish what the contract was, the parties themselves not having fully stated the terms of their contract.

2. Implying Terms in Law

Terms implied in law are those terms imposed on the contracting parties, regardless of their intentions. It is the desire of the laws to regulate certain types of contracts in the interests of protecting the parties.

3. Implying Terms by Trade Customs

A term implied by trade customs shall not be inconsistent with an express term in the contract.[2] However, not all trade customs will be implied into a contract. In *Eggar, Forrester Offshore Ltd. v. Hong Kong United Dockyards Ltd.* [3], the court stated that to establish a trade custom, capable of being implied into a contract, it must be shown that that the custom is "notorious, certain and reasonable".

III. Summary

i. Similarity

In the circumstance where the loan term is not specified or unclear, the handling approach is similar between the Chinese Mainland and Hong Kong. The lender can negotiate to fix a repayment date with the borrower. If failed on renegotiation, the loan term may be implied in fact or by trade customs. If no loan term is so fixed or implied, the lender can demand repayment from the

---

[1] [1999] 2 HKCFAR 255.

[2] *Palgrave, Brown and Son Ltd. v. Owners of SS Turid* [1922] 1 AC 397.

[3] [1987] 1 HKC 318.

borrower at any time within a reasonable time.

ii. Difference

The Chinese Mainland and Hong Kong take different approaches in defining the reasonable time allowed for the borrower. In Hong Kong, it is limited to the time necessary for the mechanics of payment. In the Chinese Mainland, however, the determination of reasonable time shall take into account relevant factors such as the identity of the lender and the solvency of the borrower. The purpose of the reasonable time is not limited strictly to payment mechanics. The court is left with more discretion comparing to Hong Kong.

Chapter VI

Comparison of Legal Rules on Security Contracts

Section One Validity of Security Contracts When the Loan Contract is Invalid

I. Laws in the Chinese Mainland

It is normal in the private lending practice that a lender and a borrower enter into a loan contract together with a security contract such as mortgage contracts, pledge contracts, guarantee contracts or other contracts with the security function[1], so that the lender can enforce the secured property and take priority in the repayment of debt when the borrower cannot pay off the debt due. As a loan contract may be invalidated by reasons of relending of credit funds at high interest rates, concluding for illegal purposes, relending by means of illegal fund raising or professional private lending, the validity of the security contract becomes the core of the controversy between the lender and the borrower.

i. Connotation, Classification and Nature of Security Contracts

1. Connotation and Classification

The conception of security contracts can be divided into broad sense and narrow sense. Pursuant to Article 388 of the *Civil Code*, the security contracts in narrow sense include mortgage contracts, pledge contracts and other contracts with the security function. The mortgage contracts and pledge contracts, as the name indicated, are contracts that create security rights of mortgage and pledge.

---

[1] There are considerable differences between the laws in the Chinese Mainland and Hong Kong with regard to the security system. Although Chinese Mainland and Hong Kong may adopt certain identical legal terminologies, the concrete definitions and meanings of certain terms are quite distinct in their respective security system. Due to limitations on expression of legal terminologies in English, readers should pay attentions to the distinctions with regard to the definition and meaning of these legal terminologies.

"Other contracts with the security function" is a generic term used to describe a contract that can function as security not specified in the *Civil Code*, and it mainly encompasses assignment guarantee, retention of ownership, financial leasing contracts, factoring contracts and so forth. These types of atypical security do not fall within the scope of security rights expressly regulated by the *Civil Code*, but they do practically function as security by means of transfer of ownership or assignment of right. The validity of atypical security is recognised by the laws in the Chinese Mainland, but these sorts of security cannot be utilised to act against third parties unless they are perfected by publicity processes such as registration. The security contracts in broad sense include guarantee contracts as well. Since it is prevalent in private lending practice that a borrower creates security by means of real security, personal security or other security types, the broad definition is adopted when referring to the security contract in this book.

The security system in the Chinese Mainland divides the security types into two main types, the typical security and the atypical security. The typical security encompasses mortgage[1], pledge[2], lien[3] and guarantee[4]. The atypi-

---

〔1〕 Mortgage (抵押) is a security that created by a debtor or a third party over his property without transferring the possession. If the debtor fails to pay due debts or any circumstance as stipulated by the parties concerned for realising the mortgage right occurs, the creditor will have the right to seek preferred payments from mortgaged properties.

〔2〕 Pledge (质押) is a security that created by a debtor or a third party over movable property by transferring possession. If the debtor fails to pay due debts or any circumstance for realising the pledge right as stipulated by the parties concerned occurs, the creditor will have the right to seek preferred payments from the movable property.

〔3〕 Lien (留置) is a security that if a debtor fails to pay off the due debt, the creditor will be empowered to acquire the possession of movable property that is lawfully possessed and to have the right to preferred payments from such movable property.

〔4〕 Guarantee (保证) is a security created by consensual agreement concluded by the guarantor and the creditor that if the debtor fails to perform the obligation on time or if circumstances agreed upon by the parties occur, the guarantor will perform the obligation or assume liability to ensure the realisation of the obligation.

cal security generally involves assignment guarantee[1], financial leasing[2], retention of ownership[3] and so forth. Article 388 of the *Civil Code* provides that "to create a security interest, a security contract shall be entered into in accordance with the provisions of this Code and other laws". This means, except for a security right directly created by operation of law, the creation of security is preconditional on the establishment of a security contract. Pursuant to Paragraph 1 of Article 400, Paragraph 1 of Article 427 and Paragraph 2 of Article 736 of the *Civil Code*, the parties shall enter into a mortgage or pledge contract in writing to create right of mortgage or pledge; a contract for financing lease shall be made in writing. Apart from the compulsory requirement of written forms, the *Civil Code* sets out specific statutory formality requirements for the creation of different types of security interests. For example, a mortgage on real property shall be created upon registration; a pledge on moveable property is created upon delivery of the pledged property; a pledge on a right is created upon delivery of the certificate of such a right or upon registration.[4] It follows that registration is a necessary condition for valid creation of mortgages on real property and pledges on certain rights. Besides, registration also serves the function of asserting and acting against bona fide third parties. For instance, a mortgage on movable property shall be created at the time when the mortgage contract enters into effect and such mortgage may not be asserted against a bona

---

[1] Assignment guarantee (让与担保) will be discussed in detail in Part 2 of this chapter.

[2] Financial leasing (融资租赁) is sort of atypical security type in combination of trade and credit, capital financing and chattel financing, which upon the lessee's selection of vendors and lease items, the lessor will purchase the lease items from the chosen vendor and provides them to the lessee for its use, and the lessee will then pay the rent.

[3] Retention of ownership (所有权保留) means contractual parties agree in the hire purchase transactions or deferred payment transactions that the vendor remains the ownership of the subject matter of the purchase and sale contract until the purchase price is paid in full. If the purchaser fails to make the payment pursuant to the contract, the vendor will be entitled to take back the subject matter.

[4] Article 402, Article 429, Article 441, Paragraph 1 of Article 443, Paragraph 1 of Article 444, Paragraph 1 of Article 445 of the *Civil Code*.

fide third party without registration.[1] To sum up, the creation of security rights not only requires the fulfilment of general requirements, but also demands the parties to complete the statutory formality requirements.

2. The Secondary Nature

The security contract is accessory to the loan contract. Pursuant to Article 388 and Article 682 of the *Civil Code*, the security contract is secondary in nature and such fundamental nature is statutory. Except for the statutory exceptions, contractual parties cannot exclude this essential nature by agreement. The secondary nature of the security contract is reflected in the following four aspects: the establishment, validity, modification and extinguishment.

(1) The establishment of security contract is secondary. The security contract cannot stand on its own and its formation is premised on the establishment and validity of the loan contract.

(2) The validity of security contract is secondary and it is mainly shown in the following aspects. Firstly, the validity of security contract is subject to that of the loan contract. If the loan contract is void, the security contract will be determined void as well. The nullity of the loan contract will cause both the security contract and the guarantee clauses in the loan contract void. The contractual parties cannot preclude the secondary nature by making a consensual agreement. Secondly, the scope and strength of security contract cannot exceed those of loan contract. The liability of a surety relies upon the accountability of the debtor. Hence, when the surety is required to bear the responsibility, the surety is also entitled to claim defences which the debtor has against the creditor, exercise the right to defend, offset or rescind against the creditor and refuse to undertake the corresponding responsibility to the extent that the debt is offset and rescinded.

(3) The modification of security contract is secondary. The modification of

[1] Article 403 of the *Civil Code*.

the loan contract will affect the validity of the security contract in the following facets. Firstly, if a creditor and a debtor do not acquire the surety's written consent to the alteration of the principal contract which aggravates the surety's liability, the surety bear no responsibility for the aggravated part of the debt. But if the alteration reduces the surety's liability, the surety only needs to bear the responsibility for the altered debt. Secondly, if a creditor transfers all or part of the creditor's right without notification to the surety, the transfer shall be of no effect on the surety. If a debtor assigns all or part of his obligation without the creditor's consent, the surety is no longer responsible for the transferred obligation, unless otherwise agreed upon by the creditor and the surety. Thirdly, the security contract cannot be solely assigned. If the loan contract is assigned, the security contract must be assigned accordingly.

(4) The extinguishment of security contract is secondary. When the loan contract is extinguished by performance, escrow, waiver of debt, merger of claims and obligations, or mutual offset, the security contract will be extinguished as a result.

ii. Legal Consequences of Security Contracts Nullified by the Invalidity of the Loan Contract

Where the security contract is rendered void due to the invalidity of the loan contract, the liability of the surety depends on whether the surety is at fault or not. Pursuant to Paragraph 2 of Article 388 and Paragraph 2 of Article 682 of the *Civil Code*, where a security contract is determined to be invalid, the debtor, the surety or creditor who are at fault shall each bear civil liability in proportion to their respective fault. The criteria for determining whether the surety is liable for the damages caused by the nullity of the security contract and the proportion of liability is regulated in Article 17 of the *Interpretation of the Relevant Guarantee System*. According to Article 17, in the circumstance where the invalidity of the loan contract results in the invalidity of the security contract provided by the third party, if the surety is not at fault, the surety has no compensatory liability; if the surety is at fault, the surety will assume compensatory liability which shall not exceed one-third of the part which the debtor is unable to discharge.

The surety bears no civil liability if he is not at fault. "The surety is not at fault" means that the surety does not know or should not have known that the loan contract is invalid, or that the surety does not facilitate the formation of the loan contract. Notably, when the surety is at fault, he is not at fault for the invalidity of the loan contract. As is required by the principle of privity, the contractual parties of the loan contract are the creditor and the debtor, and the surety is obviously not a party of the loan contract. The situation where the surety is deemed at fault and thus bears civil liability refers to circumstances where the surety provides security with clear knowledge that the loan contract is invalid, or where the surety acts as intermediary to facilitate the formation of the contract with full awareness of the invalidity of the loan contract.[1] For example, party A and B entered into a loan contract agreeing that A made a loan of ¥1 million to B. After providing B with the loan money, A concluded a security contract with C who would be liable if B failed to duly perform his obligations of discharge of the principal and interest. After the expiration of the loan term, B failed to repay the principal and interest, and therefore A brought legal actions claiming for repayment of debt by B and liability under the security contract by C. If the court found that A was actually a professional money lender who had provided loans to multiple borrowers for profit without obtaining the qualification for money lending and that C still provided security with such knowledge, C should bear the corresponding civil liability in proportion.

---

[1] See the Second Civil Division of the Supreme People's Court, *Understanding and Application of the Interpretation of the Supreme People's Court of the Application of the Relevant Guarantee System of the Civil Code*, People's Court Press, 2021, p. 210.

When determining the allocation of compensatory liability, it is necessary for the court to consider the faults of the surety as well as the contractual parties of the loan contract. The reason is that the security contract is void due to the invalidity of the loan contract and the parties of the loan contract are blameable without doubt. Therefore, the creditor's loss should be calculated on the basis of equal division among the creditor, debtor and surety. The liability of the surety should be limited to one-third of the proportion that the debtor is unable to repay.

II. Laws in Hong Kong

i. Types of Security and Security Contracts

1. Types of Security

Types of security are more diverse and various in Hong Kong than those in the Chinese Mainland. In terms of the security created over personal credits, the borrower or surety can provide security in the form of guarantee, indemnity, letter of comfort [1], standby letter of credit [2] and performance bond [3]. When a security is created over real estate, chattel or rights, the borrower or surety can create security interests in the subject matter through methods such as

---

[1] Geraldine Andrews, Richard Millett, *Law of Guarantees*, 7th Edition, Sweet & Maxwell, para. 14-010. Letters of comfort are normally used in a circumstance where a third party is unable or unwilling to provide a guarantee for a loan made to a borrower, but is prepared to give a written assurance to the lender of its continued support for, interest in, or dealings with the borrower which indicates the borrower's ability to repay the loan. It is common that parent company provides a letter of comfort to assist its subsidiary to obtain a loan.

[2] Standby Letter of credit is sort of arrangement that the issuing bank acts at the request and on the instruction of an applicant for the credit to make a payment to the beneficiary or accept bills of exchange drawn by the beneficiary, provided that the terms and conditions of the credit are complied.

[3] Geraldine Andrews, Richard Millett, *Law of Guarantees*, 7th Edition, Sweet & Maxwell, para. 16-001. Performance bonds (or performance guarantees or demand guarantees as they are sometimes known) are essentially unconditional undertakings to pay a specified amount to a named beneficiary, on demand or on the presentation of certain specified documents.

mortgage, charge or pledge.

2. Security Contracts

Under the security system in Hong Kong, a security contract is not a necessary condition for establishing a security interest. The creation of different types of security requires the surety to satisfy different formality requirements. Generally speaking, the formality requirements for creation of security includes conclusion of written security contracts and delivery of secured property or certificate of property.

(1) Taking the Form of Writing

When the surety creates security with personal credits, the surety must enter into a written security contract with the lender.

When creating a security interest over land,[1] the surety can create security interests by legal charge (or legal mortgage[2]), equitable mortgage or equitable charge. The adoption of legal charge requires the surety to comply with Section 44(1) of the *Conveyancing and Property Ordinance* and take the form of deed to create security. Equitable mortgage and equitable charge require the surety to create security interests in the form of written agreements which ought to include a clear and express intention to create security.

When creating a security interests over chattels, the surety is required to take the form of bill of sale and abide by the registration requirements set out in the *Bills of Sale Ordinance*. If the surety intends to create an equitable mortgage or equitable charge over chattels, the surety can create such security either in writing or by oral agreement. In addition, if the pledge is chosen by the surety,

---

[1] Section 2 of the *Conveyancing and Property Ordinance* defines the meaning of "land", which includes (a) land covered by water; (b) any estate, right, interest or easement in or over any land; (bb) the whole or part of an undivided share in land and any estate, right, interest or easement in or over the whole or part of an undivided share in land; and (c) things attached to land or permanently fastened to anything attached to land.

[2] The laws in Hong Kong do not differ legal mortgage from legal charge, which are often used interchangeably.

it is essential to adopt written form to create security.

(2) Taking the Form of Delivery

When creating an equitable charge over land, the surety can create security interests by depositing the title deed. For creation of equitable mortgage and equitable charge over chattel or the benefit of chose in action, the surety can take the form of delivery of secured property or certificate of property. For example, the surety can create equitable mortgage over share by depositing share certificates.

ii. Legal Consequences of the Security Contract Affected by the Unenforceability of the Loan Contract due to Violation of the *Money Lenders Ordinance*

As mentioned in previous chapters, there are two common scenarios where the loan contract is unenforceable: first, the money lender does not hold a money lender licence; second, the interest rate agreed in the loan contract is excessive. When a loan contract is determined unenforceable, whether the lender can enforce the security contract to demand repayment from the surety and reduce the loss becomes the lender's key concern.

1. Lack of Money Lender's Licences

Section 23 (1) of the *Money Lenders Ordinance* provides: "No money lender shall be entitled to recover in any court any money lent by him or any interest in respect thereof or to enforce any agreement made or security taken in respect of any loan made by him unless he satisfies the court by the production of his licence or otherwise that at the date of the loan or the making of the agreement or the taking of the security (as the case may be) he was licensed." Such section strictly regulates the conduct of unlicensed money lending. Only if a money lender's licence is legally obtained can the lender carry on the business as a money lender. Otherwise, it is less likely for the lender without a licence to have access to remedies when the defence of unlicensed money lender is successfully raised by the borrower who refused to pay off the principal and interest of the loan. Generally speaking, when a loan contract is unenforceable due to lack of money lender's licences, the court will determine whether the security contract is unenforceable as well.

The case of *Re Kwai Chung Town Lot No.* 358 [1] illustrates Hong Kong courts' firm position of refusing the enforceability of a loan contract and its security contract which breached the mandatory provisions of the *Money Lenders Ordinance*. The appellant in this case was Official Trustee in Bankruptcy of Queensland in Australia and the respondent was SH Lock (Hong Kong) Ltd. The debtor Antonios Stamatellos was adjudicated bankrupt by an Australian court. His other mortgagee exercised power of sale and sold the property for repayment of debt, and the surplus of the proceeds were then paid into Hong Kong court after satisfying the debt. The respondent used to grant credit facilities to the debtor and acquired a legal charge and a guarantee in favour of the respondent. Moreover, in another legal proceedings against the debtor, the respondent as drawer under the bills paid off the bills on demand by the judgement creditor and thus obtained the corresponding creditor's right. As the holder of the bills in due course and pursuant to the guarantee entered into by the debtor, the respondent claimed the funds held by the court. The respondent was successful at first instance, but the decision was then appealed by the appellate claiming that the loan and security granted by the respondent were illegal and irrevocable on the grounds that the respondent did not hold money lender's licence in breach of Section 23 of the *Money Lenders Ordinance*. The High Court after trial was satisfied that the respondent was not a licensed money lender and held that the legal charge entered into by the respondent was unenforceable by virtue of illegality, and therefore the respondent's application to be enti

[1] [1987] 2 HKC 434.

tled to the surplus proceeds must fail.[1]

2. Excessive Interest Rate

The *Money Lenders Ordinance* explicitly prohibits lenders from stipulating excessive interest rate in loan contracts. The effective interest rate shall not exceed 48% per annum, otherwise the lender commits an offence. Section 24(2) provides: "No agreement for the repayment of any loan or for the payment of interest on any loan and no security given in respect of any such agreement or loan shall be enforceable in any case in which the effective rate of interest exceeds the rate specified in subsection (1), namely 48% per annum." Such provision straightforwardly bans the enforceability of the loan contract and its security contracts which contain excessive interest rate clauses.

In *Wong Kwai Fun v. Li Fung*[2], the defendant in financial difficulties borrowed HK $ 150,000 from the plaintiff on April 2, 1986, but only received HK $ 148,850 after deduction of legal service fees. In the course of borrowing, the defendant also executed a power of attorney in favour of Ho Sum Wah, which enabled him to sell the house on behalf of the defendant. On April 17, 1986, the defendant failed to repay the agreed amount. On April 18, 1986 the defendant entered into a sale and purchase agreement with Wong Kwai Wing that he agreed to sell the property at the price of HK $ 600,000 and that he was entitled to cancel the agreement once he paid off the debt of HK $ 245,000 to Wong Kwai Wing before the settlement date of July 3, 1986. But prior to this date, the defendant and his family suffered from various threats and intimidation of debt collection. On August 6, 1986, the plaintiff entered into another sale and purchase agreement on the same property with the defendant agreeing to sell the property at the price of HK $ 490,000. On September 8, 1986, Wong Kwai Wing and Ho Sum Wah assigned the defendant's property to the plaintiff

[1] *Re Kwai Chung Town Lot No.* 358 [1987] 2 HKC 434, p. 428.

[2] [1994] 1 HKC 549.

free from any encumbrance and then the plaintiff brought an action for possession of defendant's property.

The High Court firstly found that the defendant had no genuine intention to sell the property to the plaintiff and that the power of attorney and the sale and purchase agreement were executed for securing the repayment of the loan and interest.[1] Secondly, the High Court held that since the effective interest rate of the loan made by the plaintiff was over 400% per annum which materially exceeded the interest rate permitted by the *Money Lender Ordinance*, the loan, the sale and purchase agreement and the security for it must be illegal and unenforceable as being in contravention of Section 24. Hence, the power of attorney and the sale and purchase agreement, both of which were executed as security for repayment of the loan and interest, were illegal, unenforceable and void.[2]

iii. Other Circumstances

Apart from the aforementioned statutory circumstances rendering a loan contract unenforceable, the loan contract may be invalidated and then determined unenforceable for other reasons. For example, a loan agreement may be invalid due to fraud, mistake regarding the subject matter of the loan agreement, misrepresentation, duress, undue influence and lack of capacity. When a loan contract is invalidated due to aforesaid reasons, whether the lender can still enforce the security contract to obtain repayment depends on the security forms chosen.

1. By Mortgage, Charge or Pledge

The creation of mortgage, charge or pledge is collateral or accessory to the

---

[1] *Wong Kwai Fun v. Li Fung* [1994] 1 HKC 549, p. 569.

[2] *Wong Kwai Fun v. Li Fung* [1994] 1 HKC 549, p. 572.

principal loan contract. If a borrower creates security interests by mortgage[1], charge[2] and pledge[3] to assure the performance of the obligation under the loan contract, the invalidity of the loan contract will directly render the security unenforceable.

Taking mortgage as an example. *Halsbury's Laws of Hong Kong* illustrates the secondary nature of mortgage as follows: "A mortgage consists of two parts, namely a personal contract for payment of a debt and a disposition or charge of the mortgagor's estate or interest as security for the repayment of the debt and that every mortgage implies a debt and a personal obligation by the mortgagor to pay it."[4] It is clear that the loan contract is the prerequisite for the creation and existence of a mortgage and the validity of the mortgage is subject to that of the loan contract. As the Court of Appeal mentioned in *Easy Fortune Property Ltd. v. Yung Chun Him*[5], when deciding the issue of whether it was inequitable not to enforce the security, it was necessary to take the merits into further consideration. If it was inequitable not to allow the plaintiff to recover from the defendant the reduced principal amount of the loan, it would follow that it would be inequitable not to enforce the security to the same limited extent.[6] Therefore, the extent to which the security to be enforced completely relies on that of the loan contract. Similar to mortgage, charge and pledge are accessory to the loan contract as well. When a loan contract is determined void and unenforceable, it is normal for the court to simultaneously come to a deci-

---

〔1〕 A mortgage is a disposition of property as security for a debt or the discharge of some other obligation.

〔2〕 A charge is the appropriation of real or personal property for the discharge of a debt or other obligation.

〔3〕 A pledge is a security created by contract and effected by the bailment of a chattel or document of title to the creditor, to be kept by the creditor until the debt is discharged.

〔4〕 See *Halsbury's Laws of Hong Kong*, Lexis Nexis Hong Kong, [230.632] Characteristics of a Mortgage.

〔5〕 [2019] HKCU 3671, [2019] HKCA 1055, [2020] 4 HKC 1.

〔6〕 *Easy Fortune Property Ltd. v. Yung Chun Him* [2020] 4 HKC 1, para. 67.

sion that the mortgage, charge or pledge created for securing the performance of obligations under the loan contract are unenforceable as well.

2. By Guarantee

Guarantee is a security that the guarantor and the creditor agree to assure the realisation of debt that if the debtor fails to perform the obligation under the loan contract, the guarantor will substitute for the debtor to repay the debt.

A guarantee contract is accessory to the principal contract. The contractual obligation borne by a guarantor is a secondary obligation. This means that the performance of obligation as a guarantor is contingent on the default of the principal. The guarantor will be liable only if the borrower defaults and fails to repay the principal and interest under the loan contract. The performance of obligation as a guarantor requires the compliance of the co-extensiveness principle that the guarantor's liability is no greater and no less than that of the principal, in terms of amount, time for payment and the conditions under which the principal is liable.[1] The existence of the guarantee contract is contingent on that of the principal contract and thus the nullity of the principal obligation will cause the guarantor not liable under his guarantee of the principal's obligation thereunder.[2]

When a guarantee contract is void by virtue of the invalidity of the loan contract, in principle the guarantor will not be liable under the guarantee. However, there are certain statutory exceptions to the general principle and the guarantor will still be liable notwithstanding the invalidity of the loan contract. For instance, the guarantor cannot refuse to perform his obligation with an excuse

---

[1] Geraldine Andrews, Richard Millett, *Law of Guarantees*, 7th Edition, Sweet & Maxwell, para. 6-002.

[2] Geraldine Andrews, Richard Millett, *Law of Guarantees*, 7th Edition, Sweet & Maxwell, para. 6-020. *Canara Bank v. Excel Triumph Ltd & Anor* [2021] HKCU 6123, [2021] HKCFI 3747 (CFI), para. 27.

that the debtor is a minor when the contract was made,[1] or the director should be accountable for guarantee given in respect of a contract entered into beyond his authority.[2]

It is noteworthy that although an independent provision regarding the guarantee liability is deliberately contained so as to preserve the liability in any event[3], such practice is not applicable where the principal contract is a loan contract. Since the consideration for the guarantee is the act of the creditor in entering or performing the principal contract, the guarantee liability will not be preserved notwithstanding the inclusion of the independent provision regarding the guarantee liability.[4] Hence, when the principal contract of the guarantee contract is a loan contract, the parties cannot break through the general principle that the invalidity of principal contract will cause the guarantee contract void by agreeing on an independent provision regarding the guaranty liability.

3. By Indemnity

Indemnity is a security used in the circumstance where the indemnifier (or

---

[1] Section 3 of the *Age of Majority (Related Provisions) Ordinance* provides that the guarantee shall not be unenforceable against the guarantor for the reason that the debtor was a minor when the contract was made.

[2] The principle of no constructive notice is regulated in Section 120 of the *Companies Ordinance* that a person is not to be regarded as having notice of any matter merely because the matter is disclosed in the articles of a company, a return or resolution kept by the Registrar. Hence, a contract entered into by a third party and the company will not be void by company's assertion of lack of authority by the agent.

[3] For example, a preserving provision or a severability provision can be added in the guarantee contract so that the guarantor is to remain liable notwithstanding defects in the principal contract rending it void, voidable or unenforceable. Such provision can preserve the guarantee liability in spite of the defects of the principal contract for the following two reasons: firstly, the contract is in substance regarded as one of indemnity; secondly, the guarantor is estopped from denying his liability by reason of defects in the principal contract.

[4] Geraldine Andrews, Richard Millett, *Law of Guarantees*, 7th Edition, Sweet & Maxwell, para. 6-028.

indemnitor) promises to hold the creditor harmless from any loss.[1] The contractual obligations borne by the indemnifier is a primary obligation and is not preconditional on the breach of the principal contract.[2] If the agreed conditions under the contract are fulfilled, the creditor may demand the indemnifier to undertake the primary obligation. Therefore, when a borrower provides security by the form of indemnity, the legal effect of an indemnity contract will not be affected by defects of the principal loan contract. The indemnity contract will not be invalidated by the nullity of the loan contract.

In general, the validity and enforceability of an indemnity contract are not affected by those of the loan contract. When the indemnity contract is validly established and the conditions agreed in the contract are fulfilled, the creditor can require the indemnifier to bear his obligations under the indemnity contract. In *Kwung Tung Hui Li Investment Ltd. v. Wong Man Pan*[3], the plaintiff brought an action to demand the defendant to perform his obligation for payment of outstanding indebtedness on so called "deed of irrevocable guarantee". The defendant made a defence that the loan contract was void and thus unenforceable for the charging of interest at higher than 10% per annum which was forbidden under the relevant law in the Chinese Mainland. The so called "deed of irrevocable guarantee" which arose out of an underlying transaction that was void, was also void and unenforceable. The Court of First Instance firstly determined that the true nature of the so called "deed of irrevocable guarantee" was indeed an indemnity contract. It was not the name but the construction of the terms should be stressed on when ascertaining the true nature of a security contract. Despite the name so called "deed of irrevocable guarantee", the terms in the deed essentially reflected the nature and characteristics of an indemnity:

---

[1] See *Halsbury's Laws of Hong Kong*, Lexis Nexis Hong Kong, [200.191] Nature and Definition of Indemnity.

[2] *Moschi v. Lep Air Services Ltd.* [1972] 2 All ER 393; [1973] AC 331.

[3] [2003] HKCU 1352.

Clause 1 of the deed provided that the contract was intended to be unconditional and irrevocable; Clause 2 stipulated that that the defendant undertook joint and several liability towards the plaintiff; Clause 11 said that the legality and validity of the deed would not be affected even if the whole or any part of the loan agreement were illegal, invalid or unenforceable.[1] Hence, the Court of First Instance held that the true nature of the "deed of irrevocable guarantee" should be conceived as indemnity. In addition, when determining the issue of whether the invalidity of the principal loan agreement will affect the validity of the indemnity contract, the Court of First Instance further held that the indemnity contract was valid and enforceable regardless of the validity of the underlying loan agreement under the laws in the Chinese Mainland, unless there were some other grounds affecting the validity or enforceability of the indemnity in Hong Kong.[2]

Due to its peculiar characteristic of independence, the indemnity contract is not affected by the validity of the loan contract. This causes a concern as to whether a lender can circumvent and escape from the regulation of the *Money Lenders Ordinance* by taking the form of indemnity as security. In response to this concern, on the one hand, the *Money Lenders Ordinance* expressly and strictly prohibits the enforcement of any security which includes indemnity. For example, a loan contract and its security in contravention of Sections 18, 22, 23 and 25 of the *Money Lenders Ordinance* are unenforceable, unless the court exercises its discretion on account of equity and fairness. On the other hand, when a loan contract is invalid due to illegality or violation of public policy, the indemnity contract may be deemed void or unenforceable by virtue of the doctrine of tainting.[3]

---

[1] *Kwung Tung Hui Li Investment Ltd.* v. *Wong Man Pan* [2003] HKCU 1352, para. 15 – 16.

[2] *Kwung Tung Hui Li Investment Ltd.* v. *Wong Man Pan* [2003] HKCU 1352, para. 17 – 18.

[3] Hugh Beale, Richard Hooley, Louise Merrett, Graham Virgo, *Chitty on Contracts*, 35th Edition, Sweet & Maxwell, para. 19 – 053.

III. Summary

i. Similarity

Firstly, in the vast majority of circumstances, the laws in the Chinese Mainland and Hong Kong both consider that security is accessory in nature. The laws in the Chinese Mainland expressly provide in statutes that the security contract is secondary in nature and cannot stand alone the loan contract. The laws in Hong Kong provide that the creation of guarantees, mortgages, charges, and pledges is contingent on the conclusion of the loan contract and that the extent to which the surety is liablc under the security contract depends on the scope of obligations under the principal loan contract.

Secondly, generally speaking, when a loan contract is determined void (or unenforceable), the laws in the Chinese Mainland and Hong Kong both negate the validity and enforceability of security contracts. The laws in the Chinese Mainland clearly stipulates that if the loan contract is invalid, the security contract will be void by its invalidity. The laws in Hong Kong provide that if a loan contract is determined unenforceable by reasons of lack of money lender's licences or charging interest at excessive interest rate, the security to the loan contract is unenforceable as well. Additionally, if a loan contract is deemed invalid or unenforceable for reasons other than those prescribed by the *Money Lenders Ordinance*, the guarantees, mortgages, charges, or pledges created by the surety will also be unenforceable.

ii. Difference

Firstly, there is inconsistency between the Chinese Mainland and Hong Kong on exceptions to the general principle that the invalidity of a loan contract will cause the security contract void. The laws in the Chinese Mainland require strict compliance of the secondary nature of security contracts and no statutory exception is stipulated regarding the general principle. While in Hong Kong, there are statutory exceptions to the co-extensiveness principle. Moreover, if the security is created in the form of indemnity, by virtue of its peculiar characteristic of independence, the legal effect of indemnity contract will not be affected by the invalidity of the loan contract.

Secondly, when a security contract is determined void (or unenforceable) due to the invalidity of the loan contract, there is inconsistency between the Chinese Mainland and Hong Kong on the exceptions to the surety's liability. The laws in the Chinese Mainland provide that when the invalidity of the loan contract causes the security contract void, the surety will be liable only if the surety is at fault, and the liability borne by the surety is limited to one-third of the proportion that the debtor is unable to repay. In accordance with the laws in Hong Kong, if the surety creates security by the form of indemnity and if the indemnity contract is validly concluded and the conditions agreed upon are fulfilled, the lender can demand the indemnifier to perform his obligations under the indemnity contract.

Section Two　Validity of Assignment Guarantee

I. Laws in the Chinese Mainland

In private lending activities, apart from providing security through traditional means such as mortgages, pledges and third-party guarantees, a borrower may also provide security by entering into a separate sales contract when concluding a loan contract, or by transferring the ownership of the subject matter (i. e. the secured property) to the lender so as to increase the likelihood of realising creditor's rights. This sort of atypical security can be divided into two kinds in light of the sequence of transfer of ownership of the subject matter—assignment guarantee and post-assignment guarantee.

i. Assignment Guarantee

Assignment guarantee is a form of atypical security. A debtor or a third party enters into a contract with a creditor agreeing that the debtor or the third party will transfer the ownership of the subject matter to the creditor without any consideration payable by the creditor and that if the debtor fails to pay off the debt upon maturity, the creditor can get repaid in respect of the secured property.

1. Form and Characteristic of Assignment Guarantee

There are two forms of assignment guarantee: trading-based assignment guarantee and transferring-based assignment guarantee. Trading-based assignment guarantee is when a debtor transfers ownership of the subject matter by means of sale, yet in substance providing security in the name of a sales transaction, with an agreement that the debtor can repurchase the subject matter in the future. Transferring-based assignment refers to a form of security that in order to assure the repayment of debt, a debtor passes the ownership of the subject matter and makes an agreement with the creditor that the ownership will be returned once the debtor pays off the debt; but if the debtor fails to repay the debt after the expiration of time for repayment, the creditor will get repaid in respect of the subject matter.

Regardless of the variation in forms, assignment guarantee generally has the following basic characteristics: firstly, when an assignment guarantee is created, the surety needs to provisionally pass the ownership of the subject matter to the creditor who will then become the nominal owner of the subject matter; secondly, the creditor usually enters into a loan for use contract or a lease contract to assure the enjoyment of right of continuous use of the subject matter; thirdly, when the debtor duly performs the obligation pursuant to the contract, the creditor shall restitute the ownership to the debtor; fourthly, the debtor and the creditor reach an agreement that if the debtor fails to repay the debt after the expiration of time for repayment, the creditor is entitled to the ownership of the subject matter.[1]

A common practice in assignment guarantee involves repurchase clauses, in which a debtor and a creditor reach agreements that the ownership of the subject matter will be passed to the creditor and repurchased by the debtor or a designated third party (usually for the principal plus a premium) after a certain period of time, and that if the debtor fails to repurchase the subject matter on the due date, the ownership will be directly vested in the creditor. For example, a trust and investment company makes loans to a transferor by means of purchase of specific assets such as real estate development projects. Consentient agreements are reached between the parties that the company, as the transferee, will hold the specific assets and pay the purchase price to the transferor, and that after the expiration of the time allowed for performance, the transferor will repurchase the specific assets from the company at the price of contract purchase price plus a fixed proportion of the premium. In this circumstance, although the company and the transferor express no explicit intention that this arrangement serves as a security for the loan, it effectively functions as such, which is substantially consistent with the basic characteristics of the assignment guarantee. The repurchase clauses agreed upon are for the purpose of ensuring the repayment of debt instead of acquiring the ownership of the specific assets. From the perspective of the transaction mode, the time for repurchase agreed upon corresponds to the allowed time for performance of repayment of the debt in the principal contract and the repurchase price consisting of principal plus premium actually corresponds to the debt and related costs in the principal loan contract.

[1] See the Second Civil Division of the Supreme People's Court, *Understanding and Application of the Interpretation of the Supreme People's Court of the Application of the Relevant Guarantee System of the Civil Code*, People's Court Press, 2021, p. 635.

2. Legal Effect of Assignment Guarantee

Although the *Civil Code* does not specifically regulate in respect of assignment guarantee, it clearly stipulates that security interests can be created by conclusion of other contracts with a security function, which includes assignment guarantee contracts. Both the practice field and the academic field incline to recognise the validity of the assignment guarantee contracts.

First of all, the validity of assignment guarantee contracts is recognised based on the principle of numerus clausus and the principle of distinction between the property right and the creditor's right. The connotation of the principle of numerus clausus is that the types, contents, legal effect and publicity processes of property right shall only be prescribed by law, which in principle shall not be stipulated either by regulatory documents or by agreements freely agreed upon. In accordance with the principle of distinction between the property right and the creditor's right, the validity of contracts is not affected by the principle of numerus clausus. Besides, the validity of assignment guarantee contracts is not determined differently simply because of its peculiar atypical nature and thus whether an assignment contract is valid or not shall be determined pursuant to the general requirements for establishment of valid contracts provided in the *Civil Code*.

Furthermore, the validity of assignment guarantee contracts satisfies the general requirements for establishment of valid contracts. For one thing, the assignment guarantee contract itself does not violate mandatory requirements of laws and administrative regulations, public orders and good morals.[1] For another, assignment guarantee is a combination of acts of creating security and passing ownership, and such transfer of ownership is conducted with true and

[1] Article 153 of the *Civil Code*.

genuine intention.[1] The agreement on vesting of ownership in the creditor in the event of debtor's failure to repay the due debt is in substance an exchange of value of the secured property with the ultimate purpose of obtaining debt repayment rather than property ownership. Therefore, the true intention behind the transfer of ownership is to create a security interest, and this intention is neither conspiratorial nor false. The validity of an assignment guarantee should not be negated on the grounds of false expression of intent.[2]

Last but not least, the prohibition on pactum commissorium does not affect the validity of assignment guarantee contracts. In accordance with Article 401 and Article 428 of the *Civil Code*, although the creditor and the debtor reach an agreement that the mortgaged or pledged property shall belong to the creditor if the debtor fails to pay the due debt, such agreement takes no legal effect and the creditor may only have the right of obtaining repayment in priority in respect of the mortgaged or pledged property. These provisions only explicitly nullify the legal effect that pactum commissorium clauses result in changes in property rights, but do not negate the validity of contracts arising from the freedom of contracting. Therefore, the clauses regarding the vesting of property ownership in the event of failure to repay debts shall be deemed invalid, but these have no influence on parties' true and genuine intentions to create security and the validity of the whole assignment guarantee contract as well.[3]

3. Enforcement of Assignment Guarantee

The prohibitive provisions of Article 401 and Article 428 of the *Civil Code* negate the effect of an agreement in the assignment guarantee contract that if the

---

[1] See the Second Civil Division of the Supreme People's Court, *Understanding and Application of the Interpretation of the Supreme People's Court of the Application of the Relevant Guarantee System of the Civil Code*, People's Court Press, 2021, p. 635.

[2] See Xie Zaiquan, *Theory of Property Rights in Civil Law (Volume II)*, China University of Political Science and Law Press, 2011, p. 1105.

[3] See Chen Yongqiang, *New Development and Interpretation of the prohibition of Liquid Pledge in the Civil Code*, Law and Economy, Issue 5 (2020), 35 - 45.

debtor fails to repay the debt at the expiration of repayment due date, the ownership of the secured property will be vested in the creditor without any liquidation process. The legislative intent of these prohibitive provisions is to prevent the creditor from taking advantage of the dilemma suffered by the debtor and abusing his dominant position to profiteer by maliciously pushing down the value of the secured property. For these concerns, Article 68 of the *Interpretation of the Relevant Guarantee System* specifies clear procedures for the enforcement of assignment guarantees.

Certain mandatory legal procedures must be complied with to enforce assignment guarantees. For one thing, the courts should examine the agreement which the creditor reaches with the debtor or a third party. Since the *Civil Code* explicitly bans the pactum commissorium clauses, the courts should focus on examining clauses regarding the vesting of ownership and the right of obtaining repayment in priority in respect of the secured property. For another, the publicity of property rights is the core process that entitles the creditor to the right of obtaining repayment in priority and thus the parties of assignment guarantee contract shall complete the publicity processes to demonstrate the changes in property rights, which requires to accomplish the delivery of chattels and the registration of real property and the benefit of a chose in action such as equity rights. There are generally three types of agreements reached by the parties in assignment guarantee contracts.

The first type of agreement is that the debtor or a third party will ostensibly pass the secured property to the creditor who will be entitled the right to be repaid from the property's valuation or the proceeds of its auction or liquidation if the debtor fails to repay the debt. Such agreements are inclined to be determined as valid by the courts. If the publicity process regarding the changes in the property right is completed and the debtor fails to repay the due debt, the creditor will be entitled to apply to the courts for obtaining priority for repayment in respect of the secured property in accordance with the relevant provisions regarding the security interest in the *Civil Code*.

The second type of agreement is that the debtor or a third party will ostensibly pass the secured property to the creditor who will be vested with the ownership of the property if the debtor fails to repay the due debt. Such agreements are inclined to be determined as void by the courts, but the voidness will not affect parties' intention of providing security. If the publicity process regarding the changes in the property right is completed and the debtor fails to repay the due debt, the creditor cannot claim for the ownership of the secured property. However, the courts incline to uphold the creditor's claim for obtaining priority for repayment from the valuation of the property or the proceeds of the auction or liquidation of the property in accordance with the relevant provisions regarding the security interest in the *Civil Code*. When the debtor pays off the debt, the creditor should restitute the property.

The third type of agreement is that the secured property will be ostensibly passed to the creditor and repurchased by the debtor or a designated third party with purchase price plus premium after a certain period of time, and that if the debtor fails to perform the repurchase obligation, the ownership of the property will be vested in the creditor. Such agreements are inclined to be determined as void by the courts. If the subject of repurchase never exists, the courts will handle the case in light of the substantive legal relationship.

ii. Post-Assignment Guarantee

1. Form and Nature of Post-Assignment Guarantee

The manifestation form of post-assignment guarantee in transactions is that the creditor and the debtor enter into a loan contract together with a sales contract which agrees that if the debtor fails to repay the principal and interest at the expiration of repayment due date, the debtor shall perform the obligations under the sales contract and that the subject matter of the contract will be utilised to offset the debt.[1] Therefore, post-assignment guarantee can be seen as a variant form of trading-based assignment guarantee.

(1) Similarity between Post-Assignment Guarantee and Assignment Guarantee

There is no substantial difference between post-assignment guarantee and assignment guarantee in terms of the nature, value, function, and classification. For these two sorts of security, the purpose of transferring the ownership of the subject matter is to assure the fulfilment of the creditor's rights rather than to obtain the ownership. This differs from the traditional conduct of property transfer, which the purchaser bears the main obligation to pay the purchase price and enjoy the essential right to obtain entire ownership. Therefore, if security is created by the form of post-assignment guarantee or assignment guarantee, the transferee of the subject matter is usually not required to pay the contract price and does not have the right of disposition and complete ownership before the expiration of repayment due date.

(2) Difference between Post-Assignment Guarantee and Assignment Guarantee

The only difference between post-assignment guarantee and assignment guarantee is the sequence of transfer of ownership. For assignment guarantee, the ownership of the subject matter is passed to the creditor at the beginning of creation of security, while for post-assignment guarantee the ownership will be passed only if the debtor fails to pay off the debt as agreed in the contract.[2] In other words, as the creditor of the assignment guarantee has already obtained the ownership of the subject matter by prior transfer of ownership, the creditor's right to the subject matter is in a completely vested state. As the creditor of the

---

[1] See Yang Lixin, *Post-Assignment Guarantee: A Security Interest Developing from Customary Laws*, China Legal Science, Issue 3 (2013).

[2] See Yang Lixin, *Post-Assignment Guarantee in Judicial Practice and its Application*, People Rule of Law, Issue 9 (2015).

post-assignment guarantee can only acquire the ownership of the subject matter in the event of the debtor's default, the creditor merely obtains a contingent right rather than a present and complete property right.

2. Dealing with Post-Assignment Guarantee Disputes

The adoption of post-assignment guarantee often causes numerous disputes despite the recognition of its security function by the *Civil Code*. For instance, if a borrower provides a post-assignment guarantee to a lender but fails to repay the principal and interest of the loan at the expiration of repayment due date, the lender (vendor) will often bring a claim for specific performance of the sales contract and require the borrower (purchaser) to complete the conveyancing and registration so as to get repaid by direct acquisition of ownership of the subject matter of the sales contract. In this regard, the borrower often rejects to continue performing the sales contract and argues that there is a considerable discrepancy between the value of the property and the loan amount, or that the value of the property is seriously inconsistent with the market price, or that the sales contract is invalid. To cope with these cases, Article 23 of the *Provisions on Private Lending* (2020 *Second Amendment*) specifies the approach of how to handle post-assignment guarantee disputes.

(1) Adhering to the Adjudication Principle of Substantive Legal Relationships

When confronted with cases where it is difficult to distinguish private lending contracts from sales contracts, the courts shall adhere to the adjudication principle of substantive legal relationships and figure out whether the true intention of the parties is to create security for the private lending contract by entering into a sales contract or to obtain the ownership of the subject matter of the sales contract through payment of consideration.

When there is a dispute arising between the parties over the same sum of money which is claimed to be the purchase price by the lender but is asserted to be a loan by the borrower, the courts should determine the nature of the disputed sum of money in light of the evidence. For this sort of disputes, there are three kinds of handling scenarios in judicial practice:

Firstly, if a party proves that a private lending contract and a sales contract both exist and that the sales contract is concluded for the purpose of creation of security for the private lending contract, the court will tend to find the case fact of providing security and adjudicate on the basis of the legal relationship of private lending.

Secondly, if the evidence adduced by the parties proves the existence of the sales contract, but it is unable to prove that of private lending, the courts will tend to find that the conclusion of sales contract is parties' true intention and adjudicate on the basis of the legal relationship of sales contract.

Thirdly, if the evidence adduced by the parties is sufficient to proves the existence of both the private lending contract and the sale contract, but not sufficient to prove that the sales contract is concluded for the purpose of creation of security for the private lending contract, the nature of the sales contract should be determined according to particular circumstances in each case. For example, when the loan term agreed in the contract expires or the borrower is unable to repay the debt, the lender enters into a sales contract with the borrower so as to offset the debt. In this circumstance, if the purchase price agreed in the sales contract is reasonable, the sales contract is generally conceived as a valid contract. This is because the conclusion of the sales contract is in substance a transformation of creditor-debtor relationship under the private lending contract, or can be seemed as an additional method for the debtor to repay the loan instead of a pre-agreed security created for the loan.

(2) Handling of the Claim for Performing the Sales Contract

When the court determines that the case shall be heard on the basis of the legal relationship of private lending which is inconsistent with the party's claim of sale contract relationship, the court shall adjudicate with concentration on the issue of whether the legal relationship disputed between the parties is a private lending legal relationship or a sales contract relationship so that the parties' right to debate can be fully safeguarded. During the court proceedings, the party may amend the claim from seeking performance of the sales contract to requesting for repayment of principal and interest of the loan by the debtor. Alternatively, the party may also insist on the original claim and if so, the court will not require the party to make any amendment to the claim and will make a decision accordingly, which will not prevent the party from bringing another new action based on the legal relationship previously determined by the court.[1]

3. Enforcement of Post-Assignment Guarantee

In the circumstance where the court determines that the sales contract between the lender and the borrower is in substance concluded and served as security for a private lending contract, the lender can apply for the auction of the subject matter of the sales contract to get repaid only after the lender obtains an effective judgment rendered on the basis of the legal relationship of private lending and the borrower fails to fulfil the monetary obligation determined in the valid judgment.[2] If there is a difference between the auction proceeds and the payable principal and interest, the lender or the borrower has the right to claim restitution or compensation. If the auction proceeds exceed the repayable principal and interest, the difference shall be returned to the borrower. In contrast, if the auction proceeds are insufficient to repay the principal and interest, the lender can make another claim for making up the shortfall from the borrower,

---

[1] Article 53 of the *Provisions on Evidence in Civil Procedures* provides that the course of litigation, if the nature of the legal relationship or the effectiveness of the civil act claimed by a party is inconsistent with the determination made by the people's court based on the facts of the case, the people's court shall try the nature of the legal relationship or the effectiveness of the civil act as the issue, unless the nature of the legal relationship has no effect on adjudicative reasoning and results, or the relevant issue has been fully debated by the parties. Under circumstances in the preceding paragraph, if the party modifies its claims based on the court trial, the people's court shall grant the modification, and may specify another time limit for proof according to the specific circumstances of the case.

[2] Paragraph 2 of Article 23 of the *Provisions on Private Lending* (*2020 Second Amendment*).

such as applying for enforcement of the borrower's other assets.[1]

Although the lender may apply to the court for auction of the subject matter of the sales contract to get repaid after obtaining an effective judgement and in the event of the borrower's failure to perform the obligations determined by the judgment, this does not mean that the lender is naturally entitled to the right of obtaining repayment in priority in respect of the proceeds from the auction of the subject matter of the sales contract. If the parties merely conclude a sales contract without creating a mortgage or pledge over its subject matter or transferring ownership, no publicity effect operates on a third party. Due to the absence of the publicity of changes in property rights, the third party is unable to decide whether a transaction deserves to be entered into with the borrower. In this circumstance, if the lender still has the right of obtaining repayment in priority in respect of the auction proceeds, it will cause injustice to the borrower's other creditors and have adverse influence on transaction safety. Instead, if the parties not only conclude a sales contract but also complete the formality requirements for changes in property rights such as delivery of chattels and registration of transfer of property ownership, it already has publicity effect on a third party and thus it is reasonable to determine that the lender enjoy the right of obtaining repayment in priority in respect of the auction proceeds.

II. Laws in Hong Kong

In the lending activities in Hong Kong, it is prevalent for borrower to obtain loans by creating security similar to assignment guarantee. Due to the urgent need of raising funds or the financial deterioration, a borrower may create security by transferring his property to a lender before the conclusion of a loan

---

[1] See the First Civil Division of the Supreme People's Court, *Understanding and Application of the Provisions of the Supreme People's Court on Several Issues Concerning the Application of Laws in the Trial of Private Lending Cases*, People's Court Press, 2021, p. 350.

contract, or by entering into a separate sales contract after the conclusion. For such transactions conducted for the creation of security for loan contracts, Hong Kong laws do not name these types of security specifically. When determining whether these transactions in substance perform the function as security, the courts in Hong Kong adopt a similar stance to the courts in the Chinese Mainland, recognising that transactions conducted before or after the conclusion of the loan contract can perform as security in the lending activities.

i. Transactions Conducted Before the Conclusion of Loan Contracts

The creation of security by transfer of secured property from the borrower to the lender before the conclusion of a loan contract is for the purpose of building up the lender's confidence in repayment of debt. For the borrower's transaction of property transfer conducted before the conclusion of the loan contract, the courts in Hong Kong apply a holistic approach to determine whether such transaction is able to function as security. If the courts are satisfied that the substantive features in the transaction match the usual features in a loan and security contract after considering the entire transaction process of loan making and property transfer, the courts will recognise that the transaction of property transfer does function as security for the loan made subsequently.

In the case of *Ding Huirong v. China Times Securities Ltd. and Another*[1], the plaintiff used shares he owned in a listed company as security to raise funds in April 2017. On May 8, 2017 the plaintiff opened an account with the first defendant and deposited the secured shares into the account. The first defendant kept the shares in custody pursuant to a collateral agency agreement with the plaintiff. In accordance with the secured loan and pledge agreement dated June 1, 2017, the second defendant issued a funding notice to the plaintiff and transferred the first tranche of the loan to the plaintiff on June 3, 2017. After mak-

---

[1] [2021] HKCU 1328, [2021] HKCA 419.

ing the first advance, the second defendant did not issue the other three tranches but instead sent a notice to the plaintiff informing that the second defendant had acquired the right to exercise all right with respect to the security pursuant to the agreement due to the occurrence of an event of default. The plaintiff therefore commenced an action on the grounds of fraud and deceit, and violation of the *Securities and Futures Ordinance* and the *Money Lenders Ordinance*. The plaintiff also submitted a claim based on his right in equity to redeem the secured shares.

After trial the Court of First Instance held that the transfer of shares before the conclusion of loan agreement should be determined as security arrangement which entitled the plaintiff the right of redemption and that the terms of the loan agreement constituted an unlawful clog on the equity of redemption. The defendants appealed against the decision of the first instance on the grounds that the decision erred in characterising the transaction as a security agreement and the conclusion drawn that the terms of the loan agreement constituted an unlawful clog on the equity of redemption.

For the appeal grounds raised by the defendants, the Court of Appeal determined that the Court of First Instance was correct in characterising the transaction of share transfer as security for the loan made in subsequence. When ascertaining the true legal nature of a transaction, the Court of Appeal stressed on the need to pay close regard to the contractual frame work under the agreement and look at the provisions in the agreement as a whole so as to decide on the substance of the transaction. By applying the approach, the Court of Appeal concluded that the transfer of secured shares into the first defendant's account prior to the conclusion of loan agreement was security for due performance of the agreement for the following reasons. Firstly, all the terms and expressions used to describe the parties' relationship in the preamble and the recital pointed towards a borrower-lender relationship, and the description regarding the second defendant's interests in the shares indicated that the transfer of shares was in substance a sort of security arrangement.[1] Secondly, the provisions in the body of the agreement clearly reflected substantive features in the transaction of a loan and security arrangement. Due to the provisions on collateral interest in securing the due performance of the obligations under the agreement, the obligation to top up security and the change in collateral safeguard, the transfer of shares between parties obviously was not apt to the general features of sale and repurchase of shares.[2] Thirdly, the obligation on the part of the plaintiff to pay interest and the provisions designed to protect the interest of the second defendant with respect to the event of default and remedies thereof strongly indicated that the transaction was a loan.[3]

Hence, if the transfer of property between the lender and the borrower, which is viewed from a holistic perspective, satisfies the essential characteristics of loan transactions, the courts will incline to determine that despite the property transfer conducted before the conclusion of the loan contract, such transaction was in substance conducted for creation of security rather than for a genuine sale or voluntary transfer.

ii. Transactions Conducted After the Conclusion of Loan Contracts

Another common practice in the lending activities to create security by means of transactions is that the lender requires or the borrower voluntarily enters into a separate sales contract after the conclusion of the loan contract. In the sales contract, it is agreed that if the borrower fails to repay the principal and interest on the repayment due date, the lender can require the borrower to perform his obligations under the contract. However, whether this kind of practice is able to function as security for the loan contract concluded prior to the sales

---

[1] *Ding Huirong v. China Times Securities Ltd and Another* [2021] HKCU 1328, para. 29 – 30.

[2] *Ding Huirong v. China Times Securities Ltd and Another* [2021] HKCU 1328, para. 31 – 32.

[3] *Ding Huirong v. China Times Securities Ltd and Another* [2021] HKCU 1328, para. 33.

contract becomes the core issue in the dispute between the lender and the borrower. With regard to this issue, the courts in Hong Kong generally determine the true nature of the sale transaction by taking into all specific circumstances of the transaction into consideration.

In *Lee Leo v. Cheong Oi Sum Ader*[1], the district court held that the transfer of flat occurred after the conclusion of loan contract was in deed security provided by the borrower and such transfer of flat was a transaction within the regulated scope of the *Money Lenders Ordinance*. In this case, the plaintiff agreed to lend HK $110,000 to the defendant although the defendant only received a net amount of HK $75,665. When the loan was due, the defendant could not repay the loan and thus transferred her flat to the plaintiff for a consideration less than its real value. The plaintiff sold the flat at a substantial profit in the next year. In earlier proceedings, the court found that the loan money had been lent to the defendant at an effective interest rate of 216% and was unenforceable due to the violation of Section 24 of the *Money Lenders Ordinance*. The plaintiff then submitted a claim asking for the court to exercise its discretion to reopen the transaction by relying on Section 25(1).

With regard to the plaintiff's claim, the district court summarised the essential issue was whether the transfer of flat by the defendant to the plaintiff was a "transaction" falling within the scope of Section 25 of the *Money Lenders Ordinance* which enabled the court to exercise its discretion to reopen the transaction. In response to this issue, the plaintiff argued that the transfer of flat was unconnected with the loan and that the "transaction" provided in Section 25 must be confined to the original loan or any security given at the time of loan, and should not be extended to subsequent transactions. However, the court rejected the plaintiff's argument and held that the "transaction" used in Section 25 was not limited to loan agreements or security expressly stated in the statute and

---

[1] [1993] 2 HKC 736.

that the transfer of the flat, which was conducted for creation of security for loan, was a transaction falling within the scope of Section 25 for the following reasons.[1] First of all, as the *Money Lenders Ordinance* was a piece of remedial legislation, the court should be slow and cautious to place a restricted contraction upon the language of such legislation when determining the scope of "transaction" used in Section 25.[2] Furthermore, when deciding whether the transfer of flat was a "transaction", it was necessary for the court look to the substance of the transaction instead of its mere form. After comprehensively considering all the circumstances, the court was satisfied that there was contemplation between the parties that the flat would be used to repay, or used as security for repayment of the loan. Firstly, the transfer was not the act of a willing defendant at a freely negotiated or fair price and the defendant did not receive the stated deposit from the plaintiff; secondly, the plaintiff became the owner and obtained vacant possession thereof without paying the outstanding balance for the flat; thirdly, although the plaintiff agreed to give an option to repurchase the flat, the plaintiff knew that the defendant would be unlikely to be able to do so because of the nature and extent of the financial pressure she was under; fourthly, during the discussions regarding the loan, the defendant had offered her flat as a form of security and the plaintiff had asked for details and checked with the Land Office before he agreed to make the loan.[3]

When confronted with the circumstance where a lender enters into a separate sales contract with a borrower after the conclusion of the loan contract, the courts in Hong Kong incline to regard the sales contract as a form of security for the loan contract. However, this inclination is not universal, which means that not all sales contracts concluded after loan contracts will be considered as security.

---

〔1〕 *Lee Leo v. Cheong Oi Sum Ader* [1993] 2 HKC 736, p. 741.

〔2〕 *Lee Leo v. Cheong Oi Sum Ader* [1993] 2 HKC 736, p. 740.

〔3〕 *Lee Leo v. Cheong Oi Sum Ader* [1993] 2 HKC 736, p. 741.

In the case of *Cheung Bing Sum Juana v. Lee Leo*[1], the respondent Lee Leo lent HK $ 15,000 to the appellant Cheung Bing Sum Juana who failed to repay the loan later on. Trapped in financial embarrassment, the appellant proposed that she would have to sell her flat and offered to sell it to the respondent at the price of HK $ 380,000. The respondent accepted the offer, paid a deposit of HK $ 25,000 to the appellant and said that he would deduct the sum owing from the balance of the purchase price. The respondent was then given a receipt which contained a description of the flat and other details. Due to the appellant's failure to complete the transaction in accordance with the agreement for sale and purchase, the respondent commenced proceedings for specific performance.

As the court at first instance rejected the appellant's defence that the payment of HK $ 25,000 to the respondent was in fact a loan, the appellant appealed to the Court of Appeal. The appellant made a defence that the loan was in contravention of Section 24(1) of the *Money Lenders Ordinance* and that the agreement for sale and the loan were unenforceable under Section 24(2) because the sale of the flat was security given in respect of the loan. The Court of Appeal rejected such defence and held that the loan and the agreement for sale and purchase of the flat were two separate transactions[2] and thus the appellant sought appeal to the Privy Council[3].

The Judicial Committee of the Privy Council endorsed the decision given by the Court of Appeal and held that the conclusion of agreement for sale and

---

[1] [1996] 4 HKC 130.

[2] *Cheung Bing Sum Juana v. Leo Lee* [1994] 3 HKC 132, para. 138A.

[3] This case was appealed to the Privy Council as it took place before the return of Hong Kong. The Judicial Committee was established in 1833, which consisted of the Lord President of the Council, the Lord Chancellor, ex-Lord Presidents, the Lord of Appeal in Ordinary and other members of the Privy Council. The Committee had the jurisdiction to hear appeals from courts in any colony. Prior to July 1, 1997, the Committee could receive and hear cases appealed from the Supreme Court and Court of Appeal for Hong Kong.

purchase of the flat was an independent transaction and such agreement was not entered into for the purpose of creation of security for the loan for the following reasons. Firstly, there was no evidence that the respondent had persuaded the appellant to sell him the flat, that the sale was at an undervalue, or that the purpose of the transaction was to provide the respondent with security for the repayment of his loan. Secondly, the only link between the loan transaction and the sale of the flat was that, having agreed to buy the flat, the respondent agreed not to demand immediate payment of the money due but to set off the loan debt against the balance of the purchase price. Putting the matter at its highest, it may be said that whatever the motive for the transaction, the respondent's right to a conveyance of the flat combined with his right to set off the loan debt constituted security for repayment of the loan. Thirdly, the respondent did not seek to rely upon such security, namely not seek to exercise the set-off right, but was willing and able to pay the whole price less the deposit instead. Based on these circumstances, the Judicial Committee considered that it was unnecessary to decide whether there may be said to be security provided by the potential set-off which was rendered unenforceable by Section 24(2) of the *Money Lenders Ordinance*.[1]

In conclusion, when determining whether a sales contract is essentially concluded as security for a loan contract, on the one hand, the courts ought to consider all circumstance where the lender and the borrower enter into the loan contract, such as whether the effective interest rate agreed upon is extortionate, and whether the loan contract is drafted in accordance with Section 18 of the *Money Lenders Ordinance*. On the other hand, the courts ought to take into account peculiar features and facts occurred in the course of the transaction, such as whether the purchase price agreed in the sales contract is market price, whether the lender pays the deposit as the purchaser, whether the lender or the

[1] *Cheung Bing Sum Juana v. Leo Lee* [1996] 4 HKC 130, p. 134.

borrower expresses intentions to regard the sales contract as security to the other party and whether the claim brought by the lender is for enforcement of the security or for specific performance of the sales contract. If there is an excessive interest rate agreed in the loan contract, a clear intention expressed by the borrower who will sell the property as security for due performance, a significantly low purchase price agreed in the sales contract subsequently entered into, and non-payment of deposit by the lender, it is sufficient for the courts to determine that the sales contract concluded by both parties is in essence a security for the loan contract.

III. Summary

i. Similarity

Firstly, there is a practice of assignment guarantee (or creating security by transactions) in both Chinese Mainland and Hong Kong and their manifestation forms are basically the same. Moreover, the laws in the Chinese Mainland and Hong Kong both recognise that assignment guarantee (or creating security by transactions) can perform function as security. In lending activities, it is common for the borrower to transfer the ownership of the secured property to the lender or to enter into a separate sales contract to create security for loan contract previously or subsequently concluded. The laws in the Chinese Mainland and Hong Kong both recognise security function can be created and performed by means of transferring the ownership of property or entering into a separate sales contract.

Secondly, there are similarities in handling disputes regarding post-assignment guarantee. When resolving post-assignment guarantee disputes, the laws in the Chinese Mainland and Hong Kong both consider it is essential to ascertain the substance of the transaction of entering into a sales contract between the lender and the borrower, namely whether the parties have the true intention to engage in sales. If parties' true intention to the transaction is deemed to genuinely concluding a sales contract, the court will generally support the lender's claim requiring the borrower to continue performing his obligations under the sales contract. Laws in the Chinese Mainland expressly stipulate that if the evidence adduced by the parties proves the existence of the sales contract, but it is unable to prove that of private lending, the courts will tend to find that the conclusion of sales contract is the parties' true intention and to adjudicate on the basis of the legal relationship of sales contract. The case laws in Hong Kong clearly point out that the nature of a transaction should be ascertained in light of its substance rather than its form, which requires the court, based on case facts, to determine whether the sales contract between the lender and the borrower is intended to provide security for the loan contract previously concluded, and not to be confused by its external form.

ii. Difference

There are differences in the classification of assignment guarantee in judicial practice between the Chinese Mainland and Hong Kong. In the Chinese Mainland, assignment guarantee is specifically subdivided into assignment guarantee and post-assignment guarantee based on the sequence of the transfer of ownership. Under this categorisation, assignment guarantee can be further divided into trading-based assignment guarantee and transferring-based assignment guarantee. The laws in Hong Kong make no specific distinctions or classification regarding this security created by means of transaction in lending activities. The laws instead focus on the determination of true nature of the transaction in light of peculiar case facts. The timing of conclusion of loan contracts and that of property transfer are generally not considered as decisive factors for the determination of true legal nature.

Chapter VII

Comparison of Legal Rules on Marital Debts

Section One Laws in the Chinese Mainland

I. Revision History

i. The Previous *Marriage Law* (*2001 Amendment*) and Relevant Judicial Interpretations

Article 41 of the *Marriage Law* (2001 *Amendment*) stipulates that upon divorce, community debts incurred for the married life shall be paid out of community property. In accordance with Article 24 of the previous *Interpretation of the Supreme People's Court about Several Problems Concerning the Application of the Marriage Law of the People's Republic of China* (*II*) issued in 2003, debts incurred by the spouse in his or her personal name during the marriage shall be deemed as community debt, unless the non-debtor spouse proves that the creditor and the debtor have explicitly agreed that such debt is a personal debt, or that the circumstance falls within the scenario stipulated in Paragraph 3 of Article 19 of the *Marriage Law* (*2001 Amendment*)[1]. The above provisions place the burden of proof on the non-debtor spouse to prove that the debt in question was not incurred for the married life, and failing that, the spouse who has not raised the debt shall also be liable for repayment.

ii. The Previous *Interpretation on Marital Debt*

The structure, types, amount and categories of family property of urban and rural residents in the Chinese Mainland have undergone significant changes along with the economic and social development in recent years, so are the

[1] Where the spouses agree that property owned by each of them separately, debts incurred by either of them shall be repaid by their own property provides that the creditor is aware of such agreement.

methods of financial management. Cases have consistently and prominently emerged in which one spouse incurs substantial debts due to entrepreneurship, investment or even colluding with creditors, causing the non-debtor spouse to be jointly liable. Such situation has led to calls for further standardisation and refinement for the criteria of determining community debt.

To reasonably allocate the burden of proof and strike a balance between the interests of the creditor and the non-debtor spouse, the Supreme People's Court issued the *Interpretation on Marital Debt* in 2018. The Interpretation clarified the criteria and rules for determining community debt. Debts incurred by one of the spouses in his or her own name, especially those exceeding the family's daily needs, shall not be deemed as community debt unless the creditor can prove that such debt has been used for the married life or production and business operation by the spouses, or that such debt is incurred by the spouses through mutual consent. Debts cannot be determined as community debt if creditors fail to provide such proof. The burden of proof of community debt has, since then, shifted from the non-debtor spouse to the creditor.

iii. The *Civil Code*

1. Community Debt Regime

(1) Types of Community Debt

The *Civil Code*, incorporating the relevant content of the *Interpretation on Marital Debt*, provides a clear legal basis for resolving community debt disputes. Article 1064 provides for three typical types of community debt, namely, debts incurred through the spouses' mutual consent, debts incurred for the family's daily life, and debts proved to be community debts by the creditor.

(2) Repayment of Community Debt

Article 1089 of *the Civil Code* provides for the discharge of community debts. In the case of divorce, community debts shall be jointly discharged by the spouses. Where community property is insufficient for repayment of community debts, or where property is owned by each spouse separately, the spouses shall work out an agreement on repayment.

2. Matrimonial Property Regime

The community of acquisition regime is the default matrimonial property regime in the Chinese Mainland, and meanwhile the laws also provide the contractual property regime as an option. Article 1062 of the *Civil Code* provides for the following five types of community property that are jointly owned by the spouses: (1) wages, bonuses, and remunerations received from services rendered; (2) proceeds obtained from production, business operation, and investment; (3) proceeds arising from intellectual property rights; (4) property inherited or given as a gift, except as otherwise provided in a will or gift contract as belonging to only one party; and (5) other property that shall be jointly owned by the spouses. Apart from that, Article 1065 of the *Civil Code* stipulates that the spouses may enter into a matrimonial agreement stating that their premarital property and the property acquired during their marriage are to be owned separately or jointly, or partially-separately and partially-jointly.

II. Principles For Determining Community Debts

i. Debts Incurred Through the Mutual Consent by Spouses

Mutual consent of the spouses can be expressed through joint signature or subsequent ratification by the other spouse, commonly known as the "co-signing" rule. Debts incurred following the "co-signing" rule are debts raised by more than one person or legal entities, reflecting the principles of autonomy of the will and privity of contract in civil law.

The implementation of the "co-signing" rule imposes an obligation of risk control on creditors with comparatively advantageous position which can effectively avoid the loss caused by inability to prove community debt and ensure transaction security. From another point of view, compliance of such rule protects the spouse's right to know and consent to the disposition of the family's major property by the other spouse, which can effectively protect either spouse from being indebted unknowingly and reduce disputes to the greatest extent.

It should be noted that valid methods for subsequent ratification include not only written contracts, but also other communication means capable of carrying relevant content, such as telephone recordings, text messages, WeChat messages, mails and so forth.

ii. Debts Incurred for the Family's Daily Life

1. Types of Community Debt Based on the Statutory Agency for Daily Family Affairs

The statutory agency for daily family affairs between the spouses is the right of either spouse, for the family's daily life, to represent one another in certain civil juristic acts with a third party. Such acts performed for satisfaction of the family's daily life are deemed to have been performed by mutual consent of the spouses and both of them shall bear the legal consequences arising therefrom.

Debts incurred based on the statutory agency for daily family affairs include expenditures on food and clothing, child education, caring for the elderly and family medical expenses. In the case of (2021) Beijing 01 Civil Final No. 9731 Private Lending Dispute, Beijing First Intermediate People's Court held that the debt in question, incurred by the defendant's spouse, should be community debt because the evidence had shown that the defendant's spouse was the breadwinner of the family and the debt was used for their underaged child studying abroad. In the case of (2019) Jiangsu 01 Civil Final No. 3461 Private Lending Dispute, Nanjing Intermediate People's Court of Jiangsu Province found that the money borrowed from the respondent by WANG (the defendant at first instance) in his own name constituted community debt because the money was used for milk powder, diapers, clothes, toys and other supplies for the family.

However, what should be stressed on is that the expenditures on the family daily needs shall be reasonable and necessary for sustaining family life. The criteria for determination of whether the amount is reasonable and necessary should be updated in line with economic and social development, accumulation of family wealth and changes of lifestyles.

2. Legal Consequences of the Statutory Agency for Daily Family Affairs

Article 1060 of the *Civil Code* stipulates that a civil juristic act performed by one of the spouses to meet the daily needs of the family is binding on both spouses. That is to say, the spouses shall bear the legal consequences including rights and duties arising from a civil juristic act performed by either spouse through the exercise of the aforesaid agency.

In the case of (2021) Beijing 01 Civil Final No. 9731 Private Lending Dispute mentioned above, since the debt incurred by the defendant's spouse was determined to be community debt, the defendant should be liable for repaying the debt after the death of her spouse. In the case of (2019) Jiangsu 01 Civil Final No. 3461 Private Lending Dispute mentioned above, the debt in question, being determined as community debt, should be repaid jointly by the appellant and the defendant at first instance

iii. Debts Proved to be Community Debts by the Creditor

1. Types of Community Debts Creditors Need to Prove

Apart from exercising the statutory agency for daily family affairs, the spouses may incur other debts with third parties during their marriage such as large loans, gifts and purchase of real estate. According to the *Civil Code*, debts incurred by either spouse in his or her own name beyond the family's daily needs are presumed not to be community debt.

However, in order to balance the interests of all parties, the *Civil Code* retains the possibility of such debt being determined as community debt by allocating the burden of proof on creditors. Creditors need to prove that such debt is used for the married life, production and business operation by the spouses, or that such debt is incurred by the spouses through mutual consent, and failing that the debt will only be borne by the spouse raising it.

Such allocation of burden of proof urges creditors to exercise sufficient duty of care by requesting the signature of the debtor's spouse, which ensures that the debt is incurred through the spouses' mutual consent and reduces disputes in this regard. Besides, it avoids collusions between one spouse and the creditor which undermine the rights and interests of the other spouse, and ultimately protects the rights and interests of creditors.

2. Three Dimensions of the Creditors' Burden of Proof

(1) Where creditors can prove that the debt has been used for the married life

It should be noted that married life includes but is not limited to the daily life of the family, and the creditor is required to prove that the proportion of debt beyond the daily needs of the family yet still falls within the scope of married life, such as purchase of real estate, investment and start-up. Such debt all in substance falls within the scope of married life as it may be used for mutual consumption, formation of community property, or management of community property for the interest of the spouses.

(2) Where creditors can prove that the debt has been used for production and business operation by the spouses

It is quite complicated to determine whether the spouses indebt for production and business operation by the spouses. Generally, if the spouses make resolutions for production and business operation together or if either spouse does so with the authorisation from the other, the debt incurred should be deemed for production and business operation by the spouses. Therefore, it is vital to consider the nature of the business and the role of the spouses in the business when deciding whether the business in question pertains to production and business operation by the spouses. Debts incurred for production and business operation by the spouses are normally used for industry, commerce, investment and purchase of production materials in which the spouses jointly engage.

In the case of (2019) Guangdong Civil Retrial No. 373 Sale and Purchase Contract Dispute, Guangdong High People's Court held that the mere fact that the defendant HE was the shareholder and legal representative of the defendant company LI could not sufficiently lead to the conclusion that the company LI's income was indeed HE's personal income. Although the defendant LEE, HE's wife, was a financial staff of the company LI, she was neither a shareholder nor an executive of the company and thus the situation did not fall within the scope of production and business operation by the spouses. As a result, the sale of goods proceeds in question could not be considered as HE's personal income or the joint income of HE and LEE. In the case of (2022) Zhejiang 07 Civil Final No. 2755 Sales Contract Dispute, Jinhua Intermediate People's Court of Zhejiang Province held that the gravel payment and its interests claimed and disputed by the appellant was not the community debt of the respondent ZHU and YE due to the creditor's failure to prove the joint operation of the construction project by ZHU and YE. In addition, the WeChat records and call recordings between the appellant and YE could not indicate YE's clear intention to be jointly liable for the debt. Therefore, the disputed debt was then held to be personal debt of ZHU.

(3) Where creditors can prove that the debt is incurred through mutual consent of the spouses

In the case of (2021) Guangdong 06 Civil Final No. 9425 Private Lending Dispute, Foshan Intermediate People's Court of Guangdong Province applied the *Interpretation on Marital Debt* and found that the disputed debt of more than ¥3,000,000 far exceeded the daily needs of the family and was not determined as community debt. The reasons for such determination were that the creditor failed to prove the usage for the married life, production and business operation by the spouses, and that the debtor's spouse neither gave consent nor subsequently ratified the incurring of the debt.

The allocation of burden of proof on creditors urges them to exercise sufficient duty of care by complying with the "co-signing" rule while lending out money, especially large amount of money. The implementation of such rule helps to raise public awareness of market risk and strikes a balance between the interest of the creditor and the non-debtor spouse, which can prevent disputes at the source and protect transaction security.

Section Two　Laws in Hong Kong

Hong Kong implements a different matrimonial property regime from that of the Chinese Mainland. The matrimonial property regime in Hong Kong is set out in the *Marriage Ordinance* (Cap. 181), the *Married Persons Status Ordinance* (Cap. 182) and the *Matrimonial Proceedings and Property Ordinance* (Cap. 192). Among these, the relevant provisions in the *Married Persons Status Ordinance* are most commonly referred to, but this Ordinance is not applicable to property division in divorce proceedings. It is now commonly acknowledged that separate property regime is the default matrimonial property regime in Hong Kong.

I. Separate Property Regime

i. Independent Status of Married Women

Section 3 "capacity of married women" of the *Married Persons Status Ordinance* stipulates: (1) Subject to this Ordinance, a married woman shall — (a) be capable of acquiring, holding and disposing of, any property; (b) be capable of rendering herself, and being rendered, liable in respect of any tort, contract, debt or obligation; (c) be capable of suing and being sued, either in tort or in contract or otherwise; and (d) be subject to the law relating to bankruptcy and to the enforcement of judgements and orders, in all respects as if she were unmarried. (2) A married woman may act as a trustee or personal representative in all respects as if she were unmarried. Section 4 "property of married women" stipulates: (1) Subject to this Ordinance, all property which — (a) immediately before 20 March 1936 was the separate property of a married woman or held for her separate use in equity; or (b) belonged or belongs at the time of her marriage to a woman married after that date; or (c) after that date has been or is acquired by or devolved or devolves upon a married woman, shall belong to her in all respects as if she were unmarried and may be disposed of accordingly. No restriction upon anticipation or alienation attached, whether before or after the commencement (commencement date: October 7, 1971) of this Ordinance, to the enjoyment of any property by a woman which could not have been attached to the enjoyment of that property by a man shall be of any effect.

In conclusion, laws in Hong Kong clearly provide that a married woman bears independent property rights and obligations, and has the capacity to acquire, hold and dispose of property, to render herself or to be rendered liable, and to act as a trustee or personal representative. A woman's right to property that she has owned or is owning will not be changed by her being married.

ii. Separate Liabilities

Section 10 of the *Married Persons Status Ordinance* provides: Subject to this Ordinance, the husband of a woman shall not, by reason only of his being her husband, be liable — (a) in respect of any tort committed by her whether before or after the marriage, or in respect of any contract entered into, or debt or obligation incurred, by her before the marriage; or (b) to be sued or made a party to any legal proceedings brought in respect of any such tort, contract, debt or obligation.

It can be drawn from the above section that, unless otherwise stipulated, married couples in Hong Kong are separately responsible for their own property, debts and obligations during their marriage. A husband is not liable only by reason of him being a husband for torts committed by his wife before or during the marriage, or for contracts, debts and obligations entered into by his wife before marriage.

iii. Abolition of Agency of Necessity

The *Married Persons Status Ordinance* abolishes the wife's agency of necessity. Section 11 stipulates: Any rule of law or equity conferring on a wife authority, as agent of necessity of her husband, to pledge his credit or to borrow money on his credit is hereby abrogated. Such agency of necessity is kind of similar to the agency for daily family affairs in the Chinese Mainland law.[1] It can be inferred from this section that there is no application of agency for daily family affairs in Hong Kong. However, the abolition of the wife's agency of necessity by the *Married Persons Status Ordinance* will not affect the establishment of other agency validly in law between the spouses.

iv. Share of the Spouse in the Improvement of Property

Section 9 of the *Married Persons Status Ordinance* provides: It is hereby declared that, where a husband or wife contributes in money or money's worth to the improvement of real or personal property in which or in the proceeds of sale of which either or both of them has or have a beneficial interest, the husband or wife so contributing shall, if the contribution is of a substantial nature and subject to any agreement between them to the contrary express or implied,

---

[1] See Ran Keping, *Discussion on Community Debts Incurred for the Family's Daily Life*, Jianghan Forum (Volume 7 2018).

be treated as having them acquired by virtue of his or her contribution a share or an enlarged share, as the case may be, in that beneficial interest of such an extent as may have been then agreed or, in default of such agreement, as may seem in all the circumstances just to any court before which the question of the existence or extent of the beneficial interest of the husband or wife arises (whether in proceedings between them or in any other proceedings).

It can be implied from the above section that the implementation of separate property regime in Hong Kong does not mean an absolute and unchangeable division of property between the spouses, nor is registration of property a definite determinative factor of property title. Where there are contributions by either spouse in money or money's worth to the improvement of property, the contributing spouse will acquire a share or an enlarged share in the beneficial interest in that property. That is to say, the contributing spouse may acquire a share of the beneficial interest in the property he or she does not originally hold a title, or the extent of the contributing spouse's beneficial interest in the property may be enlarged as a result of his or her contribution to the improvement of the property.

v. Protection of Creditors

Section 12 of the *Married Persons Status Ordinance* regulates the circumstance in which gifts are made in fraud of creditors. It stipulates: Nothing in this Ordinance shall be construed as validating—(a) as against creditors of the husband, any gift, by a husband to his wife, of any property which, after such gift, continues to be in the order or disposition or reputed ownership of the husband or any deposit or other investment of moneys of the husband made by or in the name of his wife in fraud of his creditors; or (b) as against creditors of the wife, any gift, by a wife to her husband, of any property which, after such gift, continues to be in the order or disposition or reputed ownership of the wife or any deposit or other investment of moneys of the wife made by or in the name of her husband in fraud of her creditors, and any such money so deposited or invested may be followed as if this Ordinance had not been passed.

It can be drawn from the abovesaid that this section aims to protect transaction security and to safeguard the interests of creditors. Gifts between spouses made for the purpose of evading debts or defrauding creditors are invalid and recoverable. This section eliminates the possibility of unscrupulous people taking advantage of the separate property regime to infringe on creditors' interests by making fake gifts.

vi. Separate Property Regime in Lending Disputes

Due to the separate property regime in Hong Kong and the non-application of community debt regime and agency of necessity between spouses, unless the spouses have acted as co-borrowers and signed together, creditors can only claim against the one who has signed the loan contract but not his or her spouse. In the absence of a special cause of action, such as fraudulent concealment of property, fraudulent transfer of assets or joint tenancy of family home, the listing of the debtor's spouse as a co-defendant by the creditor may be struck out by the court. However, in exceptional cases, the court may still find a non-signatory spouse to be a co-borrower after looking through the whole process of contract formation. [1]

II. Resolution of Property Disputes

i. Statutory Approach

According to Section 6 and Section 7 of the *Married Persons Status Ordinance*, if there arises any question between the spouses as to the title to or possession of property, including the circumstances in which one claimed that the

[1] *Chow Yu Heung Elsa v. Li Muk Ming* [2006] HKCU 1664.

other spouse has had in his or possession or under his or her control money to which, to a share of which, property to which, or to an interest in which, he or she was beneficially entitled, the spouse may apply by summons or otherwise in a summary way to a judge to determine the question. The judge, if satisfied that certain conditions are met, may order the spouse to pay to the other spouse as the judge may consider appropriate.

ii. Equity Approach

In Hong Kong, joint tenancy of spouses can be determined through constructive trust in equity. In the case of (2016) Shanghai 02 Civil Final No. 2239 Property Title Dispute, the Shanghai First Intermediate People's Court determined the ownership of the house in question by applying Hong Kong's law of equity. In this case, the appellant XU and the respondent ZHANG were Hong Kong permanent residents and got married in Hong Kong in 1987. XU purchased the house in question in Shanghai and paid the purchase price and the bank loan. The house had always been registered in XU's name, and there was no matrimonial property agreement between XU and ZHANG. ZHANG claimed for confirmation of his fifty percent of share in the house.

The Shanghai First Intermediate People's Court held that the dispute between XU and ZHANG over the title of the house was, in effect, a property dispute arising out of their marriage, and therefore Article 24 of the *Law of the People's Republic of China on Choice of Law for Foreign-Related Civil Relationships*[1] shall be applied to determine the applicable law. Since there was no agreement on choice of law between XU and ZHANG, according to Article

[1] As for the property relation between husband and wife, the parties concerned may choose the applicable laws at the habitual residence, of the state of nationality or at the locality of the main properties of one party by agreement. If the parties do not choose, the laws at the mutual habitual residence shall apply; if there is no mutual habitual residence, the laws of the mutual state of nationality shall apply.

15 of the *Interpretations of the Supreme People's Court on Issues Concerning Application of the Law of the People's Republic of China on Choice of Law for Foreign-Related Civil Relationships* (*I*) (Revised)[1], the place where XU and ZHANG got married shall be determined as the habitual residence for the determination of applicable law. Therefore, the dispute in this case should be governed by the laws of Hong Kong.

Both XU and ZHANG had confirmed that, the statutory law of Hong Kong has adopted the separate property regime as the matrimonial property regime. However, under equity or case laws, if there exists a constructive trust, the title of the property can be determined as being jointly held by spouses regardless of the registration in the name of mere one spouse. The house in question was acquired during the marriage between XU and ZHANG but registered in XU's name only. Without an agreement on the title of the house between XU and ZHANG, pursuant to the statutory law, the house in question belonged to XU only. While in equity, the focus of the dispute should be whether there was a constructive trust between XU and ZHANG on the title of the house.

The legal opinion issued by a Hong Kong lawyer in this case states: According to the laws of Hong Kong, the disposal of a couple's marital property shall comply with the rules of the separate property regime, except where there is an express agreement between the spouses or where there is a constructive trust. Constructive trust can be created through express or implied agreement: firstly, there must be a mutual consent to jointly hold the property; and secondly, the party claiming the constructive trust has an interest in the property by virtue of any agreement, arrangement, etc. Constructive trust means that, with-

[1] For a place where a person has continuously lived for a period of not less than one year as his or her life center at the time of the occurrence, change or termination of any foreign-related civil relationship, the people's court may determine such place as the habitual residence as prescribed in the *Law on Choice of Law for Foreign-Related Civil Relationships*, except medical treatment, labor dispatch, official duty and other similar circumstances.

out any trust agreement (oral or written), a property may become a trust property under the principles of equity in which one party is the trustee and the other (or both of them) is the beneficiary. That is to say, the party holding the legal title of the property may not be the sole owner of the beneficial interests in that property or own the entire beneficial interests, but holds all or part of the beneficial interests on behalf of the beneficial owner as the trustee. Common intention constructive trust is applicable to marriage. To establish common intention constructive trust, the following two conditions shall be met: firstly, at any time prior to acquisition of the property, or exceptionally at some later date, there is an agreement, arrangement or understanding reached between the parties on the property to be held jointly; and secondly, there is detrimental reliance of one party on such agreement, arrangement or understanding, i. e. one has paid the amount for the purchase of, or the amount of the mortgage of, the property. It is then possible for a common intention constructive trust to be established even in the absence of any written agreement between the paying party and the other party.

After contemplating whether there was a mutual consent between XU and ZHANG to jointly hold the house and whether there was contribution or detrimental reliance of ZHANG on such agreement, the Shanghai First Intermediate People's Court held that the house in question was solely owned by XU.

Section Three Summary

I. Similarity

Firstly, the laws in the Chinese Mainland and Hong Kong both stipulate that debts incurred through mutual consent of the spouses shall be repaid by both of them.

Secondly, the laws in the Chinese Mainland and Hong Kong both stipulate that debts incurred by one of the spouses in his or her own name which exceed the daily needs of the family do not generally fall within the scope of community debts.

II. Difference

Firstly, the Chinese Mainland and Hong Kong implement different matrimonial property regimes. The default matrimonial property regime in the Chinese Mainland is the community of acquisition regime, with contractual property regime as an option. Hong Kong, however, implements a separate property regime and only in exceptional cases matrimonial property is determined to be held jointly.

Secondly, the Chinese Mainland and Hong Kong implement different matrimonial debt regimes. In the Chinese Mainland, debts incurred through mutual consent of the spouses and debts incurred by one of the spouses in his or her own name for the family's daily life both fall within the scope of community debts. Debts exceeding the daily needs of the family shall not be deemed as community debts, unless the creditor can prove that such debt is used for the married life, production and business operation by the spouses, or that such debt is incurred by the spouses through mutual consent. There is no such concept and even description of community debt in Hong Kong laws. There is no statutory agency for daily family affairs between spouses in Hong Kong neither. Debts incurred by one of the spouses in his or her own name are generally determined as personal debts.

Chapter Ⅷ

Comparison of Legal Rules on Limitations

Section One Laws in the Chinese Mainland

The *Civil Code* regulates the limitations in the Chinese Mainland, including provisions on limitation periods, the limitation period for instalment debts, the commencement of limitation periods, the suspension and interruption of limitation periods, the legal effects of the expiration of limitation periods, etc.

Assuming A was the lender and B the borrower, the agreed amount of loan was ¥500,000, and the loan term started from May 20, 2023 and ended on May 20, 2024. The following parts of this section will interpret the various provisions on limitations based on the above elements (hereinafter referred to as the sample case).

I. Limitation Period

i. General Limitation Period

According to Article 118 of the *Civil Code*, the general limitation period in the Chinese Mainland is three years, which also applies to private lending disputes. Take the sample case for example. If B failed to repay the debt by May 20, 2024, the limitation period of this case would start from May 20, 2024 and would end on May 20, 2027. The *Civil Code* does not specially provide for the limitation period of secured debts, to which the general limitation period also applies.

ii. Special Limitation Period

Special limitation periods are provided in some special laws and apply to certain kinds of disputes. For example, the *Insurance Law* provides for a five-year limitation period for the insured or the beneficiary of a life insurance policy to claim payment of the insurance benefit from the insurer. The *Maritime Law* stipulates that the limitation period for claims against the carrier for damages of the carriage of passengers by sea is two years. The provisions of special limitation periods provided in special laws shall prevail over those of the general limitation period in the *Civil Code*. Special limitation periods do not apply to private lending disputes.

II. Commencement of Limitation Period

Article 188 of the *Civil Code* stipulates that the limitation period starts to run from the date on which the right holder knows or should have known that his right has been infringed and who the infringer is. According to this article, three conditions need to be met for the limitation period to start running: Firstly, the right is objectively infringed upon. Secondly, the right holder knows or ought to have known that the right is infringed upon. The test for "ought to have known" is that the right holder as an ordinary person is able to apprehend the infringement in the given circumstance. Thirdly, the right holder knows or ought to have known who the infringer is. In practice, when the limitation period starts to run shall be determined based on the circumstances of each case. In lending disputes, the limitation period generally starts to run from the expiration of the loan term, but it differs in the following two situations.

i. Repayment Date Specified

Article 675 of the *Civil Code* stipulates that the borrower shall repay the loan within the agreed period. Therefore, for cases where there is an agreed loan term, the limitation period starts to run from the expiration date of the loan term. Take the sample case for example. Since the agreed loan term started from May 20, 2023 and ended on May 20, 2024, the limitation period started to run from May 20, 2024.

ii. No Repayment Date Agreed Upon

Where there is no agreed repayment date, the *Civil Code* and other relevant laws and regulations [1] provide for the following handling processes. Firstly, if the loan term can be determined in accordance with Article 510 of the *Civil Code*, the limitation period will start to run from the expiration date of the determined loan term. Secondly, if the loan term cannot be so determined, the borrower may repay the loan at any time, and the lender can also demand the borrower to repay at any time, but reasonable time for the preparation of repayment shall be given. The limitation period will start running from the expiration date of the reasonable time given by the lender. Thirdly, if the borrower explicitly refuses to fulfil the obligation at the first assertion of right by the lender, the limitation period starts to run from the refusal date.

Take the sample case as an example. If A and B had not agreed on the loan term, and it could not be subsequently determined, B could repay the loan at any time from May 20, 2023 onwards. A could also demand repayment from B at any time, but must give B a grace period. For example, if A made the demand on January 1, 2024 with a grace period of 7 days, the limitation period started to run on January 8, 2024. If B refused to repay on January 1, 2024, then the limitation period started to run on the same day.

In practice, the court will determine whether the limitation period has started running based on the content of the loan contract, the timing of the lending

[1] Article 675 of the *Civil Code* provides that a borrower shall repay the loan within the agreed period. Where there is no such agreement, or the agreement is unclear, and cannot be determined according to Article 510 of the *Civil Code*, the borrower may repay the loan at any time, and the lender may demand the borrower to repay the loan within a reasonable period of time. Article 4 of the *Provisions on the Application of Statute of Limitations*: The limitation period starts to run from the expiration date of the grace period which the creditor gives while demanding performance from the debtor. If the debtor clearly rejects to perform his obligations when the creditor makes the first demand, the limitation period starts to run from the rejection date.

and the conduct of both parties. In the case of (2021) Shandong 02 Civil Final No. 12526 Private Lending Dispute, Qingdao Intermediate People's Court of Shandong Province held that the limitation period had not started running in this case since there was no agreed repayment date between the parties, and the creditor had never claimed repayment from the debtor.

iii. Instalment Debts

Article 189 of the *Civil Code* stipulates that when the parties agree that the debt is repaid by instalment, the limitation period starts to run from the date when the last instalment is due. Take the sample case as an example. If A and B agreed to repay the debt in three instalments within the one-year loan term in which the first instalment was due on August 20, 2023, the second on January 30, 2024, and the last on May 20, 2024, and B defaulted on every payment, the limitation period would start to run from May 20, 2024.

It is important to pay close attention to the difference between instalment debts and periodic debts which formed regularly through contracts entered into on a termly basis. The total amount of an instalment debt is fixed at the time of contract formation, with the debt discharged through instalments. In contrast, the total amount of periodic debts is generally not determined at the time when the obligation arises as each debt is separate from each other.

iv. Mortgage, Guarantee and Suretyship

1. Mortgage

According to Article 419 of the *Civil Code*, a mortgagee shall exercise his right to mortgage within the limitation period for claiming debts in the principal contract. In other words, the duration of a mortgagee's right to the mortgage is subject to the limitation period of debts in the principal contract. The suspension, interruption and extension of the limitation period of debts in the principal contract will accordingly affect the duration of the mortgage right. Take the sample case as an example. If B used the real estate under his name as the collateral for the loan of ¥500,000, A should exercise his right to the collateral within the limitation period of the ¥500,000 debt.

2. Guarantee and Suretyship

(1) Guarantee

According to Paragraph 1 of Article 694 of the *Civil Code*, the limitation period of actions of guarantee starts to run from the date when the guarantor's right to refuse to assume the responsibility is extinguished. This is consistent with the guarantor's right of discussion. Take the sample case as an example. If C provided guarantee for the ¥500,000 loan with a guarantee period of six months, and B failed to repay the loan before May 20, 2024, A should first claim against B through litigation or arbitration within six months starting from May 20, 2024, and then proceed with the enforcement of B's property according to the laws. If B was still unable to repay the debt after court enforcement actions, A could then require C to assume the guarantee responsibility. To be more specific, the limitation period of A's claim against C only started to run if the following two conditions were met: ① the court's enforcement actions against B were completed; ② the debt had still not been fully discharged. In addition, if B's conduct satisfied any of the four scenarios [1] listed in Article 687 of the *Civil Code*, A could claim against C from date of the occurrence of such scenarios.

(2) Suretyship

According to Paragraph 2 of Article 694 of the *Civil Code*, when a creditor secured by the suretyship demands the surety to assume the responsibility before

[1] A guarantor has the right of discussion, except under any of the following circumstances occurs: (1) the debtor's whereabouts is unknown and there is no property available for enforcement; (2) the court has accepted the debtor's bankruptcy petition; (3) the creditor has proved that the debtor has insufficient assets to repay all his debts or that the debtor is insolvent; (4) the guarantor waives his right of discussion in writing.

the expiration of the suretyship period, the limitation period starts to run from the date of the demand. Unlike guarantors, a surety has no right of discussion, the creditor does not need to exhaust all remedies against the debtor before proceeding against the surety. Take the sample case as an example. If C provided suretyship for the loan, with a term of six months, and B failed to repay the loan before May 20, 2024, A could demand C to assume the responsibility within the suretyship period of six months starting from May 20, 2024, the limitation period started to run from the date of the demand.

III. Calculation of Limitation Period

i. Commencement of Time Period

Article 201 of the *Civil Code* provides for the calculation of time periods. Where a time period is counted by year, month and day, the day on which the period begins shall be excluded, and the following day is counted as the first day. Take the sample case as an example. The limitation period of A's claim against B started to run from May 20, 2024, which means that the day of May 20 should be excluded, and the earliest day on which A could file a case against B is May 21, 2024.

ii. End of Time Period

According to Article 203 of the *Civil Code*, where the last day of a time period falls on a public holiday, the next working day shall be deemed as the last day of the period. For example, where the last day of a limitation period falls on Sunday, the following Monday shall be deemed as the last day of the limitation period. Where the last day of the limitation period falls on October 1 (which is generally the first day of the National Holidays), then October 8 (which is the next day following the last day of the National Holidays) shall be deemed as the last day of the limitation period.

Ⅳ. Suspension, Interruption, and Extension of Limitation Period and the Maximum Time Length

i. Suspension of Limitation Period

The suspension of limitation period means that during the course of the limitation period, the obligee is prevented from exercising his right of claim due to the occurrence of certain prescribed incidents and thus the calculation of the limitation period pauses until the elimination of the incident. Article 194 of the *Civil Code* provides for five kinds of incidents which will suspend the limitation periods: (1) where there is a force majeure; (2) where the obligee is with no or limited capacity for civil juristic acts and has no legal representative, or where the legal representative deceases or loses the capacity for civil juristic acts or the authority of agency; (3) the successor or administrator has not been determined or appointed after the commencement of succession; (4) the obligee is controlled by the obligor or any other parties; (5) other scenarios in which the obligee is unable to claim his right. The suspension will take effect only if the prescribed incidents occur within the last six months of the original limitation period. The limitation period will resume and keep running for another six months upon the elimination of the prescribed incidents. If, in the sample case, A became a person with limited capacity for civil juristic acts due to illness on Marth 20, 2027 (which was within the last six months of the original limitation period starting to run on May 20, 2024) and failed to claim his rights against B, the limitation period was suspended from Marth 20, 2027 and resumed from the date of appointment of A's legal representative with recalculation of another 6 months.

ii. Interruption of Limitation Period

The interruption of limitation period means that the occurrence of certain prescribed incidents during the limitation period overturns the basis for the existence of the original limitation period, nullifies the elapsed time of the original limitation period and thus causes the limitation period to restart. Article 195 of the *Civil Code* provides four kinds of incidents which will interrupt the limitation periods: (1) the obligee has demanded performance from the obligor; (2) the obligor has agreed to perform; (3) the obligee has initiated a litigation or arbitration proceeding against the obligor; (4) any other circumstances which are of equivalent effect as initiating litigations or arbitrations. If, in the sample case, A demanded repayment from B on May 21, 2025 (which was within the three-year limitation period starting from May 20, 2024), the limitation period would be interrupted and restart running from May 21, 2025 for another three years.

In the case of (2023) Jiangsu 13 Civil Final No. 639 Private Lending Dispute, Suqian Intermediate People's Court of Jiangsu Province held that the limitation period in this case had not expired for the reason that although the debtor was unable to repay within a reasonable period after the first demand of repayment by the creditor, the witness affirmed to the court that the creditor had come to the debtor's dwelling and asked for repayment every year before the initiation of the litigation. The creditor's active exercise of rights by annually demanding repayment resulted in the interruption of the limitation periods. Therefore, notwithstanding the fact that there was no agreed loan term and no repayment from the debtor upon the first repayment demand, the limitation period in this case had not expired.

iii. Maximum Length of Limitation Period and the Rule of Extension

According to Article 188 of the *Civil Code*, the maximum length of limitation periods is twenty years. Such time period is calculated objectively, starting from the date when the right is infringed and without regard to whether and when the obligee is aware of the infringement and the identity of the obligor.

The abovementioned rules of suspension and interruption of limitation periods do not apply to the calculation of the maximum length. No judicial protection can be sought upon the expiration of maximum length of twenty years since the date of infringement, except for extension granted by the court in exceptional circumstances. That is to say, the rule of extension applies only to the maximum length of limitation periods and does not apply to the general limitation period. Take the sample case for example. The limitation period of A's claim against B started to run from May 20, 2024. Notwithstanding any incidents causing suspension and interruption, A would not be able to seek judicial protection for his claim against B since May 20, 2044.

In the case of (2019) Hebei Civil Final No. 2671 Life, Health and Body Rights Dispute, the plaintiff got an electric shock at the age of 6, and after that his father passed away and his mother remarried. The plaintiff was raised by his grandfather who was severely disabled and his grandmother who was mentally handicapped. Such upbringing put an adverse impact on the intellectual development of the plaintiff. The 20-year maximum length of limitation period had expired when the plaintiff sued for damages for the electric shock. Baoding Intermediate People's Court of Hebei Province granted an extension to the limitation period by considering the plaintiff's suffering by virtue of several significant family changes and no fault subjectively committed by the plaintiff regarding the expiration of the limitation period.

V. Invoking the Limitation Period

i. The Court

According to Article 193 of the *Civil Code*, the court must not invoke the stipulations on limitation periods without pleading from the litigants. The rationale is that the right to plead limitation periods is, in essence, a private right of the obligor, the exercise of which falls within the scope of the obligor's autonomy. The court shall not take the initiative in applying the limitation period, including actively invoking and explaining all relevant stipulations, or actively applying the rules of suspension, interruption, and extension of limitation period. A party who is tried in absentia or served by publication is deemed to have waived his right to defend and the court must not apply the stipulations on limitation period on its own initiative as well. In the sample case, if A filed a case against B on March 1, 2028 (which fell without the 3-year limitation period starting from May 20, 2024), and B did not appear and defend, the court should not dismiss the claim on the ground of expiration of the limitation period.

ii. The Litigant

A plea of the limitation period may be raised by the parties who are to benefit directly from the expiration of limitation periods, generally including debtors, guarantors, sureties and mortgagors. The *Provisions on Statute of Limitations* provides the timing and circumstances in which a party may plead the limitation period.

Firstly, a party shall plead the limitation period at first instance. A party's plead of the limitation period during the appeal will be dismissed by the court, unless there is new evidence proving the expiration of the other party's right of claim. A petition for retrial on the ground of expiration of the limitation period or a plea with the limitation period as a defence during retrial will be dismissed by the court if the party has not pled the limitation period during first instance.

Secondly, if the obligors consent to perform their obligations or have voluntarily performed their obligations after the expiration of the limitation period, the plea of the limitation period as a defence will be dismissed.

Thirdly, if the limitation period for debt in the principal contract has expired, the relevant guarantor (surety or mortgagor) will have the right to plead the limitation period as the debtors do. A guarantor (surety or mortgagor) who has repaid the debt in the principal contract without pleading the limitation period cannot recover from the principal debtor afterwards.

VI. Legal Effects of Expiration of Limitation Period

i. Right to Plead the Limitation Period

According to Article 192 of the *Civil Code*, upon expiration of the limitation period, the obligor may use it as a defence to not perform his obligation. In private lending disputes, the legal effect of the expiration of the limitation period is that the borrower gains the right to plead the limitation period, and the creditor is barred by enforcing his claim by legal actions. To be specific, the creditor can still initiate a proceeding against the debtor and the court shall accept the case. If the debtor does not plead the limitation period or waives his right to plead the limitation period, the creditor will still be able to recover the debt through litigations. However, if the debtor plead the limitation period, the creditor's claim will be dismissed by the court.

ii. Waiving the Right to Plead the Limitation Period

As mentioned before, the right to plead the limitation period is a private right of the obligor, the exercise of which falls within the scope of the obligor's autonomy. Therefore, an obligor may choose to waive this right after the expiration of the limitation period. Methods of waiving the right include consent to perform and voluntary performance. It should be noted that according to Article 19 of the *Provisions on Statute of Limitations*, if the obligor waives the right to plead the limitation period, he cannot invoke it again, including pleading the expiration of the limitation period as a defence, or demanding the obligee to return the voluntarily repaid loan. In the sample case, if A filed a case against B on March 1, 2028 (which fell out of the 3-year limitation period starting from May 20, 2024), and B repaid the debt after service by the court, then B could not plead the limitation period or demand the recovery from A.

Section Two Laws in Hong Kong

The *Limitation Ordinance* provides for the limitation periods in Hong Kong, categorising different limitation periods for different classes of action. For example, the limitation period for actions to recover contribution in respect of any damage from any other person under Section 3 of the *Civil Liability (Contribution) Ordinance* is 2 years. The limitation period for actions founded on simple contract or on tort, actions to enforce a recognizance, and actions to enforce an award is 6 years. The limitation period for actions to recover money secured by a mortgage or charge is 12 years. The limitation period for actions to recover land by the Crown is 60 years.

I. Limitation Period

i. Limitation Period for Actions Founded on Simple Contract

Section 4(1) of the *Limitation Ordinance* stipulates that actions founded on simple contract or on tort shall not be brought after the expiration of 6 years from the date on which the cause of action accrued. In the case of actions founded on contract, time runs from the moment when the breach occurred. Accordingly, an action for breach of contract shall be brought within 6 years of the breach. Such 6-year limitation period applies to common lending disputes. It should be noted that this section shall not be applied to any claim for specific performance of a contract, an injunction, or other equitable relief.

ii. Limitation Period for Actions to Recover Money Secured by a Mortgage or Charge

Section 19(1) of the *Limitation Ordinance* stipulates that no action shall be brought to recover any principal sum of money secured by a mortgage or other charge on property after the expiration of 12 years from the date when the right to receive the money accrued. Accordingly, in lending disputes where the debt is secured by a mortgage or other charge on property, the limitation period to recover the principal sum of the debt is 12 years. In practice, the specific types of "other charge on property" to which this section applies are left to the court to exercise the discretion in light of different circumstances in each case.

iii. Limitation Period for Actions to Recover Interest Payable in Respect of Any Sum of Money Secured by a Mortgage or Other Charge

Section 19(5) of the *Limitation Ordinance* stipulates that no action to recover arrears of interest payable in respect of any sum of money secured by a mortgage or other charge shall be brought after the expiration of 6 years from the date on which the interest became due. When the mortgagee's claim for the principal is barred, the interest claim is barred.[1] In addition, relevant English authorities have ruled that although an action by a mortgagee for mortgage interest which has remained unpaid for longer than six years from the date on which it became due is barred by virtue of this sub-section, a mortgagor as a condition of redeeming or receiving the proceeds of sale of the mortgage security must pay all arrears of interest, however old.

II. Commencement of Limitation Period

In the case of actions founded on contract, time runs from the moment when the breach occurred.[2] For lending disputes, it begins on the date the borrower fails to repay the loan as agreed.

---

[1] See *Cap. 347 Limitation Ordinance with Annotation*, Lexis Nexis Hong Kong, para. 4.20. Elder v. Northcott [1930]2 Ch 422, [1930] All ER Rep 398.

[2] *Yeung Shu v. Alfred Lau & Co.* (*a Firm*) (*Chang Pao Ching*, *Third Party*) [1996] 1 HKC 562 (CFI).

i. Repayment Date Specified

In an action for money lent, if a time is specified for repayment or any condition for repayment is imposed, the limitation period runs on the expiration of the time specified or on the happening of the condition.[1]

ii. No Repayment Date Agreed Upon

The common law position is that where the date of repayment of a loan is not agreed upon, it will be due immediately and the cause of action accrues at that time. The position will be the same even if the loan is said to be repaid on demand. The cause of action for repayment of the loan will still accrue once the loan is made. In *Lee Siu Fong Mary v. Ngai Yee Chai*[2], the Court of Appeal of the High Court applied this rule. In this case, the plaintiff claimed that eight loans were made to the defendant between 1994 and 1995, but the defendant had only made partial payment to settle the loans. The plaintiff commenced the action against the defendant in 2002, and the defendant said he was not liable to repay it on the ground that the claim was barred by the 6-year limitation. The court found that the plaintiff had only given four loans to the defendant in 1994. Since no date of repayment was agreed upon the loans were due immediately and the plaintiff's cause of action accrued on the dates when the four loans were made in 1994 and would be barred on the respective dates in 2000.

iii. Instalment Debts

If in an agreement for the repayment of an existing debt by instalments it is provided that on default of payment of any instalment, the whole debt is to be

---

[1] See *Halsbury's Laws of Hong Kong*, Lexis Nexis Hong Kong, [245.042] Actions Founded on Contracts of Loan. *Lim Ban Thoon v. Chin tung Securities Ltd.* [1991] 2 HKC 204 (CA).

[2] [2006] 1 HKC 157 (CA).

recoverable, time runs as to the whole debt from the time of the first default in payment of an instalment.[1] Where, however, in the event of default in payment of any instalment the whole debt is to be repayable "on demand", the limitation period as to the whole debt does not run from the date of the first default, unless the lender in fact demands payment of the whole debt.[2]

iv. Actions to Recover Money Secured by a Mortgage or Other Charge

Section 19(1) of the *Limitation Ordinance* stipulates that no action shall be brought to recover any principal sum of money secured by a mortgage or other charge on property after the expiration of 12 years from the date when the right to receive the money accrued. This subsection was amended in 1991. Before amendment, the limitation period was 20 years.

In *Broada Ltd. v. Chow Cheuk Yin*[3], the High Court, upon the application by the plaintiffs, declared that a mortgage dated August 26, 1957 was no longer of effect. In this case, the principal amount advanced under the mortgage was HK $3,000 and repayable on February 26, 1958. In 1976 the plaintiffs' predecessor-in-title made a declaration to the effect that he was desirous of building a house on the property, and for that reason had undertaken with the Hong Kong Government to obtain the necessary consent from the mortgagee (the defendant). He further declared that he had not seen the defendant for many years and was unable to locate the defendant. The declaration was registered at the Land Registry on January 23, 1976. It would follow that no payment of interest or principal or any part thereof had been made for many years before 1976 and certainly not since then. On these facts, the court held that the

---

[1] See *Cap. 347 Limitation Ordinance with Annotation*, Lexis Nexis Hong Kong, para. 4.08.

[2] See *Halsbury's Laws of Hong Kong*, Lexis Nexis Hong Kong, [245.042] Actions Founded on Contracts of Loan.

[3] [1997] 3 HKC 168.

defendant is no longer able to maintain an action to recover the principal sum secured by the mortgage, nor maintain any foreclosure action nor any claim to interest by reason of Section 19 of the *Limitation Ordinance*. Since the cause of action accrued before July 1, 1991, the appropriate limitation period in this case was 20 years.

In determining the date when the right to receive the money accrued, it should be noted that such date is not a simple result of calculations, but should be determined on a case-by-case basis by considering relevant factors, such as the repayment condition of the secured debt and the date when the cause of action for the secured debt accrued. *In Siu Wing Yee Angeline v. Earning Yield Ltd.* [1], the Court of First Instance of the High Court held that time did not run from the date of creation of the legal charge but from the date when the cause of action accrued. In *Alpha Star Enterprises Ltd. v Personal Representative of Tang Mei Shin (deceased)*[2], the Court of First Instance of the High Court held that the burden was on the plaintiff to show that the mortgagee had been time-barred from claiming against the mortgagor and/or the suit property. In addition, Section 19(3) of the *Limitation Ordinance* stipulates that the right to receive any principal sum of money secured by a mortgage or other charge and the right to foreclose on the property subject to the mortgage or charge shall not be deemed to accrue so long as that property comprises any future interest or any life insurance policy which has not matured or been determined.

v. Actions to Recover Interest Payable in Respect of Any Sum of Money Secured by a Mortgage or Other Charge

Section 19(5) of the *Limitation Ordinance* stipulates that no action to recover arrears of interest payable in respect of any sum of money secured by a

---

[1] [2013] 6 HKC 281.

[2] [2002] 4 HKC 218.

mortgage or other charge shall be brought after the expiration of 6 years from the date on which the interest became due. Accordingly, the limitation period runs from the date, according to the loan agreement, when the lender can first bring an action to recover the interest and not from the date when it is due to be paid.[1]

vi. Calculation of Time Period

In computing this period, the date on which the cause of action accrued is excluded. When on the last day of the period the Court office is closed all day, the time is extended to the first day on which the office re-opens.[2] Once time has begun to run it will, as a general rule, continue to do so and will not be broken by any subsequent disability. This general principle, discernible as early as *Prideaux v. Webber*[3], can be ousted only by a statutory provision. In the absence of the parties' agreement that the limitation period shall be suspended during negotiations, time does not stop running.[4]

III. Extension or Postponement of Limitation Period

The *Limitation Ordinance* provides for the extension or postponement of the period of limitation: (1) in cases where the plaintiff was under a disability at the time when the cause of action accrued; (2) in cases of an acknowledgment of the cause of action in writing or part payment by the defendant or his predecessor or agent; (3) in cases where the action is based on fraud or the right of action was deliberately concealed or where the action is for relief from the consequences of a mistake.

---

[1] See *Cap. 347 Limitation Ordinance with Annotation*, Lexis Nexis Hong Kong, para. 19.13.

[2] See *Cap.* 347 *Limitation Ordinance with Annotation*, Lexis Nexis Hong Kong, para. 4.06.

[3] [1661] 1 Lev 31.

[4] *Ho Cheung Electrical Engineering Co. Ltd. v. Ko Wai Sun* [2017] HKCU 661.

i. Disability

Section 22(1) of the *Limitation Ordinance* stipulates that if on the date when any right of action accrued for which a period of limitation is prescribed by this Ordinance, the person to whom it accrued was under a disability, the action may be brought at any time before the expiration of 6 years from the date when the person ceased to be under a disability or died, whichever event first occurred, notwithstanding that the period of limitation had expired.

According to Section 22(3), a person shall be deemed to be under a disability while he is an infant or of unsound mind. According to Section 3 of the *Interpretation and General Clauses Ordinance* (Cap. 1), an infant or minor means a person who has not attained the age of 18 years. As to the meaning of "disability", there are authorities indicating that liberal approach should be taken in the context of this section so that a person of "unsound mind" is not confined to a mental health patient only but should cover cases where a person cannot manage his own affairs.[1] For the purposes of this, a person shall be conclusively presumed to be of unsound mind while he is detained in pursuance of any Ordinance or imperial enactment authorising the detention of persons of unsound mind, including persons convicted of offences or awaiting trial, or while he is receiving treatment voluntarily under the provisions of the *Mental Health Ordinance* (Cap. 136).

ii. Acknowledgment or Part Payment

Section 23(1) of the *Limitation Ordinance* stipulates that where there has accrued any right of action (including a foreclosure action) to recover land or any right of a mortgagee of personal property to bring a foreclosure action in respect of the property, and the person in possession of the land or personal prop-

[1] See *Cap. 347 Limitation Ordinance with Annotation*, Lexis Nexis Hong Kong, para. 22.05.

erty acknowledges the title of the person to whom the right of action has accrued, or in the case of a foreclosure or other action by a mortgagee, the person in possession as aforesaid or the person liable for the mortgage debt makes any payment in respect thereof, whether of principal or interest, the right shall be deemed to have accrued on and not before the date of the acknowledgment or payment.

It can be seen that the types of actions to which this section applies are limited to actions to recover land (including foreclosure actions) and foreclosure actions by mortgagees in respect of personal property. In lending disputes, the possible scenario for this section to apply is a foreclosure action by a mortgagee against mortgaged land or personal property where the debtor fails to repay the debt which is secured by a mortgage.

It should be noted that this section has clearly listed the applicable types of actions, the application of which cannot be extended straight away to including acknowledgment or part payment in different scenarios. However, whether acknowledgment or part payment in other scenarios may actually result in the "extension" of limitation periods under other statutes or legal principles (such as fixing another time or condition for repayment which is, in essence, modifying the loan contract) should be determined in accordance with relevant laws on a case-by-case basis.

iii. Fraud, Concealment or Mistake

Section 26(1) of the *Limitation Ordinance* stipulates that where the action is based upon the fraud of the defendant, or any fact relevant to the plaintiff's right of action has been deliberately concealed from him by the defendant, or the action is for relief from the consequences of a mistake, the period of limitation shall not begin to run until the plaintiff has discovered the fraud, concealment or mistake (as the case may be) or could with reasonable diligence have discovered it.

1. As to the meaning of "fraud" for the purpose of this section

It is an essential ingredient of the cause of action, and its definition is generally consistent with that of fraud under common law, although some authorities perceive that it could be extended to include "unconscionable behaviours".

2. As to the meaning of "concealment" for the purpose of this section

Subsection (3) provides that deliberate commission of a breach of duty in circumstances in which it is unlikely to be discovered for some time amounts to deliberate concealment of the facts involved in that breach of duty.

3. As to the application of "mistake" for the purpose of this section

It applies to an action at common law to recover money paid under a mistake of fact or to an analogous claim in equity for money paid under a mistake of fact or law.[1]

4. As to what constitutes "reasonable diligence"

In *Peco Arts Inc. v. Hazlitt Gallery Ltd.*[2] (a case involving the purchase of what was believed to be a valuable work of art but was subsequently discovered to be a reproduction), it was held that "reasonable diligence" did not mean the doing of everything possible, but the doing of that which an ordinarily prudent buyer of a valuable work of art would do in the circumstances. In *Baron v. Hartford Fire Insurance Co.* & Ors.[3], the Court of Appeal of the High Court applied the same test. The burden is on the plaintiff to establish that he cannot have discovered the fraud, without exceptional measures which he cannot reasonably have been expected to take.[4]

---

[1] *Re Diplock, Diplock v. Wintle* [1948] Ch 465, [1948] 2 All ER 318.

[2] [1983] 1 WLR 1315, [1983] 3 All ER 193.

[3] [1995] 1 HKC 149.

[4] *Paragon Finance Plc v. DB Thakerar & Co. (A Firm)* [1999] 1 All ER 400.

IV. Pleading the Limitation Period

Rule 8 of Order 18 of the *Rules of the High Court* stipulates that a party must in any pleading subsequent to a statement of claim plead specifically any matter, for example, performance, release, any relevant statute of limitation, fraud or any fact showing illegality. That is to say, the defence of the limitation period must be specifically pleaded, even if it appears on the face of the statement of claim that, since the cause of action accrued, the period of limitation has expired.

V. Legal Effect of Expiration of Limitation Period

In the usual case, upon the expiration of the relevant limitation period, the effect of the *Limitation Ordinance* is to bar the remedies by action but not the right. In *Lee Siu Fong Mary v. Ngai Yee Chai*[1], the Court of Appeal of the High Court held that since no date of repayment was agreed upon the loans were due immediately and the plaintiff's cause of action accrued on the dates when the four loans were made in 1994 and would be barred on the respective dates in 2000. Since the plaintiff had only commenced the action against the defendant in 2002, the court held that the defence of limitation must defeat the plaintiff's claim and dismissed the plaintiff's claim against the defendant.

It should be noted that the expiration of the limitation period only bars the remedies by action but leaves the right otherwise untouched. If a creditor whose debt is statute-barred has any means of enforcing his claim other than by action, the Ordinance does not prevent him from recovering by those means.[2]

---

[1] [2006] 1 HKC 157 (CA).

[2] See *Halsbury's Laws of Hong Kong*, Lexis Nexis Hong Kong, [245.031] Cases Where the Remedy is Barred and not the Right.

Section Three Summary

I. Similarity

Firstly, the legal effects of expiration of limitation period are similar between the Chinese Mainland and Hong Kong. Both bar the remedy by action but leave the right otherwise untouched.

Secondly, statutes in the Chinese Mainland and Hong Kong both provide that the defence of the limitation period must be specifically pleaded.

II. Difference

Firstly, the limitation periods are different between the Chinese Mainland and Hong Kong. In the Chinese Mainland, it is provided that a three-year limitation period is generally applicable. The statutes in Hong Kong, however, specify different limitation periods applicable to different classes of action. The applicable limitation period to lending disputes is three years in the Chinese Mainland and six years in Hong Kong. Furthermore, there is no specifically applicable limitation period for guarantee (mortgage or suretyship) in the Chinese Mainland, while there is specific limitation period for actions to recover money secured by a mortgage or other charge (for principal sum is 12 years, for interest is 6 years) in Hong Kong.

Secondly, the rules for commencement of limitation period are different between the Chinese Mainland and Hong Kong due to different rules on the accrual of the cause of action. For example, for loan contract without a repayment date, the laws in the Chinese Mainland provide for a reasonable period for repayment and the limitation period starts running on the expiration of the reasonable period. In Hong Kong, the cause of action for repayment of the loan will accrue once the loan was made and the limitation period starts running then.

Thirdly, the rules for breaking the original limitation period are different between the Chinese Mainland and Hong Kong. In the Chinese Mainland, the rules for suspension and interruption of limitation period are generally applicable, while the rule of extension only applies to calculation of the maximum length of time with no specific scenario prescribed, and empowers the court to extend the maximum limitation period in exceptional cases. In Hong Kong, there are no generally applicable rules of suspension and interruption of limitation period, but specific scenarios are prescribed for the application of extension or postponement of limitation period.

Fourthly, the maximum length of time for limitation period is generally applicable in the Chinese Mainland, while there is no such rule in Hong Kong.

Epilogue

Rule of law ensures the best business environment. As the legal system with the closest connection to the business activities of commercial entities, the laws and regulations on private lending are not only a guideline for regulating the capital financing conduct, but also serve as a shield to protect the rights and interests of lenders and borrowers. This book compares the laws between the Chinese Mainland and Hong Kong from the following eight pivotal themes as the "micro entry points", including the statutory interest rate cap, the calculation of principal and interest, the determination of professional money lenders, the marital debts and so forth. The comparative study demonstrates that the Chinese Mainland and Hong Kong share a consensus on respecting the autonomy of will and safeguarding commercial justice, and a solid and profound ground has been laid down for the alignment of commercial legal rules. This not only lays the foundation for exploring the beneficial path of rule alignment in the Greater Bay Area but also fosters strong confidence in further deepening the rule alignment in the future.

The alignment of legal rules in the Greater Bay Area is not a task that can be accomplished overnight but should be continuously updated and explored in conjunction with the demand of judicial practices and the revision of legal rules. This book takes the private lending disputes prominently arising in the Hong Kong-related commercial trials as the research target, which comprehensively displays the similarities and differences of the rules in legal theories and judicial practices so as to preliminarily explore a feasible path for integrating the substantive rules of commercial affairs and thereby accumulate methods and experience for the follow-up of rule alignment. In the future, the Shenzhen Qianhai Cooperation Zone People's Court will continue to adhere to the principle of "one country" and make good use of the advantages of "two systems". Standing on the practice of commercial trials, the Shenzhen Qianhai Cooperation

Zone People's Court has been expanding the depth and breadth of comparative research on cross-border legal rules so as to provide cross-border investors with a more comprehensive and detailed guide with regard to the legal rule alignment. In order to contribute its strength to advance the high-quality integrated development of Guangdong-Hong Kong-Macao, the Shenzhen Qianhai Cooperation Zone People's Court hereby has been devoted to promoting the "soft connectivity" of commercial legal rules and facilitating the "deep integration" of the economic development between the Chinese Mainland and Hong Kong.

In the end, special thanks go to Barrister Frederick H. F. CHAN and Barrister CHOW Lap San, Edward for their assistance in the compilation of this book. Meanwhile, special thanks are extended to research interns Qi Ying and Yu Yujuan for their assistance in translation of this book.